Social Marketing
Theoretical and Practical Perspectives

ADVERTISING AND CONSUMER PSYCHOLOGY
A series sponsored by the Society for Consumer Psychology

Social Marketing
Theoretical and Practical Perspectives

Edited by

Marvin E. Goldberg
Pennsylvania State University

Martin Fishbein
University of Illinois, Champaign–Urbana
Centers for Disease Control and Prevention

Susan E. Middlestadt
Academy for Educational Development,
Washington, DC

LEA   LAWRENCE ERLBAUM ASSOCIATES, PUBLISHERS
1997   Mahwah, New Jersey   London

Lawrence Erlbaum Associates, Inc., Publishers
10 Industrial Avenue
Mahwah, New Jersey 07430

Library of Congress Cataloging-in-Publication Data

Social marketing : theoretical and practical perspectives / edited by
Marvin E. Goldberg, Martin Fishbein, Susan E. Middlestadt.
    p.   cm. — (Advertising and consumer psychology)
    Papers presented at the Role of Advertising in Social Marketing
Conference held in Atlanta, Ga., May 17–19, 1995.
    Includes bibliographical references and index.
    ISBN 0-8058-2499-5 (cloth : alk. paper)
    1. Social marketing. I. Goldberg, Marvin E. II. Fishbein,
Martin. III. Middlestadt, Susan E. IV. Role of Advertising in
Social Marketing Conference (1995 : Atlanta, Ga.) V. Series.
HF5415.122.S637   1997
658.8—dc21   96-36833
                                                               CIP

Books published by Lawrence Erlbaum Associates are printed on acid-free paper, and their bindings are chosen for strength and durability.

Printed in the United States of America
10 9 8 7 6 5 4 3 2 1

Contents

Preface

For both academics and practitioners who are involved with social marketing, the domain remains in its infancy. And, as is typically the case with any new applied field, while programs and approaches are being developed and implemented by practitioners, academics are expending considerable effort on defining "what it is," "where it comes from" (i.e., What are the contributing or underlying disciplines from which it borrows?), and "where it is going." The last includes an assessment of current work and the direction that work is taking.

Implicit in much of the work that is done is the assumption that educated, well-intentioned professionals, usually but not always funded by government, can effectively address a variety of societal problems and, in so doing, successfully improve the lives of specific communities within society, either domestically or abroad. Of course how one "improves the lives" of these targeted others and, even more basically, what constitutes "improving the lives" of others is a phrase that much like "beauty" lies in the "eye of the beholder."

Consider two examples: For some, efforts to rid society of guns may be part of a worthwhile social marketing intervention to reduce violence, whereas for others, encouraging citizens to arm themselves may be the perceived route to the same goal. Similarly, for some, condoms may be a critical weapon in efforts to reduce sexually transmitted diseases, yet for others (who may prefer to encourage abstinence), condoms may be viewed as an instrument that is likely to encourage sex and hence increase sexually transmitted diseases. Although some of these differences may be put to an empirical test, some differences occur at the level of basic values, and one is hard-pressed to reason through such issues "pragmatically." Even where empirical tests might potentially provide an answer, the answer (as perhaps in the issue of violence above) may be a long time in coming, making those supporting one position or the other reluctant to wait. Inevitably then, both the content and processes associated with social marketing, and the very parameters used to define it, are open to debate.

This position reflects the tenor of the discussion that took place at the Role of Advertising in Social Marketing Conference held in Atlanta GA, May 17–19, 1995. This book incorporates many of the presentations made at the conference, part of the continuing Advertising and Psychology series sponsored by the Society for Consumer Psychology. As is evident from a quick perusal of the table of contents, the conference attracted a wide variety of professionals from academia, government, and nongovernment organizations, who addressed a highly diverse and interesting set of societal problems. Unfortunately, this preface can touch only briefly on the various chapters. The reader is urged to reflect on the meaning and import of each.

A number of the chapters underscore the need for theory in social marketing. Alan Andreasen (chapter 1) focuses on the need for marketers to employ theory-driven planning models, highlighting Prochaska and DiClemente's stage model. Andreasen calls for the incorporation of emotional factors into such cognitive models. His chapter includes an interesting taxonomy of the behaviors that social marketing typically tries to influence.

Bill Smith (chapter 2) argues that "the acid test for (defining) social marketing is the demonstrated integration of product, place, price, and promotion . . ." (p. 27). He reminds us that we are in an era of shrinking government spending, an era that shakes some basic tenets of social marketing and its sources of support. It is in this climate that social marketers are forced to adopt a sharper customer focus. Part of this focus is clarifying the distinctions among regulatory (advocacy), information (advertising), and marketing approaches.

The core of marketing's contribution is its insistence on adopting the consumer's perspective. One example of this approach and its utility is Joel Cohen's chapter (15). Government has insisted that the cigarette companies provide tar and nicotine ratings in their advertising. Have consumers used this information to their advantage? Cohen presents results of a survey of smokers. The data indicate that smokers have little understanding of these ratings, even with regard to their own cigarettes. Nor do they have much understanding of the relative risks associated with different tar levels. Cohen argues that the FTC ought to use more realistic (less optimistic) estimates of tar yields and communicate these estimates through category-descriptive labels rather than absolute numbers, which can be readily misconstrued.

A second core contribution of marketing is its emphasis on "the four *p*s." These serve to remind social marketers that to be successful, their interventions need to consider not just *promotion*, but also *price*, *place* and *product*. Lynn Kozlowski and Christine Sweeney (chapter 14) focus on the product—light and ultra light cigarettes. To understand the attraction of these products for many smokers and how they may be undermining efforts to get people to stop smoking, we need to carefully examine the product itself. Kozlowski and Sweeney demonstrate that the tar numbers provided in cigarette advertising are misleadingly low, in part because of smokers' tendency to intentionally or inadvertently block micro-vents which are instrumental in lowering the tar levels.

Darren Dahl, Gerald Gorn, and Charles Weinberg (chapter 11) focus on both price and place in an interesting set of field experiments. They find that a percentage-off coupon for condoms can be effective if the percent is high enough and the coupon is distributed in the right place—in front of the cooperating pharmacy (and not at other test sites, e.g., at a ballpark or the condom shelf itself).

Although the costs and benefits of a particular sought-after behavior may be relatively immutable, shifting the salience of the benefits relative to the costs, or highlighting a particular benefit, is often a more achievable objective; hence the frequent emphasis on promotion/advertising by social marketers.

Cornelia Pechmann (chapter 12) argues that communications are competitive, and at least one antismoking message is needed for every four cigarette ads. She suggests that the failure to attain this ratio is partly responsible for the failure to achieve reductions in the rate of underage smoking over the past few decades. Examining a number of relevant field and lab experiments, Pechmann concludes that properly designed antismoking messages can be successful, particularly if used in coordination with school education programs. These messages are most effective when they focus on the short-term costs that teens regard as most salient.

In his insightful chapter, Bob Hornik (chapter 4) examines the reasons for the success or failure of large scale public health interventions. Hornik suggests the following exchange theory: When benefits are high and/or costs are low we can expect to see the target consumers change. Witness how quickly parents changed from aspirin to alternative pain remedies for their children when aspirin was implicated in Reyes syndrome. A simple substitute (low cost) and a clear-cut benefit made for a rapid change in the population's behavior.

Why do the macro experiments like the COMMIT study typically show very little effects of huge intervention efforts? Hornik argues that these interventions typically fail to add very much exposure beyond that which is already produced by the background public discourse. People may not respond to the few extra exposures produced by the formal structured interventions. They may have already responded to the much heavier dose of health information on the same issues broadcast on Good Morning America and its like, and to the informal conversations that such shared exposures stimulate.

Martine Stead and Gerard Hastings (chapter 3) use examples such as the introduction of fluoride in Northern England to show the effectiveness of lobbying key individuals and key institutions as a low cost alternative to expensive mass advertising. They suggest that it is difficult to compete with the private sector which may have greater expertise and considerable resources.

Segmentation is yet another core contribution that marketing makes to the study of social marketing. Michael Swenson and William Wells (chapter 7) point to the availability of lifestyle data from the DDB Needham Lifestyle surveys to segment markets psychographically. As an example, they identify items used to describe consumers who are more environmentally sensitive. This segment is then examined in terms of their associated behaviors and media interests.

Cynthia Currence (chapter 8) provides a detailed case study in identifying, describing, and reaching one segment—poor, older women—in an effort to persuade them to get mammograms. Geodemographics—census data, buyer behavior data, and media behavior data—are used to locate and describe high concentrations of poor women in the Atlanta area and the most convenient mammogram centers they might access. (To the program's credit, they realize that persuading the women is not the sole answer. The availability of mammogram services for these women is also examined and found lacking, highlighting the need to impact the social/structural environment as well as the target individual.)

June Flora, Caroline Schooler, and Rosalind Pierson (chapter 20) consider "communities of color," with the underlying thesis that an understanding of the racial and cultural differences among these groups can enhance health promotions targeted to them. They detail a number of useful bases for segmenting these populations, including immigration status, family structure, degree of assimilation or accommodation to the majority culture, language use, and health beliefs and practices.

With an eye on the research methodologies that accompany social marketing efforts, George Balch and Sharyn Sutton (chapter 5) argue persuasively that social marketers ought to pay as much (or more) attention to "formative" and "process" research as to "outcome" or "impact" research. They detail the manner in which evaluations of social marketing systems ought to be part of an "interactive, iterative, ongoing system" (p. 61). Formative research should be more strategic, and even quantitative, as needed, to answer strategic questions for program decision making. And process evaluation needs to be more diagnostic, even qualitative, as needed, to tell us what, if anything, our program delivered, to whom, and how—to be able to understand and adjust it intelligently.

Jonathan Baggaley (chapter 6) describes an innovative research methodology that facilitates the collection of consumer data to assist in all stages of program development from formative research, through concept and material testing and monitoring. He shows how his computer-based interactive data collection methodology can be used in a range of cultures and can provide rapid, reliable, inexpensive, and culture-free results.

As the primary sponsoring agency, the CDC's participation in the conference was critical. To portray a sampling of the CDC's work in social marketing, Fred Kroger (chapter 16) gathered some key contributors who described a number of CDC programs. These include The Tobacco Control Programs (McKenna); The Prevention Marketing Initiative, a broad ranging effort to prevent the spread of HIV and other STDs among people under 25 (Shepherd); The Nutritional and Physical Activity Communications Project (NUPAC; Howze & associates); The Brokering and Dissemination of Public Health Information (Knight); and the CDC's nascent efforts to market the merits of essential public health services (Kroger).

Sometimes, to compensate for a lack of resources, and almost always to increase the effectiveness of an intervention, researchers seek to involve local individuals and institutions. One example is the effort reported by Martin Fishbein and colleagues (chapter 9). Described as a theory-based community-level intervention, the CDC's AIDS Community Demonstration Projects is a field experiment designed to reduce AIDS-related risk behaviors in populations that typically do not come in contact with public (or private) health services: injecting drug users (IDUs), the female sex partners of IDUs, commercial sex workers, men who have sex with men but who do not gay-identify, and youth at high risk. The specific goals are to increase both the use of condoms and the use of bleach to clean needles and other injecting drug paraphernalia. The strategy is to use community volunteers to develop and distribute targeted, theoretically based small media materials (e.g., local community flyers, pamphlets). Fishbein presents significantly positive interim results from this long-term project.

In chapter 17, Middlestadt, Schechter, Peyton, and Tjugum discuss the community partnership strategies AED has used in their work on HIV prevention, child survival, the environment, and other social issues, both domestically and internationally, in developing countries. Increasingly, social marketers are being asked to design programs under conditions of local control, ownership, and community participation. The chapter outlines the different definitions and assumptions underlying social marketing and community mobilization models and presents recommendations for behavioral science and technical assistance tools to assist social marketers in meeting the challenge.

In an era of declining budgets, many have found that forming partnerships with the private sector can be an effective strategy. Jim Mintz and his associates at the Canadian Department of Health (chapter 13) describe how promotional efforts for Health Canada now involve a Partnership Network Expansion: government alliances with for-profit and not-for-profit organizations to maximize effectiveness of mass media interventions in Canada.

Paul Bloom and his colleagues (chapter 18) describe the private sector's involvement in independent efforts to conduct social marketing campaigns. They suggest that corporate social marketing initiatives can often be more effective than those sponsored by governmental agencies or nonprofit organizations and discuss the strengths and drawbacks of each approach. The chapter then presents 11 case studies of corporate initiatives on diverse topics including a bran cereal campaign by a food company to encourage a high-fiber, low fat diet; a breast cancer crusade promoting early detection by a cosmetic firm; and an anti-violence against women program by a shoe manufacturer.

In his description of social marketers' efforts to promote and sell subsidized contraceptives in 43 developing countries, Phil Harvey (chapter 10) emphasizes that the success of the effort is keyed to small management teams operating flexibly and autonomously within the private sector.

The final part of this book points to the very diversity of topics addressed by social marketers. Jeffrey Prottas (chapter 21) addresses perhaps the most daunting challenge raised in this book—increasing the rate of organ donation. He considers the utility of social advertising as a vehicle for accomplishing this goal and concludes that, notwithstanding the difficulties and inherent limitations, it is a strategy worth pursuing.

Marvin Goldberg, Ozlem Sandikci, and David Litvack (chapter 19) consider the thesis that violence in sports reflects violence in society. Focusing on the role of communications, they argue (following Bandura's social learning model), that professional sports, and in particular hockey on TV, provide influential violent role models for young hockey players. They propose to test this hypothesis by exposing various young hockey teams to videotapes of either violent hockey fights or scoring highlights just before game time and measuring how violently these young teammates play. They also propose strategies for reducing such violence.

Jerome Kernan and Teresa Domzal (chapter 22) examine the challenge of public health advertising from a postmodern perspective. They detail the shift from a simpler, traditional (top-down) world of doctors and hospitals as sole (sacred) holders of the public's trust regarding definitions of health and illness to today's postmodern cacophony of influences, including most saliently, commercial influences.

As indicated by this brief overview of some of the presented papers, the May 1995 Atlanta Conference provided a forum for academics, governmental, and nongovernmental professionals to interact, exchange ideas, and learn about a number of social marketing approaches and programs. And, whereas some of the discussion addressed the questions of "What is social marketing?" and "Where is it going?", the primary focus of the conference was on research, program development, and evaluation. Perhaps because of this and the mix of attendees, considerable interest was expressed in similar exchanges in the future. The forum for such exchanges was considered, with the possibility that a continuing series of such conferences would be initiated.

ACKNOWLEDGMENTS

As this book goes to press, the third annual conference, Innovations in Social Marketing, is scheduled for Spring 1997. Considerable credit for this ongoing effort goes to the conference's various sponsors, in particular the CDC. Fred Kroger of the CDC is owed a particular debt of gratitude for his encouragement and support of both the conference series and this book. Lastly, we also wish to acknowledge the help of Ann Bellochio, staff assistant at Penn State University, with regard to the preparation of both the 1995 Atlanta conference and this book.

—Marvin E. Goldberg
—Martin Fishbein
—Susan E. Middlestadt

Part I

PARADIGMS/PERSPECTIVES

Chapter 1

Challenges for the Science and Practice of Social Marketing

Alan R. Andreasen
Georgetown University

Twenty-five years ago, marketing scholars, led by the "Northwestern School" (Elliott, 1991) began to look at possible applications of commercial sector marketing beyond its traditional confines (Kotler & Levy, 1969; Kotler & Zaltman, 1971). The first wave of interest was institutional. In the 1970s, marketing scholars focused on adapting marketing mind-sets, processes, and concepts to a wide range of nonprofit enterprises, initially universities, performing arts organizations, and hospitals. In the 1980s and 1990s, however, an increasing number of scholars and practitioners shifted away from this institutional focus toward what might be called a *program focus*. They recognized that the basic goal of marketing is to influence behavior, whether that behavior is buying a Big Mac, flying United Airlines, practicing safe sex, or getting one's child immunized (Andreasen, 1993). In each case, marketers mount programs to bring about these behaviors. Some programs, like that of United Airlines or the National High Blood Pressure Education Program, are very long term. Others, like many new cereal introductions and some health care interventions, are shorter lived.

This perception that marketing constitutes a proven and potentially very powerful technology for bringing about socially desirable behaviors is the engine motivating the growth of what might be called "the social marketing movement" over the last 15 years. This movement has established social marketing as a distinct subdiscipline within the general field of academic marketing. At the same time, it has led to the adoption of the technology by a wide range of private, public, and private-nonprofit organizations and institutions, including the Centers for Disease Control and Prevention, the U.S. Agency for International Development, the U.S. Department of Agriculture, and the National Cancer Institute. There are now social marketing textbooks (Andreasen, 1995; Fine, 1981; Kotler & Roberto, 1989; Manoff, 1985), readings books (Fine, 1990), chapters within mainstream texts (Kotler & Andreasen, 1996), and a Harvard teaching note (Rangun & Karim, 1991). There have been reviews of the accomplishments of social marketing (Fox & Kotler, 1980; Malafarina & Loken, 1993) and presidential addresses for two different consumer behavior organizations calling to researchers and academics to become more deeply involved in studies of social marketing (Andreasen, 1993; Goldberg, 1995). Centers for social marketing are present or proposed in Florida, Ottawa, Scotland, and South Africa.

Social marketing is now sufficiently established that it has earned its own critics. For example, Wallack (1990) argued that social marketing is too costly and time consuming and that its individual-level approach fails to remove the noxious environments that are the true causes of the behaviors it is trying to change. Wallack proposed media advocacy as the most cost-effective way to bring about important social changes. He concluded that "the effectiveness of social marketing remains limited" (p. 376).

Despite the healthy skepticism of its critics, social marketing is now both deepening and broadening its market penetration. For this reason, it is important for those who feel custodial responsibility for the field to insure that this growth is healthy. The challenges facing the field depend on whether one is broadening or is deepening the application.

BROADENING SOCIAL MARKETING APPLICATIONS

Social marketing in its formative years was primarily associated with health problems as represented by two of the most important early applications, contraceptive marketing and high blood pressure (National Heart, Lung, & Blood Institute, 1992; Rangun & Karim, 1991). However, in the last 5 years, although health applications continue to dominate, there has been a broadening in the application of the technology to other areas. Andreasen and Tyson (1993) applied social marketing to get builders to plant or save more trees on the residential lots they develop. Others used social marketing ideas to get householders and businesses to recycle more often, and to get families to adopt more difficult-to-place children. Still others developed programs to get politicians and school administrators in Asia to increase the educational opportunities for girls (Schwartz, 1994), to encourage rural economic development, to reduce spousal abuse, and to lobby U.S. congressional representatives (Novelli, 1995).

As many authors and speakers have made clear, the principles of social marketing can apply to an extremely diverse set of social problems wherever the bottom line is influencing behavior (Andreasen, 1995; Kotler & Roberto, 1989). However, as managers and funding agencies begin to use social marketing in more and more disparate domains, it is important to repeat the following cautions about basic principles, which—in their haste to adopt the very latest social engineering fad—they may ignore.

Social marketing is about behavior change. It is not about education and propaganda, and individuals should not imagine they are doing social marketing if their *primary* goal is informing the public or trying to change some basic values. These are laudable goals and they may precede social marketing. But they are not social marketing! As a corollary, social marketing is not social advertising. Although communications tools are often central to social marketing programs, social marketing is much more than just communications.

Social marketing is not a grab-bag of concepts and tools (like focus group research) randomly used as needed or peppered throughout traditional approaches like health education. It is, first of all, a specific mind-set that puts customers at the center of everything the marketer does. Second, it is a process of doing social marketing. This process involves constantly going back and forth to the target market before and after planning and before and after implementation. And it is, finally, a set of coordinated interventions that do not rely only on communications.

Social marketing is not a panacea. It often must deal with huge problems where the expectations of funding agencies, governments, and the general public is very high. Yet, these very same problems typically involve very fundamental behaviors, attitudes, and values. Changing the way Pakistani men treat young women in their society is a lot more difficult than getting more kids in the United States to eat Froot Loops. As various scholars have noted (Bloom & Novelli, 1981; Kotler & Andreasen, 1991; Rothschild, 1979), social marketers have several special issues with which to deal:

Nonexistent demand—for example, where targets of a contraceptive social marketing program are members of a particular religious group who believe that children are "God's plan" and cannot be prevented or spaced.

Negative demand—for example, where drivers feel that driving under 55 mph or wearing a seat belt is unduly restrictive.

Intense public scrutiny—for example, where village leaders feel that a new breast feeding or oral rehydration program is a hostile Western attempt to eliminate traditional values and social patterns.

Nonliterate and/or extremely impoverished target markets—for example, when villagers cannot afford either the cost of condoms or, alternatively, the time to go to a health clinic to get free ones.

Highly sensitive issues—for example, where one wishes to ask Muslim women about their sexual behaviors in order to develop a more effective safe sex campaign.

Invisible benefits—for example, where one is promoting driving under 55 mph or getting a child inoculated but where success means that nothing happened (i.e., no accidents, no measles), which makes it hard for the target audience to see a connection between the recommended behavior and specific outcomes.

Benefits are often to third parties—for example, where one is trying to get individual households to recycle even though they do not directly benefit and, in fact, pay real costs.

Benefits are often hard to portray—for example, where one would like to show the outcome of safe sex or family planning without using clichéd pictures of happy, healthy individuals and families.

Social marketing is not mass marketing. Indeed, as is noted later, one of social marketing's important contributions is to insist that markets almost always need to be segmented, and in many cases segmented in unconventional ways.

Finally, changing behavior in many cases is only the first step. Too many programs are short lived, designed as one-time campaigns. For the difficult behaviors with which many social programs are involved, such quick fixes are likely to have equally quick lifetimes.

DEEPENING SOCIAL MARKETING INTERVENTIONS

Social marketing has been around long enough so that there are a number of organizations now in existence that have 15 to 20 years experience implementing and/or advising about social marketing. They have become better practitioners of this new technology and through newsletters, monographs, and manuals have sought to share their findings and insights with others in a range of formats: general management guides (Cabañero-Verzosa et al., 1989), manuals for communications campaign planning and executions (e.g., HealthCom, 1995), guidelines for a range of marketing functions (Elder, Barriga, Graeff, Rosenbaum, & Boddy, 1991; Seidel, 1993; SOMARC, n.d.), narrative histories of particular programs (Browne, 1994; Saade & Tucker, n.d.), program evaluations (Seidel, 1992; SOMARC III, 1994), and conference reports (Women, Infants, & STDs, 1991).

A review of this literature suggests that, if the field is to deepen its applications, attention must be paid to each of the three central elements of the social marketing approach. Progress can be made in widening the use of the customer mind-set, introducing new theory-driven planning models, and developing more sophisticated concepts and tools.

Widening the Use of the Customer Mind-Set

The essence of the social marketing mind-set is a fanatical devotion to being customer driven. And, most sophisticated social marketers have little difficulty being customer driven when it comes to their target markets. They thoroughly understand the need for customer research at various stages of the process. They know they must segment their markets (although often not as creatively as might be imagined). They can craft programs that directly address the needs, wants, and perceptions of the segments they select. And, they know they must pay careful attention to both cognitive and behavioral responses of those targets before, during, and after implementation.

However, where these marketers often fail is when they focus on other than final target markets. For example, it is commonly asserted that most social marketing programs can only succeed if they enlist the help of others to carry out program activities. Social marketers have limited budgets and, typically, immense challenges. So they must work with physicians, retailers, government bureaucrats, politicians, and the media to achieve their goals. Yet, when dealing with these potential partners, they often forget the customer mind-set that made them so successful in the first place. They forget that the bottom line of social marketing is influencing behavior and the cooperation of others is simply just another kind of behavior to be influenced. Thus, attempts to influence such audiences must also start with these audiences' needs, wants, and perceptions.

Yet, it has been my experience that too many program managers seek cooperation from important partners by arguing as persuasively as they can that the program needs the help. These myopic marketers describe the immense challenges they face and point out how cooperating partners can be instrumental in helping the social marketer achieve success. They say over and over again that help is desperately needed! The social marketers seem to think that the targets will be flattered by this call for help. But, even though they seldom realize it, the basic message they are sending out is: "You should act in the ways we want because *we* will benefit from it!" The social marketer would never act this way when addressing final consumers. But, they will often act this way with television news directors, nurses, or pharmacists. They adopt a classic *organization-centered approach* (Andreasen, 1984).

Of course, what these social marketers need to learn to do instinctively is to cast the desired behavior and its consequences in terms of each audience's needs and wants. They have to show the news director how the news director's audience will be enthralled by a story about the social marketing program (especially if they provide a photogenic child for interviewing). They have to show nurses that participating in the program will help them learn new skills and increase their efficiency in their sphere of work. They have to show the pharmacists that participating will not only mean more sales and profits but will enhance their prestige in the community as a source of important new innovations and sage advice.

The principles are the same. Social marketers just seem to forget how widely they can be applied.

Introducing New Theory-Driven Planning Models

Most mature social marketing organizations have developed some form of boxes-and-arrows planning model to guide their operations. These models typically start with a formal situational analysis with a heavy emphasis on consumer research. This is then followed by planning, pretesting, and implementation, with the planning stage further subdivided to address major subcomponents of the program (e.g., segmentation, positioning, developing the marketing mix). The implementation stage is typically followed by some form of monitoring that then leads back in a recursive fashion to more planning, pretesting, implementation, and so on. Programs with finite lives and outside funding agencies also typically build into their model some form of final evaluation for the entire activity (Seidel, 1992).

These linear process models function very much like checklists. They indicate the steps and tasks that a careful social marketer is to follow if a program is to have a successful outcome. But, what is missing from most of the process models is any kind of underlying theoretical framework. The models tell managers what to do and in what sequence. But, they do not tie these steps to any particular framework that makes clear how what they do is supposed to work to impact critical social behaviors. This is a role, however, that can be played by one or more of the available social science theories discussed throughout this volume (e.g., Lutz & Bettman, 1977; Wilkie & Pessemeir, 1973).

Sophisticated social marketing managers are well aware of these theories of behavior change. But, the design and execution of social marketing programs is seldom driven by underlying theoretical models.

Why would a grounding in such theories be helpful? The simplest answer lies in the fundamental mission of all social marketing programs: They are "in business" to influence one or more behaviors that society deems to be a potential (or actual) source of problems. Whatever social marketers implement as part of their strategy is designed to impact those behaviors. It seems obvious, therefore, that if a social marketer had some sort of mental roadmap or social science model about how what they do may have its effect, then they could design strategies with a higher probability of succeeding.

As Hornik (1992) and others (Fishbein et al., in press) pointed out, there exist a significant array of midrange theories that can form the basis for such a model. One group of models focuses on individual cognitive activity. They include the Theory of Reasoned Action (Fishbein & Ajzen, 1975), the Health Belief Model (Rosenstock, 1990), the Theory of Planned Behavior (Ajzen, 1991), the Theory of Trying (Bagozzi & Warshaw, 1990), the Theory of Self-Regulation and Self-Control (Kanfer, 1970; Kanfer & Shefft, 1988), Protection Motivation Theory (Rogers, 1983; Maddux & Rogers, 1983), the Theory of Subjective Culture and Interpersonal Relations (Triandis, 1972, 1977), Social Learning Theory (Bandura, 1977), the Stages-of-Change—or transtheoretical—Model (Baranowski & Jenkins, 1989–1990; Prochaska & DiClemente, 1983), and Innovation Adoption Theory (Rogers, 1983; Kotler & Roberto, 1989).

Another group of models draws on the work of Skinner and focuses not on cognition but on the behavior itself and its direct modification (Graeff, Elder, & Booth, 1994). Finally, a third set of models or approaches focuses not on individuals but on communities or cultures as the potential point of impact (Wallack, 1990). Whereas each group of models has a distinctive focus, they have many points of intersection. The challenge is to translate the models, or some useful subset of them, into a framework that social marketing managers can use to guide strategy. Such a framework would provide an important missing bridge between the more esoteric world of scholarship and the real world of practitioners interested in making an impact on society's problems. As John Dewey has said, nothing is so practical as a good theory! But, what might such a framework look like?

Consider the following serviceable, portable framework for social marketing programs drawing on several of the social science sources already suggested. Although not a definitive approach, it shares communalities with recent work by Baranowski and Jenkins (1992–1993), Maibach and Cotton (1995), and Fishbein (1995). Put very simply, the model is as follows:

1. It is assumed that the behaviors that social marketers are attempting to influence are of a class called *high involvement* (Celsi & Olson, 1988);

2. Consumers come to take and maintain high involvement actions through a series of stages. In a simplification of the Prochaska and DiClemente (1983) model, four stages are labeled Precontemplation, Contemplation, Action, and Maintenance. The Contemplation Stage is further divided into Early and Late Contemplation stages.

3. At the Precontemplation Stage, the major social marketing challenge is to overcome one or both of two problems. In precontemplation, target audience members do not see the proposed behavior as relevant to their own needs and wants. There are typically two reasons for this. Either the consumers were unaware of the new behavioral opportunity and/or they

believe it is not appropriate for someone like them. The reason for the latter is often that the behavior is perceived to contravene important values, including religious ones ("my people do not practice family planning"). A crucial problem here is a Catch-22, consumers' tendencies to selectively ignore and/or screen out social marketing messages that do not address an issue of relevance to them. The principal techniques a social marketer must use here are education (Glanz, Lewis, & Rimer, 1990; AIDS Education, 1989), propaganda (Bush, Ortinau, & Bush, 1994), and media advocacy (Wallack, 1990).

4. After the Precontemplation Stage, behavior is driven and maintained by many factors, principally perceived benefits, perceived costs, perceived social influences, and perceived behavioral control.

5. To get consumers to move from the Contemplation Stage to Action and Maintenance, the model makes clear that marketers must increase perceived benefits, decrease perceived costs, increase perceived social pressure, and increase perceived behavioral control.

6. Once the consumer has taken initial action, then behavioral models become more important than cognitive models. To maintain new behavioral patterns, consumers must feel rewarded. They must also be subject to regular reminders until the new behaviors become an ingrained way of life and the old behavior is no longer an option.

This is not the only social science framework one can use to inform marketing strategies. However, it is important to have *some* framework. Frameworks provide a basis for both research and strategy. They tell marketers what to ask about when they study consumers. Using the model presented here, they tell them they need to know the stage in which the target market is, what they perceive the consequences of the behavior to be, what they think others want them to do, and whether they think they can actually make the behavior happen. Such data will tell marketers in broad terms how to segment the market, what positioning to take and what messages and other marketing mix elements have to be in place to move the target toward the ultimate goal of maintained behavior. The model has the advantage that it provides a structure and a checklist of what needs to be done that is grounded in how people act!

Developing More Sophisticated Concepts and Tools

The proper program-wide mind-set and a theory-grounded strategic plan are only two of the requirements for deepened social marketing. But, the devil is in the details of particular tactics and strategy. It is here that much more needs to be done. Both academics and commercial practitioners have available a number of tools that are now well accepted in the private sector that have seen only limited use in social marketing. Some of these tools need to be adapted for the new context. Most do not need such adjustment.

Segmentation by Lifestyles. Although segmentation is now common in social marketing, the approach typically used is based on relatively rudimentary demographics. Such an approach is, of course, simple to comprehend and allows marketers to make use of census data and other secondary source material in order to estimate market sizes and locations. The difficulty with the approach, however, is that it forces social marketers to make assumptions about what their target market needs, wants, and perceives. Further, it provides little insight into just who these people are—other than to say, for example, that they are women 18 to 45 years old living in major metropolises with a husband at home and at least one child under age 5. This description helps a strategist to some extent, but it says little about how the target market might be portrayed in advertisements or how they might be spoken to. One-on-one interviews can help flesh out this portrait, but this solution is very expensive and slow, especially when dealing with a great many segments.

The commercial sector long ago recognized the need for a research technique that combined the efficiency of large-scale survey research with the richness and detail of one-on-one depth interviews or "motivation research" (Wells, 1989). The solution they developed was labeled *psychographic* or *lifestyle segmentation.* This approach collects detailed information on the activities, interests, and opinions (AIOs) of probability samples of households and then clusters target audiences into groups similar in AIO profiles. Such groupings are often referred to as *lifestyle segments* and are typically given vivid labels to characterize their central features (e.g., "the New Bohemians"). Lifestyle profiles yield rich insights into the target audience's particular interests, media habits, leisure patterns, and so forth. These insights are very valuable in creating messages that "speak to" specific target audiences. And recent approaches that profile lifestyle segments by geographic location ("geoclustering") solve a major problem of earlier work, namely, how to reach a given lifestyle segment (cf. Riche, 1989).

Lifestyle research can be particularly valuable in addressing social behaviors in upscale audiences. Indeed, geoclustering is already being explored by the marketing specialists at the American Cancer Society for income development purposes and is planned for use for interventions to affect cancer prevention, detection, and treatment. Where lifestyle research has not been used is in studying the social behaviors of the lowest income groups that are often a particular interest of many social marketing programs, especially in developing countries. Low income markets have been studied by anthropologists at some length. However, to date, no one has tried to use the quantitative technique of lifestyle research.

The potential for such an approach was revealed in interviews conducted in Jakarta, Indonesia, in 1994. There, informants suggested that the poor in Jakarta could be partitioned into four groupings along two dimensions depending on whether they were legal or illegal residents of the city and whether their principal source of income was from entrepreneurial effort or working for others. These demographics were associated with differences in lifestyle patterns that potentially would be better than the demographics themselves as the main focus of any social marketing campaign. Thus, for example, informants suggested that the "illegal entrepreneurials" were more likely to live on the outskirts of the city along highways or railroad tracks. All members of the family hustled. This implies that mothers would not have much time for traveling to health care centers for treatment or for counseling, say, on breastfeeding or prenatal care. On the other hand, their success motivation may make them responsive to appeals about actions that would better their lives and that of their children (e.g., "breastfed children are less trouble for the busy mother and grow into active, healthy workers").

On the other hand, informants said that the legal poor who worked in factories in the city often had single incomes. Wives did not work. And, because Jakarta is so crowded and their incomes are so low, they had very tiny homes and seldom stayed indoors in the evenings; meals were typically eaten out at corner stands. This suggests that mothers would have more leisure time to attend to health programs and seek treatment. It also implies that the way to reach them may well be by street corner presentations in the evenings, perhaps through new forms of entertainment education (Rogers, Aikat, Chang, Poppe, & Sopory, 1989).

The potential for richer intervention strategies based on lifestyle segmentation would appear to be substantial. Of course, the measurements of lifestyles that would be used in such research would differ from those applied in upper quintile markets. The following are among the questions to be addressed for low income markets:

What are the activities, interests, and opinions that span the lifestyles of a given low income target population?

What are the dimensions that underlie the lifestyles?

Do the underlying activities, interests, opinions, and dimensions vary across countries or subpopulations (e.g., ethnic groups) within countries?

How many clusters seem to capture the total populations and do these clusters vary across subpopulations?

How well do the clusters predict present social behaviors and likely responses to future socially desirable behaviors? Is this prediction better than that from traditional socioeconomic characteristics?

Enriching the Cognitive Model. The model proposed above has only four major cognitive components (benefits, costs, the influence of others, and self-efficacy) set within the stages-of-change framework. Clearly, there are other factors that influence behavior that could be introduced. A "theorist's workshop" conducted in the early 1990s among several of the leading figures in behavioral theory concluded that there were eight such factors that should be within the "finite set of variables to be considered in any behavioral analysis" (Fishbein et al., in press). These are intention, environmental constraints, skills, anticipated outcomes, norms, self-standards, emotion, and self-efficacy. Three of these factors—self-efficacy, anticipated outcomes (benefits and costs), and norms (influence of others)—are included in the model proposed here. Further, Fishbein et al. suggested that "intention" may be considered a proxy for stages of change.

The remaining four factors (environmental constraints, skills, self-standards, and emotion) merit exploration in future research in social marketing. Environmental constraints are the conditions in the target audience's surroundings that make it impossible for the behavior to be performed. These constraints presumably are especially important as consumers move through the Contemplation Stage toward Action. Equally important are the skills necessary to perform the behavior. These two components have a major influence on self-efficacy, that is, the consumer's perception that they can actually carry out the behavior. The distinction, however, is important because it has implications for social marketing programs and for future theory development. Obviously, if behavioral constraints are the critical component of a lack of self-efficacy, then action must be taken to remove the constraints, such as improving condom availability, broadening the hours at which a clinic is open, or establishing a new waste recycling system. On the other hand, if skills are crucial, then training must be provided directly or indirectly to improve perceived self-efficacy.

From a conceptual standpoint, it is important to understand whether these two factors are, indeed, the major determinants of self-efficacy as compared to personal self-confidence. Correcting constraints and skill deficiencies is clearly easier than trying to bolster individual self-confidence, although approaches to the latter are available in both the popular and scientific press.

The third additional component proposed is self-standards. This factor reflects Kanfer's work proposing that people decide what to do in part based on whether the action fits with their conception of who they are. In order to act, the person must perceive "that performance of the behavior is more consistent than inconsistent with his or her self-image, or that its performance does not violate personal standards that activate negative self-sanctions" (Fishbein et al., in press, p. 10). If this factor is found to be an important determinant in some behavioral situations, this has implications for message strategies in the Contemplation Stage (i.e., showing the individual that the behavior is "something people like you are doing"). It also has implications for the Action and Maintenance stages where Kanfer emphasized the critical role that self-regulation and self-reward play in maintaining a behavior once it has begun. Conceptually, it raises questions about the multidimensionality of the role of others in influencing behavior. Others not only communicate information, but they also reflect norms and set standards for the individual to emulate. Sorting out these inter-personal influences in specific situations can advance the understanding of how to bring social pressure to bear on behavior.

The last "new" factor, emotion, is also critical to behavior. As Fishbein et al. pointed out, individuals are much more likely to perform a behavior if they have a positive rather than a negative "gut feeling" about doing it. This is critical to social marketing which is concerned with high involve-ment decisions involving attitudes and behaviors that are very important, or central, to individuals. Efforts to change these behaviors may arouse significant emotional reactions (Cohen & Areni, 1991). Emotional benefits and costs are, indeed, central in programs dealing with AIDS, family plan-ning, drug use, gang membership, child and spousal abuse (and many other crimes), weight control, and many others. This may be the best way to introduce emotional factors into behavior change modeling.

However, it must be recognized that emotions can get in the way of planned behavior. For example, many people targeted in AIDS or family planning programs claim their runaway emotions are the prime reason they failed to carry out what they were convinced rationally was a sound course of behavior, that is, using a condom. In this context, emotion acts as an internal constraint on behavior.

The lack of research on emotion in social marketing is consistent with the relatively low status affect and emotion have had in basic psychology (Cohen & Areni, 1991; Isen & Hastorf, 1982). Bagozzi and Moore (1994), however, suggested some useful beginnings. Drawing on the work of Laz-arus (1991), Shaver, Schwartz, Kirson, and O'Connor (1987), and Watson and Tellgren (1985), Bagozzi and Moore explored the role of emotions in explaining the effects of public service advertisements (PSA) on indi-viduals' decisions to help others in child abuse cases. They found that PSAs work through empathy, either directly or through negative emotions, to influence the decision to help. They found that the stronger the negative emotion (anger, sadness, fear, and tension), the stronger the empathetic response. Bagozzi and Moore encouraged other researchers to extend the approach to other social behaviors and one could recommend extending it to positive as well as negative emotions.

A New Taxonomy of Behaviors.   One of the problems in the literature on behavior change is that researchers and modelers tend not to make dis-tinctions among types of behavior change. For example, Triandis (1972) and others suggested that environmental constraints are important influences on behavior. Whereas it is clear how such constraints might play a role in adopting a new behavior, it is not so clear what their role might be when one is attempting to stop a behavior. As suggested elsewhere (Andreasen, 1993), social marketing behaviors differ in important ways along measurable dimensions and these distinctions are worth paying attention to on both theoretical and practical grounds. That is, the role that benefits, costs, others, and self-efficacy (and/or the other factors Fishbein et al. proposed) may be very different depending on the type or category of behavior with which one is dealing.

How, then, might target behaviors for social marketing be categorized? Consider the following as a starting point:

Behaviors that are new to the world versus behaviors that are new to the individual. Diffusion-of-innovation theory (Rogers, 1993) suggests that those who try something early in its lifecycle (innovators or early adopters) may be very different from those who consider adopting it later. Thus, a man contemplating quitting smoking in Thailand in 1996 is likely to be very different from a man contemplating quitting in the United States at the same time. Baranowski (1992–1993) suggested that, because Late Majority and Laggards are likely to have personalities that attribute locus of control (Rotter, 1955) externally, they are more likely to be influenced by normative factors throughout the behavior change process. On the other hand, Innovators and Early Adopters are more likely to exhibit internal locus of control and so pay more attention to personal costs and benefits. Clearly, the role of the key behavioral determinants will systematically vary across these situations.

Behaviors facing serious competition versus behaviors having no serious competition. Marketers pay a great deal of attention to competition in the real world and argue that one cannot develop a good strategy without understanding the competition. For some behaviors of interest to social marketers, the competitive behavior might be thought of as "the status quo." Those who are not exercising do not think of the decision to start to be a choice between one desirable alternative and another, they think of it as doing something versus doing nothing. On the other hand, a marijuana-smoking high-schooler does think of stopping using marijuana as a choice between two lifestyles, each of which has its pros and cons. In the latter setting, a good social marketer and a good behavioral modeler ought to measure the behavioral determinants of both behaviors in order to develop a sound strategy.

Behaviors with personal benefits versus behaviors with third-party benefits. Many social marketing behaviors have important personal benefits, such as losing weight, getting off drugs, and spacing children. On the other hand, an important subset of behaviors have costs to the individuals, but the benefits produced are largely accruing to others. Obeying the speed limit and recycling are clear cases of the latter. One would expect that the role of significant others may always be critical in the latter category but not always so in the former. It may also be possible that the benefit component may play virtually no role at all in cases where third parties are involved, despite what most theorists—and much common sense—would predict.

Behaviors that are public versus behaviors that are private. Some social marketing behaviors are very obvious to the world either in the act itself (e.g., recycling or stopping smoking) or in its outcome (e.g., weight loss). Other behaviors are largely private and unobservable to others (e.g., a bachelor switching to a low cholesterol diet). Again, this distinction will have an important systematic effect on the role of outcomes (benefits/costs) versus the role of significant others in influencing behavior change. It is also likely that self-rewards will be more important in private behaviors than external rewards.

Behaviors that are one-time versus behaviors that are continuing. Some behaviors, such as getting a vaccination against measles, are a one-time event. Most social marketing behaviors, however (such as quitting smoking), require repeated actions (or substitute actions). Presumably, the risk that the behavior will be "wrong" will be a more important determinant in the first case as contrasted to the risk that accrues to not taking the behavior. In the latter, the reverse may be true.

Behaviors that are carried out alone versus behaviors that require the participation of others. Some behaviors, such as driving 55 mph, are totally within the control of the individual. For such behaviors, to achieve a sense of self-efficacy, they only need to have personal competence. For other behaviors (such as condom use), which require the participation of others, self-efficacy issues involve *inter*personal competence. The skills required will be markedly different in each case. (There may be a third category of behaviors here that does not require the participation of others but could benefit from it. Such would be the case for someone seeking to cut cholesterol who is dating a burger fanatic or a smoker trying to quit while living within a household of continuing smokers. In such cases, it would be important to understand the factors that determine whether the individual decides to go it alone or enlist the aid of important others.)

It clearly would be fruitful in future modeling efforts to develop a catalog of modifications or adjustments to behavioral determinants that need to be made to accommodate variations in the class of behaviors one is modeling or seeking to influence. Such work would go a long way toward furthering an understanding of the extent to which social marketing can be treated as a generic methodology.

REFERENCES

AIDS education—A beginning. (1989). *Population reports, issues in world health*, September, Series L, No. 8.

Ajzen, I. (1991). The theory of planned behavior: Some unresolved issues. *Organizational Behavior and Human Decision Processes, 50*, 179–211.

Andreasen, A. R. (1993). Presidential address: A social marketing research agenda for consumer behavior researchers. In M. Rothschild & L. McAlister (Eds.), *Advances in consumer research* (Vol. 20, pp. 1–5). Provo, UT: Association for Consumer Research.

Andreasen, A. R. (1994). Social marketing: Definition and domain. *Journal of Marketing and Public Policy*, Spring, 108–114.

Andreasen, A. R., (1995). *Marketing social change*. San Francisco: Jossey-Bass.

Andreasen, A. R. & Tyson, C. B. (1993). *Improving tree management practices of homebuilders: A social marketing approach*. Washington, DC: American Forests.

Bagozzi, R., & Moore, D. J. (1994). Public service advertisements: Emotions and empathy guide prosocial behavior. *Journal of Marketing, 58* (January), 56–70.

Bagozzi, R. P., & Warshaw, P. (1990). Trying to consume. *Journal of Consumer Research, 17*, 127–140.

Bandura, A. (1977). *Social learning theory*. Englewood Cliffs, NJ: Prentice-Hall.

Baranowski, T. (1992–1993). Beliefs as motivational influences at stages in behavior change. *International Quarterly of Health Education, 13*(1), 3–29.

Baranowski, T., & Jenkins, C. D. (1989–1990). Reciprocal determinism at the stages of behavior change: An integration of community, personal, and behavioral perspectives. *International Quarterly of Health Education, 10*(4), 297–327.

Bloom, P., & Novelli, W. D. (1981). Problems and challenges in social marketing. *Journal of Marketing, 45* (Spring), 79–88.

Brown, J. (1994). Evaluation of the impact of the protector condom campaign in Malawi. *SOMARC Occasional Paper* (19, May).

Bush, R. P., Ortinau, D. J., & Bush, A. P. (1994). Personal value structures and AIDS prevention. *Journal of Health Care Marketing, 14*(1, Spring), 12–20.

Cabañero-Verzosa, C., Bernaje, M. G., De Guzman, E. M., Hernandez, J. R. S., Reodica, C. N., & Taguiwalo, M. M. (1989). *Managing a communication program on immunization*. Washington, DC: U.S. Agency for International Development.

Celsi, R. L., & Olson, J. C. (1988). The role of involvement in attention and comprehension processes. *Journal of Consumer Research, 15* (September), 210–224.

Cohen, J., & Areni, C. (1991). Affect and consumer behavior. In T. S. Robertson & H. H. Kassarjian (Eds.), *Handbook of consumer behavior* (pp. 188–240). Englewood Cliffs, NJ: Prentice-Hall.

Elder, J. P., Barriga, P., Graeff, J., Rosenbaum, J., & Boddy, P. (1991). *Nothing to sneeze at: Integrating research into the Honduran ARI communication program*. Washington, DC: HealthCom Project.

Elliott, B. J. (1991). *A re-examination of the social marketing concept*. Sydney: Elliott & Shanahan Research.

Fine, S. (1981). *The marketing of ideas and social issues*. New York: Praeger.

Fine, S. (Ed.). (1990). *Social marketing: Promoting the causes of public and nonprofit agencies*. Boston: Allyn & Bacon.

Fishbein, M. (1995, May). Luncheon address, marketing and public policy conference, Atlanta, GA.

Fishbein, M., & Ajzen, I. (1975). *Belief, attitude, intention, and behavior: An introduction to theory and research*. Reading, MA: Addison-Wesley.

Fishbein, M., Triandis, H. C., Kanfer, F. H., Becker, M., Middlestadt, S. E., & Eichler, A. (in press). Factors influencing behavior and behavior change. *Handbook of health psychology.*

Fox, K. F. A., & Kotler, P. (1980). The marketing of social causes: The first ten years. *Journal of Marketing, 44,* 24–33.

Glanz, K., Lewis, F. M., & Rimer, B. K. (Eds.). (1990). *Health behavior and health education.* San Francisco: Jossey-Bass.

Graeff, J. A., Elder, J. P., & Booth, E. M. (1993). *Communication for health and behavior change: A developing country perspective.* San Francisco: Jossey-Bass.

HealthCom. (1995). *A tool box for building health communication capacity.* Washington, DC: Academy for Educational Development.

Hornik, R. (1992). Alternative models of behavior change. In J. Wasserheit, K. Holmes, & S. Aral (Eds.), *Research issues in human behavior and sexually transmitted disease in the AIDS era.* Washington, DC: American Society for Microbiology.

Isen, A. M., & Hastorf, A. H. (1982). Some perspectives on cognitive social psychology. In A. H. Hastorf & A. M. Isen (Eds.), *Cognitive social psychology* (pp. 1–31). New York: Elsevier, North-Holland.

Kanfer, F. H. (1970). Self-regulation: Research, issues, and speculations. In C. Neuringir & J. L. Michael (Eds.), *Behavior modification in clinical psychology* (pp. 178–220). New York: Appleton-Century-Crofts.

Kanfer, F. H., & Shefft, B. K. (1988). *Guiding the process of therapeutic change.* Champaign, IL: Research Press.

Kotler, P., & Andreasen, A. R. (1996). *Strategic marketing for nonprofit organizations* (5th ed.). Englewood Cliffs, NJ: Prentice-Hall.

Kotler, P., & Levy, S. (1969). Broadening the concept of marketing. *Journal of Marketing, 33,* 10–15.

Kotler, P., & Roberto, E. (1989). *Social marketing.* New York: The Free Press.

Kotler, P., & Zaltman, G. (1971). Social marketing: An approach to planned social change. *Journal of Marketing, 35,* 3–12.

Lazarus, R. S. (1991). *Emotion and adaptation.* New York: Oxford University Press.

Lutz, R. J., & Bettman, J. R. (1977). Multi-attribute models in marketing: A bicentennial review. In A. Woodside, J. Sheth, & B. Bennett (Eds.), *Consumer and industrial buying behavior* (pp. 137–150). New York: North Holland.

Maddux, J. E., & Rogers, R. W. (1983). Protection motivation and self-efficacy: A revised theory of fear appeals and attitude change. *Journal of Experimental Social Psychology, 19,* 469–479.

Maibach, E. W., & Cotton, D. (1995). Moving people to behavior change: A staged social cognitive approach to message design. In E. W. Maibach & R. L. Parrott (Eds.), *Designing Health Messages* (pp. 41–64). Newbury Park: Sage.

Malafarina, K., & Loken, B. (1993). Progress and limitations of social marketing: A review of empirical literature on the consumption of social ideas. In M. Rothschild & L. McAlister (Eds.), *Advances in consumer research* (Vol. 20, pp. 397–404). Provo, UT: Association for Consumer Research.

Manoff, R. K. (1985). *Social marketing.* New York: Praeger.

National Heart, Lung, and Blood Institute. (1992). *The fifth report of the Joint National Committee on Detection, Evaluation, and Treatment of High Blood Pressure.* Bethesda, MD: Author.

Novelli, W. D. (1995, May). Remarks made to the conference on The Role of Advertising in Social Marketing, Atlanta, GA.

Prochaska, J. O., & DiClemente, C. C. (1983). Stages and processes of self-change of smoking: Toward an integrative model of change. *Journal of Consulting and Clinical Psychology, 51,* 390–395.

Rangun, V. K., & Karim, S. (1991). *Teaching note: Focusing the concept of social marketing.* Cambridge, MA: Harvard Business School.

Riche, M. F. (1989). Psychographics for the 1990s. *American Demographics*, July.

Rogers, E. M., Aikat, S., Chang, S., Poppe, P., & Sopory, P. (1989). *Proceedings from the Conference on Entertainment-Education for Social Change.* Los Angeles: Annenberg School of Communications.

Rogers, R. W. (1983). Cognitive and psychological processes in fear appeals and attitude change: A revised theory of protection motivation. In J. T. Cacioppo & R. E. Petty (Eds.), *Social psychophysiology* (pp. 153–176). New York: Guilford.

Rosenstock, I. M. (1990). The health belief model: Explaining health behavior through expectancies. In K. Glanz, F. M. Lewis, & B. K. Rimer (Eds.), *Health behavior and health education* (pp. 39–62). San Francisco: Jossey-Bass.

Rothschild, M. D. (1979). Marketing communications in nonbusiness situations or why it's so hard to sell brotherhood like soap. *Journal of Marketing*, Spring, 11–20.

Rotter, J. B. (1955). The role of the psychological situation in determining the direction of human behavior. In M. R. Jones (Ed.), *Nebraska symposium on motivation.* Lincoln: University of Nebraska Press.

Saade, C., & Tucker, H. (n.d.). *Beyond pharmacies: New perspectives in ORS marketing.* Washington, DC: PRITECH.

Seidel, R. E. (1992). *Results and realities: A decade of experience in communication for child survival.* Washington, DC: U.S. Agency for International Development.

Seidel, R. E. (1993). *Notes from the field in communication for child survival.* Washington, DC: U.S. Agency for International Development.

Shaver, P., Schwartz, J., Kirson, D., & O'Connor, C. (1987). Emotion knowledge: Further exploration of a prototype approach. *Journal of Personality and Social Psychology*, 52, 1061–1086.

SOMARC. (n.d.). *A program manager's guide to media planning.* Washington, DC: The Futures Group.

SOMARC III. (1994). SOMARC's special study evaluates effectiveness of several condom social marketing interventions addressing HIV/AIDS prevention. *SOMARC III Highlights* (9, February).

Schwartz, B. (1994, May). Social marketing for gender equity in Bangladesh. *Social Marketing Quarterly*, 1, 3.

Triandis, H. C. (1972). *The analysis of subjective culture.* New York: Wiley.

Triandis, H. C. (1977). *Interpersonal behavior.* Monterey, CA: Brooks/Cole.

Wallack, L. (1990). Media advocacy: Promoting health through mass communication. In K. Glanz, F. M. Lewis, & B. K. Rimer (Eds.), *Health behavior and health education* (pp. 370–386). San Francisco: Jossey-Bass.

Watson, D., & Tellgren, A. (1985). Toward a consensual structure of mood. *Psychological Bulletin*, 98, 219–235.

Wells, W. D. (1989). *Planning for R.O.I.: Effective advertising strategy.* Englewood Cliffs, NJ: Prentice-Hall.

Wilkie, W. L., & Pessemeir, E. A. (1973). Issues in marketing's use of multiattribute attitudes models. *Journal of Marketing Research*, 10(4, November), 428–441.

Women, infants and STDs. (1991). Arlington, VA: John Snow.

Chapter 2

Social Marketing: Beyond the Nostalgia

William A. Smith
Academy for Educational Development, Washington, DC

The future of social marketing is more interesting than ever. For the past two decades, the focus has been on the "marketing" part of social marketing. Theorists have tried to explain, to sell, to carry out, to evaluate, and to accommodate the basic premises of a marketing mentality to a robust social sector, largely dominated by public investment in disease prevention, the protection of the environment, and the control of human fertility. The problem has been to explain the theory of exchange, the concepts of segmentation, target marketing, consumer research, and positioning to a deeply committed, but often very skeptical, audience of people trying to do good in the world.

Today, it is the "social" in social marketing that is under attack. The question is no longer, why use social marketing to help people, but rather why help people? And, if you have to help them, why use government? The reinvention of the social contract between government and the people forces social marketers to fundamentally reassess their role and their future in the world. America's eroding leadership role in the world; a widespread sense that for the first time in history children may not be better off than their parents; the endless stream of intimately reported murders, rapes, and psychosis reported on the nightly news; and a growing impatience with the regulation of American life by "health Nazis" and "tree huggers" has created an anti–safety net mentality. The relentless "sell" of nutrition, exercise, safe sex, and the regulation of discrimination and the protection of the environment have led to a backlash, even among many who want to live long healthy lives in harmony with nature. The most vocal critic of AIDS prevention at the moment is an AIDS psychotherapist by the name of Walter Odets. Odets believed that gay men have been traumatized as much by the demand to change their lifestyle as by the epidemic itself. He argued that gay men should be given the chance, through prevention programs, to choose between a shorter, happier life of condom-free sex, versus a longer life bound to the fear and anxiety of the condoms and AIDS (see Suggested Readings).

Social marketing rests on the assumptions that there are behaviors worth changing and that it is society's responsibility to help people make the right choices. The consensus on both of these propositions is eroding. Social marketing is, after all, a robust technology of behavior change. Hardly perfect, but impressive in its strategic coherence, nonetheless. But the political consensus that supported and funded much work is falling apart. Even for those who do not rely entirely on public funds, access to public funds made some of the best and most important work possible. The international family planning community has been one of the implementation pioneers of the social marketing field—millions of dollars have been invested in the social marketing of fertility choice, and products that make the choice possible, even for some of the poorest women and families in the world. Similarly, U.S. government support for child survival, a 15-year consensus that 6 million children need not die every year in developing countries, a commitment that produced dramatic declines in infant mortality due to diarrheal dehydration and immunizable diseases, is being eroded in a desperate attempt to balance the budget and cut back government. Domestic cuts in public programs, elimination of government agencies, and the divestiture of federal responsibility to the States is transforming the environment in which social marketing was born and has grown. How to adapt is really the question of the day. Consider first a quick status report, some continuing problems in social marketing, and a set of opportunities for the future.

A QUICK STATUS REPORT

There has been significant diffusion of the social marketing concept among many public and private agencies. The Centers for Disease Control and Prevention has just created a new office of Health Communication attached directly to the Office of the Director and adopted a sophisticated model influenced by social marketing. The USDA, the Veterans Administration, and the Department of Education have all begun to explore how to use social marketing. Private foundations are expressing interest, the American Association of Retired Persons is expressing an interest, and the World

Bank designed a 3-day workshop for its program staff on social marketing. All of these incursions are on top of what has already been accomplished in cancer communication, family planning, and HIV/AIDS by the Canadians, Australians, and English in their robust social marketing programs and societies. The presence of social marketing is expanding.

The second trend is a shift toward survival marketing. Many nongovernmental organizations, particularly nonprofits, are moving away from the social marketing of specific health or environmental behaviors, toward fund raising and public consensus building to save their organizations.

And, finally, there is a growing academic interest in social marketing. Along with the University of South Florida's excellent program, other universities (Columbia, Hopkins, Tulane, and Emory) are developing programs to train a new generation of social marketers. This is a very positive note.

SOME CONTINUING PROBLEMS

There are three continuing problems: too much "advertising" in the practice of social marketing; too much reliance on focus groups as the primary social marketing research technique; and too little science in our sales pitches, programs, and publications. And, as a field, researchers are still unclear as to what they are. The definition of social marketing is too ambiguous and all-encompassing. Anything that works is called social marketing, or the functional definition is limited—"if you don't have a slogan you don't have a social marketing program."

Andreasen (1995) tackled the definition problem. He focused on three key aspects in the definition of social marketing: its adaptation of technologies from commercial marketing, the voluntary change in behavior, and the improvement of societal welfare. But the definition itself leaves a question unanswered: What are the technologies of commercial marketing?

THE CORE COMPETENCIES OF SOCIAL MARKETING

There are four commercial technologies or competencies that should determine if a program of behavior change is truly a social marketing program:

1. Exchange Theory. Marketers believe that people give up one behavior in exchange for something else. The marketing question is not "What is it you don't understand about smoking?" but "What is it you want (that I can provide) in exchange for giving up smoking?"

2. *Competition.* This leads to a view that in marketing individuals are not competing against ignorance or lack of information, but against other behaviors that offer benefits people like. To help people change their behavior, it is necessary to compete with those benefits, not just educate, remind, or amuse. The key marketing question is "What do people really like about what they are doing now, and how can I compete with it?"

3. *Segmentation by Lifestyle.* Marketers believe people are different in ways that often cut across demographic and epidemiological boundaries. All African-American women who smoke are not alike. All Latino men who have sex with other men are not alike. All adolescents do not watch MTV. Segmentation is the process of finding out how to best group people by the similarities that are important to their behavioral choices. Sometimes demographics and epidemiology are the answers, but sometimes information on lifestyle is needed as well. The third key marketing question is "What characteristics do people share they make it easier for the marketer to influence them as segments rather than isolated individuals?"

4. *Marketing Mix.* And, finally, marketers should believe that there is more to behavior change than messages. If people are going to make difficult changes in their life, they need new products and services, at lower cost, with easier access (and yes, clever, compelling messages matter too). The final marketing question is "What mix of products, services, cost, access and promotion is right for this audience, this behavior and this point in time?"

BUT . . . IT'S TIME TO RECOGNIZE THAT "THE CUSTOMER IS ALWAYS RIGHT"

The following are all paraphrased comments or direct quotes:

> "After a lot of thought I figured out what I don't like about social marketing. . . . I just don't believe that mass media can change behavior."
>
> "Social marketing is not about advertising . . . It is about good advertising."
>
> "Social marketing is a subset of Health Communication and Health Promotion."
>
> "Ultimately marketing is manipulation. . . . It deals with situations in which someone has decided for someone else what is good for them. It never gives all the information people need to make an objective choice—It only gives them the information the program directors believe will lead them to make a specific choice."
>
> "Social marketing is about individual behavior—It is about "blaming the victims" of systems that push bad products and bad behaviors at them

all the time. The solution is not to blame the victim, but advocate for the victim. It is not to change the individual, but make it more difficult for the individual to be victimized."

"We may understand and describe our efforts within the context of exchange theory, but in truth, there is rarely an actual trade between marketer and market. What we're after is change—not exchange."

Tired debates continue to confuse the practice of social marketing: manipulation, victimization, banality, and *advertising über alles*. After years of trying to understand and promote strategic social marketing, forget nostalgia for what was possible.

It was once thought possible, and frankly necessary, to have an architect for the new community being built. Marketing was the place in which the architects were to be trained and nurtured. But the community, both clients and practitioners, has decided it prefers artisans—craftspersons who are better at carpentry than electrical, better at foundations than roofs, better at windows than at doors. Some clients want campaigns and slogans and messages, and advertisers give it to them. Other clients want policy change and regulation of industry and advocates who give it to them. Some clients want distribution systems and product marketers give it to them.

Marketers may think of themselves as architects, but in fact they are general contractors, trained as artisans, often prejudiced in their judgment of what is needed by what they know best how to supply. But, for the most part, they are also quite competent general contractors, and so for the most part their contributions are welcome, useful, and even beneficial.

It is time to get over the nostalgia for what was possible; it is tiring to talk about and write about "strategic" social marketing only to go back to find oneself working on yet another message campaign, or embroiled in an argument over whether mass media changes behavior, or having another endless discussion about manipulation. Labels matter less than actions. It is better to talk about individual strategic approaches rather than to define such a wide range of practical options under the single discipline of social marketing.

GIVING CUSTOMERS CHOICE

What customers care about is what people do to protect themselves and their environment from bad things. They care about people continuing to do good things despite temptations to do bad things. They care about people deciding to do better things rather than continuing to do harmful things. They care about human behavior. And they have several choices in how to go about influencing one behavior or another. To tell them social marketing is the best answer, or the only answer, or the answer that leads them to all other answers may or may not be true, but it is not helpful. It leads only to more discussions about "what is social marketing?"

Choices that make sense, and not a new ideology of behavior change, are necessary. For the most part, they do not have the managerial opportunities and resources to be marketing architects. But, they are nonetheless engaged in building important behavioral houses throughout the United States and the world. They need to understand their choices. They have four broad models from which to choose. They allow us to talk to clients about choices and to give them much more specialized professional help.

Regulatory approaches tackle important structural forces external to the individual. Typically they take one of two different forms. Public power is translated into *direct regulations* (no smoking on airplanes or public places) or *indirect regulations* (no cigarette advertising permitted on TV). Both use the technologies of advocacy, media advocacy, and public relations to shape human behavior indirectly through public policy, law, and social control. It has been argued that advocacy is a subset of marketing and perhaps officially it is. But the point is not where it goes on an organizational chart, but rather what it brings to the technologies of change. Regulatory approaches do offer a unique set of tools and technologies that require significant specialization. Therefore, advocacy should be considered, for practical purposes, a distinct class of interventions, independent of social marketing.

Information approaches are certainly the most widespread form of behavioral intervention in the world today. Here, the central belief is that people do not protect their health because they do not know something, or because they do not feel the need for the new behavior deeply enough. It is certainly true that simply publicizing immunization programs has increased their use. It is also true that emotional appeals (e.g., fear) have been shown to work on some behavior in some contexts. The power of information and what should be called "social advertising" can be critical. Again, there are those who would argue that this is a subset of marketing, but they do an injustice to both advertising and marketing. Of course, good marketing would always look for advertising potential, but by separating them clearly in this categorization, there is greater opportunity for clients to understand that advertising is not the only marketing strategy.

Marketing approaches are differentiated from other intervention strategies by a focus on benefits resulting from an improvement in services, price, or access considerations. Marketing unique contribution is the orchestration of services to provide better benefits, at lower cost, and with greater access. The acid test for social marketing is the demonstrated integration of product, place, price, and promotion decisions, which distinguishes social marketing from other forms of behavioral intervention.

Decision-making and counseling models do not have any one answer to promote. The problem is complex. Take pancreatic cancer, for example. Choices here between surgery, medication, or no care are complex and not clearly defined. There is no single "product" to offer. Judgment is required. Value decisions must be made by the individual after full consideration of all the alternatives. People must take control of the decision-making process. Regulators and marketers do not have a single best answer. Until recently, this domain was confined largely to one-on-one encounters. Today, and even more tomorrow, interactive computer technology offers to make the counseling function available on a mass scale. It is definitely a much larger arena to consider than ever before.

Each of these models has an implicit assumption about people:

Regulators see people as evil, needing to be controlled, or as victims, needing to be protected from evil forces.

Information folks see people as students who need to be motivated to go to class or lovers waiting to be seduced by emotion.

Marketers see people as consumers, making choices between one brand and another.

Counselors assume people are information managers, able to acquire wisdom and make reasoned, difficult judgments.

The best programs, of course, recognize that people are all of these things. They understand that most complex behavior involves the need for new technologies, new policy, and new perceptions of both the new technology and the new policy.

THE PROBLEM IS BEHAVIOR, NOT MARKETING

This chapter has argued that it is better to be specific about different behavior change strategies than to lump them all under a single new approach to behavior change called social marketing. Regulatory means, both direct and indirect, offer useful alternatives. Information approaches have been shown to be effective, although there is strong evidence that marketers have relied much more heavily on them than they should. And there are situations where decision making is complex, and people must have all the available information to make a difficult health or environmental decision, rather than be "marketed" the benefits of a single solution.

It is best for clients to have choices, to begin with the behavior they care about, not with the change technology marketers love to practice best. It is about a process of helping individual clients consider and choose a strategy that best fits their readiness for action, their resources, and their behavioral problem. This is an era of eroding support for social control and government "interference." Social marketing theory must remain broad, but the practice of social marketing should become ever more specialized and professional to meet these new challenges.

SUGGESTED READINGS

AIDS education and harm reduction for gay men: Psychological approaches for the 21st century, by Walt Odets. *AIDS & Public Policy Journal*, Frederick, Maryland. Spring, 1994.

Bottom-up marketing by Al Ries & Jack Trout. New York: McGraw-Hill. 1989.

Marketing for health care organizations by Philip Kotler & Roberta N. Clarke. Englewood Cliffs, NJ: Prentice-Hall. 1987.

Marketing health behavior: Principles, techniques, and applications by Lee W. Frederiksen, Laura J. Solomon, & Kathleen A. Brehony. New York: Plenum. 1984.

Partners in action: Environmental social marketing and environmental education by Michele Archie, Lori Mann, & William Smith. Washington, DC: Academy for Educational Development. 1993.

Reinventing government: How the entrepreneurial spirit is transforming the public sector by David Osborne & Ted Gaebler. Reading, MA: Addison-Wesley. 1992.

Results and realities: A decade of experience in communication for child survival. A summary report of the communication for child survival or HEALTHCOM project by Renata Seidel. Washington, DC: Academy for Educational Development. 1992.

Social marketing: Promoting the causes of public and nonprofit agencies by Seymour H. Fine. Allyn and Bacon. 1990.

Social marketing: Strategies for changing public behavior by Philip Kotler & Eduardo L. Roberto. New York: The Free Press. 1989.

Strategic marketing for nonprofit organizations by Philip Kotler & Alan Andreasen. Englewood Cliffs, NJ: Prentice-Hall. 1987.

Strategies in AIDS prevention. Washington, DC: Academy for Educational Development. 1992.

Chapter 3

Advertising in the Social Marketing Mix: Getting the Balance Right

Martine Stead
Gerard Hastings
University of Strathclyde, Glasgow

ABSTRACT

Social marketing continues to be equated, by many practitioners and even by some academics, with social advertising. Overstating advertising's importance in social marketing threatens the discipline in several ways: Nonpromotional elements of the social marketing mix are neglected, social marketing is restricted in practice, distracting arguments are generated, social marketing is blamed for advertising's limitations and is subject to ethical misgivings. Some have argued that the dominance of social advertising in social marketing is inevitable because the intangibility and immutability of social marketing's products leave promotion as the only mix variable open to manipulation. However, social marketers can change their products, as a UK social marketing initiative promoting water fluoridation to the public, policymakers, and the media demonstrates. Creative thinking is needed to prevent social marketers believing that all they can change is promotion and all they can do is social advertising.

From the early days of social marketing, theorists and practitioners have cautioned that social marketing "is a much larger idea than social advertising" (Kotler & Zaltman, 1971, p. 5) and encompasses more than the design and use of mass media campaigns (Kotler, 1994; Sutton, 1991; Young, 1988–1989). Yet, the tendency to label what is essentially social advertising activity as social marketing persists at practitioner level, as Andreasen (1994) noted: "Too many practitioners are really doing social advertising and calling it social marketing" (p. 9). Papers and textbooks continue to be written that, by citing mass media advertising campaigns as their main social marketing case studies, perpetuate the tendency for the two to be seen as synonymous despite assertions to the contrary (e.g., Forman, 1991; Maibach, 1993; Manoff, 1985; Mintz, 1988–1989; Wyld & Hallock, 1989). This conflation threatens both the development of the discipline and its application in practice.

This chapter examines these threats, and then discusses why social advertising and social marketing are so often confused. It argues that this is not inevitable, as Elliott (1995) suggested, but is a result of social marketers taking too narrow and inflexible a perspective on the challenges they face.

THREATS TO SOCIAL MARKETING

Confusing social advertising with social marketing can cause five types of problem:

1. The basic marketing concepts become obscured and neglect of the nonpromotional elements of the social marketing mix is encouraged.
2. The use and practice of social marketing is restricted.
3. Distracting interdisciplinary arguments are generated.
4. Social marketing is blamed for the limitations and misapplications of social advertising.
5. Ethical doubts about advertising are transferred to social marketing.

Problem Type 1

The central principles of social marketing are *consumer orientation* and *exchange* (Lefebvre, 1992a; Lefebvre & Flora, 1988; Ling, Franklin, Lindsteadt, & Gearion, 1992). The marketing philosophy calls for agencies to be aware of and responsive to consumer needs at all stages (Lefebvre & Flora, 1988) and "sees consumers as active participants in the search for a mutually beneficial outcome" (Hastings & Haywood, 1994, p. 60).

Initial needs analysis guides decisions about how to segment and target consumer groups, what product offerings are needed and are likely to be adopted, and how to structure the marketing mix. This analysis may indicate that promotion is the most important "P" and therefore that a social advertising campaign is required, or it may not; it may instead indicate that equal or greater attention needs to be paid to the price, product, or place, and therefore that different methods are required. The social marketing process does not prejudge which mix elements should be prioritized, but simply provides a framework within which strategic decision making can take place (Lefebvre, 1992b). Smith (1991) described the "balancing act that program managers must go through to choose the most important of the four inputs" (p. 4); some *P*s may need very little attention, others may require the bulk of the social marketer's efforts, but "the point is, the mix . . . varies from one problem and one audience to another" (Smith, 1991, p. 4).

Jumping to a social advertising solution therefore undermines social marketing in two ways. First, it ignores the most fundamental premise of marketing, that decision making should be based on a clear understanding of consumer needs. The best or most effective offering to meet these needs may not comprise or even include mass media advertising. Second, it draws attention away from other elements of the marketing mix that may have a crucial part to play in increasing the acceptability of the offering.

Problem Type 2

An overemphasis on mass media advertising encourages the tendency for social marketing to be seen as an inaccessibly expensive alternative. Mass media advertising is extremely costly. Bloom and Novelli (1981) highlighted this and it remains true today. Developing and running a major UK television campaign can cost several million pounds, and the mass media program budgets of government agencies are still a tiny fraction of the amount spent by the producers of just one health-damaging product, the tobacco industry. For example, in the UK, it is estimated that the tobacco industry spends £70m annually on advertising. By contrast, the Health Education Authority (HEA), the national health promotion body for England, has a budget of just over £20m for all its activities, of which advertising is only a part.

An overemphasis on advertising as the output of social marketing reinforces the idea that social marketing is an expensive club open only to agencies with large budgets and from which smaller, poorer organizations are excluded. Of course, conducting social marketing research or developing social marketing programs also requires resources and expertise, but does not necessarily demand the intimidating budgets required for large-scale advertising. Social marketing is a mind-set, not a collection of compulsory, expensive activities. As Andreasen pointed out, "Social marketing is a point of view. Even if we don't have a big budget we can do social marketing with what we have because it's a way to address a problem" (Sutton, 1991, p. 46). Similarly, Elliott and Hastings (1993) argued that, in road safety, the social marketing approach can be used even where time and budgets are limited: "No matter how small the available road safety budget, the strategy and tasks to be completed can be based on consumer orientation" (p. 50). This may mean channeling limited research resources into qualitative research rather than into evaluation, and setting pragmatic and modest goals that will not foster unrealistic expectations, but it does make social marketing, and its benefits in terms of decision making, planning, and implementation, accessible even to those with the smallest budgets.

However, not everyone endorses this low budget, pragmatic approach to social marketing. The call is frequently made for the discipline to strengthen its scientific credentials, particularly through the establishment of large-scale rigorously controlled trials "to demonstrate its superiority (in any comparative way) to other approaches and techniques" (Lefebvre, 1995, p. 1). Although obviously the greater the social marketing research base the better, the increasing iteration of the call "bigger research, larger trials" can have an inhibiting, paralyzing effect on smaller scale practitioners struggling to apply social marketing first and foremost to very practical problems.

Furthermore, the underlying assumption that controlled environment clinical trials can be replicated in the real world, or can provide the information needed, may be flawed (Balch & Sutton, 1995; Sutton, 1991). As Walsh, Rudd, Moeykens, and Moloney (1993) expressed it, there is something of a clash of "world views and professional identities" among social marketers on this issue. On one level it is perhaps no more than the expected academic versus practitioner divide, encapsulated in Young's (1988–1989, p. 3) perspective that social marketing is "less a package of techniques than it is a way of thinking." However, Walsh et al. hinted that by its very nature social marketing contains two conflicting impulses, one stressing technological precision in evaluation, the other stressing intuition and pragmatism. The latter instinct says that if a program seems not to be working, and continuous consumer research and feedback say that needs or the environment have changed, then be flexible enough to change direction—an approach that is not compatible with the requirement of a major experimental trial for a program to stay its course for 3, 5, or 10 years in order to provide uncontaminated and comparable data (Walsh et al., 1993, p. 115).

One reason large-scale mass media campaigns have dominated thinking about social marketing is because they appear to answer the need for such data. They are clearly defined, predictable, easily controlled and high profile. Impact and effect can be measured in a relatively straightforward manner, using tried and tested procedures. In this way, mass media campaigns become linked with elaborate and expensive research designs, making them even less accessible to small agencies, who cannot even afford the research budget.

Problem Type 3

Confusing social marketing with social advertising prompts two unfounded criticisms from other disciplines. The first asks "What's new about this? Why do we need it if we've already got social communication/mass media theory?" (e.g., Tones, 1994), and perceives social marketing as a "me too"; the second, seeing limitations to social advertising, sets up alternative disciplines and strategies to meet what are perceived to be social marketing's shortcomings. In particular, social marketing has been accused of failing to act "upstream," of emphasizing individual change strategies, and of neglecting the social and political environment (Wallack, 1990).

Neither argument can survive the wider view of social marketing. Tones' notion of social marketing as a "me too" for mass communication theory collapses when other elements of the marketing mix as well as promotion are considered, or exchange theory and consumer orientation are factored in. Similarly, Manoff (1990) argued that Wallack confused social marketing with one of its important components, social advertising, and that the media advocacy he proposed is just another component; Manoff criticized the fragmentation of effort that results when one approach is pitted against another in this way.

But whereas many (although not all) social advertising campaigns are underpinned by an individual behavior change focus, social marketing can and already has been proven to act upstream. Social marketing approaches have been advocated in the alcohol policy arena (Murray & Douglas, 1988), and have been used in the UK to lobby successfully for the withdrawal of a tobacco advertising campaign (Hastings, Ryan, Teer, & MacKintosh, 1994), to convince local and national government and private industry to introduce water fluoridation (Hastings, Smith, & Lowry, 1994), and to reorientate the dental profession to a major change in service provision through the social de-marketing of general dental practice general anesthesia (Hastings, Lawther, et al. 1994; Lawther & Lowry, 1995). None of the latter three programs involved the promotion of individual consumer health behavior change, or had a large mass media component. One is examined further as a case study.

The argument here is that Tones and Wallack cannot be blamed for misrepresenting social marketing, and criticizing it in an inappropriate way, given the tendency for social marketing to become confused with social advertising even within the discipline.

Problem Type 4

As well as being expensive, social advertising is difficult to do well, can only perform relatively limited tasks, and is often misused. Social marketing will be blamed for these shortcomings if it is confused with social advertising.

Difficult to Do Well. There have always been problems with transferring advertising from the commercial to the social sector. There is a lack of expertise in social advertising and insufficient freedom and flexibility to use advertising to its full potential. The lack of expertise comes about because, whereas there are many people who know about advertising and many who know about social marketing issues such as health promotion, there are few who know about both.

The lack of freedom and flexibility in social advertising can be illustrated by a case history. In 1993, the English HEA developed a national television advertising campaign on smoking cessation featuring the comedian and actor, John Cleese. The campaign was developed on sound principles, using careful formative and pretesting research. The result was high quality, expensive looking, and enjoyable, with Cleese being particularly popular.

At the same time, however, the message was a very traditional one, highlighting the negative consequences of smoking, such as the health risks to smokers' children. As is usually the case with this sort of advertising (e.g., Leathar, 1981), it generated some unease and defensiveness among the target audience (Eadie, Goodlad, Hastings, MacKintosh, & Avan, 1993).

What was the tobacco industry doing at the time? It had created "Reg," a deliberately downbeat, ostensibly unattractive poster campaign for Imperial Tobacco's Regal brand of cigarettes, featuring a fat, ugly middle-age man. The campaign antagonized many adult smokers because they did not understand or relate to it (Hastings, Ryan, et al., 1994). It looked obscure, cheap, and off target, which is the antithesis of the HEA's high quality television campaign.

Of course the "Reg" campaign was not off target at all; Imperial Tobacco had designed a campaign and character that, intentionally or otherwise, appealed not to adults but to schoolchildren. This was demonstrated by later research, also funded by the HEA. The research indicated that Reg appealed to young people's rebelliousness, humor, and peer group values and, using branding, reinforced their smoking. It made them feel good about both their habit and themselves. The research findings were used in a lobbying campaign against the tobacco industry and led to the Reg ads being withdrawn.

Thus, the HEA had produced in the John Cleese advertisements a high quality but conservative and—in health education terms—safe campaign. Its limited resources, and the fact that these came from the public purse, made innovation and risk taking very difficult. The tobacco industry did not face these sort of limitations and were able to produce, in Reg, an extremely innovative and appealing campaign. In short, it was very difficult for the HEA to beat the commercial sector at their own game.

In contrast, the HEA was much more successful in its lobbying campaign, which was low profile and required only limited resources. As noted earlier, this lobbying can also be seen as a piece of social marketing. The HEA commissioned research to examine the needs being satisfied by Reg, exposed these to public scrutiny and satisfied the regulatory authority's need for clear evidence that the campaign appealed more to children than adults. It also succeeded in working upstream, and changing people's smoking environment.

Limited Achievements. Advertising alone is best suited to performing a fairly limited range of communication tasks, a limitation that has been widely recognized. The field of drug misuse provides a typical example. Although it is agreed that well-targeted and credible media campaigns can be effective in raising awareness and providing information (Dorn & Murji, 1992), increases in knowledge can be short term (de Haes, 1987) and may even be counter-productive in the sense that drug use and experimentation can increase following a campaign (Polich, Ellickson, Reuter, & Kahan, 1984).

There is even less evidence that media-only campaigns can be effective in changing attitudes and behavior. Backer, Rogers, and Sopory (1992), after reviewing the drugs prevention field in the United States, concluded that "more effective campaigns combine mass media with community, small group and individual activities, supported by an existing community structure" (p. 30). Dobson (1992), making a comparative review of drugs education in Belgium, the Netherlands, and the United Kingdom, recommended avoiding single tactic approaches in favor of "a comprehensive one including multiple components representing a wide variety of approaches to prevention" (p. 73).

These are clear calls for social marketing instead of social advertising, and the credibility of the discipline will inevitably be damaged if, by confusing the two, it continues to offer social advertising as a stand-alone behavior change mechanism.

Inappropriate Use. Overstating the importance of social advertising encourages its misuse in an all-too-public arena. Social marketing is then blamed for the resulting flawed campaigns. Drug misuse again provides powerful examples.

"Just Say No" in the United States and the Australian Drug Offensive have been severely criticized for not segmenting their target markets. Although they may have successfully reinforced the antidrug feelings of those who were already antidrug, they offered nothing to those with different attitudes and experiences, with the result that the messages were totally inappropriate for existing drug users and those who were knowledgeable about drugs (Makkai, Moore, & McAllister, 1991; Strasburger, 1989). The message of Just Say No was also attacked on the grounds that there is a fundamental illogicality and educational unsoundness about telling young people to be responsible and make their own decisions, but then to supply the decision ("say no") anyway (Strasburger, 1989).

Despite the lack of segmentation and the weakness in the Just Say No message, which surely would not have survived pretesting, critics will see this and others as social marketing campaigns and criticize them accordingly.

Problem Type 5

The predominance of advertising also affects the moral acceptability of social marketing. There is a tendency for the public sector to mistrust advertising, to see it as manipulative and dishonest, pushing people to buy things they do not need—despite the fact that there is ample evidence that advertising is nowhere near as powerful as this view would suggest (e.g., Glover, 1984; Lannon & Cooper, 1983). These feelings are frequently transferred to generic and social marketing (e.g., Brieger, Ramakrishna, & Adeniyi, 1986–1987; Buchanan, Reddy, & Hossain, 1994), a process that is encouraged by an overemphasis in social marketing campaigns on advertising. This problem is exacerbated by the tendency for politicians to be overly enthusiastic about social advertising because it provides a glamorous and highly visible quick-fix solution to social problems (Elliott, 1995), as with the drug misuse examples mentioned earlier.

When politicians approach social marketers with big budgets, proposing to use advertising to solve major social problems, the value of this approach must be questioned. First, it is unlikely to work. Advertising alone rarely stops people using drugs or having unsafe sex, any more than it makes them buy cars. Second, it will devalue social marketing in the eyes of these politicians, who know advertising is not that powerful. Third, it will compound the moral doubts of others working in the social sector about the value of social marketing, who will see significant budgets being frittered away in superficial, ineffective, and even counterproductive campaigns. Instead of being cautious about advertising, however, social marketers are all too enthusiastic about it.

In summary, overstating the importance of social advertising in the social marketing mix threatens the discipline in a variety of ways. It obscures its strengths, restricts its use, encourages unfounded theoretical and practical criticism, and generates mistrust. In view of these problems, why do social marketers continue to blow their advertising trumpet so loud? The answer is not, as Elliott (1995) suggested, because it has to be so, but because social marketers do not respond imaginatively enough to the challenges.

WHY HAS SOCIAL MARKETING BEEN DOMINATED BY SOCIAL ADVERTISING?

The literature suggests that the dominance of social advertising is inevitable, given the nature of social marketing. Specifically, commentators have blamed both the intangibility and immutability of social marketing products. But, neither explanation holds water, and this chapter rejects the suggestion that social marketing's overdependence on advertising is inevitable.

Intangibility

Young (1995) suggested that social marketing is dominated by social advertising because, in the absence of a tangible product and of an actual trade between marketer and market, mass media is perceived to be the only channel where social marketers can exert influence. Conscientious practitioners and theorists then find themselves "constantly at pains" to locate their promotional work within "the broader marketing mix."

This last comment, however, shows that intangibility does not make the advertising option inevitable, but merely the easiest approach. Bloom and Novelli (1981) wrote that

> Because doing anything to the product strategy is difficult for social marketers, many will ignore this aspect of marketing planning and instead concentrate their efforts on developing advertising and promotion strategies for the product they have been told to sell. However, social marketers should recognize that although they may be unable to adjust the performance characteristics of their products, they may be able to adjust the perception characteristics of their products and achieve significant results. (p. 83)

Going one step further, social marketers can and should manipulate the performance as well as the perception characteristics of their products to meet consumer needs, but this runs contrary to the second explanation for the dominance of social advertising: the immutability of social marketing products.

Immutability

Elliott (1995), noting the tendency for social marketing efforts to be dominated by social advertising campaigns, argued that this is an inevitable result of the lack of scope in social marketing to alter the nonpromotional elements of the marketing mix—in particular, the product—leaving as the main variable open to change by the social marketer "the communication of the idea/product" (p. 2), that is, promotion. This, Elliott (1995) argued, is why there is so much emphasis on social advertising: Where a commercial marketer would seek to change the offering if faced with a negative reaction, the social marketer's product, often conceived outside the market place, is usually an unalterable given, driving the program manager largely into the business of selling or advocacy.

This notion can be disputed on four grounds. First, the pressure of a "given" product is just as evident in commercial marketing as in social marketing. Commercial marketers do not change products when faced with a negative reaction. The tobacco industry provides a resonant example here. Despite knowing for at least 40 years that cigarettes are carcinogenic

(Glantz et al., 1995) and coming under immense political and social pressure as a result, the industry has steadfastly stuck to its product; and, yet, has been heavily (and judging by profitability, successfully) involved in marketing in its broadest sense, not just in promotion. Indeed, it has used marketing in an environment where promotional activity has been increasingly restricted, if not forbidden altogether.

Of course, this oversimplifies the argument. The tobacco industry has responded to market need and altered its products. Low tar cigarettes and filters are obvious examples. The point is that these are relatively minor alterations on the periphery of the product, rather than full-scale abandonment of it. Social marketing is just as capable of this type of product flexibility. In UK HIV/AIDS education, for example, it was rapidly accepted that messages of absolute safety, recommending behaviors such as celibacy and complete abstinence from injecting drugs, simply would not sell. They have been replaced by messages of relative safety—safer sex and safer drugs use. Interestingly, these compromise messages bring with them a need for products (such as condoms and clean syringes) as well as for media communication.

The second problem with the idea that social marketers are hamstrung by given products is that, as with an overdependence on advertising, it undermines both the application and the concept of the marketing mix. The question of the marketing mix's applicability to social marketing continues to exercise academics and practitioners. On the one hand, it is felt to be too broad to apply to what is primarily communication activity (Elliott, 1995), and, on the other hand, too narrow a concept, with calls being made to add yet more Ps such as politics, policy, and public relations (e.g., Kotler, 1994; Weiner & Samuels, 1995).

Simply sidestepping these arguments and reiterating the agreement with Lefebvre (1992a), the mix provides a framework for strategic decision making. It is not a straightjacket (and certainly should not be seen as synonymous with social marketing itself; Maibach, 1993), but a tool to aid thinking. If seven Ps help this process, use them; if only one is appropriate, apply it, but, do not prejudge on the basis that there is no choice.

According to the third argument, case histories show that the product can be changed. For example, in the United Kingdom, a recent social marketing initiative to advance water fluoridation (Hastings, Smith, & Lowry, 1994) has put particular emphasis on the product, and next to none on promotion.

The health authorities concerned saw fluoridation as a means of improving dental health, particularly among the disadvantaged, in a way that was far more effective and efficient than any of the alternative products such as distributing free fluoride drops, promoting dietary change, or encouraging better tooth brushing. In addition, fluoridation is government policy, and health authorities are ultimately responsible to the government.

In short, fluoridation could satisfy both their public health and their political needs. The health authorities' initial intent, having decided to try social marketing, was to run a high profile mass media campaign—because that is what they felt social marketing comprised. A step back, and an examination of their consumers, showed that this would not only be ineffective but positively counterproductive.

Introducing water fluoridation in the United Kingdom is a complex process. Local health authorities request (but do not tell) water companies to start adding fluoride to the water once they have formally consulted the public and the relevant local government authorities. This suggested there were at least three consumer groups—the public, the local government, and the water companies—each of whom were researched. Research with the general public found that they were largely supportive of fluoridation and would need to be kept informed of developments, but confirmed they had little role to play in actively progressing the initiative. This would depend on the different professional agencies, research with whom revealed quite different needs and perceptions.

The local government authorities were not interested in public health, at least for its own sake, and being Labor dominated had no love for health authorities or their (Conservative) government-inspired policies. Their main concern was to represent and meet the needs of their constituents. If they were going to buy fluoridation, their interest in and ownership of it would need to be stimulated by emphasizing the benefits that fluoridation would bring to their voters and by reminding them that the first UK fluoridation schemes, back in the 1960s, had been introduced by local authorities, not health authorities. In short, if they were going to buy it, fluoridation had to meet their political needs.

Similarly, the private water companies were not interested in public health. They wanted to provide their customers with clean, wholesome water, and their shareholders with a reasonable return. However, they were interested in helping the government carry out its policies, retaining good relationships with public health professionals in their area and positive public relations. At a more practical level, they also needed a fluoridation product that met their technical requirements: that would suit their existing plant and have an acceptable safety standard, for example. They needed more than the basic "benefit to the public" product that would satisfy the local authorities.

The case illustrates two points. First, social advertising had only a minor role to play, in informing the public of the health authority's plans. Second, actively advancing fluoridation required manipulation of the product. The varying needs of the target groups had to be met by offering them different fluoridation products: a basic public benefits product to the local authorities, and a more complex product for the water companies, with a range of technical add-ons that would meet their logistical needs. Returning to the analogy of tobacco, this seems no different than the tobacco industry retaining customers who would otherwise reject the basic product, by offering low tar options.

In the alcohol policy area, Murray and Douglas (1988) similarly identified how the product of alcohol policy advice has different policymaker target groups: legislators; sponsors of alcohol-related events; federal, state, and provincial government bodies; sellers and distributors of alcohol; and so on. For each of these, the benefit or exchange is concerned with an increased understanding of their own liability in legal matters relating to alcohol sale and distribution. Adding to this the concepts of the product life cycle and adoption, Murray and Wyld suggested further product benefits can be identified for different product adopter groups, such as internalizers, identifiers, and compliers. Both cases illustrate that, in practice, the social marketing product can be changed.

The final argument with immutability is that it strikes at the heart of social marketing. If social marketers cannot change their offerings, how meaningful are the basic marketing concepts of exchange and consumer orientation? Walsh and colleagues (1993) encapsulated this point when they concluded their overview of the field with

> social marketing . . . challenges health specialists to think in new ways about consumers and product design. Entering the marketing world requires abandoning the expert's mind-set that the product is intrinsically good, so that if it fails to sell, the defect must reside in uninformed or unmotivated consumers who need shrewder instruction or louder exhortation. (p. 117)

More fundamentally still, if social marketers cannot change their product, how can they move forward? At the end of the day, even the tobacco industry will stop producing cigarettes if no one buys them. Saying that products cannot be changed ignores this ultimate pressure and condemns social marketers to stagnation. They will become like latter-day snake oil sellers, hawking their wares long after everyone has ceased to value them.

CONCLUSIONS

Social advertising is an important part of social marketing, but it is not a synonym for it, nor should it inevitably dominate or even be involved in all social marketing activity. This chapter began by examining the dangers inherent in the overimportance of social advertising. It obscures the strengths of social marketing, restricts its use, encourages unfounded theoretical and practical criticism, and generates mistrust. In short, it damages social marketing.

It has also argued that the current predominance of social advertising in the discipline is not inevitable, and cannot be blamed on the intangibility and immutability of social marketing products. The problem of intangibility simply requires a more ingenious search for solutions that go beyond advertising; the problem of immutability has to be rejected if social marketing is to pay more than lip service to the ideas of consumer orientation and mutually beneficial exchange. Cases in alcohol policy and water fluoridation show that social marketing products can be altered in response to consumer demand.

However, this debate is only helpful if it leads to clearer planning and better projects. This can be achieved by thinking about the product more creatively and sensitively. By becoming more responsive in thinking about products, benefits, and in the long term consumer relationships, marketers will perhaps fall less regularly into the trap of thinking that all they can change is promotion and all they can do is social advertising.

REFERENCES

Andreasen, A. R. (1994). Social marketing: Its definition and domain. *Journal of Public Policy and Marketing, 13*(1), 108–114.

Backer, T. E., Rogers, E. M., & Sopory, P. (1992). *Designing health communication campaigns: What works?* Newbury Park, CA: Sage.

Balch, G., & Sutton, S. (1995, May). *Keep me posted: A plea for practical evaluation. The role of advertising in social marketing.* Paper presented at 1995 Society for Consumer Psychology Conference, Atlanta.

Bloom, P. N., & Novelli, W. D. (1981). Problems and challenges in social marketing. *Journal of Marketing, 45,* 79–88.

Brieger, W. R., Ramakrishna, J., & Adeniyi, J. D. (1986–1987). Community involvement in social marketing: Guineaworm control. *International Quarterly of Community Health Education, 7*(1), 19–31.

Buchanan, D. R., Reddy, S., & Hossain, Z. (1994). Social marketing: A critical appraisal. *Health Promotion International, 9*(1), 49–57.

de Haes, W. (1987). Looking for effective drug education programmes: Fifteen years exploration of the effects of different drug education programmes. *Health Education Research Theory and Practice, 2*(4), 433–438.

Dobson, B. E. (1992). *A comparison of the delivery and effectiveness of drug education in Belgium, the Netherlands and the United Kingdom—A feasibility study.* Manchester: Tacade.

Dorn, N., & Murji, K. (1992). *Drug prevention: A review of the English language literature.* ISDD Research Monograph Five. London: Institute for the Study of Drug Dependence.

Eadie, D. R., Goodlad, N. R., Hastings, G. B., MacKintosh, A. M., & Avan, S. H. (1993). *Qualitative pre/post-test of the HEA's 1993/94 family and adult smoking campaign—main findings.* Centre for Social Marketing, University of Strathclyde.

Elliott, B. (1995, May). *The limits to marketing: On the side of the angels. The role of advertising in social marketing.* Paper presented at 1995 Society for Consumer Psychology Conference, Atlanta.

Elliott, B. J., & Hastings, G. B. (1993). Social marketing practice in traffic safety. In *Marketing of traffic safety: Report prepared by an OECD scientific expert group* (chap. 3). Paris: Organization for Economic Co-operation and Development.

Forman, A. (1991). In AED, *Social Marketing: Views from inside the government. 30th Anniversary Seminar Series* (pp. 16–24). Washington, DC: Academy for Educational Development.

Glantz, S. A., Barnes, D. E., Bero, L., Hanover, P., & Slade, J. (1995). Looking through a keyhole at the tobacco industry—The Brown and Williamson documents. *Journal of the American Medical Association, 274*(3), 219–224.

Glover, D. (1984). *The sociology of the mass media.* Ormskirk, UK: Causeway Press.

Hastings, G. B., & Haywood, A. J. (1994). Social marketing: A critical response. *Health Promotion International, 9*(1), 59–63.

Hastings, G. B., Smith, C. S., & Lowry, R. J. (1994). Fluoridation—a time for hope, a time for action. *British Dental Journal,* May, 273–274.

Hastings, G. B., Lawther, S., Eadie, D. R., Haywood, A. J., Lowry, R. J., & Evans, D. (1994). General anaesthesia: Who decides and why? *British Dental Journal, 177,* 332–336.

Hastings, G. B., Ryan, H., Teer, P., & MacKintosh, A. M. (1994). Cigarette advertising and children's smoking: Why Reg was withdrawn. *British Medical Journal, 309,* 933–937.

Kotler, P. (1994). Reconceptualizing marketing: An overview with Philip Kotler. *European Management Journal, 12*(4), 353–361.

Kotler, P., & Zaltman, G. (1971). Social marketing: An approach to planned social change. *Journal of Marketing, 35,* 3–12.

Lannon, J., & Cooper, P. (1983). Humanistic advertising: A holistic cultural perspective. *International Journal of Advertising, 2*(3), 195–213.

Lawther, S., & Lowry, R. (1995). Social marketing and behaviour change among professionals. *Social Marketing Quarterly, 2*(1), 10–11.

Leathar, D. S. (1981). Defence inducing advertising. In "Taking Stock: what have we learned and where are we going?" *Journal of the Institute of Health Education, 19*(2), 42–55.

Lefebvre, R. C. (1992a). Social marketing and health promotion. In R. Bunton & G. MacDonald (Eds.), *Health promotion: Disciplines and diversity* (pp. 153–181). London: Routledge.

Lefebvre, R. C. (1992b). The social marketing imbroglio in health promotion. *Health Promotion International, 7*(1), 61–64.

Lefebvre, R. C. (1995, May). *Sustaining the growth of social marketing: The need for a research base. The role of advertising in social marketing.* Paper presented at 1995 Society for Consumer Psychology Conference, Atlanta.

Lefebvre, R. C., & Flora, J. A. (1988). Social marketing and public health intervention. *Health Education Quarterly, 15*(3), 299–315.

Ling, J. C., Franklin, B. A. K., Lindsteadt, J. F., & Gearion, S. A. N. (1992). Social marketing: Its place in public health. *Annual Review of Public Health, 13,* 341–362.

Maibach, E. (1993). Social marketing for the environment: Using information campaigns to promote environmental awareness and behaviour change. *Health Promotion International, 8*(3), 209–224.

Makkai, T., Moore, R., & McAllister, I. (1991). Health education campaigns and drug use: The "drug offensive" in Australia. *Health Education Research Theory and Practice, 6*(1), 65–76.

Manoff, R. K. (1985). *Social marketing: New imperative for public health.* New York: Praeger.

Manoff, R. K. (1990). What influences one person may not influence another. *World Health Forum, 11,* 157–158.

Mintz, J. (1988–1989). Social marketing: New weapon in an old struggle. *Health Promotion,* Winter, 6–12.

Murray, G. G., & Douglas, R. R. (1988). Social marketing in the alcohol policy arena. *British Journal of Addiction, 83,* 505–511.

Polich, J., Ellickson, R., Reuter, P., & Kahan, J. (1984). *Strategies for controlling adolescent drug use.* Santa Monica, CA: RAND.

Smith, W. A. (1991). In AED, *Social marketing: Views from inside the government. 30th Anniversary Seminar Series* (pp. 1–5). Washington, DC: Academy for Educational Development.

Strasburger, V. C. (1989). Prevention of adolescent drug abuse: Why "Just Say No" just won't work. *Journal of Pediatrics, 114*(4, 1), 677–681.

Sutton, S. M. (1991). In AED, *Social marketing: Views from inside the government. 30th Anniversary Seminar Series* (pp. 36–47). Washington, DC: Academy for Educational Development.

Tones, K. (1994). Marketing and the mass media: Theory and myth. Reflections on social marketing theory. *Health Education Research Theory and Practice, 9*(2), 165–169.

Wallack, L. (1990). Improving health promotion: Media advocacy and social marketing approaches. In C. Atkin & L. Wallack (Eds.), *Mass communication and public health* (pp. 147–163). Newbury Park, CA: Sage.

Walsh, D. C., Rudd, R. E., Moeykens, B. A., & Moloney, T. W. (1993). Social marketing for public health. *Health Affairs,* Summer, 104–119.

Weiner, L., & Samuels, S. E. (1995). Expanding the definition. *Social Marketing Quarterly, 2*(1), 12.

Wyld, D. C., & Hallock, D. E. (1989). Advertising's response to the AIDS crisis: The role of social marketing. *AIDS and Public Policy Journal, 4*(4), 193–205.

Young, E. (1988–1989). Social marketing: Where it has come from; where it's going. *Health Promotion,* Winter, 2–6.

Young, E. (1995, May). *From persuasion to attraction: Building loyalty and involvement in social marketing campaigns. The role of advertising in social marketing.* Paper presented at 1995 Society for Consumer Psychology Conference, Atlanta.

Chapter 4

Public Health Education and Communication as Policy Instruments for Bringing About Changes in Behavior

Robert Hornik
University of Pennsylvania

ABSTRACT

This chapter outlines selected evidence that public health education and communication have affected important health behavior. Three questions are addressed: What programs are public health communication interventions? What are their effects on behavior? Under what conditions are such programs effective? This is an exemplary rather than a comprehensive review that should not be read as suggesting that such efforts always or usually have such effects. The nature of the available evidence precludes any such conclusion. Rather, it shows that at least in some cases there have been effects.

The investigation begins by contrasting the Stanford Five City Project and the National High Blood Pressure Education Program. The first is a landmark, a well-controlled, carefully developed program that may have had only small or no effects on behavior. The second is a national multi-component program with an uncontrolled evaluation that probably produced a massive reduction in stroke mortality. It goes on to review other apparently successful cases (e.g., AIDS campaigns in Netherlands and Switzerland, Reye's Syndrome, Sudden Infant Death Syndrome, smoking, immunization in the Philippines). The chapter closes with an analysis of the conditions of success: when the recommended behavior is supported by the health system, when much of the audience is reached repeatedly, when sponsors expect the process of change to reflect slow social norm change rather than individual effects of direct message exposure, and when new behaviors fit easily with the existing pattern of behavior.

There are contradictions in the way the medical world thinks about public health communication. On the one hand, an image of powerful advertising promises rapid changes in health behavior. This image is reflected in an ambivalent admiration for commercial advertisers: "If Coca Cola can do it why can't we?" On the other hand, the failure of some people who "know" healthy behavior to do healthy behavior leaves other observers skeptical about the utility of public education as an intervention tool. Most people know about the transmission of HIV, for instance, but many still engage in high risk behavior.

Both of these contradictory views grow out of the same naive expectation of effects. The fact is that despite Coca Cola's massive promotion budgets, changes in market share are only slowly achieved: a 1% or 2% add-on to market share would be an extraordinary success. Few health promotion activities have been capable of measuring so small a change, never mind being ready to accept it as a sufficient outcome of a campaign. However, such small declines may have immense consequences for public health status, even if they do not represent complete success.

There is a thoroughgoing contradiction in the available evidence about the role of public health communication in affecting health status. On the one hand, there is possibly the best-known project in the field, the Stanford Five City Project. This program features a well-defined implementation and a careful evaluation. However, the evaluation so far suggests only limited effects, effects that may not be large compared to the secular trend. On the other hand, there are some activities (difficult to call them projects) that have relied heavily on public health communication, and are associated with quite substantial changes in behavior. However, the evaluations of these activities are much less controlled and the attribution of their effects is much more problematic.

It is tempting to attend only to well-controlled studies and suggest that if the latter evaluations had been done with better controls, then they would also have been unconvincing as to the power of public health communication. However, there is an alternative view about such programs: The circumstances in which public health communication has a large success make it exceedingly difficult to do definitive evaluation.

Any program that makes use of mass communication in a major way and that does or is meant to affect health behavior falls into this discussion. This includes many different programs. Some use mass media alone. Others add complementary efforts with and through health professionals. Yet others include direct outreach to communities. Some programs stimulate demands on the health system such as increasing immunization visits, whereas others address autonomous behavior such as quitting smoking. Some programs are focused on a single behavior like obtaining a mammography; others address a set of related behaviors or behaviors that have to be maintained over time such as quitting smoking, engaging in exercise, or changing one's diet. Some work in a focused geographic area and others include the entire nation. Some use the mass media as a channel for broadcast of prepared materials; others use the media by encouraging attention to issues by existing news and other shows so as to either discourage unacceptable behavior or encourage desired behavior. Still others use the media as an element of a program of public advocacy, to stimulate legal or policy change by influencing and organizing the climate of public opinion.

EVIDENCE FROM CONTROLLED EVALUATIONS

First, consider the Stanford program, which has been a central model of public health campaigns. The Stanford Five City Project provided 5 years of mass media and community organization cardiovascular risk reduction education to two small cities in Northern California. The "treatment" cities were compared with two roughly similar control cities on their rates of change on relevant risk factors. This project and its predecessor, the Stanford Three Community Study, have been the catalyst for many other projects and for the growth of the community health education approach. The educational efforts have been serious, based in a theory of behavior change, and have incorporated the careful development and implementation of educational programs, including television and radio spots, printed materials, classes, contests, and correspondence courses. The project estimates that each adult in the treatment communities would have been exposed to around 5 hours of education each year (Farquhar et al., 1990).

The evaluation, done with great care, is still a messy affair. The treatment and control cities were not equivalent beforehand and two different methods of evaluation give quite different results. However, a reader disposed to take a skeptical view would conclude that the effects of the program were either small or not established. A look at differences between the independent, rather than cohort, samples of the first and last measurement waves finds that only two of six risk factors showed a significantly ($p < .05$) larger effect for the treatment cities than the control cities. In addition, the cumulative rates of change for estimated all-cause mortality risk, or coronary heart disease risk, were not different for the treatment and control cities. Other ways of framing the data can give a more optimistic view. Not-yet-reported follow-up data gathered in each community 4 years after the end of the formal educational activity and estimates of changes in morbidity and mortality may give still a different picture. However, for the moment, the evaluation suggests uncertainty as to outcomes and allows room to doubt the significance of a treatment-city advantage.

The best light to put on such results is to ask: Even if the effects were small, were they worthwhile? Will the likely benefit outweigh the cost?

Farquhar et al. (1990) revealed that the cost "to our group" was about $4 per person per year, excluding research costs and, assumedly, donated media time and volunteer time, crucial elements in the project's operation (p. 364). At that rate, if a continuing high quality program could be delivered, even a small benefit could justify continuation.

However, the smallness of any treatment-attributable changes appears in the context of some substantial secular trends, either estimated from the control group or from external sources. For example, the treatment cities were declining at the rate of .016 mmol/L per year in cholesterol level, which was quicker than the decline in the control cities. However, in the 4-year period after the post survey reported here, the two control cities declined at the rate of about .05 mmol/L per year, three times the rate during the treatment period. That was a period when cholesterol presumably increased its presence on the national media agenda (Frank, Winkleby, Fortmann, Rockhill, & Farquhar, 1992).

Other, similar studies show equally mixed results. The earlier Stanford Three Community Study and a parallel project in Finland show somewhat larger effects than did the Five City Study. The Finnish study demonstrated a sharper rate of decline in mortality in the treatment community of North Karelia than was shown elsewhere in the country (Puska et al., 1989). Another U.S. program, Minnesota Heart Health (a heir to the Stanford effort), has also failed to show substantial community effects (Luepker et al., 1994).

These projects are perhaps more important for the community health promotion movement they have catalyzed than as models for replication. They require talent and concentrated effort on a scale not easily reproduced. Thus, even if the benefit–cost ratio justified their operation despite small effects, the securing of even limited funds for regional or national versions of these programs, and the organization and maintenance of the community efforts they require may put them beyond feasibility.

EVIDENCE FROM UNCONTROLLED EVALUATIONS

The National High Blood Pressure Education and Control Program (NHBPEP) contrasts with the Stanford model. If Stanford is a carefully constructed, carefully evaluated, and geographically focused program associated with small effects, the NHBPEP has been a kitchen sink sort of program that has been associated with massive effects.

The decline in stroke mortality has been an "extraordinary public health achievement" (McGovern et al., 1992). However, attribution of the decline remains controversial (Casper, Wing, Strogatz, Davis, & Tyroler, 1992; Jacobs, McGovern, & Blackburn, 1992; Kannel & Wolf, 1992; McGovern et al., 1992). Nonetheless, the consistency of evidence from controlled trials and the matched timing of stroke mortality decline, increasing control of hypertension, and initiation of the National High Blood Pressure Education and Control Program in 1972 does draw attention. Although the decline in stroke mortality had begun before 1972, the rate of decline accelerated rapidly for the decade after the beginning of the NHBPEP. Between 1960 and 1972, the age-adjusted stroke mortality rate declined at 1.6% per year for all U.S. Whites; from 1972 to 1984, the rate was 5.9% per year (McGovern et al., 1992).

Whether one definitively attributes all or only some of the decline in stroke mortality to changing patterns of treatment of high blood pressure, there was massive change in attention to and treatment of hypertension after the launch of the NHBPEP. Eighteen percent of 25- to 59-year-old male hypertensives in the Minnesota Heart Survey were under treatment in 1973–1974, but 41% were under treatment in 1980–1982. For women, comparable numbers were 36% growing to 56% (McGovern et al., 1992). Evidence from other sources about the United States as a whole is consistent with these findings (Casper et al., 1992).

How is such a large change in behavior to be explained? The NHBPEP involved many activities: institutional consensus building, education of health professionals, some public education through community organizations, and major efforts in mass media education. These media efforts included distribution of public service announcements for broadcast on radio and television and stimulation of coverage of hypertension by various media outlets. This has been a multicomponent program, and it may well have been its scale that has made it successful. It is beyond any evaluation to sort out just which elements of the program were effective. More important, it is likely to be misleading to attribute to a particular focused set of actions what may well have been a massive norm change within a society.

One can imagine how the process of change occurs: A person sees some public service announcements and a local TV health reporter's feature telling her about the symptomless disease of hypertension. She checks her blood pressure in a newly accessible shopping mall machine, and those results suggest a problem. She tells her spouse who has also seen the ads and encourages her to have it checked. She goes to a physician who confirms the presence of hypertension, encourages her to change her diet, and then return for monitoring. Meanwhile, the physician has become more sensitive to the issue because of a recent article in the *Journal of the American Medical Association*, some recommendations from a specialist society, and a conversation with a drug detailer, as well as informal conversations with colleagues and exposure to television discussion of the issue. The patient talks with friends at work or family members about her experience. They also increase their concern and go to have their own pressure checked. She returns for another checkup and her pressure is still elevated although she has reduced her use of cooking salt. The physician decides to treat her with medication. The patient is ready to comply because all the sources around her—personal, professional, and mediated—are telling her that she should.

The program is effective in this explanation not because of a PSA or a specific program of physician education. It is successful because the NHBPEP has changed the professional and public environment as a whole around the issue of hypertension. There is some evidence that the National Cholesterol Education Program similarly affected consumption of high cholesterol foods.

If the best public communication has its effect because it changes the public environment as a whole, then controlled evaluation may be difficult. Even the multifaceted Stanford program and its successors, which do reach their communities in many of the ways just described, must maintain control areas. Thus, they can only change a part of the environment, that part isolated from the regional and national media and professional worlds. For the residents of their treatment cities, the 5 hours of annual exposure may only be a fraction of all their exposure to relevant information on the national media. For the health professionals of their communities, the local education may come in the context of a larger dose of national or regional information. In this context, it may be no surprise to see the experimental and control cities changing at only slightly different rates.

There are other examples of large observed changes in behavior associated with the operation of public communication programs, but also in a context where there can be no definitive attribution of cause and effect. The Swiss Stop AIDS campaign and the Netherlands AIDS program used mass media heavily to reach audiences believed to be at risk of infection with HIV (deVroome et al., 1990; Dubois-Arber, Lehmann, Hausser, Gutzwiller, & Zimmermann, 1989). There were two sides to the mass media activity. Government authorities carefully developed television and radio advertisements, billboards, and newspaper inserts whose content was quite explicit in encouraging the use of condoms for protection. At the same time, as in much of the rest of the world, mass media were full of coverage of AIDS. In both countries, the operation of the programs was associated with a period of substantial change in use of condoms. Self-reported use of condoms with all "casual" partners in the previous 6 months increased from 8% to 48% in Switzerland and from 9% to over 40% in the Netherlands between early 1987 and late 1989. These are self-reported behaviors with the risks of such indirect measurement. However, the growth in usage rates was supported in a general way by evidence about condom sales.

From a policy view, one would hope to be able to separate the effects of the deliberate educational efforts from the massive natural media coverage of AIDS. Would the natural coverage have produced these effects without the deliberate campaign? Would the deliberate campaign have had these effects without the natural coverage? An answer can only be speculative. However, patterns of behavior in other countries where the natural coverage was also heavy, but where the educational campaign was less intense and less explicit, are suggestive. The rates of change in behavior were apparently less (Brorsson & Herlitz, 1988; Forrest & Singh, 1990; Moran, Janes, Peterman, & Stone, 1990; Sonenstein, Pleck, & Ku, 1989). The natural coverage alone seems insufficient to explain the Swiss and Dutch rates of change. On the other hand, it is sensible to speculate that the deliberate educational campaign, with its explicit action recommendations, was successful because of the context of AIDS consciousness and fears engendered by natural coverage. Such coverage made people susceptible to such recommendations.

Two other cases are parallel to both the NHBPEP and the AIDS campaigns in that they show large effects associated with the initiation of deliberate educational efforts as well as natural media coverage of issues, but concern less common diseases: Reye's Syndrome and the use of aspirin, and SIDS and placing infants to sleep on their backs.

Soumerai, Ross-Degnan, and Kahn (1992) tell the story of the virtual disappearance of Reye's Syndrome over a short period. Their narrative shows how debate in the scientific community and the health policy community was played over media outlets. The attention over both professional and, particularly, public communication channels were closely associated with the decline in disease incidence. They make a convincing case that the decline was not primarily associated with the timing of declared changes in policy or particular recommendations made to physicians, or even with the warnings placed on aspirin bottles. Rather, the decline followed immediately on increased coverage on these issues in the mass media. This is sensible, because much use of aspirin was independent of visits to physicians, and thus would be most sensitive to sources of change in public knowledge.

A parallel pattern is the rapid decline in Sudden Infant Death Syndrome (SIDS) associated with publicity about the risk of the prone sleeping position for infants. Thus far, the evidence comes from other countries, but perhaps it will soon be repeated in the United States. There is credible evidence that publicity has produced rapid change in the frequency of the prone sleeping position. An earlier campaign in the Netherlands that favored the prone position had produced an increase in its use from 10% to 55%–65%; this fell to 27% within a year of antiprone publicity (Engelberts, de Jonge, & Kostense, 1991). In the Otago District of New Zealand, the use of the prone position fell from 44% to 3% after 3 years of publicity (Taylor, 1991).

Available reports do not detail the nature of the publicity, but programs seem to include both media coverage of health authority announcements on the issue and, in some cases, deliberate publicity efforts and advice to health professionals. Guntheroth and Spiers (1992) noted that such publicity has been "associated with reduction in SIDS by 20% to 67%, paralleling the reduction in use of the prone position" (p. 2359).

The Reye's Syndrome and SIDS examples have at least one feature in common that may explain why the relevant behaviors have changed so rapidly with only low to moderate amounts of publicity. In both cases, the original behavior (aspirin use and the use of the prone position) was replaced by a roughly equivalent substitute (the adoptions of aspirin substitutes and the side or back position). The changes demanded little from the changer and promised a large benefit. In that context, knowledge gained from public communication is rapidly turned into behavior.

Each of the previously described programs involved some mix of mass media promotion and coverage, but usually there was simultaneous professional education and outreach and other activities. A common question is then whether mass communication without use of complementary activities can be successful. Obviously, no mass media campaign would influence behavior without required support from a health professional. Increased demand for mammograms without a ready mammography clinic to supply them will not produce any behavior change. However, it is still pertinent to ask whether mass media can influence the rate of behavior change. In some cases, healthier behavior does not require health system action. In others, the health system is ready to meet any demand created by mass media promotion. There are at least some major media efforts whose effects appear to be independent of other organized efforts.

With this in mind, health communication programs can be seen in terms of two types. One type of program intends to animate changes in autonomous health behavior (e.g., quitting smoking or reducing salt intake). The other seeks to increase demand for specific health services such as immunization, high blood pressure testing, or mammograms. Both these types of programs have shown success in some instances.

A well-known program aimed at individual behavior is the televised smoking counteradvertising campaign between 1967 and 1970. It can be argued that this campaign is among those offering the greatest public health benefit of any U.S. health communication effort. The television networks were required by the "Fairness Doctrine" then in force to match cigarette manufacturers' commercials with antismoking commercials. The period of broadcast of frequent antismoking commercials was associated with a reduction of 10% in per capita projected use of cigarettes. Attribution of this change to the counteradvertising effort is strengthened by the finding that when the counteradvertising effort was eliminated, per capita consumption increased 5%, returning to a trend present before the counteradvertising began (Erickson, McKenna, & Romano, 1990; Warner, 1981).

Another frequent use of mass media is to stimulate demand for services provided by the health system. The 1989–1990 Communication for Child Survival campaign in the Philippines used heavy television and radio advertising to encourage early immunization. Children with timely complete coverage increased from 32% to 56% in 1 year (Zimicki et al., 1994). There was evidence that the mass media programming was essential in this shift. Despite some outreach efforts to vaccination providers, service practice changes were insubstantial. Also, better vaccination rates were substantially associated with caretakers' knowledge levels, which, in turn, were closely associated with their exposure to the mass media materials. Much of the effect of this program was to reduce delay in coming in for vaccination with a smaller effect in reaching children who otherwise would have remained unvaccinated.

Other demand stimulation programs have encouraged mammography, blood pressure screening, and early visits to emergency rooms with heart attack symptoms. For example, the percentage of women over 49 who had a screening mammogram within the last year increased from 26% to 38% during 1987. A small part of that increase was associated with the American Cancer Society's spring media campaign; the larger part with fall press coverage of Nancy Reagan's breast cancer diagnosis (MMWR, 1989).

A final type of health communication program focuses attention less on addressing health behavior directly than on efforts to use mass media to organize public opinion. Media advocacy programs like Mothers Against Drunk Driving hope to change individual decisions, such as the one to drink and drive. However, they also want to influence the policy environment around drunk driving. They intend to ready legislatures to add tough laws, encourage strict enforcement by police and influence judges to give more severe punishments for drunk driving offenses. Programs such as this, which often incorporate events created to gain media attention, serve to catalyze public opinion around an issue or at the least raise the image of public concern about an issue.

WHAT IS ASSOCIATED WITH PROGRAM SUCCESS?

Many of the cases presented are successes. Nonetheless, this presentation does not lend itself easily to definitive policy conclusions about the worth of public heath communication. Three issues get in the way. First, the cases examined cannot be said to be entirely representative. The universe of published results from which the sample of cases is chosen is biased toward successful programs and the cases selected from that universe were purposefully chosen. Second, it is difficult to attribute changes in behavior to specific aspects of education and communication campaigns. The claims of successes rely on the chronological association of the introduction of public communication interventions and changes in health behaviors and/or morbidity. Also, the communication interventions are sometimes intertwined with other elements of programs so that their independent effects cannot be estimated. Third, the cases examined here have only their use of mass media in common. They are very different in other aspects, including how they operate and the type of behavior they seek to influence. A single conclusion about public communication could not have much specificity.

Nonetheless, the pattern of results does suggest a useful operating assumption. At least some of the time, public communication programs have been able to influence behavior. On that ground, their applicability to specific behaviors, in specific contexts, is worth some consideration. Some speculation about the elements of programs that may enhance success, based on these experiences and others, may enrich this operating assumption:

1. Programs that stimulate demand on the medical system, or assume that the medical system will provide support for the messages of a public education effort, must assure that such support is available. The NHBPEP had its success, if it did, because all elements of the system were offering coordinated messages. The Philippines vaccination campaign improved timely immunization because the health system had adequate supplies and trained staff available in its clinics.

2. Reach and frequency are vital. A basic principle of advertising is that, all else being equal, the more people who are reached with a message and the more frequently they hear it, the more likely they are to respond. Health programs that intend to influence behavior, but then choose to rely on unpaid public service announcements that are broadcast rarely and in late-night hours, should not be surprised at failure. The Defense Department has spent upward of $120 million in a year to locate recruits. Health and Human Services is usually expected to make do with air time contributed by broadcasters. Public and private health agencies have had to become adept at gaining media attention through provision of press releases and video materials and other means of encouraging coverage of their concerns. However, the budgets to buy media time might increase their ability to gain public attention.

3. There are two complementary models of behavior change implicit in many public health education campaigns. One focuses on individuals as they improve their knowledge and attitudes and assumes that individual exposure to messages affects individual behavior. The complementary model focuses on the process of change in public norms, which leads to

behavior change among social groups. The models contrast direct effects of seeing mass media materials from indirect effects. The first assumes a viewer sees a public service announcement (PSA) about the role of condoms in safe sex, for instance, and then decides to follow the advice. The second assumes that discussion within a social network is stimulated by PSAs or media coverage of an issue and that discussion may produce changed social norms about appropriate behavior, which affects the likelihood that each member of the social network will adopt the new behavior. If the second model is most correct, if a social process dominates the process of a behavior change, then individuals' detailed knowledge about the benefits of a new health behavior may be less important than their belief that it is an expected behavior. In that case, substantial attention in the public environment, with multiple channels saying the same thing (as in the NHBPEP), may be central to success.

4. Straightforward substitution of behaviors, when possible, may allow more rapid change than attempts to introduce new behaviors. Both the Reye's Syndrome and SIDS cases testify to the success of direct substitution programs. In both cases, rapid acceptance of a new behavior occurred. However, they were very easy behaviors to change and adoption of the new behavior sharply reduced the risk of a rare but devastating event. In contrast, new behaviors like regular exercise and seat belt use have been resistant to public promotion efforts.

This is a specific instance of a more general principle. Programs flounder unless recommendations for behavior change fit with the circumstances and the world view of the target audience. Thus, the Philippines program worked through increasing knowledge about the appropriate age for measles vaccination; knowledge about the dangers of measles was already prevalent.

5. Public promotion efforts require reasonable goals. The benefit–cost ratio can be quite large even though the absolute number of people who benefit may be only a small portion of those who might benefit. For example, cigarettes per capita now declines at 1.5% per year. Assume that $50 million per year advertising could move that to 2.5% per year for 10 years. Given the strong association between smoking and morbidity, the likely return on investment in extended life and lowered health costs would be large.

If expectations for change are large, and measurement tools are only able to detect quite substantial effects, it is likely that many mass educational interventions with worthwhile effects would be rejected as unsuccessful, effects comparable to benefits achieved by other interventions.

A final issue is cost. Early in a public epidemic, as for HIV, or if there is a need for short-term immediate action only, as for the swine flu immunization, it may be possible to shift substantial costs to private agencies.

In the case of HIV, television stations were willing to broadcast public service announcements at prime time; their news programs were full of information (as well as some hysteria) about risks for HIV transmission. In this kind of context, some of the cost of public health education can be borne by in-kind contributions by private agencies. However, as time goes on, and as the health issue loses its hold on public attention, although not its need for educational intervention, in-kind contributions are reduced. In the broadcast arena, PSAs are relegated to late-night, less valuable broadcast time and much of the audience will be lost without the direct purchase of advertising time. A similar problem occurs with other forms of public health education: Programs that rely on in-kind contributions through mobilizing volunteer efforts, on unpaid peer educators at work places, or on outreach workers going house to house may find volunteer enthusiasm difficult to maintain. The in-kind contributions may have to be replaced by direct expenditures, or else the outreach will fade well before the need for it is gone.

CONCLUSIONS

There have been some successes in public health education as well as a largely undocumented number of likely failures. This chapter describes some important cases. There are others that could be cited, although they are few in number.

The idea that public education is a potent policy strategy for affecting adult health can be supported. Some of the principles that make success more likely were detailed earlier. They include assuring that the recommended behavior is supported by the health system, reaching much of the audience repeatedly, expecting individual change to be related to social norm change rather than to direct message exposure, and expecting larger changes when new behaviors fit with the existing pattern of behavior and world view.

This chapter also recognizes that, in general, natural media coverage and media advocacy may play no less a role in the process of behavior change than do formal efforts at influencing behavior through deliberate educational efforts.

Finally, successful programs may require substantial expenditures and particularly, well-organized institutional foundations and skilled personnel. It should be noted that this has some special policy implications for campaigns in developing countries. Institutional and financial efforts may well pay off in improved health; however, in many developing countries, major efforts in the child survival area have been maintained only through foreign funding. Certainly, it will be appropriate to make an assumption that many developing countries will be slow to absorb the costs of large-scale public health education for adults into domestic budgets.

A final caveat is implied by the fact that this is a restricted review. By and large it stays with the published literature, although that literature tends to ignore failed programs. It examines programs that are relatively coherent entities, thus leaving out what is surely the greatest portion of such health education: the individual efforts of health professionals counseling patients. It considers programs with mass audiences, but ignores pilot or small-scale efforts with focused audiences, even though many published studies, particularly those with only face-to-face education, are eliminated by this criterion. Thus, de facto, it becomes a review of programs that made some use of mass media. It also includes only programs for which there is evidence about behavior change, ignoring studies restricted to evidence about knowledge or attitude change. The representativeness of the sample of studies examined is further limited by the subjectivity in with which the cases within these criteria were chosen. The chosen cases seemed particularly intriguing or unusually suggestive. An evaluation of the arguments presented here needs to take into account the nature of the programs examined.

REFERENCES

Brorsson, B., & Herlitz, C. (1988). The AIDS epidemic in Sweden: Changes in awareness, attitudes and behavior. *Scandinavian Journal of Social Medicine. 16*(2), 67–71.

Casper, M., Wing, S., Strogatz, D., Davis, C. E., & Tyroler, H. A. (1992). Antihypertensive treatment and US trends in stroke mortality, 1962 to 1980. *American Journal of Public Health, 82*(12), 1600–1606.

deVroome, E. M., Paalman, M. E., Sandfort, T. G., Sleutjes, M., de Vries, K. J., & Tielman, R. A. (1990). AIDS in the Netherlands: The effects of several years of campaigning. *International Journal of STDs and AIDS, 1*(4), 268–275.

Dubois-Arber, F., Lehmann, P., Hausser, D., Gutzwiller, F., & Zimmermann, E. (1989). *Evaluation of the Swiss preventive campaigns against AIDS: 2nd assessment report.* Lausanne: Institute Universitaire de Medecine Sociale et Preventive.

Engelberts, A. C., de Jonge, G. A., & Kostense, P. J. (1991). An analysis of trends in the incidence of sudden infant death in the Netherlands 1969–89. *Journal of Paediatrics and Child Health, 27*(6), 329–333.

Erickson, A. C., McKenna, J. W., & Romano, R. M. (1990). Past lessons and new uses of the mass media in reducing tobacco consumption. *Public Health Reports, 105*(3), 239–244.

Farquhar, J. W., Fortmann, S. P., Flora, J. A., Taylor, C. B., Haskell, W. L., Williams, P. T., Maccoby, N., & Wood, P. D. (1990). Effects of communitywide education on cardiovascular disease risk factors: The Stanford Five-City Project. *Journal of the American Medical Association, 264*(3), 359–365.

Forrest, J. D., & Singh, S. (1990). The sexual and reproductive behavior of American women, 1982–1988. *Family Planning Perspectives, 22*(5), 206–214.

Frank, E., Winkleby, M. A., Fortmann, S. P., Rockhill, B., & Farquhar, J. W. (1992). Improved cholesterol-related knowledge and behavior and plasma cholesterol levels in adults during the 1980s. *Journal of the American Medical Association, 268*(12), 1566–1572.

Guntheroth, W. G., & Spiers, P. S. (1992). Sleeping prone and the risk of sudden infant death syndrome. *Journal of the American Medical Association, 267*(17), 2359–2362.

Jacobs, D. R., Jr., McGovern, P. G., & Blackburn, H. (1992). The US decline in stroke mortality: What does ecological analysis tell us? *American Journal of Public Health, 82*(12), 1596–1599.

Kannel, W. B., & Wolf, P. A. (1992). Inferences from secular trend analysis of hypertension control. *American Journal of Public Health, 82*(12), 1593–1595.

Luepker, R. V., Murray, D. M., Jacobs, D. R., Mittelmark, M. B., Bracht, N., Carlaw, R., Crow, R., Elmer, P., Finnegan, J., & Folsom, A. R. (1994). Community education for cardiovascular disease prevention: Risk factor changes in the Minnesota heart health program. *American Journal of Public Health, 84*(9), 1383–1393.

McGovern, P. G., Burke, G. L., Sprafka, J. M., Xue, S., Folsom, A. R., & Blackburn, H. (1992). Trends in mortality, morbidity, and risk factor levels for stroke from 1960 through 1990: The Minnesota heart survey. *Journal of the American Medical Association, 268*(6), 753–759.

MMWR. (1989). Trends in screening mammograms for women 50 years of age and older—behavioral risk factor surveillance system, 1987. *Morbidity and Mortality Weekly Reports, 38*(9), 137–140.

Moran, J. S., Janes, H. R., Peterman, T. A., & Stone, K. M. (1990). Increase in condom sales following AIDS education and publicity, United States. *American Journal of Public Health, 80*(5), 607–608.

Puska P., Tuomilehto, J., Nissinen, A., Salonen, J. T., Vartiainen, E., Pietinen, P., Koskela, K., & Korhonen, H. J. (1989). The North Karelia project: Fifteen years of community-based prevention of coronary heart disease. *Annals of Medicine, 21*(3), 169–173.

Sonenstein, F. L., Pleck, J. H., & Ku, L. C. (1989). Sexual activity, condom use and AIDS awareness among adolescent males. *Family Planning Perspectives, 21*(4), 152–158.

Soumerai, S. B., Ross-Degnan, D., & Kahn, J. S. (1992). Effects of professional and media warnings about the association between aspirin use in children and Reye's syndrome. *Milbank Quarterly, 70*(1), 155–182.

Taylor, B. J. (1991). A review of epidemiological studies of sudden infant death syndrome in southern New Zealand. *Journal of Paediatrics and Child Health, 27*(6), 344–348.

Warner, K. E. (1981). Cigarette smoking in the 1970's: The impact of the antismoking campaign on consumption. *Science, 211*(4483), 729–731.

Zimicki, S., Hornik, R. C., Verzosa, C. C., Hernandez, J. R., De Guzman, E., Dayrit, M., Fausto, A., & Lee, M. B. (1994). Improving vaccination coverage in urban areas through a health communication campaign: The 1990 Philippines experience. *Bulletin of the World Health Organization, 72*(3), 409–422.

Part II

METHODOLOGICAL ISSUES/ PSYCHOGRAPHIC SEGMENTATION

Chapter 5

Keep Me Posted:
A Plea for Practical Evaluation

George I. Balch
University of Illinois–Chicago

Sharyn M. Sutton
U.S. Department of Agriculture

WHY EVALUATE?

The root purpose of evaluating is to see what, if anything, can be done better than what is being done or was done. It is inherently practical. This chapter contends that, despite the very practical intent of evaluation efforts in social marketing, the evaluations designed and conducted are often not useful. At times, they stand in the way of evaluation efforts that would be useful. At times, summative evaluations—with the randomized controlled experiment as the gold standard—impede the development and management of social marketing programs. As a result, program results suffer from inappropriate evaluation-related actions or through the opportunity cost of missed program improvements. Social marketers should apply the kind of practical marketing research perspective and procedures that commercial marketers apply to their programs.

Evaluations of social marketing programs are most useful if they are integrated into programs in an interactive, iterative, ongoing system. Successful evaluation provides program direction as relevant, accurate, timely, and cost-effective "feedforward" and feedback on program objectives, target audiences, processes, and results. It not only guides program improvements, but also communicates program value to outside authorities. It is decision-driven research for consumer-based programs.

Meaningful evaluation research requires evaluators to become key program team members who raise and answer questions that will improve the program demonstrably (Balch & Sutton, 1995). This often contrasts with the practices of outside evaluators whose primary commitment is not to program success, but to passing verdicts on programs or to publishing in academic journals.

A PRIMER OF TRADITIONAL EVALUATION

First, consider the basic terms used in evaluation research. *Formative evaluation* is the research that is presumably done when preparing a program. It usually involves exploratory qualitative work: focus groups, in-depth interviews, and so on. It includes pretesting. It may also involve activities like setting baselines and segmenting audiences.

Process evaluation measures how the program is working. It looks at how often the message got out, how many media impressions were created, how many brochures were mailed, and so forth. It is used, presumably, to learn what actually happens during the program and whether the program really delivered what it was supposed to. This may include "monitoring" the program to make sure it is delivered according to plan.

Summative research is "accountability research," the research done to prove that a program has really done something. Typically, summative research is divided into *outcome* and *impact* summative evaluation. Outcome research looks at the direct outcome of the program; impact evaluation assesses measures related to social marketing objectives or the reasons for the program's existence. For example, outcome evaluation might consider whether your audience understood the message; impact evaluation might look at whether their morbidity or mortality rates have changed as a result.

Evaluation research addresses three questions: What should we do? How are we doing? Did we do it? It is that simple. These questions need to be answered or time is being wasted. They must be answered in real time for management decisions that affect the communications and other program components.

UPDATING TRADITIONAL EVALUATION
FOR SOCIAL MARKETING

In social marketing, formative research tends to be exploratory, qualitative research—research looking for ideas with a need to be in touch with consumers—but it does not really try to measure anything. It usually stops on the exploratory side. That is a mistake. More *strategic* formative research for program decision making needs to be done.

This formative research must be focused on the basic strategic questions of who should be the target and what are they like, what should the communication persuade the target to do (the "action"), what benefit will the target find most rewarding about this action (the "benefit"), what will make the promise of that benefit most credible, how can that target be reached for the greatest persuasive effect, and what image should the communication convey. These are some strategic questions that commercial marketers ask to develop communications to achieve their marketing objectives (Wells, 1989; Moore & Wells, 1991). Social marketing formative evaluation should and can do the same (Sutton, Balch, & Lefebvre, 1995).

It is not good enough to do focus groups and learn that consumers are confused or unaware of health or environmental problems and solutions. For example, marketers must know *how many* people hold a misconception before they commit resources to a program designed to rectify the problem. Formative research is not equivalent to qualitative research. Marketers need the "hardest" information obtainable and that also requires quantitative methods. The sounder the basis for what the marketing team should be doing, the more readily they can agree on and they pull together to do it—and to measure how well they are doing it.

On the other side of the coin, process evaluation needs to be more *diagnostic*. Too much time is spent wanting to know how many brochures went out, how many calls came in, how many "exposures" or "impressions" were made—and this exactness lends the weight of summative evaluation to process data. This bean counting can also miss much of the qualitative process information that can be diagnostically invaluable for real-time program adjustment. It is necessary to know what the program being delivered really is—what, if anything, it delivered to whom, and how—if it is to be understood and adjusted intelligently.

With summative evaluation, more of both exploratory/qualitative and quantitative research is needed. But it must be done in ways that answer the questions that are realistic and important to social marketers. Most important, the focus must be on the *actions* that the communications attempt to persuade target consumers to take. And *real-time feedback* is necessary for real-world management and results.

To sum up this viewpoint, formative research is foremost. It provides more value for the effort than any other kind of research. It answers the questions that guide the whole social marketing effort. It directs the team's efforts toward the target, action, benefit, openings, and image that will have the best chance of achieving the social marketing objective. Process is pivotal. Unless marketers understand what the social marketing efforts are—communications and other elements—they cannot know what is working well or badly. Yet they cannot pretend that just delivering brochures or media impressions is all they are about. Therefore, outcome is optimal.

Outcome evaluation is the research that focuses on the objectives that can be realistically expected from communications or other program elements. This is the kind of summative research to which marketers need to hold their efforts accountable. Finally, impact is overrated. It sounds ideal to be able to show the contribution of a social marketing communication—or any other program element—to improvements in morbidity, mortality, environmental protection, or other social marketing objectives. But it is very difficult or impossible, expensive, and time-consuming to do. It may cost more than the program itself. It may interfere with making the program successful. And by the time marketers have the answer, it may no longer be useful (Sutton, 1992).

SOME COMMON AND CRITICAL OBSTACLES
TO DOING PRACTICAL EVALUATION

Common obstacles to doing practical evaluation include: failure to agree on realistic communication objectives, some irrelevant (academic) questions, failure to design action-oriented research, and a misguided reliance on an experimental/"hard science" paradigm.

Unrealistic Communication Objectives

Evaluation studies of communications in social marketing may not be directed at a realistic, agreed on communication objective—the action marketers want the target audience to take as a result of the communication. Instead, they may be directed at objectives for the entire program (impact). Or evaluators may expect communications alone to achieve complex behavior change. This is especially inappropriate when the social marketing effort is limited to communications alone. Social marketing principles have always maintained that promotion is only part of the "marketing mix." Other factors influence the consumer, particularly product, price, and distribution (Andreasen, 1994a, 1994b).

Authorities may expect an ad campaign to achieve such social objectives as reducing the volume of solid waste sent to landfills or reducing the morbidity and mortality rates due to breast cancer. Yet, the volume of solid waste in landfills depends on more than getting people to recycle; it also depends on variables such as the recyclability of waste items and the market price of recyclables and their regular pickup and delivery. The rates of recycling depend on more than a communication program that encourages it; they also depend on variables such as the relative ease of using new recycling procedures, the consumer price of separating and sorting versus just discarding waste, how much consumers pay for the pickup of their trash, whether and how much they are paid for the recyclables they deliver, and the nearby availability of drop-off boxes or regular curbside pickup. The rates of breast cancer and death from it depend on more than getting women to have mammograms; they also depend on variables such as the conditions that cause breast cancer, as well as medical facilities available to treat it. And the rates of mammography depend on more than a communication program; they also depend on variables such as how women are treated at the mammography location, how much they are charged, and how far they have to travel to get there. Unless communication is an integral part of an overall social program to create and facilitate behavior change, it should not be evaluated based on measures of such program objectives.

Reasonable behavior change expectations for which communications can be held accountable and evaluated to some extent include the usual hierarchy of effects: awareness, knowledge, attitudes, intentions, reported behavior, and behavior. The further down this list, the more other variables come into play, such as the price, quality, and availability of products and services. The more important the noncommunication variables, the further up on the hierarchy the communication objective should be set—and the more closely evaluation research should take account of those other variables. Another way to look at possible communication objectives or "actions" is moving from one "stage of change" to another. Stages may range from "precontemplation," or "unawareness," to "maintenance" of the desired behavior as a self-sustaining practice (Andreasen, 1994b; Prochaska & DiClemente, 1984). Picking the right kind of communication objective is no small or easy matter.

Irrelevant (Academic) Questions

Academic authorities have also posed their share of misguided evaluation questions, such as, "Does advertising (or communication) work?" Then they may design a study, for example, to persuade college students to buy a product—invariably ignoring the critical communication strategic questions (who is the intended target audience, what is the intended action, etc.) and the critical executional issues (was the advertising on strategy, was it attention getting, novel, etc.)—and conclude from that study that advertising does not work (Thorson, 1992). Then they conclude communications or advertising should not be included in social marketing programs.

Well, the answer to the question is sometimes advertising works and sometimes it doesn't. A more useful question to ask, as commercial marketers do, is "Did *this* ad work to achieve my objectives with my target consumers?" or "Did *this campaign* work to do that?"

Another favorite academic question is "Which works better, communications or community interventions or both?" Well, the answer is both. A more useful question to ask, as commercial marketers do, is "What is the optimal marketing mix for this product in this market now?" or "What is the optimal integration of advertising, sales promotion, public relations, and direct marketing for this product in this market now?"

Nonaction Orientation

Another set of obstacles comes from a failure to treat evaluation studies as action-oriented research. Some research evaluation is designed with theoretical questions in mind. Some is done as general exploration. And some is done just because that is how it was done before, as in "Let's start with a Knowledge–Attitudes–Practices" study. These are the kinds of research that generate data that provoke questions like, "What am I going to do with these data?" Often marketers do not know what some of their most important research questions are until they are doing something in the market. By then, they do not have the resources to answer them. Yet there may be money for a summative evaluation at the end of the project. At that point, it will do nothing for the people marketers were trying to help. It may not do much for any future efforts, either, because it evaluates a project that went begging for research help while it was under way.

Inappropriate Research Paradigm

The final obstacle is an inappropriate research paradigm. In that paradigm one starts with basic research, ideally in a laboratory. Marketers learn what the basic causal mechanism is, such as a virus. Then they may do some behavioral research to identify the behavior pattern that people should be following in order to compensate or to take care of themselves. Then they design an intervention to test it, ideally, by randomized clinical trials. Having found an experimental effect in this artificial setup, they then take it out to the rest of the world.

The gold standard evaluation method of the logical positivist or "hard science" paradigm is the clinical trial, which is essentially a large, randomized controlled experiment. Its most touted strength is its perceived ability to answer causal questions of the "A (program) caused B (outcome)" variety, such as "Did this program cause this outcome?" This strength comes from its ability to control sources of variation other than chance. It does so by fixing on a particular sample of units, treatments, observations, and settings (Cronbach, 1982). When these do not vary much or quickly, experiments are a strong basis for inferring their relevance and application to particular situations, such as the agricultural ones for which they originated.

However, humans, unlike seed plots, are both reactive and highly variable. Effective evaluation aims at moving targets, real programs in operation in various places among various populations over time. The more tightly controlled the experiment, the less generalizable it is to real-world social settings for the causal question that it addresses. Its results are "merely a historical fact" (K. J. Conrad & K. M. Conrad, 1995). Experiments on interventions cannot automatically translate into "magic intervention bullets," which can be rapidly fired into communities for effective implementation (Kreuter, 1992). The "hard science" model even has its limits in the biological world, which is turning out to be more dynamic than expected. Consider the rapid evolution of TB and HIV viruses, for example, or the recently completed mammogram trials that were based on technology no longer in use.

The behaviors marketers are trying to change in a society today will not be the same as yesterday's or last year's. Nor should the ad campaigns. And some research on communications and social interventions can take 5, 10, or 20 years. Most of those studies started in a social world that no longer exists. That may be why some of the more recent community interventions, such as the Stanford Five City Project, are less effective than the earlier interventions in California and Finnish communities (Balch, 1995; Contento et al., 1995).

HOW DO COMMERCIAL MARKETERS
REALLY EVALUATE?

Social marketing is about marketing, not about research. And market research is also about marketing action, not about research. Of course, causal research is important. Nevertheless, it helps marketers only over the long run. It does not help particular marketers doing a particular program while they are doing it. It does not help the people whom the social marketer is trying to help. People die while waiting.

So, what kinds of things do effective (social or commercial) marketers need to do to evaluate their advertising and the rest of their program? They may do test marketing, but fewer and fewer do that these days in commercial marketing; it is too costly, too time consuming, too hard to read reliably, and it may tip your hand to competitors.

If they do not test it in the market, then they may test it *before* they take it to market. They bring in all sorts of strategic research—focused formative research—to identify appropriate target markets/audiences, realistic communication objectives, and so on. They apply something like Wells' ROI process in commercial marketing (Moore & Wells, 1991; Wells, 1989) or its Consumer-based Health Communication version (Sutton, Balch, & Lefebvre, 1995) in social marketing. They arm themselves with a well-researched strategy.

Based on that strategy, they do lots of formative research to develop concepts, products, communications, and promotions. They do focus groups, one-on-ones, product–concept tests, and even some lab tests. They have consumers take the products home and try them themselves. They know it is a lot more cost effective to get it right before it goes to market.

Then they may "roll out" into some markets or "go national" at once. This is a real market test. They observe it intensely to see what needs to be fixed, fine-tuned, emulated, or deep-sixed. They track awareness, attitudes, and usage. They track distribution and inventory. They track competitive efforts. They track sales and add up profits (or losses). They track quarterly, monthly, or even weekly or daily to keep posted for the unexpected things that happen in the real world of events, be they historical events (such as changes in political actors or laws), natural events (such as extreme weather), or competitive events (such as sales or coupon drops). They look for problems. They look for opportunities. When they identify a problem or opportunity in a particular market, they want to be ready to respond.

Then they may decide to stay where they are until they get it right, or they expand further, or they just forget the whole thing before it becomes a national disaster. They do not do a 5-year-long randomized controlled experiment. The closest thing to that is a BehaviorScan market test. That is not very close. And commercial marketers do not commission research to get grant money, to publish, or to write papers that gather dust on shelves.

With rare exceptions, the decision to "go national" is a decision to stay in the market for the long haul. It is not an experiment to evaluate after a year or two—or even five. And it is not a decision to "monitor" how the marketing plan is being carried out just to keep it unchanged and "right" as the marketer originally planned it. The market keeps changing and so must the marketer's actions. So, they do more tracking and exception reporting and listening to the sales force and to consumers' product or service complaints. They do surveillance, not monitoring. They try to make improvements continually. At the same time, they do proactive research and development for new campaigns for these products. And they develop new and better products—preferably before competitors do.

Commercial marketers make plenty of time-sensitive decisions based on informed judgment, not just research. When they make judgments about a commercial, they look at the commercial, not just at the research data. Storyboards and scripts appear in their reports.

Some activities that prepare commercial marketers to make needed changes are: listening to the sales force; paying special attention—with rapid turnaround studies—to geographic areas above or below average in performance (to learn what does and does not work); trying out modifications of the plan in particular geographic areas; developing alternatives in the bullpen (e.g., ad campaigns, media schedules, product improvements or replacements, pricing alternatives, new possibilities for distribution); and implementing some of the more attractive alternatives as tracking of attitudes and sales indicate the need for them. They keep listening, learning, and changing.

There is a subtle, but crucial, difference between this kind of evaluation and the "monitoring" of the marketplace. It is analogous to Drucker's distinction between management and leadership. The idea of "monitoring" is to watch to make sure that things are done "right"—as planned in the protocol, or as efficiently as possible (Rossi & Freeman, 1985). This, of course, is a good thing to do. It is good management. But the kind of surveillance that savvy marketers conduct helps them prepare to jump in and change the procedures if it looks like something better is needed or possible. That is good leadership.

The marketplace is a jungle, not a laboratory. It is fiercely competitive and keeps changing. A marketer who keeps posted is prepared for those changes with relevant actions. A marketer who fails to do that, who relies complacently on prior or current successes, commits marketing myopia (Levitt, 1960). That person pays for it. Just look at WalMart, the retail market leader, and Sears and KMart, which were the former leaders.

WHAT SHOULD SOCIAL MARKETERS DO?

The social marketplace is no more comfortable than the commercial one. Indeed, the literature suggests that the "high involvement" behaviors often aimed at in social marketing are harder to change than the "low involvement" ones more typical in commerce (Rothschild, 1979). There are also more diverse tasks, such as community development and institution building. And there are more diverse audiences, such as political and community leaders, media decision-makers, and some of the youngest and oldest, poorest, and least commercially attractive consumers—and more limited resources. Moreover, social marketers often need to be accountable to government agencies. Surely, then, marketers must be at least as thoughtful, creative, and flexible in their social marketing as in their commercial ventures. The Pawtucket Heart Health Program is one example that engaged in many of the self-correcting evaluation activities mentioned here. They began their community intervention by approaching community organizations. After a disappointing rate of progress, they also went directly to the public via mass media and special events (Lefebvre, Lasater, Assaf, & Carleton, 1988).

Fortunately, many practical techniques in evaluation have been gaining broad acceptance and use. They can be found, for example, in the work of Wholey and colleagues and in the work of Green and Kreuter (1991). These works offer a set of tools that guide and refine programs as they operate. Here are some components that make them useful.

Collaboration: Involving Key Decision Makers and Stakeholders

Drawing on successful evaluation cases, Newcomer and Wholey (1989) noted key opportunities for management involvement at various stages of the evaluation process. Effective evaluation is a result of collaboration between program managers and evaluators. Managers must be involved from the start, both in agreeing on the role of communications and in setting relevant, realistic measurable objectives. Useful programs or evaluations are highly unlikely without consensus on the definition of success. Sensitivity to timing is crucial; deadlines both create openings and close them. Involvement of program managers is greatest in the evaluation planning stage. Adding other stakeholders, such as different beneficiaries and overseers, also helps. It can provide different perspectives on particular issues.

Feedforward: Diagnostic/Strategic Program Research

Particularly helpful is forward-looking research, starting with "diagnostic" (Green & Kreuter, 1991) or "strategic" research of the sort mentioned earlier.

When You Can't Start at the Start: Preevaluation

In government programs (as well as private sector programs) there may not be agreement or clarity of goals and objectives, or on steps by which people expect to their achievement. Without such agreement, one cannot design a useful evaluation. *Preevaluation,* called "evaluability assessment" by Wholey (1987), is a fast, mainly qualitative research process that involves key stakeholders in building consensus on program goals; on the steps in the program intended to achieve them; and realistic, measurable objectives and indicators by which to evaluate their achievement. It has been widely used in government to provide "preliminary evaluations," to suggest program improvements, and to communicate program successes to authorities that authorize and fund them. This helped keep the WIC program alive for many years (Wholey, 1970, 1983, 1987; Wholey et al., 1989).

Pretesting

As messages are developed in communication programs, it is advisable to subject messages and materials to pretesting of concepts and executions, with an eye to making them attention getting, clear, meaningful, relevant, believable, important, interesting, memorable, and persuasive to the target audience (DDB Needham, 1988; National Cancer Institute, 1989). If the communication strategy is strong and the executions communicate it as intended, then a cost-efficient measure of communication effectiveness has been achieved. Additionally, this kind of communication research can help explain and justify the executions to key stakeholders who are not part of the target audience, such as policy makers and scientists.

Process Research: Opening the Black Box

Process research goes beyond merely counting up the materials that the agency produced or sent out. It starts with collecting the actual communication materials: the posters, ads, news releases, brochures, and so on. It includes measuring how the materials were distributed to channels, how much exposure they achieved among target audiences, and the extent to which they actually reached the target audience's consciousness (Gentry & Jorgensen, 1991). A strong strategy with effective implementation is a cost-efficient and practical guarantor of program impact (Roper, 1993).

A diagnostic process evaluation can identify achievements, shortcomings, and opportunities that a summative evaluation might not notice. For example, a process evaluation of a comprehensive community health intervention in Florence, South Carolina, recently showed that apparent participation by community leaders was less than it appeared; some leaders did not even know about the program. Similarly, the evaluation identified missed phases planned but not accomplished, and some intermediate benefits that community participants appreciated that had not yet produced changes in health outcomes. Overall, the process evaluation showed what might be done better next (Goodman, Wheeler, & Lee, 1995).

Researching Backward

A process called *researching backward* (Andreasen, 1985) or *utilization-focused evaluation* (Patton, 1986) eliminates the considerable waste that occurs when data and studies go begging for uses after they have been done. The process starts by identifying the actual users of research and determining how they intend to use the research results. It asks decision-makers, stakeholders, and other information users what they would do based on each possible research outcome prior to gathering data. Research methods and analytical techniques are then designed and deployed to fit those uses. Studies of variation in the levels of usage of research have consistently shown the effectiveness of this approach (Patton, 1986, 1990). Similarly, Green and Kreuter (1991) began their health promotion planning and evaluation at the end—at the quality of life outcome(s) desired.

Staying Flexible: Moving With the Program

In the evaluation process itself, effective evaluators work closely with managers to identify acceptable decision rules that guide the process. This ensures ownership in the projects. Rather than plan an elaborate, long-term evaluation of a complicated and changing program in a changing environment from inception all the way through its impact on policy goals and impacts (morbidity, mortality, environmental safety, etc.), managers usually find it more useful to start with smaller scale, quick turnaround "rapid feedback evaluation" (Wholey, 1983). Using focus groups, in-depth qualitative interviews, small-scale surveys, multiple measures and methods, nonstandard levels of statistical significance, and the like, rapid feedback evaluation produces a preliminary assessment and a design for fuller evaluation. The preliminary assessment may be sufficient to justify changing, maintaining, or dropping the program. It may raise additional questions requiring further research in successive iterations as the program and its environment change.

Make Summative Review Part of a Process, Not Just an End Point

Summative research that leads to program decisions is needed. A useful summative evaluation is like a useful personnel review: It should be the final step in a process of continual feedback with opportunities for improvement and rewards for success, with no surprise about the need to pull the plug on the program if the results warrant it. And both the communication program and the evaluation should be routinely and easily available for others who are likely to do similar programs.

CONCLUSIONS

As pointed out earlier, the root purpose of evaluating a campaign or program is to see what, if anything, can be done better. It is inherently practical. Social marketers can and should plan and evaluate evaluations based on their practical results: What decisions do they help us make? As Wells (1993) would ask of any research, "All kidding aside, what does this really mean?" (p. 498). It is time for "evaluation" to be accountable.

REFERENCES

Andreasen, A. R. (1985). "Backward" market research. *Harvard Business Review, 63,* 176–182.
Andreasen, A. R. (1994a). Presidential address: A social marketing research agenda for consumer behavior researchers. In M. Rothschild & L. McAlister (Eds.), *Advances in Consumer Research, 20,* 1–5.
Andreasen, A. R. (1994b). Social marketing: Its definition and domain. *Journal of Public Policy and Marketing, 13,* 108–114.

Balch, G. I. (1995). *Nutrition education for adults: A review of research.* (U.S. Government Printing Office No. 1995-386-40/20030). Alexandria, VA: Office of Analysis and Evaluation, Division of Food and Consumer Service, U.S. Department of Agriculture.

Balch, G. I., & Sutton, S. M. (1995). Putting the first audience first: Conducting useful evaluation for a risk-related government agency. *Risk Analysis, 15*, 163–168.

Conrad, K. J., & Conrad, K. M. (1994). Reassessing validity threats in experiments: Focus on construct validity. In K. J. Conrad (Ed.), *Critically evaluating the role of experiments in program evaluation: New directions for program evaluation* (pp. 5–25). San Francisco: Jossey-Bass.

Contento, I. R., Balch, G. I., Bronner, Y. L., Paige, D. M., Gross, S. M., Bisignani, L., Lytle, L. A., Maloney, S. K., White, S. L., Olson, C., & Swadener, S. S. (1995). The effectiveness of nutrition education and implications for nutrition education policy, programs and research. *Journal of Nutrition Education, 27.*

Cronbach, L. J. (1982). *Designing evaluations of educational and social programs.* San Francisco: Jossey-Bass.

DDB Needham Worldwide. (1988). *1989 directory of advertising testing services.* Chicago: Author.

Gentry, E., & Jorgensen, C. M. (1991). Monitoring the exposure of "America Responds to AIDS" PSA campaign. *Public Health Reports, 106*, 651–655.

Goodman, R. M., Wheeler, F. C., & Lee, P. R. (1995). Evaluation of the Heart to Heart Project: Lessons from a community-based chronic disease prevention project. *American Journal of Health Promotion, 9*, 443–455.

Green, L. W., & Kreuter, M. W. (1991). *Health promotion planning: An educational and environmental approach.* Mountain View, CA: Mayfield.

Kreuter, M. W. (1992). Human behavior and cancer: Forget the magic bullet! National Conference on Cancer Prevention and Early Detection, Chicago, IL.

Lefebvre, R. C., Lasater, T. M., Assaf, A. R., & Carleton, R. A. (1988). Pawtucket Heart Health Program: The process of stimulating community change. *Scandinavian Journal of Primary Health Care* (Suppl. 1), 31–37.

Levitt, T. (1960). Marketing myopia. *Harvard Business Review, 38*, 45–56.

Moore, J., & Wells, W. D. (1991). *ROI guidebook: Planning for relevance, originality, and impact in advertising and other marketing communications* (2nd ed.). Chicago: DDB Needham Worldwide.

National Cancer Institute. (1989). *Making health communications work: A planner's guide* (NIH Publication No. 89-1493). Rockville, MD: U.S. Department of Health and Human Services, Public Health Service, National Institutes of Health.

Newcomer, K. E., & Wholey, J. S. (1989). Conclusion: Evaluation strategies for building high performance programs. In J. S. Wholey, K. E. Newcomer, & Associates (Eds.), *Improving government performance* (pp. 195–208). San Francisco: Jossey-Bass.

Patton, M. Q. (1986). *Utilization-focused evaluation* (2nd ed.). Beverly Hills, CA: Sage.

Patton, M. Q. (1990). *Qualitative evaluation and research methods* (2nd ed.). Newbury Park, CA: Sage.

Prochaska, J. O., & DiClemente, C. C. (1984). *The transtheoretical approach: Crossing the traditional boundaries of therapy.* Homewood, IL: Dow Jones-Irwin.

Roper, W. L. (1993). Health communication takes on new dimensions at CDC. *Public Health Reports, 108*, 179–183.

Rothschild, M. D. (1979). Marketing communications in nonbusiness situations or why it's so hard to sell brotherhood like soap. *Journal of Marketing, 43*, 11–20.

Rossi, P. H., & Freeman, H. E. (1995). *Evaluation: A systematic approach* (3rd ed.). Beverly Hills: Sage.

Sutton, S. M. (1992). Evaluation research: Opportunity or obstacle to good communications? In *Proceedings: Evaluation research* (pp. 6–21). Washington, DC: Office of Disease Prevention and Health Promotion, U.S. Department of Health and Human Services.

Sutton, S. M., Balch, G. I., & Lefebvre, R. C. (1995). Strategic questions for consumer based health communications. *Public Health Reports, 110,* 725–733.

Thorson, E. (1992). *Effects of alcohol advertising: Four under-explored aspects.* National Institute on Alcohol Abuse and Alcoholism Working Group on the Effects of the Mass Media on the Use and Abuse of Alcohol. Washington, DC: National Institute on Alcohol Abuse and Alcoholism.

Wells, W. D. (1989). *Planning for ROI: Effective advertising strategy.* Englewood Cliffs, NJ: Prentice Hall.

Wells, W. D. (1993). Discovery-oriented consumer research. *Journal of Consumer Research, 19,* 489–504.

Wholey, J. S. (1979). *Evaluation: Promise and performance.* Washington, DC: The Urban Institute.

Wholey, J. S. (1983). *Evaluation and effective public management.* Boston: Little, Brown.

Wholey, J. S. (1987). Evaluability assessment: Developing program theory. In L. Bickman (Ed.), *Using program theory in evaluation* (pp. 77–92). New Directions for Program Evaluation, No. 38. San Francisco: Jossey-Bass.

Wholey, J. S., Newcomer, K. E., & Associates. (1989). *Improving government performance.* San Francisco: Jossey-Bass.

Chapter 6

From Madison Avenue to the Field: Cross-Cultural Uses of Media Research Technology

Jonathan P. Baggaley
Athabasca University, Alberta

ABSTRACT

This chapter includes three audience research studies representing successive stages in the implementation of educational media campaigns, from the initial needs assessment stage to the product's development and its eventual delivery. Each study indicates the particular problems that arise when the developers and the intended consumers of educational material come from different cultures, and the obstacles this presents for the pilot-testing process. To deal with these problems, the studies used a computer-based data collection methodology of a type more commonly associated with North American advertising research. The chapter outlines uses of this methodology, known as Time-Scaling™, by community educators working with Somali refugees living in Canada, farmers in the fields of Mount Kenya, and townspeople and villagers of Ukraine.

OVERALL METHODOLOGY

Conventional media evaluation methods commonly fail to overcome problems associated with cross-cultural testing. The need arises for a rapid, reliable, inexpensive, and culture-free method of surmounting linguistic and literacy barriers, and the wide geographic dispersion of test audiences, in order to ensure that social marketing and development communications programs achieve the goals they intend.

Commercial advertisers have long since streamlined the process of media evaluation through the use of automated research methods that collect

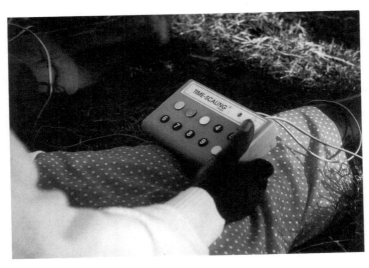

FIG. 6.1.   A data collection hand-unit.

audience responses to their pilot productions with immediacy and precision. The three current projects made use of a data collection system known as Time-Scaling™, which allows respondents to make nonverbal, anonymous responses by pressing buttons on personal hand-units connected to a laptop computer (Fig. 6.1). Data collection and analysis are both instantaneous, and reactions to presentations can be obtained on a second-by-second basis. The system's software plots the reactions graphically, providing simultaneous, continuous feedback of a presentation's impact.

North American educational media researchers have utilized the Time-Scaling™ evaluation methodology since 1991. A schools commission media unit in Maryland, for example, uses the method to obtain formative evaluation data from its target audiences in the classroom. The U.S. Government has used it in the design and evaluation of its national educational media campaign "America Responds to AIDS." In the latter context, the methodology has been used to collect data from low-literacy, high-risk audiences in inner city areas, for whom the usual focus-group methods were completely inappropriate (Baggaley et al., 1992). The current chapter describes three new projects that took the methodology into field settings far removed from the Madison Avenue-type settings in which it first evolved.

STUDY 1: ASSESSING THE NEEDS
OF SOMALI REFUGEE CHILDREN IN CANADA

The first study illustrates the earliest stage of educational program evaluation—the *initial needs assessment*.

Refugee immigrants to North America have customarily encountered problems in adjusting to their new lives. The common barriers to their integration are cultural and linguistic. With children, these problems are exacerbated by their immaturity and inability to articulate their problems. The effort to cater to young refugees' needs by the formulation of educational and immigration policies is often thwarted by the fact that these needs go unexpressed.

In February 1994, the International Children's Institute sought to overcome these typical communication obstacles in a study at Kingsview Village School in Etobicoke, Ontario. To cope with the influx of Somali refugee children to the school, a refugee integration program had been established. Although the program itself was perceived to be effective, the children had not as yet been able to provide systematic, confidential feedback about the integration process and their adjustment to Canada.

Evaluation Methodology: Somali Study

On February 15, 1994, 25 refugee children at the school were presented with a series of questions about themselves, their lives in Canada, and any problems they might have experienced since arriving in the country. They were invited to give anonymous and confidential responses to these sensitive questions via the push-button hand-units of the Time-Scaling™ evaluation system.

The sample comprised 58% girls and 42% boys, all of whom had been in Canada for at least 1 year. Of the 25 children tested, 12 were 10 years old and 13 were 11 years old. Pretest questions established that only six (24%) of the children spoke English on a regular basis. Sixteen (64%) of them spoke Somali most frequently, two (8%) spoke Punjabi, and one (4%) spoke Hindi.

The director of the International Children's Institute, Madeline-Anne Aksich, moderated the sessions which included the administration of a questionnaire and a 5-minute "continuous response" task (Baggaley, 1987). The questionnaire was designed to elicit information about the children's attitudes to life in Canada, their psychosocial coping skills, and their social network: The test also included questions about the children's demographics and about their reaction to the computer-based data collection method. The continuous response task was designed to provide information about the children's moment-by-moment reactions to a TV program regularly viewed at the school (Canadian *Sesame Street*), so that the school could decide whether or not the program was appropriate for use with these students in the future.

In a 5-minute briefing session, Ms. Aksich instructed the children on how to use the hand-units to respond to the series of multiple-choice questions. During the *Sesame Street* segment, the children used a 4-point Likert scale to indicate their responses as follows: *dislike a lot* (Button 6), *dislike a little* (Button 7), *enjoy a little* (Button 8), and *enjoy a lot* (Button 9). They were told they could change their responses to the video as often or as seldom as they wished.

Findings: Somali Study

Analyses of the data revealed that in general the Somali children like their life and the activities available to them in Canada. The nonverbal, confidential aspect of the methodology also allowed them to give sensitive information: For example, 17 (68%) of them indicated that, since arriving in Canada, they had experienced problems with children from countries other than their own—especially with the local Canadian children. Seventeen (68%) of the 25 children also revealed that they had trouble understanding their teachers.

The continuous responses of the children to Canadian *Sesame Street* were analyzed by synchronizing their second-by-second input with an animated computer graphic superimposed on the video presentation. The responses were never overwhelmingly positive, probably owing to the children's age (i.e., 5 years older than the program's target age-group). Examination of the continuous (second-by-second) responses revealed that the boys were more negative about the puppets featured in the video than were the girls. The segments with music and visuals received a more favorable response than a subsequent segment lampooning a Canadian news broadcast. The average responses of the sample as a whole became negative 14 seconds into the latter segment, at a reference to Canadian shipping history. They remained negative until the end of the segment.

After the continuous response task, 11 (44%) children gave push-button responses indicating that they had enjoyed the program a lot, 4 (16%) enjoyed it a little, and 8 (32%) expressed no opinion. With respect to the methodology, 9 (36%) children indicated that they preferred the hand-unit system to conventional discussion. Three children (12%) preferred discussion, and 13 (52%) would have preferred a combination of discussion and hand-units.

Conclusions: Somali Study

The principal of Kingsview Village School, Naomi Emmett, who attended the evaluation, considered the methodology useful in revealing attitudes to school life that the children had not hitherto expressed, in some cases over periods as long as a year. She stated that in developing effective programs for refugee children, it is vital but often difficult to take into account the children's changing needs, and that the evaluation had been useful in identifying those activities that can help refugee children adjust to their new lives.

For example, the teachers had previously been unaware that many of the children endure unpleasant experiences at the hands of their Canadian schoolmates, for such reports are relatively unlikely to emerge in classroom discussion. The principal regarded the anonymity and confidentiality of the push-button data collection method as having particularly valuable implications for studies of preadolescent and latency-age children, who are more reticent about expressing themselves than are younger children. She also welcomed the methodology's ability to give continuous feedback of responses to educational video materials: "You can literally go back frame by frame and see where the kids liked it, where they didn't, and where they found the subject matter sensitive."

Similarly, Madeline Aksich of the International Children's Institute felt that a prime benefit of the evaluation was its ability to "develop programs based on the children's attitudes and opinions." The push-button method was clearly easy for the children to use, and could be used repeatedly to evaluate and refine educational materials in different contexts.

Often, the development of children's educational programming neglects the input of the children themselves. Data collection methodologies such as Time-Scaling™ can obviously provide very specific feedback about children's feelings, and about the specific moments at which media presentations succeed or fail to convey their intended messages. On the basis of this study, Ms. Aksich stated that she was able to see "whether our messages are understood and whether the children's attitudes have been changed as a result." The study demonstrates, moreover, that this crucial information can be obtained in an effective and nonthreatening manner.

STUDY 2: EVALUATING EDUCATIONAL RADIO WITH KENYAN FARMERS

The second study illustrates the *formative evaluation* phase of program development, conducted during the production of educational materials.

The development of educational media materials for developing countries is often a hit-and-miss process. The lack of budget, time, and evaluation expertise often makes it impossible for materials to be pilot-tested in the field and modified, if required, before distribution. In February 1993, the International Development Research Centre (IDRC) confronted these problems in the course of developing methods to encourage farmers to apply the results of agricultural research.

FIG. 6.2. A Kenyan Radio Listening Group.

The IDRC's study allowed an educational radio producer, Ms. Mary Ngechu of the University of Nairobi, to pilot-test five agricultural radio tapes with 199 nonliterate, nonnumerate farmers with no English skills, in their Mount Kenya villages. The project was undertaken in collaboration with the College of Education and External Studies of the University of Nairobi, as part of its research into the use of Radio Listening Groups (RLGs) as a community education and development technique (Fig. 6.2). The author was engaged to collect and analyze the data for the project, using the computer-based Time-Scaling™ methodology.

Background of the Study

The preparatory work for the Kenyan evaluation project had spanned many years. The co-investigator (JB) had first used electronic advertising research methods with rural audiences in 1982. With an extension film producer, Kirk Smith, he took an instructional film produced for the Canadian Government's Department of Fisheries and Oceans into fishing communities in remote parts of Newfoundland (Baggaley & Smith, 1982). The fishermen's reactions to the film, using an earlier audience response system, were constructively critical, and were immediately acted upon by the producer. The resulting discussion in the fishing community led directly to the formation of the Canadian Seal Fishermen's Association, and to a Royal Commission on the future of the sealing industry in Canada.

Kenya, similarly, has focused much attention on the education of its rural farming communities, and on the development of their agricultural practices through research on improved farming methods. However, prior to the present project, no research had been conducted in the country on farmer education using participatory, grass-root methods, or appropriate communication technologies. It is perhaps not surprising, therefore, that although 71.3% of Kenya farmers have radio sets and listen to some of its content (25% average listenership per program), the following for agriculture education programs is very low. The prime reason for this appears to be that farmers do not consider these programs relevant to their needs.

A feasibility study carried out in the Nyeri and Embu districts of Kenya by Mary Ngechu in 1990 had revealed that rural small-scale farmers—of which 80% are women—have little access to the existing ministry-provided agricultural extension services. Many villagers (48.8% of the male population and 59.4% of the female) are poor and illiterate. Extension services delivered through individuals, mainly men, and media such as pamphlets, are therefore largely inaccessible to them. The chiefs' *barazas* (meetings) are viewed by extension agents as prime sources of information dissemination, but relatively few villagers attend them.

The RLG project assumes that farmers will listen to radio programs whose content and format are based on their needs and interests. Radio Listening Groups are used in the project as a participatory method designed to (a) aid distance learning and the exchange of ideas, (b) provide access to new information that farmers need, and (c) improve farming methods, productivity, and farmers' well-being. The radio provides rural farmers with an opportunity to share the research experiences of other farmers and researchers. The significance of the RLG project is that it is directed and shaped by the farmers themselves, through "feed forward" as well as feedback methods. In this respect the project is unlike other community development projects in which outside agencies determine the content and delivery of the educational materials that are produced. The RLG initiative considers it vital that rural communication be both participatory and adaptive, and that the listening groups themselves truly be designed by farmers for farmers.

The project also assumes that its radio programs should embody the highest broadcast communication standards. To ensure this, Mary Ngechu required an evaluation method which would enable Kenyan villagers who lack literacy and numeracy skills to respond freely to the pilot tapes without feeling intimidated. The process of data collection would have to be simple because repeated visits to the regions would be both time-consuming and costly. In addition, analysis of results would have to be instantaneous, to allow for immediate, informed discussion of the findings by the production team and the villagers. The Time-Scaling™ data collection system was selected as a cost-effective means of meeting these requirements with accuracy and speed.

Evaluation Methodology: Kenya Study

Between February 15 and 23, 1993, 199 farmers from 13 Mount Kenya villages evaluated a series of five tapes. Each tape was presented in a different village, to an intact group of between 10 and 22 people accustomed to gathering once a week, either in a field or a community meeting hut, as a Radio Listening Group (Fig. 6.2, Fig. 6.3). The 13 groups met in Gachoka, Githimna, Icuga, Kaburaini, Kalichen-Lusoi, Kiamariga, Kianjokoma, Kirairi, Kiriti, Mufu, Muitathiini, Muuri, and Ruthanji. Dr. Nancy George, IDRC Project Officer, and the author attended the first five sessions. Ms. Ngechu acted as the Kiswahili-language moderator for all sessions, with computer assistance by researcher Steven Gruber (Concordia University, Montreal). Because none of the villages had electricity, the laptop-based Time-Scaling™ system was powered from the cigarette lighter of the project team's car (see Fig. 6.3).

On their team's arrival at each session, the moderator explained to the villagers that their feedback was needed in order to improve the radio programs. She introduced the computer system, and told the villagers that it would allow her to give them full and immediate feedback about their responses. On this basis, none of the village communities refused to use the hand-unit methodology. Indeed, many villagers clearly welcomed the opportunity to criticize the tapes without speaking!

The five pilot tapes were entitled *Beans, Implements, Maize, Tomatoes/A,* and *Tomatoes/B,* and averaged 12 minutes in length. Using the Time-Scaling™ hand-units, the team collected the pretest and posttest responses by the farmers to the tapes, and also second-by-second reactions that provided

FIG. 6.3.   Farmers respond to the pilot tapes using the push-button response units.

guidelines for the tapes' modification. The buttons of each hand-unit were color-coded using symbols meaningful to the communities. Pressing an orange button, for example, indicated a *yes* response, blue indicated *no*, and white *don't know*. These three colors were chosen in view of their associations for the villagers with sun, sky, and peace, respectively. To convey their positive or negative feelings on a second-by-second basis during the tapes, the villagers pressed buttons bearing plus and minus signs. This formative evaluation feedback was available to the producer on the laptop screen in the instant that the farmers gave their push-button responses.

The pretest questions were designed to determine the farmers' prior knowledge of the radio tapes' agricultural content. The posttest questions examined (a) whether the tapes had increased the farmers' knowledge, (b) whether their agricultural practices were likely to be affected by the tapes, (c) the audiences' overall reactions to the tapes, and (d) their age, sex, and literacy levels. The moderator used the instant feedback of the groups' responses (Fig. 6.4) in leading debriefing discussion sessions with the farmers. The Time-Scaling™ software also provided her with printouts combining and comparing the data collected in each session with those collected previously.

Findings: Kenya Study

Of the 199 people tested in the 13 villages, 34% were male and 66% female. The predominant mother tongue was Kikuyu, followed by Kiembu. Because the sample contained many individuals with no numeracy skills, age levels were inferred from a question relating their farming experience to their memory for significant historical events in Kenya. From these questions, the researchers found that 42% of villagers had been farming since before 1963 and 28% had been farming for at least 40 years.

The responses to the five agricultural radio tapes were generally positive. The villagers unanimously agreed that the tapes were interesting, easy to understand, well paced, and believable, and that they covered important topics. Forty-three percent of the villagers felt the programs were too short, and 46% stated that they did not contain enough information.

Owing to their economic and physical conditions, the villagers felt that they would not use all of the agricultural techniques recommended to them

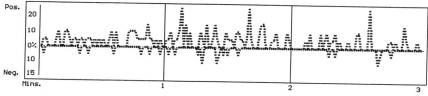

FIG. 6.4. Second-by-second responses by Kenyan farmers to an agricultural radio tape.

in the radio programs. For example, most villagers could not afford chemical fertilizer, nor did they need to harrow because Mount Kenya soil is naturally fine. One group indicated that they could not plow deep furrows in their soil because of shallow bedrock. Another suggested that they could not dig after the harvest because the effort involved at that time is too great. Finally, when asked whether they preferred conventional discussion or the hand-unit response method, between 70% and 100% of each group expressed a definite preference for the hand-unit method. One woman stated, "Sometimes we can waste a lot of time talking, and this way I can be more honest."

Conclusions: Kenya Study

In developing media education for rural communities, it is essential to take into account the people's opinions and perceived needs. Because the Time-Scaling™ evaluation method was previously untried in Kenya, the researchers were unsure as to whether the farmers would respond well to the use of the hand-unit methodology. To their great satisfaction, the farmers openly welcomed it. It was clear, however, that the research would not have been as effective without the villagers' implicit prior trust in their extension worker, Ms. Ngechu. Recognizing that Ms. Ngechu approved of the handset method, they reacted to it enthusiastically.

Having seen that the automated method is as acceptable in the fields of Kenya as in the fishing villages of Newfoundland and the test centers of Madison Avenue, it becomes increasingly apparent that the benefits of such methodologies can be reaped in a wide range of settings. These benefits go far beyond the ability to obtain rapid feedback about the design and effects of educational media productions. The instant analysis and feedback capabilities of the Time-Scaling™ system allow rapid insights and decisions to be made in community development settings generally.

STUDY 3: EDUCATING COMMUNITIES
OF UKRAINE ABOUT AIDS

The third study illustrates the delivery and summative evaluation phase in the development of community education materials.

Background of the Study

Ukraine has one of the lowest incidences of AIDS in the world. Currently, 6 Ukrainians per 10 million are estimated to have the disease, compared to rates 10 times higher in Poland and over 200 times higher in Romania. But the spread of AIDS in Ukraine is accelerating rapidly, and, in view of the large number of high-risk groups in the country, it is regarded as a serious and escalating problem.

Since 1994, the Canada–Ukraine Partners in Health Program has conducted several projects designed to combat the spread of AIDS in Ukraine. Its most recent project has been conducted in conjunction with the President of Ukraine's National Anti-AIDS Committee (Baggaley, James, & Schatz, 1995). Established in 1992, the President's Committee has undertaken to visit communities in all regions of Ukraine, with an educational package combining medical and preventative information about AIDS and HIV infection. The Committee's program brings together medical and educational specialists with actors, musicians, and singers to present the Ukrainian public with a wide range of AIDS awareness messages.

As the main delivery medium for its program, the Committee has adopted a method pioneered in Ukraine over 75 years ago—the educational train. The power of the railway to spread information was first harnessed in 1918, to unite the new Soviet by disseminating propaganda about the state, its ideology, and the problems facing it. The concept of *agitatsya propaganda* was born, in educational train tours networking the entire Union.

One of the primary functions of the early "agit prop" trains was to spread knowledge about health. In the 1920s and early 1930s, the trains carried popular education on topics ranging from alcoholism and tuberculosis to healthy childbirth and the improvement of working conditions. The train tours also featured sophisticated uses of educational media, in the hands of early film-makers such as Dziga Vertov and Alexander Medvedkin. In each community these pioneers filmed the people at work and at play, aiming to capture what Vertov called "fragments of reality." Editing their film by night, they would play it back to the people who gathered on the station platform the next day. The people watched themselves in stunned amazement, and were able to see their lives in new detail (Henny, 1983).

When they played back the film recorded in one village to the people of other villages, the film train pioneers found that the moving image also has the power to unify. In viewing each other's lives, the people were able to recognize that their problems were shared by many others like them. This empowering educational effect did not commend the film train tradition to the Stalinist regime, and from the 1930s onward the practice was banned. Sixty years later, the health problems tackled in the 1920s and 1930s are joined by the new threat of HIV infection and AIDS, and in 1995 the tradition of the film train was revived in respectful detail by a Canada–Ukraine AIDS education project.

Evaluation Methodology: Ukraine Study

In April 1995, a team of Concordia University educators travelled with the President's National Anti-AIDS Committee and a team of medical specialists, actors, and musicians, to schools and institutes in Kyiv and in towns and villages of Volyns'k province (Luts'k, Kovel', Bereschencko, and Shats'k). Within a 2-week period, the tour brought AIDS information and awareness to thousands of young people in 12 schools and institutes. Sometimes the team visited schools and other centers in the community; at other times, the community came to the educational train, to view films in the traveling classroom or to visit the discotheque.

The Canadian team included a 3-person video crew, which recorded discussions about AIDS by the members of each community and played them back to the villagers, and later to the members of other villages. Whereas 60 years ago the vital process of video feedback would take 12 hours, today it is immediate. In the 1995 project, feedback was further enhanced by the use of the Time-Scaling™ system. Using the system's push-button hand-units, the project team collected evaluation data from 384 students between the ages of 12 and 27. The on-site analysis capability of the system allowed the team to give the students immediate feedback about their knowledge and opinions, in the course of lectures about the spread of HIV infection.

Findings: Ukraine Study

By providing instant feedback of the groups' responses, the project's methodology allowed the Ukrainian students to relate directly to the issue of AIDS, and to assess the issue's personal relevance to them. Data collected from them reflected a community that had already taken a firm stance with respect to AIDS prevention. The findings also reflected a teenage population whose sexual activity is firmly moderated by a solid framework of community values, and which has a commendable sense of urgency regarding the importance of AIDS prevention in their communities. Questions aimed at students 15 years and older revealed sensible attitudes toward the prevention of HIV infection in their sexual conduct and a compassionate understanding of the problems of persons with AIDS. The team gathered this information directly from the students themselves, in discussions on subjects ranging widely from abstinence to nonpenetrative sex.

Naturally, public discussion of such topics is as embarassing and inhibiting in Ukraine as it is anywhere in the world. In this respect, the Time-Scaling™ hand-units were a welcome addition to the project, allowing as many as 64 students at once to respond to questions about AIDS and sexual practice nonverbally and anonymously. Instantly analyzed by computer in the students' presence, the data indicated the areas of their knowledge that required immediate elucidation (see Fig. 6.5). They also provided insights into the educational messages most urgently needed by students in the different gender and age groups. (A full analysis of the findings of this study is currently in preparation.)

FIG. 6.5. Ukrainian students examine computer printouts with Dr. Jon Baggaley (center).

Conclusions: Ukraine Study

The Ukraine project illustrates the manner in which rapid data collection and analysis procedures can be employed both in the delivery of community education materials and in their simultaneous evaluation. The data collection methodology yielded an useful summative evaluation of the materials at hand and simultaneous formative insights for the developers of future materials. The instant analysis features of the methodology also allowed the communities to receive immediate feedback about their current levels of knowledge and opinion. For the protection of the evaluation's integrity, it was naturally crucial for the data to be collected prior to the feedback activity in each session. However, the data collection and feedback activities could be combined in numerous ways for purposes of, for example, action research.

The high level of AIDS awareness revealed by the current study will need to be carefully sustained in Ukraine in the months and years ahead; the information gathered in Kyiv and Volyns'k has subsequently been used in the production of educational print and video materials for this purpose. The immediacy of Ukraine's national AIDS education campaign for the communities receiving it is heightened by the campaign's combined usage of the computer-based evaluation methodology and the time-honored film train tradition.

At present, HIV infection in Ukraine is spreading rapidly along the country's highways and rail routes to its most distant rural communities. The decision of the President's National Anti-AIDS Committee to use the national railway as a major delivery mode for the campaign is thus one that combines traditional expertise with timeliness. The film train technique preserves a vital educational ingredient not featured in other forms of mass media education: the ability to design educational programs for each community's specific needs. It allows the people to be a vital part of the educational activity, and effectively puts them "in the picture." The computer-based evaluation methodology complements this interactive capability. It is vital for this highly advanced form of national education to be maintained while there is still time to preserve the sound preventative work conducted by organizations such as the President's National Anti-AIDS Committee in Ukraine to date.

In North America and other parts of the world, community-based approaches to health education are often eclipsed by elaborate national media strategies involving massive costs but achieving only marginal public impact. International health educators can learn much from the approaches currently being revived in Ukraine, combining teaching and research, information and entertainment, in a manner as modern today as it was 75 years ago (James, 1996).

OVERALL CONCLUSIONS

The three projects demonstrate that computer-based methods of data collection more commonly associated with the advertising research industry can be used effectively in a wide range of cross-cultural research and evaluation settings. In an atmosphere of trust, they surmount the barriers of language and literacy and are capable of dramatic results. Three types of media development study have been illustrated, emphasizing needs assessment (Somali refugee study), formative evaluation of education materials (Kenya study), and the delivery and summative evaluation of materials (Ukraine study). In each study, data were collected with distinct feedback benefits for the communities that gave the data as well as for the researchers and producers in the project team.

The Ukraine study actually combines the best features of the two earlier studies, yielding confidential, frank data about students' attitudes to AIDS and sexual activity, which were instantly analyzed and fed back to the students themselves and to the designers of the national AIDS education campaign. In this way, the Time-Scaling™ methodology served teaching, needs assessment, and evaluation purposes simultaneously. The data, used for the assessment of the campaign as it unfolded and for the project's overall assessment, fulfilled both formative and summative evaluation functions. The Ukrainian government has since used the data as the basis for a cumulative research database of evolving public attitudes on health issues.

The ability to serve all of these purposes at once is due wholly to the speed and precision of data handling made possible by contemporary computer methods. Whereas by traditional interviewing and questionnaire methods it would have taken many months to conduct and report studies of the magnitude reported here, each of the current studies was completed in the few hours that it took to collect the actual data: 1 working day in the case of the Somali study, and 10 in the Kenya and Ukraine studies. The Ukraine study also used a media process that promises to generate novel benefits in the years ahead. The project's use of video as a health education tool at the community level offers distinct advantages over the conventional uses of network television for educational purposes. The method's main advantage lies in the total interaction it affords with the audience, and in its consequent ability to adjust the educational message immediately to the community's needs. The developing nations of the world should perhaps consider themselves fortunate if they cannot at this stage afford expensive mass media delivery systems for their public education campaigns, and are compelled to concentrate instead on developing community-based methods of media education and feedback.

ACKNOWLEDGMENTS

The author is grateful for the assistance of: the International Children's Institute, Montreal; the International Development Research Centre, Ottawa; the Canadian Society for International Health, Ottawa; Madeline-Anne Aksich, Helen Baggaley, John Bentley, Aaron-Henry Brauer, Naomi Emmett, Nancy George, Sheila James, Dr. Valery Iwasiuk, Mary Ngechu, Dr. David Nostbakken, Frank Roop, Paulette Schatz, Claire Sergeant, Volodimir Tarasenko, Dr. Renard Vasilinets; and to the communities of Ontario, Mount Kenya, and Ukraine, whose patience and trust made these studies possible.

REFERENCES

Baggaley, J. P. (1987). Continual response measurement in TV research. *Canadian Journal of Educational Communication, 16,* 217–238.

Baggaley, J. P., James, S., & Schatz, P. (1995). Canada–Ukraine partnership battles AIDS. *Canada–Ukraine Monitor, 3*(2), 23–24.

Baggaley, J. P., Salmon, C., Lewis-Hardy, R., Tambe, B., Siska, M., Jorgensen, C., Harris, R., & Jason, J. (1992). Automated evaluation of AIDS messages with high-risk, low-literacy audiences. *Journal of Educational Television, 18,* 83–96.

Baggaley, J. P., & Smith, K. (1982). Formative research in rural education. *Media in Education and Development, 15,* 173–176. (Republished 1982 in *Media Asia, 9,* 196–199).

Henny, L. (1983). Video and the community. In P. W. Dowrick & S. J. Biggs (Eds.), *Using video.* New York: Wiley.

James, S. (1996). Educational media and "Agit Prop": I. The Legacy of Vertov. *Journal of Educational Media, 22,* 111–123.

James, S. (in press). Educational media and "Agit Prop": II. The Vertov Process Repatriated. *Journal of Educational Media, 22,* 161–173.

Chapter 7

Useful Correlates of Pro-Environmental Behavior

Michael R. Swenson
William D. Wells
University of Minnesota

ABSTRACT

A secondary analysis of two recent national consumer surveys shows that pro-environmental behavior is correlated with some major demographic variables and with concern for the environment, cosmopolitanism, liberalism, frugality, planfulness, community involvement, health concerns, perceptions of financial distress, and dissatisfaction with life. This chapter explores how these findings can be used in developing and disseminating pro-environmental campaigns.

The first "Earth Day"—April 22, 1970—marked the beginning of sustained research on relations among demographic characteristics, personality traits, pro-environmental attitudes, and pro-environmental behavior. The outcomes of this effort have been mixed. Demographic and personality characteristics that correlated with pro-environmental attitudes in one investigation failed to correlate with pro-environmental attitudes in others. Attitudes that predicted pro-environmental behavior in one study failed in replications (Anderson & Cunningham, 1972; Belch, 1979; Buttel & Flinn, 1978a; De Young, 1985–1986; Granzin & Olsen, 1991; Hines, Hungerford, & Tomera, 1987; Kassarjian, 1971; Pickett, Kangun, & Grove, 1993; Samdahl & Robertson, 1989; Van Liere & Dunlap, 1981; Vining & Ebreo, 1990; Webster, 1975; see Antil, 1984, or Schwepker & Cornwell, 1991, for reviews).

Looking across all this work, and surveying the low and sometimes inconsistent correlations, Pickett et al. (1993) concluded that the general constructs, "pro-environmental attitudes" and "pro-environmental behaviors," are doomed to be of little use. Instead, they concluded, each micro-aspect of environmentalism (e.g., recycling newspapers, turning down the thermostat in the winter, using public transportation, and supporting strict water pollution laws, etc.) must be examined on its own. If Pickett et al. (1993) are right, a great deal of effort has been wasted. If every micro-aspect of pro-environmental behavior must be examined individually, then generalities will not be found.

Before agreeing to this pessimestic verdict, consider a reexamination of it using two recent national consumer surveys that included questions regarding pro-environmental behaviors, environmental attitudes, and a wide array of demographic, lifestyle, personality, product use, and media preference variables. The reexamination begins with reference to previous reviews of relations among demographics, global attitudes, and specific behaviors.

CORRELATES OF PRO-ENVIRONMENTAL BEHAVIOR

In most of social psychology, correlations among demographic characteristics, personality traits, global attitudes, and specific behaviors rarely exceed .40 (Ajzen, 1988). However, as Fishbein and Ajzen (1975) and Ajzen and Fishbein (1980) pointed out, correlations between attitudes toward a specific object and behavior toward that object tend to be higher, and correlations between intentions to perform a particular behavior in the near future and measures of that behavior tend to be higher still. These findings suggest that a general construct of pro-environmental behavior can provide informative background for a nomological network linking antecedants, general attitudes, specific attitudes, and specific intentions with specific behavior.

Also note that environmental organizations are not likely to have the financial resources to sponsor new research each time they decide to act. Therefore, when an organization is faced with a choice between no research, research on some other specific pro-environmental behavior, or research on the general construct of pro-environmental behavior, the research on the general construct is apt to provide the best available help.

This chapter reexamines the correlates of pro-environmental behavior, using two recent surveys conducted by the advertising agency DDB Needham Worldwide.[1] These surveys include relations among pro-environmental behavior, demographic characteristics, pro-environmental attitudes, and social and lifestyle characteristics within a large sample of U.S. con-

[1]We thank DDB Needham Worldwide, and especially Martin Horn, manager of DDB Needham's Life Style investigation, for providing the data used in this work.

sumers. The 1992 survey identified relations. The 1993 survey provided replication on an independent, demographically matched group.

The DDB Needham data have several advantages over data used in previous research. First, the samples are large: 3,922 in 1992 and 3,690 in 1993. This means that relations are likely to be more stable than relations based on the (often much) smaller samples used in earlier work. Second, the samples are demographically matched to the U.S. consumer population. This means that the data are likely to contain substantially more reliable variance than corresponding data drawn from smaller geographic regions or relatively homogeneous localities such as college towns.

Third, in addition to conventional demographic questions, the DDB Needham database contains a very wide range of psychological, attitudinal, and behavioral items, including questions on media preferences and product use. Although this rich source does not cover all of the conceptual territory of previous investigations, it covers quite a lot of it. It therefore permits conceptual, if not exact, replication of previous work.

The DDB Needham database has one important disadvantage. It was constructed by other investigators for other purposes. This means the content of the survey items was not under this study's control. Moreover, some useful items present in the 1992 were absent in 1993, and some useful items present in 1993 were absent in 1992. These changes forced some changes in the operational definition of the dependent variable, as described in the next section.

Dependent Variable

The dependent variable was a 9-item scale of pro-environmental behaviors. In the 1992 data, this scale attained a Cronbach alpha of .70. In the 1993 data the conceptually identical but somewhat modified scale attained an alpha of .60 (see footnotes on individual items). Of course, it would have been preferable to use exactly the same items both years. But, as already noted, changes in the questionnaire made this impossible. The following items appeared on the scales:[2]

1. Recycled paper products (newspapers, etc.).
2. Recycled glass bottles and containers.

---

[2]Activity questions asked for the "number of times participated in past 12 months." Seven response categories ranged from none in the past year to 52 or more times. The items on use of disposable plates and cups and the use of organic fruits and vegetables were asked of males regarding personal use, and of females regarding personal or household use. Seven response categories for these items ranged from "Don't use" to "More than once a day."

In 1993, the response options for items 1–4 were Always, Often, Sometimes, Never. Items 5 and 8 were not asked in the 1993 survey. Items 9–10 were added to the survey in 1993, and are reverse coded before adding to the scale.

3. Recycled metal cans and containers.
4. Recycled plastic bottles and containers.
5. Recycled used motor oil.
6. Boycotted a product or service because of the company's record on environmental or social issues.
7. Used public transportation to get to work.
8. Used a car pool to get to work.
9. Used disposable paper or plastic plates.
10. Used disposable paper or plastic cups.
11. Eat organically grown fruit or vegetables.

The items in this scale were intended to be congruent with previous operational definitions of pro-environmental behavior, and include behavior advocated by pro-environmental organizations. The question, then, is what demographic, psychographic, and attitude characteristics correlate significantly and reliably with pro-environmental behavior? In assessing an answer to that question, it is important to note that changes in the way the dependent variable was measured produce a conservative bias against finding the same relations both years.

Demographics

Education. In the DDB Needham data, education (Table 7.1) is positively related to pro-environmental behavior, $r = .18$. (Unless noted otherwise, all correlations reported here are significantly different from zero at $p < .001$ in both samples.) This relation agrees with the meta-analysis by Hines et al. (1987) as well as findings from Granzin and Olsen (1991). It does not agree with Vining and Ebreo (1990), and Pickett et al. (1993).

Income. In the DDB Needham data, income is positively related to pro-environmental behavior, $r = .21$. This finding also agrees with Hines et al.'s (1987) meta-analysis, and with Vining and Ebreo (1990) and Granzin and Olsen (1991). It disagrees with Pickett et al. (1993).

Community Size. Like numerous other researchers (Buttel & Flinn, 1978b; Lowe & Pinhey, 1982; Samdahl & Robertson, 1989; Tremblay & Dunlap, 1978), this study found community size was positively related to pro-environmental behavior, $r = .14$ in 1992, and $r = .17$ in 1993.

Age and Gender. Relations between pro-environmental behavior and age and gender have varied widely across studies and over time. This inconsistency led Hines et al. (1987) to conclude that there is no stable pattern. This

TABLE 7.1
Pearson Product–Moment Correlations Between
Demographic Variables and Pro-Environmental Behavior

Demographic Characteristics	Correlations 1992	Correlations 1993
Education	.18*	.19*
Income	.21*	.15*
Age	−.05	.06
Sex	.00	.02
Community size	.14*	.17*

*$p < .001$.

study agrees. It found a weak negative correlation with age of $r=-.05$ in 1992, and a weak positive correlation of $r=.06$ in 1993. Similar to Hines et al.'s (1987) meta-analysis, a correlation was found with gender of $r=.00$ in 1992 and $r=.02$ in 1993 (not significant). Although exceptions for both age and gender can be found within individual studies (most recently Granzin & Olsen, 1991; Vining & Ebreo, 1990), the general consensus is that these relations are inconsistent and very weak.

Conclusion. Considering all demographic variables, the results—based on large demographically representative samples—show strongest agreement across all demographic variables with the meta-analysis by Hines et al. (1987). This outcome supports the convergent validity of the present findings and demonstrates that conclusions drawn from a meta-analysis are likely to be more replicable than conclusions drawn from individual investigations, especially when samples in individual investigations are not large. The magnitude of the relations are discussed later on.

Pro-Environmental Attitudes

In keeping with the long-standing interest in attitude–behavior associations, this study searched the attitude, interest, and opinion section of the DDB Needham surveys for items expressing pro-environmental attitudes or intentions to act in pro-environmental ways. Six items appeared in both years. They form the following Environmental Concerns Scale with Cronbach alpha of .68 in 1992, and .70 in 1993:

- I make a special effort to buy products in packages made out of recycled materials.
- I support pollution standards even if it means shutting down some factories.

- I would switch from my usual brands and buy environmentally safe cleaning products, even if I have to give up some cleaning effectiveness.
- I would be willing to accept a lower standard of living to conserve energy.
- I worry a lot about the effects of environmental pollution on my family's health.
- The government isn't spending enough to clean up the environment.

In the DDB Needham data, environmental concern as measured by this scale was positively and significantly associated with pro-environmental behavior, $r = .27$ in 1992, and $r = .25$ in 1993. These correlations are somewhat lower than the .35 reported by Hines et al. (1987), but higher than those reported by Pickett et al. (1993) and Vining and Ebreo (1990). Thus, in both the 1992 and 1993 data, general attitudes toward the environment were positively and significantly associated with pro-environmental practices. The magnitude of this relation is explored further later on.

Approximate Replications

A cross-validated search (identifying correlates in the 1992 data, and confirming them in the 1993 data) through the remainder of the DDB Needham database revealed a number of correlates of pro-environmental behavior. When the individual items are organized into themes, conceptual if not exact replications of important previous findings emerge (Table 7.2).

Cosmopolitanism. Congruent with the work of Anderson and Cunningham (1972), and Anderson, Henion, and Cox (1974), a positive relation was found between cosmopolitanism and pro-environmental behavior. The measure of cosmopolitanism includes items like "I am interested in the cultures of other countries" and "Took an airplane trip for personal reasons" (see Appendix for a full list of the items). This scale correlated with pro-environmental behavior, $r = .19$ in 1992 and $r = .25$ in 1993.

Liberalism. Consistent with the findings of Dunlap (1975), Mazmanian and Sabatier (1981), Antil (1984), and Samdahl and Robertson (1989), it was found that pro-environmental behavior is positively associated with social liberalism ($r = .16$ and .18 in 1992 and 1993, respectively). This measure of liberalism includes attitudes toward gender roles, abortion, communism, and guns (see Appendix for full list of items).

Community Involvement. In accord with Webster (1975), it was found that pro-environmental behavior is positively associated with involvement in the community ($r = .22$ and $r = .20$ in 1992 and 1993, respectively).

TABLE 7.2
Pearson Product–Moment Correlations Between
Independent Variables and Pro-Environmental Behavior

Scale	Cronbach Alpha		Correlation		Expected Relationship
	1992	1993	1992	1993	
Environmental concern	.68	.70	.27	.25	positive
Cosmopolitanism	.64	.64	.19	.25	positive
Liberalism	.67	.69	.16	.18	positive
Community involvement	.62	.61	.22	.20	positive
Social networking	.57	.58	.23	.18	positive
Frugality	.68	.68	.14	.14	positive
Planning	.57	.57	.30	.23	positive
Perceived financial distress	.72	.73	−.13	−.16	negative
Dissatisfaction	.66	.66	−.15	−.15	negative
Healthful diet	.88	.88	.16	.20	new
Fitness exercise	.66	.66	.23	.17	new
Out-of-home entertainment	.55	.55	.24	.23	new

Note: All correlations reported in this table are significant at $p < .001$.

This measure of community involvement included items like attendance at club meetings and participation in community projects (see Appendix). In a related area we constructed a scale of social networking consisting of frequency of sending greeting cards, entertaining people at home, and giving or attending dinner parties. This scale is positively correlated ($r = .23$ and $.18$ in 1992 and 1993, respectively) with pro-environmental behavior (see Appendix).

Frugality. The investigation lends additional support to the finding of Granzin and Olsen (1991), Belch (1979), and De Young (1985–1986) that participants in environmental activities derive satisfaction from leading a "frugal" life, as distinguished from a "prosperous, comfortable" life. In the DDB Needham data, frugality was represented by items like frequency of coupon use, purchase of generic products, and shopping at wholesale clubs (see Appendix). This scale is correlated with pro-environmental behavior ($r = .27$ and $.14$ in 1992 and 1993, respectively).

Information Seeking. Similar to Belch (1979), it was found that pro-environmental behavior is positively associated with information seeking and careful planning ($r = .30$ and $r = .23$ in 1992 and 1993, respectively). In the data this construct was measured with items about consulting *Consumer Reports* and similar publications before making a major purchase and attendance of classes or seminars (see Appendix).

Security. Agreeing with Belch's (1979) finding that environmentally concerned consumers are financially and emotionally secure, it was found that a scale of perceived financial distress is negatively correlated with pro-environmental behavior ($r = -.13$ and $-.16$ in 1992 and 1993, respectively). A more general scale of dissatisfaction was also negatively correlated with pro-environmental behavior ($r = -.15$ in both samples). The Perceived Financial Distress Scale includes items like "My family is too heavily in debt." The Dissatisfaction Scale includes items like "I dread the future" and "My opinions do not count for much" (see Appendix).

Conclusion. In short, the 1992 and 1993 DDB Needham data provide approximate replications of much previous research, some more than 20 years old. These replications, in the face of changes in items and samples, and in the face of a methodological bias against replication, suggest that pro-environmental behavior is a viable construct and that much previous research still holds.

New Findings

Now consider some previously unreported relations between lifestyle variables and pro-environmental behavior.

Healthful Diet. In the DDB Needham data, pro-environmental behavior was positively associated ($r = .16$ and $.20$ in 1992 and 1993; Cronbach alpha $= .88$ in both years) with effort to eat a healthful diet as measured by the following scale:

- I am careful about what I eat in order to control my weight.
- I try to avoid foods with a high salt content.
- I try to avoid foods that have additives in them.
- I try to avoid beverages that are high in caffeine.
- I am concerned about how much sugar I eat.
- I try to avoid foods that are high in cholesterol.
- I try to avoid fried foods.
- I try to avoid foods that are high in fat.
- I try to select foods that are fortified with vitamins, minerals, and protein.
- I use a lot of low calorie food products.
- I make a special effort to get enough fiber (bran) in my diet.

Furthermore, in spite of its positive relation with frugality, pro-environmental behavior is positively related to willingness "to pay more for a product with all natural ingredients" ($r = .16$ and $.16$). And, although those scoring high on the Pro-environmental Behavior Scale report they try to avoid food containing additives, they also report that they "try to select foods that are fortified with vitamins, minerals, and protein" ($r = .10$ and $.09$).

To implement their food preferences and concerns, consumers who engage in pro-environmental behavior need to be able and willing to process information regarding food. It is therefore not surprising that they are less likely than other consumers to agree that they are "confused by all the nutrition information that is available today" ($r = -.09$ and $-.09$). In keeping with their tendency to be planful and attentive to information, they are more likely to say that they "usually check ingredient labels when buying food" ($r = .17$ and $.18$).

Fitness Exercise. Complementary to efforts to eat a healthful diet, those scoring high on the Pro-environmental Behavior Scale were also more likely to score high on the following Fitness Exercise Scale ($r = .23$ and $.17$ in 1992 and 1993, respectively; Cronbach alpha $= .66$ in both years):

- Rode a bicycle.
- Went to an exercise class.
- Did exercises at home (not at a class).
- Went to a health club.
- Jogged.
- Went swimming.
- Walked more than 1 mile for exercise.

An underlying theme that logically connects pro-environmental behavior, exercise, and diet is a concern for health. The human body can be thought of as a personal internal environment. Those who take action to control and maintain that environment are more likely to take action to control and maintain the outside environment.

Of course, it is unknown whether health concerns operate as dependent or parallel relations across internal and external environments. That is, it is unknown whether people are concerned about maintaining the external environment because it affects personal or family health—a dependent relation—or express concern about the health of the external environment for its own sake, or some of both. Because these two interpretations suggest somewhat different persuasion strategies for encouraging pro-environmental behavior, this uncertainty is an important topic for further research.

Use of Leisure Time. Pro-environmental behavior is also related to how people use their leisure time. A 5-item scale was constructed of out-of-home entertainment including items like going to movies, attending concerts, and going to art galleries or museums. Pro-environmental behavior was positively correlated with out-of-home entertainment, $r = .24$ and $.23$ in 1992 and 1993, respectively. It was also positively correlated with gardening ($r = .17$ and $.22$), working on do-it-yourself projects around the house ($r = .21$ and $.12$), and taking photographs ($r = .19$ and $.15$).

Summary. Relations between pro-environmental behavior and various attitudes and personality traits are summarized in Table 7.2. Table 7.2 shows that pro-environmental behavior is positively and significantly correlated with environmental concern, cosmopolitanism, liberalism, community involvement, social networking, seeking out-of-home entertainment, frugality, planfullness, a healthful diet, and engaging in fitness-oriented exercise. It is negatively correlated with perceptions of financial distress and dissatisfaction with life.

Media Preferences. Compared to those scoring low on the Pro-environmental Behavior Scale, those scoring high had distinct preference for print media over television, and specific preferences within media. Pro-environmental behavior is negatively related to overall level of watching television ($r = -.13$ and $-.15$), and positively related to both the number of visits to the public library ($r = .18$ and $.16$) and the number of books read in the past year ($r = .14$ and $.12$).

When media preferences were examined in finer detail, it was found that preferences for 13 out of 56 print media choices were positively related to pro-environmental behavior, whereas only 1 (*The National Enquirer*) was negatively related. In contrast, only 2 of 83 preferences for television programs, genres, or cable channels were positively related and 13 out of 83 were negatively related (see Appendix for a full list of media preferences).

Predicting Environmental Behavior Scores

To assess the predictability of pro-environmental behavior scores, the demographic variables and all of the scales and single items that survived replication at the item level were entered into a stepwise regression (except the media items). For the 1992 sample, this procedure produced a 16-variable model explaining 25% of the variance. In the 1993 sample, it produced a 15-variable model explaining 21% of the variance—significantly higher than the 13% found by Pickett, Kangun, and Grove (1993).[3] This outcome

---

[3]This is not offered as an ideal model predicting environmental behavior, because working with secondary data means researchers are certain to miss important predictive constructs like knowledge regarding the environment. The point of the regression is simply to show that a general construct of pro-environmental behavior is substantially more predictable than suggested by the results of Pickett et al. (1993).

suggests that Pickett, Kangun, and Grove may have underestimated the predictability (and underlying unity) of pro-environmental behavior.

IMPLICATIONS

R^2s of .21 to .25 seem low, and are generally considered weak. However, the practical question remains: Are relations of this magnitude strong enough to be useful in creating pro-environmental programs and advertising campaigns?

One way to answer that question is to consider the nature of the behavioral change being sought. Suppose a communication/intervention contributes to a lasting behavioral change in 2% of the adult U.S. population. In absolute terms, this seemingly small change recycles an enormous amount of waste and conserves a great deal of energy. After all, 2% of the U.S. population is approximately 5 million people. Further, changes cumulate over time. As Abelson (1985) pointed out, differences in skill account for very little (less than 1%) of the variance in the outcome of any one batting episode in a major league baseball game. However, over the course of a season or a career, those very small differences accumulate into very different outcomes for both players and teams. Accumulation over time magnifies the impact of differences that otherwise seem small.

Copy Strategies

Another way to assess implications is to consider how advertising and public relations agencies use such data to develop copy strategies. Kover (1995) found that while creating persuasive messages, copywriters conduct dialogues with internal "others" who represent target audiences. It seems obvious that the more accurately this internal "other" represents the actual target, the more effective copywriters will be in their work.

It should be easiest to persuade consumers who already engage in a variety of pro-environmental behaviors to adopt a new one, so an appropriate target would be consumers who resemble consumers who scored in the upper quartile on our Pro-environmental Behavior Scale. What copy strategies can be inferred from the set of correlates presented?

Use Strong, Fairly Detailed Scientific Arguments to Persuade This Target Audience. The target's higher level of education should enable them to understand scientific arguments. Their higher level of seeking information and planning—as evidenced by behaviors like sending away for free informational brochures, calling toll-free numbers for product information, and consulting authoritative sources before making major purchases—points out a need for information when making decisions.

Emphasize How the New Behavior Is Frugal. Although the target audience tends to have a higher income than others, they are also more conservative with their money, as evidenced by higher levels of coupon use, purchase of generic products, and shopping at warehouse stores or wholesale clubs. Many pro-environmental behaviors like driving a smaller more fuel efficient car, do in fact save money as well as improve the environment.

Endorse and Support Government Programs. In addition to engaging in more pro-environment behaviors, the target audience is also more concerned than others about issues like pollution, safety, and about the role of government in improving the environment. Therefore, capitalize on government actions that correct environmental damage or avoid environmental dangers.

Emphasize the Health Benefits of the New Behavior. An underlying theme that logically connects pro-environmental behavior, concern about pollution, exercise, and diet is a concern for health. The human body can be thought of as a personal internal environment. Members of the target audience take action to control and maintain their personal environment and also take action to maintain and improve the environment. Although clearly the personal health benefits of the new behavior are most salient, the benefits to the health of the broader community should not be ignored.

Emphasize a Sense of Community. This recommendation flows from the personal sociability of the target audience. They are more involved than others with their local community—attending club meetings, doing volunteer work, and writing letters to the editor of a local paper. They also attend and give more parties. Therefore, appeals to engage in a new pro-environmental behavior should play on the local impact of the new behavior and appeal to the target members to act as local group leaders and role models.

Emphasize the Global Implications of the New Behavior. The members of the target audience are cosmopolitan in outlook. They are interested in other cultures and travel more widely and frequently than those who do not engage in pro-environmental behavior. Because the earth is a closed system, virtually any environmental behavior has both local and global impact. This fact, combined with their greater interest in people of various cultures, can be used to make a global altruistic appeal.

Appeal to the Target Members' Action Tendencies and Their Sense of Resourcefulness. Members of the target audience are active. They have engaged in pro-environmental behaviors, are more likely than others to exercise, are more involved in their communities, and have a greater tendency to enjoy entertainment that gets them out of the house. They also have higher incomes and feel they have more financial resources than others. They are more satisfied with life. They feel more optimistic about the future, and believe their opinions do count. Therefore, persuasive messages regarding pro-environmental behavior should end on an upbeat note (as opposed to dire prediction of impending doom) and should emphasize that active individuals can have positive effects.

Media Selection

In advertising agencies, media planners use "indices" to select media vehicles. That is, they divide target exposure to each media vehicle by general population exposure to that vehicle. In reaching those scoring in the upper quartile of pro-environmental behavior, the four most selective vehicles are *Money* (index score 132), *US News and World Report* (130), *Newsweek* (121), and *National Geographic* (121). Although these indices all translate into correlation coefficients lower than .20, they are of the magnitude that media planners commonly use. Taken together, these four magazines provide 59% coverage of the target group.

Promotional Events

When examining the details of the pro-environmentalists' socializing and educational tendencies, there are possibilities for promotional events as a part of a total plan for encouraging the adoption of pro-environmental behavior.

Find Public Partners for Promotions. Museums and zoos are potential public partners that already appeal to the target audience. Although sometimes criticized by the most radical of environmentalists, zoos do speak out on behalf of wildlife conservation and preservation of natural habitats, and they do attract members of the target group. Further, most zoos have experts that can assist in educating the public about the effects of environmental changes on animal populations. Because of expertise and credibility, museums of science and/or natural history are also potential public partners.

Create Promotional Events That Include an Opportunity to Socialize. The target audience attend more dinner parties, entertain in their own home, and attend more club meetings than others. Promotional events should find ways to capitalize on this tendency to socialize.

Create Promotional Events That Include an Educational Element. Because members of the target audience attend classes, seminars, and lectures at a substantially higher rate than others, promotional events to encourage pro-environmental behaviors can quite naturally include educational components. Continuing education adds to and is encouraged by more detailed understanding of the ecological systems that govern the future of the world.

CONCLUSIONS

Even though the DDB Needham data were collected for another purpose, and even though the operational definition of the dependent variable was (of necessity) not exactly the same in 1992 and 1993, the results of this analysis provide approximate replications of previous findings and contribute new and reliable correlates of pro-environmental behavior. These correlations generate plausible inferences as to the causes of pro-environmental behavior, and help us understand the differences between those who do and do not engage in pro-environmental behavior. Further, when used in the ways such correlations are normally used in for-profit marketing, these correlations facilitate strategic planning, message construction, and media selection in pro-social advertising and public relations campaigns.

These findings therefore contradict the gloomy prescriptions of those who have concluded that each micro-aspect of pro-environmental behavior must be examined on its own. Without negating the value of aspect-specific investigations, it can be concluded that the general concept, pro-environmental behavior, is strong enough and consistent enough to provide valuable guidance in both theoretical and practical work.

APPENDIX: SCALES

The individual items that make up the following scales were all significantly related to pro-environmental behavior at $p < .001$ in both 1992 and 1993. Items were standardized before adding together in scales. The numbers following each item are the percent who agree, or who do an activity within the lower and upper quartile of the Pro-environmental Behavior Scale. These figures are from the 1992 survey.

Cosmopolitanism

- I would feel lost if alone in a foreign country (69, 54) [reverse scored]
- I prefer to vacation in the U.S. (76, 68) [reverse scored]
- I am interested in the cultures of other countries (60, 77)

- Used a travel agent for personal travel (25, 39)
- Took an airplane trip for personal reasons (31, 45)
- Stayed at an upper priced hotel while on a personal trip (21, 26)

(Cronbach alpha = .64 in both years)

Liberalism

- The father should be the boss in the house (49, 40) [reverse scored]
- A woman's place is in the home (29, 21) [reverse scored]
- I think the women's liberation movement is a good thing (56, 67)
- Men are smarter than women (17, 12) [reverse scored]
- Men are naturally better leaders than women (34, 25) [reverse scored]
- I am in favor of legalized abortions (56, 65)
- Communism is the greatest peril in the world today (36, 23) [reverse scored]
- There should be a gun in every home (35, 24) [reverse scored]

(Cronbach alpha = .67 in 1992 and .69 in 1993)

Community Involvement

- Went to a club meeting (53, 57)
- Did volunteer work (55, 68)
- Worked on a community project (30, 47)
- Wrote a letter to an editor of a magazine or newspaper (12, 25)
- I am interested in politics (40, 56)

(Cronbach alpha = .62 in 1992 and .61 in 1993)

Social Networking

- Gave or attended a dinner party (27, 47)
- Entertained people in my home (34, 55)
- Sent greeting cards (47, 63)

(Cronbach alpha = .57 in 1992 and .58 in 1993)

Frugality

- Sent in for a manufacturer's rebate (34, 60)
- Used a "price-off" coupon at a grocery store (37, 60)
- Used a "price-off" coupon at a drug store or discount store (44, 64)
- Bought a generic product (37, 53)

- Shopped at a warehouse club or wholesale club (54, 64)

(Cronbach alpha = .68 in both years)

Planning

- Before going shopping, I set down and make out a complete shopping list (56, 64)
- I consult *Consumer Reports* or other publications before making a major purchase (38, 60)
- I seldom make detailed plans (46, 35) [reverse scored]
- Used a toll-free telephone number to get information about a product or service (53, 79).
- Mailed away for a free informational or educational brochure (45, 73)
- Attended a lecture (29, 56)
- Attended a class or seminar (38, 65)

(Cronbach alpha = .57 in both years)

Perceived Financial Distress

- I pretty much spend for today and let tomorrow bring what it will (29, 22)
- Our family is too heavily in debt (40, 34)
- I am not very good at saving money (48, 41)
- Our family income is high enough to satisfy nearly all our important desires (55, 65) [reverse scored]
- No matter how fast our income goes up we never seem to get ahead (62, 55)

(Cronbach alpha = .72 in 1992 and .73 in 1993)

Dissatisfaction

- I am very satisfied with the way things are going in my life these days (63, 71) [reverse scored]
- I often wish for the good old days (60, 51)
- If I had my life to live over, I would sure do things differently (62, 55)
- I dread the future (30, 23)
- Everything is changing too fast today (68, 57)
- My opinions don't count for very much (41, 29)

(Cronbach alpha = .66 in both years)

Out-of-Home Entertainment

- Visit an art gallery or museum (32, 60)
- Went to a pop or rock concert (13, 23)
- Went to a classical concert (10, 27)
- Went to the movies (60, 78)
- Went to the zoo (27, 44)

(Cronbach alpha = .55 in both years)

Media Correlates

Newspaper Sections
- News section (91, 97)
- Business section (65, 81)
- Food section (67, 79)
- Lifestyle section (68, 83)
- Travel section (56, 75)
- Magazine section (72, 83)
- Editorial section (73, 84)

Magazines
- *Newsweek* (18, 29)
- *US News and World Report* (11, 21)
- *Money* (10, 20)
- *National Geographic* (26, 42)
- Travel magazines (15, 27)
- *The National Enquirer* (20, 13)

Television
- Documentary programs (34, 52)
- Public Broadcasting System programs (PBS) (39, 64)
- "Knots Landing" (18, 10)
- "In the Heat of the Night" (38, 25)
- "Matlock" (37, 29)
- Daytime serials/soap operas (31, 23)
- "Fresh Prince of Bel Air" (19, 11)
- National talk shows ("Donahue," "Oprah Winfrey," "Geraldo," etc.) (44, 34)
- "America's Most Wanted" (41, 29)

- "Unsolved Mysteries" (49, 36)
- "Rescue 911" (48, 34)
- Religious programs (14, 10)
- Game shows (in general) (38, 27)

Cable Channels
- Nashville Network (22, 17)
- Family Channel (27, 22)

Radio
- National Public Radio (12, 25)
- Classical music (13, 28)
- Jazz (8, 17)
- Country and western (44, 23)
- Religious/gospel (17, 12)

REFERENCES

Abelson, R. P. (1985). A variance explanation paradox: When a little is a lot. *Psychological Bulletin, 97,* 129–133.

Ajzen, I. (1988). *Attitudes, personality, and behavior.* Chicago: Dorsey.

Ajzen, I., & Fishbein, M. (1980). *Understanding attitudes and predicting social behavior.* Englewood Cliffs, NJ: Prentice-Hall.

Anderson, W. T., & Cunningham, W. H. (1972). The socially conscious consumer. *Journal of Marketing, 36,* 23–31.

Anderson, W. T., Henion, K. E., & Cox, E. P. (1974). Socially vs. ecologically responsible consumers. *AMA Combined Conference Proceedings, 36,* 304–311.

Antil, J. H. (1984). Socially responsible consumers: Profile and implications for public policy. *Journal of Macromarketing,* Fall, 18–39.

Belch, M. A. (1979). Identifying the socially and ecologically concerned segment through life-style research: Initial findings. In K. E. Henion II & T. C. Kinnear (Eds.), *The conserver society* (pp. 69–81). Chicago: American Marketing Association.

Buttel, F. J., & Flinn, W. L. (1978a). The politics of environmental concern: The impacts of party identification and political ideology on environmental attitudes. *Environment and Behavior, 10*(1), 17–35.

Buttel, F. J., & Flinn, W. L. (1978b). Social class and mass environmental beliefs: A reconsideration. *Environment and Behavior, 10*(3), 433–450.

De Young, R. (1985–1986). Encouraging environmentally appropriate behavior: The role of intrinsic motivation. *Journal of Environmental Systems, 15*(4), 281–292.

Dunlap, R. E. (1975). The impact of political orientation on environmental attitudes and actions. *Environment and Behavior, 7* (December), 428–454.

Fishbein, M., & Ajzen, I. (1975). *Belief, attitude, intention and behavior: An introduction to theory and research.* Reading, MA: Addison-Wesley.

Granzin, K. L., & Olsen, J. E. (1991). Characterizing participants in activities protecting the environment: A focus on donating, recycling, and conservation behaviors. *Journal of Public Policy and Marketing, 10*(2), 1–27.

Hines, J. M., Hungerford, H. R., & Tomera, A. M. (1987). Analysis and synthesis of research on responsible environmental behavior: A meta-analysis. *Journal of Environmental Education, 18*(2), 1–8.

Kassarjian, H. (1971). Incorporating ecology into marketing strategy: The case of air pollution. *Journal of Marketing, 35*, 61–65.

Kover, A. (1995). Copywriters implicit theories. *Journal of Consumer Research, 21* (March), 596–611.

Lowe, G. D., & Pinhey, T. K. (1982). Rural–urban differences in support for environmental protection. *Rural Sociology, 47*(1), 114–128.

Mazmanian, D., & Sabatier, P. (1981). Liberalism, environmentalism and partisanship in public policy-making. *Environment and Behavior, 13* (July), 361–384.

Pickett, G. M., Kangun, N., & Grove, S. J. (1993). Is there a general conserving consumer? A public policy concern. *Journal of Public Policy and Marketing, 12*(2), 234–243.

Samdahl, D. M., & Robertson, R. (1989). Social determinants of environmental concern: Specification and test of the model. *Environment and Behavior, 21*(1), 57–81.

Schwepker, C. H., Jr., & Cornwell, T. B. (1991). An examination of ecologically concerned consumers and their intention to purchase ecologically packaged products. *Journal of Public Policy and Marketing, 10*(2), 77–101.

Tremblay, K. R., Jr., & Dunlap, R. E. (1978). Rural–urban residence and concern with environmental quality: A replication and extension. *Rural Sociology, 43*, 474–491.

Van Liere, K. D., & Dunlap, R. E. (1981). Environmental concern: Does it make a difference how it's measured? *Environment and Behavior, 13*(6), 651–676.

Vining, J., & Ebreo, A. (1990). What makes a recycler? A comparison of recyclers and nonrecyclers. *Environment and Behavior, 22*(1), 55–73.

Webster, F. E., Jr. (1975). Determining the characteristics of the socially conscious consumer. *Journal of Consumer Research, 2* (December), 188–196.

Chapter 8

Demographic and Lifestyle Data: A Practical Application to Stimulating Compliance with Mammography Guidelines Among Poor Women

Cynthia Currence
American Cancer Society, Atlanta

ABSTRACT

Breast cancer is the number one cause of cancer deaths among women and the incidence of this disease is increasing. According to national surveys, it is women's number one health concern. In an effort to help women detect this problem early, when it is most survivable, the American Cancer Society has placed mammography screening as a core priority in their strategic plan. Cancer organizations have made great strides in increasing midincome to wealthy women's first-time use of mammography, but the behavior is much weaker among the poor population and minority groups. Traditional intervention approaches have not generated the desired behavior among these groups.

This chapter illustrates the use of geo-demographic and lifestyle data to influence mammography usage among poor, older, African-American women in central Atlanta. The Claritas PRIZM system was used to identify the market, understand the market's characteristics and needs, and select media channels and messages to influence behavior among women in this market group (Reardon, 1994). Attitudinal data was also used to refine messages. A subsequent test demonstrates the impact of nontraditional media as recommended in the previous analysis to reach the specified market.

In the 1930s, the data were available to enable organizations and individuals to predict certain human behavior and responses based on analysis of basic demographic characteristics, lifestyle habits, buyer behavior, and dominant media behavior. At that time, however, the technology was not available to perform detailed and timely analysis. Today, such power exists and several companies have blended the power of the computer with available demographic, lifestyle, and media data. Companies like Claritas, CACI, and Equifax have spent many years refining this technology and now offer dynamic marketing tools to progressive businesses based on it.

These tools can save businesses significant time and money in their efforts to identify high potential market groups and influence market behavior for a wide range of products and services. From banks to retail stores to direct mail-based companies, this technology has been used to better understand customers' needs and demands in terms of developing the best products and services and positioning these offerings to best reflect the chosen market's requirements. Given that 85% of new products fail in this country, this intelligence can be particularly valuable when trying to carve a niche for something new. It is also valuable when reshaping existing products for new markets.

There are very few nonprofit groups working with this kind of technology. The biggest barrier to its use may be the expense, but there is also a significant barrier in terms of how most nonprofits think. Few nonprofits have truly embraced the need to target their offerings and still rely largely on mass marketing strategies. Generally speaking, nonprofits have trouble "leaving anyone out." Rather than seeing targeting as a way to focus energy for greater results (be they fund raising or saving lives), it is frequently seen as withholding services from a particular group or not taking full advantage of a wider group. Until this element of strategic thinking is solidly connected with outcome results in the nonprofit sector, the players using it will probably remain few. It is hoped that this chapter will facilitate greater movement in the nonprofit sector toward use of powerful segmentation processes.

The American Cancer Society (ACS) purchased a target marketing software tool years ago from Claritas/NPDC, Inc. Part of their product, PRIZM, is a segmentation system that separates the U.S. population into 62 distinct markets that look and behave differently. The software package that manipulates the market clusters along with a vast array of demographic, lifestyle, and media characteristics is called Compass. Compass crunches census data, consumer buyer behavior data, and media behavior data in ways that help the marketer identify and locate desired markets, understand the markets, and then approach them with much greater precision.

One of the greatest benefits that the system offers ACS is tremendous savings in terms of the amount of time and money it takes to shape offerings to given markets. For example, the requirements for intervention programs have usually been based on extensive and expensive perceptual and behavioral studies, and trial and error. The Claritas product helps shorten this route to success. It enables researchers to intuit and anticipate many market needs and modify approaches by analyzing demographic characteristics, buyer behavior, and media behavior. It is important to note that the system is generally not used independent of other data and market research when tackling a marketing problem. It is one tool and is best used in conjunction with attitudinal data that address the given behavior of the market that is to be influenced.

The ACS has used this technology to influence cancer risk behavior such as tobacco use and early detection practices like mammography screening for breast cancer. It has also been used to target populations related to goals in serving patients and to identify and approach markets for income and volunteer development.

MAMMOGRAPHY APPLICATION DESCRIPTION

The application of the technology chosen for discussion is the adaptation of traditional mammography screening programs to reach the poor. In terms of saving lives from breast cancer, the ACS staff and volunteers knew through experience that existing breast cancer screening programs were not reaching the poor woman or the ethnic woman as effectively as they were reaching the middle-class woman. This assumption was validated in research commissioned by ACS—the Jacobs Institute study (Horton, Romans, & Cruess, 1992) and the Wirthlin study (Allsop & Kielpinski, 1992). The Jacobs study showed that over a 2-year period, whereas a 10% increase was measured among middle-class women having ever had a mammogram, negligible increase was detected among poor women. The Wirthlin study showed that compliance with mammography guidelines for ethnic populations lagged behind the Caucasian population. The Wirthlin study also identified several attitudinal and perceptual barriers to screening among ethnic groups. From this data, the ACS concluded that traditional mammography screening approaches were not as effective with poor and minority groups as they were for middle-income groups. It was further concluded that market-driven approaches were needed to effectively reach the poor as well as ethnic groups. These populations had to be targeted in light of their special needs and demands if a significant change was to be expected in compliance with mammography guidelines.

In order to make mammography screening more relevant to poor women, the ACS used demographic data as well as consumer buyer and media behavior data from Compass, PRIZM data, and attitudinal data regarding market attitudes about and barriers to mammography usage among poor women. The Wirthlin study was the primary source of attitudinal data on barriers. Although most of the attention is on the Compass and PRIZM data, it should be noted that the attitudinal data was a pivotal element in message development and conclusions for next steps.

Statement of Problem

It is necessary to increase the percentage of older, poor women (over the age of 50 and making less than $20,000 household income annually) in Atlanta's inner city who follow the ACS mammography guidelines.

Why Atlanta?   Atlanta was chosen because it is the site of the National Home Office for ACS where the resources for this project originated, because the Georgia division of ACS is known to have a very progressive and action-oriented staff and volunteer operation who could take next steps in attempting to prove any theory developed from the analysis, and because the area met demographic requirements for the test (significant numbers of poor, older, minority women).

Why Older Women?   Eighty percent of breast cancer is detected in women over the age of 50. As women get older, compliance with screening guidelines weakens (Behavioral Surveillance Branch, 1992). More lives can be saved by focusing on this older group.

SECONDARY DATA ANALYSIS

Demographic Data

The first step was to understand what the older, poor women in Atlanta were like and where they were concentrated using information that already existed. Through Compass, it was possible to generate a map of the Atlanta Metropolitan Statistical Area displaying census tracts with the greatest propensity of having female residents over the age of 50. By dividing the population into quintiles, shading each quintile differently and having the top quintile include tracts with the greatest percentages of older women, it was possible to literally see where the highest propensity of finding the desired age-defined group was located. Similarly, the system was used to display the tracts with greatest propensity to have households with incomes less than $20,000 per year. Both maps showed a high concentration of the desired market in the inner-city area of Atlanta as well as in the far outer ring of the Atlanta Metropolitan Statistical Area. It looked like a donut overlay of the Atlanta MSA.

The common tracts from these two maps were then analyzed to determine the types of lifestyle groups living there. A PRIZM map and report were produced to determine what types of lifestyle clusters reside in the areas of greater propensity for older, poor women. The investigation revealed five lifestyle groups meeting the description of older, poor women living in the inner-city area and four additional different groups living in the outer ring. The groups in the inner-city area were merged, as were the groups in the outer ring, to obtain two distinct combined market groups. Once this was done, the common demographic characteristics were analyzed and compared, as were consumer buyer and media behaviors of the two groups.

This analysis revealed that the two groups were quite different and would require different features and benefits to effectively influence behavior. The hope that perhaps all poor women could be treated similarly in terms of getting them to comply with mammography guidelines was effectively dismissed.

In terms of demographic characteristics, it was found that the inner-city market was four times as likely (compared to the general population) to be African American, whereas the outer ring group was more likely to be Caucasian. The inner-city group was almost three times as likely as others answering the survey on buyer behavior not to own cars. Those in the outer ring group generally had their own transportation. Both groups showed an increased propensity to be single parents, and unemployed or in low-level service jobs. And, although both groups showed an above average statistic for having less than high school education, literacy appeared to be a greater issue in the outer ring than the inner city.

It was also deduced that a sizable percentage of the market probably stayed near their residence during the day because of the increased propensity to be unemployed. However, there is still a significant shift in day-time population of given tracts. Those that were employed showed a greater than average propensity to hold low-level service jobs to which they commuted. The inner-city group traveled by public transit outside the city limits in many cases. It was possible to display this shift in day- and night-time population by showing where the concentrations of day-time population existed compared to residential population. A discussion on use statistics with Atlanta public transportation officials confirmed this travel pattern.

The Compass system also allows other databases to be imported. It was possible to map the location of types of businesses such as hospitals through the business database. Once the location of local hospitals with mammography facilities was mapped, it became apparent how important the mapping of day-time migration became in terms of solving the puzzle of attracting poor women to mammography screening. At that time, there were few mobile mammography units that could bring the screening service to women. So, mammographic screening for breast cancer had to be done at local hospitals or special facilities. The convenience factor was particularly relevant to the inner-city market, where transportation was suspected to be an issue given weak ownership of cars and strong usage of public transportation.

In summary, several market demands can be deduced from basic demographic information. Given all of the aforementioned, critical market demands for the inner-city market included transportation, day care and low reading level materials. For the outer ring group, day care was a common issue with the inner-city group, but reading level was of greater concern than in the inner-city group, and transportation was not an issue for the outer ring group.

Consumer Buyer Behavior Data

From consumer buyer behavior reports, the inner-city market was above average for buying soul/Black music and gospel music, whereas the outer ring was strong in religious music and country western. The inner-city group tended to purchase movie tickets more than four times in a 3-month period, and had a strong propensity to travel by bus and drink regular cola. The outer ring group had a strong propensity for outdoor activities, but did not rely on public transportation. The outer ring also held a propensity to watch pro wrestling, buy country or rock music, and drink regular cola.

Several actionable possibilities were derived from the consumer information. Given a strong match with Coca Cola's market for regular Coke, it was thought that Coca Cola could possibly be approached as a funder for this program. Also, collaboration with retail music stores in the local area and use of certain music personalities in promotional activities could be a supportive strategy.

Other observations from consumer data reinforced needs deduced from analysis of demographic data. The transportation issue is the biggest example for the inner-city group. Demographically, a propensity was observed in the inner city to not own cars and consumer data reflects a propensity in the inner city to travel by bus.

Media Behavior Data

In terms of media behavior, the inner-city market was three times more likely to watch Black Entertainment TV and listen to urban/contemporary radio. This group also showed almost twice the chance of being part of the heaviest day-time TV viewing audience. The outer ring group also shared high levels of TV viewership, although their program selections differed from the inner-city group. They prefer quiz shows and TV wrestling. The outer group listens to country radio and religious radio. Their highest media rating is for being in the bottom 20% for newspaper reading.

From media and consumer buyer behavior, it was determined that non-traditional media should be given high priority as a channel for reaching the inner-city group. Bus shelter posters, bus cards, local billboards, and theater trailers should be used to carry a very simple message. Given that the outer ring group did not use public transportation, radio and billboards were considered very good message vehicles for that group. Given interest and participation in religious programming and products, it was also considered a good idea to work with local churches to help deliver the screening message.

Television was rejected as a vehicle unless the local ACS office could obtain sponsorship to ensure placement and frequency of the message. Although television viewership is high, ACS did not have the means to control the placement or frequency of free TV commercials. Also, ACS did not have the budget that would permit adequate paid advertising on this medium. For these reasons, television was not deemed a good place to focus messages. Further, even though radio ranks high, because of the impact of transportation and employment issues, it is likely that a significant portion of the inner-city target group may be watching TV or riding the bus during drive-time radio periods. So, electronic media was not chosen as a viable communications channel for the inner-city group. Radio, however, was deemed a good selection of the outer ring group given the propensity to travel by car and a known degree of success in the ACS Atlanta organization in working with radio stations to secure promotion time.

Again, although demographic, consumer, buyer and media behavior have been reviewed separately, these areas work together to point to possible market needs. Several observations from media data reinforced needs deduced from analysis of consumer and demographic data. For example, the outer ring group revealed a high propensity for less than high school education in the demographic review, which was stronger than the inner-city data on that variable. The number one media behavior for this outer group was being in the bottom 20% for reading newspapers. This media indicator reinforces a probable difficulty with reading level.

Attitudinal/Perceptual Data

The next step in analysis of the data was to enrich what was found through the PRIZM/Compass data with attitudinal data. Qualitative and quantitative research conducted by the Wirthlin Group in 1992 showed that the greatest barriers to women seeking mammograms were the lack of physician referrals, cost, fear, and a realistic attitude about access to follow-up health care. Physician referral was the number one barrier across all economic levels and ethnic backgrounds. However, even if a program could satisfy concerns relating to transportation, cost, day care, and referral, the market still might not respond because of real or perceived limit to their access to further health care. In other words, it was necessary to be able to assure women they would have access to care if cancer was detected. Unless this barrier could be dissolved, some women would prefer not to know whether they had cancer and would choose not to be screened for it.

Specifically, in terms of messages, regardless of whether the women were from the inner city or the rural area, they needed a doctor or clinic to tell them to get a mammogram. They needed urgent, but hopeful messages to prompt action. And, they needed information about cost and to be reassured about access to future care.

Recommendations

The following recommendations were offered from the analysis of this data in an effort to improve the rate of poor women choosing to get mammograms in Atlanta:

Develop collaborative relations with the six hospitals in the heart of the inner-city market's residential and day-time population centers (maps were provided). Similarly, choose convenient hospitals in the rural areas with which to work when approaching the poor women in the rural community.

In cooperation with hospitals, develop a program that addresses day care and transportation needs, cost, treatment options, and low-level reading capabilities of the target market.

Create/make available low reading level literature and increase in-person contact with the market. Emphasize messages that address fear and concerns about access to care. Include local telephone number within messages with intent to have women call for information on where to go for a mammogram.

Work with area clinics to inform doctors and nurses about the availability of low cost/free screening and the availability, if possible, of treatment support to encourage them to refer women to hospitals for screening.

Use nontraditional media like bus shelter posters and cards, billboards, and theater trailers to promote the availability of mammography for the poor in the inner city. Use radio and billboards in the rural area.

Collaborate with churches in areas with high propensity for older, poor women to carry the message to their membership.

Follow-up Research

In 1993, as part of a study to test the effectiveness of paid advertising, the impact of some of these recommendations was demonstrated. The intent was to determine whether a program tailored to the needs of this market as recommended previously would perform better than the traditional screening programs in terms of attracting poor women to mammography screening facilities.

In this study, Atlanta was chosen as the experimental site and Philadelphia was chosen as a control site. Both cities share a high concentration of inner-city poor who are African American. The Philadelphia division had received numerous awards for program implementation with particular accolades for promotion and advertising support for intervention programs. Whereas this represents a minimal number of treatment and control units, and Philadelphia and Atlanta are different in many regards, this was viewed as an early and interesting test of the analysis.

Both cities executed mammography screening programs during the same 2-month window (October–November 1993) and with the same theme and attending messages. The intent of both sites was to attract poor women to call in and set up appointments for free mammography screening at local hospitals participating in the test.

Philadelphia, participating as the control site for the test, conducted its program and promotions in traditional manner with scheduled television promotions on prime time news shows, radio coverage, and literature distribution through hospitals. It was very successful in gaining coverage of the screening event.

Atlanta, participating as the experimental site in the test, conducted a modified program with promotion through nontraditional media (bus shelter posters, bus cards, billboards). Nontraditional media was purchased and served as the main promotional vehicle, although press releases were picked up by some traditional media, particularly radio.

Neither program accommodated all the needs identified in the earlier analysis. Atlanta's main alteration from the traditional promotional approach for this type of program was to shift the focus of media channels. As previously stated, they chose nontraditional media. Both cities carried identical messages: "A picture can save your life." Supporting messages dealt with urgency to get a mammogram and the percentage of women who can be cured of breast cancer if it is found early through mammography screening.

Both programs used 800 numbers to track the number of people calling for information, scheduling appointments for mammography screenings. Over the phone lines, they were able to capture basic demographic information about respondents to determine whether the number of respondents were from the target audience.

Results

The use of nontraditional media in carrying the mammography screening message to poor African-American women who are older is strongly correlated with increase in first-time mammography behavior in this test. The

Philadelphia program generated only 8 calls from people meeting the demographic descriptive of poor, African-American women over the age of 50. The bulk of their more than 2,000 total calls were from middle-income, Caucasian women. On the other hand, Atlanta received over 300 calls from poor, African-American women and minimal calls from women of other income levels.

CONCLUSIONS

Although there has been no conclusive test of all elements recommended in the initial analysis reviewed here, the combination of geo-demographic and lifestyle data with attitudinal data are powerful ingredients in program development and should be a standard part of new product development processes or product reinvention processes.

The system and attending databases provide valuable and easily accessible information that could take years and great amounts of money to acquire through traditional testing and information gathering means. In essence, the technology provides a jump start to program development and enables social marketers to have an ongoing tool to measure the effectiveness of strategies.

Further, the media focus of the follow-up research indicates strong correlation of the data to effective selection of media channels for hard-to-reach populations like the poor. These targets have not been and are not likely to be adequately reached through traditional media.

REFERENCES

Allsop, D., & Kielpinski, C. (1992). *A nationwide survey on breast health: Prepared for the American Cancer Society.* McLean, VA: The Wirthlin Group.

Behavioral Surveillance Branch. (1992). *BRFSS Summary Prevalence Report.* Atlanta: Centers for Disease Control and Prevention.

Horton, J. A., Romans, M. C., & Cruess, D. F. (1992). Mammography attitudes and usage study. *Jacobs Institute of Women's Health, 2*(4), Winter, 180–188.

Reardon, P. T. (1994, November 15). Who are you? *Chicago Tribune Magazine,* Section 10, pp. 15–28.

Part III

FIGHTING AIDS/
PROMOTING FAMILY PLANNING

Using A Theory-Based Community Intervention to Reduce AIDS Risk Behaviors: The CDC's AIDS Community Demonstration Projects

Martin Fishbein
University of Illinois, Champaign–Urbana
Centers for Disease Control and Prevention

Carolyn Guenther-Grey
Wayne Johnson
Centers for Disease Control and Prevention

Richard J. Wolitski
Centers for Disease Control and Prevention
California State University, Long Beach

Alfred McAlister
University of Texas, Austin

Cornelis A. Rietmeijer
Denver Department of Public Health

Kevin O'Reilly
World Health Organization

The AIDS Community Demonstration Projects[1]

[1]Other ACDP participants include: Ann Freeman and Marty Krepcho (Dallas County Health Department), David Cohn and Paul Simons (Denver County Health Department), Nancy H. Corby and Fen Rhodes (California State University, Long Beach), Susan Tross and Bea Krauss (National Development and Research Institute, New York), Robert Wood and Gary Goldbaum (Seattle–King County Department of Public Health), Donna Higgins and Dan Schnell (Behavioral and Prevention Research Branch, CDC), and John Sheridan (Conwal, Inc., Virginia).

The Centers for Disease Control and Prevention (CDC) is supporting a number of projects designed to implement, and evaluate the effectiveness of, interventions to reduce the risk of HIV transmission. One of these projects, the AIDS Community Demonstration Projects (ACDP), is a multisite study involving five U.S. cities: Dallas, Denver, Long Beach, New York, and Seattle. Generally speaking, the ACDP is evaluating the effectiveness of using community volunteers to deliver a theory-based intervention designed to increase consistent condom use and/or consistent bleach use in a number of ethnically diverse, traditionally hard-to-reach, high risk populations: men who have sex with men but who do not gay identify (MSM-ngi); injecting drug users (IDU) who are not recruited from treatment programs; female sex partners (FSP) of male IDU; female prostitutes or sex traders (FST); and youth in high risk situations (YHR). Each project, except Dallas, intervened with one to three of these groups; the Dallas project intervened with residents in two separate census tracts having a high rate of both STD and drug use (O'Reilly & Higgins, 1991).

Researchers from the project sites, the CDC, and expert consultants collaborated to design a common protocol that was adapted to develop site-specific and population-specific community-level interventions. The common protocol includes five key elements: the use of theories of behavioral prediction and change as a foundation for the design of a community-level, HIV prevention intervention; formative research within the project communities prior to implementing the intervention; small media materials (e.g., pamphlets, brochures, flyers) with role-model stories of individuals who are changing or have changed their risk behaviors; distribution of these small media materials, along with condoms and bleach kits, through volunteer networks of community members who reinforce positive behavior change among individuals who are at risk; and an evaluation protocol that includes both process and outcome measures and is linked to the behavioral theory of the intervention.

Several of the elements in this protocol are adapted from earlier community-level interventions such as the North Karelia Project, a community-level risk reduction program designed to prevent coronary heart disease (Puska et al., 1985; see also McAlister, 1991; McAlister, Puska, Koskela, Pallonen, & Maccoby, 1980). In order to tailor the interventions most effectively to local needs and resources, each project implemented this protocol based on the specific circumstances in their community, as well as on the particular population each intervention was designed to reach.

THEORETICAL FRAMEWORK

The ACDP is based on behavioral research, and has incorporated elements of several theories: the Health Belief Model (Rosenstock, 1974), Social Cognitive Theory (Bandura, 1986), the Theory of Reasoned Action (Fishbein & Ajzen, 1975), and the Transtheoretical Model of Behavior Change (Prochaska, DiClemente, & Norcross, 1992).

The Health Belief Model (HBM) suggests that individuals will be most likely to engage in a preventive health behavior if the individuals believe they are susceptible to (or at risk for) a given disease, that getting the disease will lead to severe consequences, that engaging in the preventive health behavior will reduce susceptibility and/or severity, and that the perceived benefits of performing the preventive behavior outweigh the anticipated barriers or costs (Becker, 1974, 1988; Rosenstock, 1974).

Bandura's Social Cognitive Theory (SCT) suggests that self-efficacy (i.e., the belief that one has the skills and abilities necessary to perform the behavior under a variety of circumstances) is a necessary component for behavior change. In addition, the individual must be motivated to perform the behavior. That is, the person must believe that the expected positive outcomes of performing the behavior outweigh the expected negative outcomes (Bandura, 1986, 1992, 1994).

The Theory of Reasoned Action (TRA) suggests that individuals' performance of a given behavior is primarily determined by their intention to perform that behavior. Two major factors influence the intention to perform a given behavior: First, the individuals' attitude toward personally performing the behavior (which is based on their beliefs about the positive and negative consequences of their performing the behavior); and second, the subjective norm concerning the behavior (i.e., the individuals' belief that "most important others" think that they should or should not perform the behavior). The subjective norm, in turn, is determined by beliefs about the normative proscriptions of specific others and the individuals' motivation to comply with those specific others (Ajzen & Fishbein, 1980; Fishbein & Ajzen, 1975; Fishbein, Middlestadt, & Hitchcock, 1991).

Perceived costs and benefits, expected positive and negative outcomes, or beliefs about positive and negative consequences can all be viewed as potential positive and negative reinforcers of a given action. In addition, Social Cognitive Theory suggests that individuals can also be reinforced vicariously through observing a model being rewarded for appropriate behavior.

The theoretical premise of the ACDP draws on these three theories and assumes there are four factors that may influence an individual's intentions and behaviors: the individuals' perception that they are personally susceptible to acquiring a given disease or illness; the individuals' attitude toward performing the behavior that is based on their beliefs about the positive and negative consequences of performing that behavior; perceived norms including the perception that those with whom the individuals interact most closely support their attempt to change and that others in the community are also changing; and self-efficacy that involves the individuals' belief that they can perform the recommended behavior under a variety of circumstances.

The relative importance of these four factors as determinants of intention and behavior is expected to vary as a function of both the behavior and the population being considered (Fishbein et al., 1992). In addition to identifying these four critical factors, the degree to which the environment facilitates or inhibits behavior change and the readiness of individuals to change their behavior are also considered.

As discussed by Fishbein et al. (1992), the presence of environmental constraints may prevent people from acting on their intentions. For example, an individual cannot use condoms or sterile injection equipment if condoms and sterile needles are not available. Thus, as part of a theory-based approach, the importance of environmental facilitation was recognized and led to an early decision to include the distribution of condoms and bleach kits as an essential part of the intervention.

It was also recognized that different behavior change interventions (or messages) would be necessary for individuals who have not even thought about adopting a given health protective behavior than for those who are trying to adopt that behavior. The Transtheoretical Stage of Change Model (SOC) directly addresses this issue.

According to this model, some individuals who are performing risky behavior may have no intention to change that behavior or to adopt a given health preventive behavior (Precontemplative Stage). Any one of several events may then lead the individual to consider change and perhaps to form an intention to adopt the preventive behavior at some time in the future (Contemplative Stage). This may be followed by the formation of an intention to adopt the new behavior in the immediate or foreseeable future and this intention should be accompanied by initial, perhaps exploratory, attempts to adopt the behavior (Preparation Stage). Then the new behavior is adopted (Action Stage) and ultimately it becomes a routine part of one's life (Maintainance Stage). Movement through the stages is assumed to be sequential although individuals may relapse (at any stage) and cycle back through the stages repeatedly before achieving long-term maintainance (Prochaska et al., 1992).

According to the SOC model, to help people change their behavior, it is first necessary to determine where individuals are on this continuum of behavior change and then develop interventions to help them move to subsequent, more advanced stages. By having discrete and immediate objectives for persons at risk of HIV infection, an intervention can be more precisely targeted to the needs of individuals. For example, it is possible to empirically determine which of the theoretical factors (e.g., norms, attitudes, self-efficacy or perceived risk) are necessary to focus on to move individuals from one stage to the next.

Generally speaking, the intervention utilized social modeling to encourage changes in one or more of the theoretcial factors underlying intention and behavior. More specifically, empirical data provided guidance to the development of role-model stories designed to move people along the SOC continuum.

In summary, the intervention is based on a theoretical foundation containing elements of several behavioral theories and the transtheoretical SOC model. Providing the projects with a firm theoretical base enhanced the development of the interventions and established a basis for both the implementation of the interventions as well as evaluation of their outcomes.

Both intervention and evaluation activities were clearly focused by defining the behavioral goals as specifically as possible. For example, formative research indicated that it was important to distinguish between using a condom with one's main (or steady) partner and using a condom with "occasional" partners (or clients). Similarly, it was important to distinguish between using a condom for vaginal sex and using a condom for anal sex. Thus, condom use was separately considered for vaginal and anal sex with main and occasional partners. This chapter focuses primarily on two of these condom use behaviors: always using a condom for vaginal sex with a main partner and always using a condom for vaginal sex with occasional partners. In addition, for those IDU who share injection equipment, the focus is on the behavior of "always using bleach to disinfect 'works' before injecting."

FORMATIVE RESEARCH

With the exception of the New York project, the AIDS Community Demonstration Projects were based in state or local health departments that had traditionally implemented clinic-based HIV prevention interventions. The ACDP attempted to implement a behavioral intervention directly in the community to reach groups participating in high risk behaviors who were less likely to come to the clinics. In order to implement this community-level behavioral intervention, the project sites needed to develop a thorough base of knowledge about the groups they sought to reach, including the geographic areas in each city where individuals in the risk groups congregate and where ACDP staff and peer network members could conduct the intervention and evaluation; the specific subpopulations within each population at risk; the risk behaviors taking place; and the theoretical variables underlying "risky" and "safer" behaviors among individuals in the risk groups.

To gather this information, project staff in each city undertook 6 months of formative, ethnographic research (Higgins et al., 1996; Goldbaum, Perdue, & Higgins, 1996). First, interviews were conducted with health department staff and local AIDS researchers to determine what they knew about the target populations. Interviews were also conducted with other professionals who have contact with these populations, such as staff at drug treatment facilities, mental health facilities, and Women, Infants, and Children (WIC) clinics, as well as police, judicial system workers, and staff of community-based organizations and other groups (depending on the city and the target population).

Based on the information gathered through these interviews, potential "gatekeepers" were identified. These individuals often serve as the link between the population at risk and the larger community. Whereas gatekeepers were sometimes members of the populations at risk, at other times they were outside of it, such as recovering IDU, or a storekeeper in an area where a large number of sex traders work the streets. These potential gatekeepers were also interviewed to gain their perspectives on the target populations.

Based on all of this information, subgroups within these populations were identified, and the target community was defined. In addition, project staff identified locations where individuals in the target communities were participating in risk-taking behaviors, and also identified other locations where members of these communities might congregate. Using a standard protocol that was modified by the sites based on local circumstances, project workers unobtrusively observed people in the identified locations to gain an understanding of those to whom they intended to direct their behavioral intervention.

Finally, through the ties previously established with the gatekeepers, project staff were able to reach individuals in the target communities. The last step in the formative research process involved interviewing the members of the community who are at risk, both individually and in focus groups. More specifically, members of the target community were asked about the types of risk-taking behaviors they engaged in, the social networks they belonged to, the people or groups who would support or oppose consistent condom use and/or bleaching, barriers and facilitators to adopting these behaviors, the advantages and disadvantages of performing these behaviors, and what respondents thought might be useful ways to help people like themselves adopt protective behaviors (Higgins et al., 1996).

These extensive qualitative data led to a better understanding of the lives of individuals in all of the target risk groups (including their behavior and motivations) from the perspective of the individuals themselves, rather than from the perspective of those outside of these populations (Harris, 1990). These qualitative data enabled the development of a common closed-item evaluation instrument to be used at all sites. In addition, by using ties to gatekeepers and members of the target populations, each site began to recruit networks of peers and other community members to deliver the intervention and to build overall community support for the intervention (Guenther-Grey et al., 1992; Guenther-Grey et al., 1996; Simons et al., 1996). Finally, the projects used the information collected at each site during this formative research stage to begin developing intervention materials that addressed the appropriate attitudes, norms, barriers, and facilitators to risk reduction among individuals in the target groups (Corby, Enguidanos, & Kay, 1996).

IMPLEMENTATION

As noted earlier, each of the five cities designed and implemented interventions for one, two, or three of the six targeted communities at risk for HIV. Dallas identified a pair of census tracts with high rates of STDs, and randomly assigned one as the intervention area and the other as comparison; a second intervention/comparison pair was added 4 months later. Denver directed an intervention to IDU, and 17 months later added an intervention for MSM-ngi. Long Beach worked with IDU, FSP, and FST. New York tailored an intervention to FSP. Seattle directed interventions to IDU, MSM-ngi, and YHR.

The five project sites followed a common protocol for the implementation of the intervention. The intervention protocol emphasized development of small media material depicting positive changes in the beliefs, attitudes, intentions and behaviors of local target population members (role-model stories); distribution of role-model stories by peer volunteers from the local community who were trained to reinforce acceptance of, and attention to, the intervention messages, as well as sucessful and unsuccessful attempts to change behavior; and environmental facilitation through the distribution of condoms and bleach. These components were chosen so that explicit prevention messages and facilitating materials could be distributed to specific populations.

The use of role-model stories was based on a technique of behavioral journalism (McAlister, in press) and the combination of social modeling in journalistic formats with grassroots networks to promote and reinforce behavior change was adapted from the North Karelia Project, a community-level intervention to prevent coronary heart disease (Puska et al., 1985; McAlister et al., 1980). Together, the media modeling and community networking provided a practical and potentially powerful vehicle for influencing the theoretical factors underlying risk reduction behavior change.

This intervention protocol was adapted for the site-specific and population-specific interventions. Some variation in the application of the intervention protocol was expected and encouraged in order to more effectively tailor the specific interventions to local circumstances.

INTERVENTION MESSAGES AND MATERIALS

The behavioral intervention materials were in the form of small media, defined here as community newsletters, brochures, pamphlets, flyers, or baseball cards containing role-model stories (Corby et al., 1996). A role-model story is an authentic story about a person within the target community that is told in the person's own language, and describes the person's stimulus and/or motivation for initiating or considering a behavior change, the type of change begun, how barriers to change were overcome, and the reinforcing consequences of the change.

The role-model stories were drawn from interviews with members of the target populations and communities, and small media materials with new stories were produced approximately once a month. The selection of messages to be emphasized in role-model stories was guided by data collected from the study populations at each site. (Specifics of the data collection process are described later.) First, these data were used to determine the relative mix of role-model stories to be distributed in a community. For example, if survey data indicated that at one site most community members were in the Precontemplative Stage for a particular behavior, most of the site's stories dealing with that behavior highlighted a change from the Precontemplative to the Contemplative Stage. Second, specific theoretical factors or beliefs were highlighted if data analysis indicated they were correlated with intentions to change or stage of change. For example, if people who were in the Contemplative Stage for consistent condom use tended to believe that condom use reduces intimacy, whereas people who were in the Ready-for-Action Stage did not hold this belief, role-model stories would address intimacy issues. Over time, the relative mix of stories produced changed for each intervention; for example, more stories highlighted the Preparation or Action stages as data from a site indicated that the target population was moving along the SOC continuum. Thus, each site produced unique media materials with role-model stories for each of its intervention populations. These role-model stories were tailored to the local populations in that they were based on real stories of local residents and written to highlight specific stages of change and theoretical factors based on local data.

In addition to the role-model stories, small media also contained basic AIDS information, instructions on the use of condoms or bleach (to clean needles), biographies of community members participating in the project, notices of community events, or information on other health and social services, such as locations of homeless shelters or needle exchanges, schedules for free meals, mammogram screening, or drug and alcohol treatment services. It was believed that community interest in and support of the program would be increased by acknowledging and addressing other relevant community concerns.

MATERIALS DISTRIBUTION THROUGH NETWORKS

These small media materials, along with condoms and bleach kits, were delivered one-on-one to people in the community. The intervention materials were distributed in part by volunteer networks of peers from the target populations or communities (Guenther-Grey et al., 1992; Guenther-Grey et al., 1996; Simons et al., 1996). In all sites except New York, a second layer of networks consisted of businesspeople, community leaders, and other persons not considered "true" peers, but who were trusted by the target groups and interacted with them on a regular basis. These network members were known as "interactors." In addition to delivering the small media materials, condoms, and bleach, all network members focused the attention of the recipients on the role-model stories, and reinforced attempts to change as well as actual change in behavior. The use of role-model stories was a key component of the intervention, and peer network members who had made efforts toward lowering high risk behavior were encouraged to provide role-model stories in which they shared their personal stories and experiences with other community members.

Network members were recruited through contact with a project outreach worker, referral from another service organization, or referral from current or former network members. Several methods were used for maintaining the networks, including offering material incentives such as small amounts of cash, food, or movie coupons, t-shirts or buttons with the project logo; providing opportunities for recognition of the network members' achievements through awards or certificates of participation; picnics, and parties; and maintaining frequent contact between outreach workers and the network members in order to provide encouragement and reinforcement for their role. Project records indicate that the sites were able to recruit and retain network members from these disenfranchised communities to intervene with the target populations, and provide HIV prevention messages in their communities (Guenther-Grey et al., 1992; Guenther-Grey et al., 1996).

Depending on the site, peer network members would distribute materials alone, in pairs, or accompanied by a project outreach worker. In addition, the protocol for the intervention allowed projects to maintain storefronts either within or near the intervention neighborhoods. Three of the project sites chose to use storefronts (Dallas, Denver, New York). These convenient locations served as a focal point for project activities such as parties for assembling intervention materials, support group meetings for peer network members or for individuals living with HIV, health screening (HIV counseling and testing, sickle cell testing), and community events such as a commemoration of World AIDS Day (Simons et al., 1996).

PROCESS AND OUTCOME EVALUATION

The multisite joint evaluation protocol included both process and outcome evaluation components. Process evaluation measures examined the implementation and diffusion of the intervention throughout the target community to determine if the intervention was reaching individuals in the targeted groups. The project sites used the following process measures: records of network recruitment and retention, and the production and distribution of materials; interviews with key observers about the changes they saw in the community and among individuals in the target populations; and records of daily outreach activities. In addition, the Dallas project obtained unobtrusive measures of discarded condoms, bleach bottles, and small media intervention materials.

As "demonstration projects," the primary outcome evaluation question was whether or not the behavioral interventions could facilitate movement toward consistent condom and bleach use in the study areas in which the intervention was implemented. More specifically, the effectiveness of the intervention in moving people along one or more stage of change (SOC) continua was evaluated.

A common outcome evaluation design was used in each city. Three basic features of the design were: The intervention was implemented in one of two geographic areas, while the other area served as a comparison condition; cross-sectional surveys were conducted in both areas, before and after the intervention began; and a common set of behavioral and cognitive variables were measured in each area during each survey period. The outcome evaluation design is best viewed as a quasi-experimental design (Campbell & Stanley, 1966; Cook & Campbell, 1979) because individuals were not randomly assigned to intervention or comparison conditions. Instead, the assignment to a condition was based on a respondent's location in a given geographic area.

Although the behavioral intervention under study was community level, the two primary behavior change objectives involved the behaviors of individuals, namely: consistent condom use and consistent cleaning of shared injection equipment with bleach. To assess change in the community, the evaluation design collected data concerning sexual and injection drug behavior from samples of individuals in the study areas. Due to different community structures, the protocols for collecting these data vary somewhat by site. Generally speaking, however, "purposive" sampling was used (National Research Council, 1991, p. 326). Locations and times for interviewing were selected to reflect the best available information about the population under study in each community. In most communities, interviewers would go to a randomly determined location within the geographic area (be it treatment or comparison) identified during formative research. For each community, a sampling protocol was developed to provide for the random selelction of respondents and/or interview sites.

Baseline and outcome evaluation data were collected through periodic cross-sectional surveys, with interviews conducted face-to-face and usually taking place in outdoor locations. Interviewers were not part of the intervention teams, but they did know which areas were receiving the intervention. Interviewers received training to assure they were able to follow the sampling protocol and correctly administer the survey instrument.

Data Collection Instruments

To collect data from the study populations, the project sites developed an interview instrument, referred to as the Brief Street Interview (BSI). The first section of the BSI "screened" individuals to determine if they were eligible for the longer interview. Eligibility required the individual to report engaging in sexual intercourse or sharing injection equipment in the recent past (30 or 60 days). If eligible, the individual received the full BSI. BSI questions assessed where individuals were on the SOC continuum with respect to consistent condom use for vaginal or anal intercourse with main or other partners and with respect to always using bleach to clean needles for injection drug use (Schnell, Galavotti, Fishbein, & Chan, 1996). Early results indicated that, with the exception of MSM-ngi, too few respondents reported anal intercourse with main and/or occasional partners to yield statistically meaningful results, and most sites dropped this section for non-MSM populations. Additional questions assessed the four key theoretical factors (i.e., attitudes toward the behaviors, perceived norms, perceived risk, and perceived self-efficacy), exposure to HIV/AIDS information, exposure to the project intervention, and other indicators of risk-reducing behaviors (carrying a condom, getting tested for HIV). Names were not collected, and confidentiality was assured. Respondents were given small amounts of cash or fast food and grocery vouchers for participating.

Once the early implementation phase began, a second, more detailed interview schedule was developed. This instrument, known as the Coffee Shop Interview (CSI) assessed behavioral beliefs about the advantages and disadvantages of consistently using condoms and bleach, normative beliefs about the proscriptions of specific individuals or groups with respect to these behaviors, and efficacy beliefs concerning one's ability to perform these behaviors under various circumstances. After completing the BSI, respondents were offered an additional small incentive to complete the CSI. Approximately 80% of all respondents agreed to participate in the second interview.

Intervention Delivery and Data Collection

Generally speaking, data collection and behavioral interventions were implemented on the following schedule: Two waves of baseline data were collected from February 1991 through June 1991. The intervention began in each city in June or July 1991, following the completion of the baseline surveys. As this behavioral intervention continued, two to three waves of data were collected each year; data collection ended in the summer of 1994. For purposes of this report, the data were summarized into three time periods (phases). The first phase, or *baseline,* was the baseline period already discussed. The second phase, or *start-up,* ran from July 1991 through May 1992 and included data from the first three waves after the intervention began. The third phase, *early implementation,* ran from June 1992 through August 1993 and included the next three data collection waves. Although not included in this report, the *full implementation* phase began in September 1993 and included the two final waves of data collection. Thus, in total, there were 10 waves of data collection.

Removal of Repeat Interviews

Data were summarized according to the baseline, start-up, and early intervention phases. Within each community, records within a phase were eliminated if they matched a previous interview within the same phase on gender, race, or ethnic group, and location and date of birth.

PRELIMINARY FINDINGS

Test of the Theoretical Model

The theoretical model underlying the ACDP is presented in Fig. 9.1. As described earlier, four factors were viewed as potential determinants of intention and behavior: perceived risk, attitudes, norms, and self-efficacy. In order to test this theoretical model, data from both the BSI and CSI

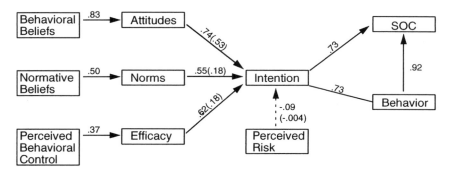

FIG. 9.1. AIDS Community Demonstration Projects: Condom use with main partner among men. Note: Numbers in parentheses are standardized regression weights.

are necessary. For illustrative purposes, data are presented from Wave 7, the first wave of data collection in which both the CSI and the BSI were administered. Figure 9.1 shows the Wave 7 interrelations among the theoretical variables with respect to males' consistent condom use for vaginal sex with their main partner. Consistent with expectations, men's intentions to "always use a condom for vaginal sex with my main partner *from now on*" are predicted with considerable accuracy ($r = .78$, $p < .001$). More specifically, attitudes ($r = .74$, $p < .001$; $\beta = .53$, $p < .001$), norms ($r = .55$, $p < .001$; $\beta = .18$, $p < .001$) and self-efficacy ($r = .62$, $p < .001$; $\beta = .18$, $p < .001$) all contribute significantly to an understanding of this behavior, although attitudes are clearly the most important determinant of this intention. In contrast to expectations based on the HBM however, perceived risk of acquiring AIDS ($r = -.09$; $\beta = -.004$) did not significantly influence the men's intentions to always use a condom for vaginal sex with their main partner.

Three other aspects of Fig. 9.1 are worth noting. First, as required by the SOC model, both behavior ($r = .92$, $p < .001$) and intention ($r = .73$, $p < .001$) contribute significantly to the SOC measure. Second, intentions are highly correlated with self-reported behavior ($r = .73$, $p < .001$). Finally, and consistent with expectations, attitudes, norms, and self-efficacy were significantly related to their underlying cognitive determinants. For example, beliefs about the consequences of "always using a condom for vaginal sex with my main partner" were significantly correlated with attitude ($r = .83$, $p < .001$), normative beliefs were significantly correlated with perceived normative pressure ($r = .50$, $p < .001$), and perceived control was found to be at least one of the factors underlying self-efficacy ($r = .37$, $p < .01$).

Such data provide guidance for the development of intervention materials. More specifically, analyses similar to the aforementioned were run in each site, and role-model stories were sought that focused on those variables that empirically had the strongest correlations with intentions and behavior.

Exposure to Project Peer Networks, Staff, and Materials

Effective delivery of the intervention to the target population is crucial to project success. Project efforts are directed toward saturating the community with prevention messages by optimizing the size and effectiveness of the peer network, engaging the cooperation of community businesses, and maximizing the allure of the message and the media through which it is distributed. Other factors that cannot be controlled by the project include characteristics of the community, such as attentiveness to prevention messages; the total number of people to be reached, and their accessibility; and migration into and out of the community. Generally speaking, these characteristics varied widely across the five cities and six types of populations involved in ACDP, and were reflected in the proportion of respondents who indicated they had been reached by project efforts.

Exposure to ACDP peer networks, staff, and materials was measured by a series of questions at the end of the Brief Street Interview (BSI). Every respondent was asked to describe HIV/AIDS materials they had seen in the community and persons who had spoken to them about AIDS. The time frame for each of these questions was "the last three months," and interviewers recorded information on up to four types of materials and three types of interpersonal contact. Responses were coded into various categories, including specific categories for exposure to ACDP materials, peer networks, staff, or storefronts (Guenther-Grey, Schnell, & Fishbein, 1995).

Respondents who spontaneously reported any exposure to ACDP materials, or who reported talking about AIDS with someone who could be identified with the ACDP, were classified as "exposed," and all others were considered "non-exposed." No distinction is made in this presentation between interpersonal contacts, such as talking with ACDP volunteers or staff, and contact with materials, such as reading a flyer or newsletter, picking up ACDP condoms or bleach kits, or visiting a storefront.

The proportions of respondents within each intervention community who reported any identifiable exposure to ACDP intervention efforts are presented by phase in Table 9.1. Exposure rates ranged from 1% to 17% during the start-up phase, and from 21% to 68% during the early implementation phase. These findings make it clear that community-level interventions, such as the ACDP, cannot be expected to have significant im-

TABLE 9.1
Exposure to ACDP Intervention by City,
Intervention Community, and Phase

City	Targeted Community	Start-Up Exposure Rates	Early Implementation Exposure Rates
Dallas	Two High STD Census Tracts	42/392 = 11%	126/414 = 30%
Denver	IDU	4/324 = 1%	60/249 = 24%
Long Beach	IDU	27/348 = 8%	178/322 = 55%
	FST	31/360 = 9%	203/300 = 68%
	FSP	11/162 = 7%	65/143 = 45%
New York	FSP	36/216 = 17%	92/212 = 43%
Seattle	MSM-ngi	2/124 = 2%	25/119 = 21%
	FST	22/165 = 13%	84/230 = 37%
	YHR	34/262 = 13%	61/263 = 23%

Note: IDU = injecting drug users; FSP = female sex partners of IDU; FST = female sex traders; MSM-ngi = men who have sex with men but who do not gay-identify; YHR = youth in high risk situations.

mediate impacts on behavior. Indeed, it took over a year before the intervention reached a substantial proportion of community members. Clearly, if the ACDP had ended after 12 months of intervention, only a small proportion of community members would have been exposed to intervention materials, and thus relatively little behavior change could have been expected.

CHANGES ASSOCIATED WITH ACDP

Success of the intervention was determined by the degree to which members of the target community moved along the Stages of Change continua toward the behavioral goals of consistent condom use for vaginal intercourse with main partners (SOC-VM), consistent condom use for vaginal intercourse with other partners (SOC-VO), and consistent bleach use when sharing works and needles (SOC-Bleach).

The quasi-experimental design of the ACDP, along with the measurement of exposure in the intervention areas, allows investigation of two issues:

1. Have intervention area respondents made more progress toward consistent condom or bleach use than comparison area respondents?
2. Were intervention area respondents who reported direct project exposure higher on the SOC scale, on average, than those who did not?

In the following discussion, the first comparison is referred to as the General Intervention Effect, and the second as the Specific Exposure Effect.

Analytical Methods

Following an empirically based algorithm (Schnell, Galavotti, Fishbein, & Chan, 1996), each individual was assigned to one of the five stages of change. More specifically, individuals were categorized as shown in Table 9.2. In the analyses described here, this stage of change measure (from 1 [Precontemplation] to 5 [Maintenance]) served as the main behavioral outcome measure (or dependent variable).

General linear models were used to evaluate the effectiveness of the ACDP intervention in moving communities toward consistent condom and bleach use. Three sets of analyses are presented: consistent condom use during vaginal intercourse with main partners (SOC-VM); consistent condom use during vaginal intercourse with other partners (SOC-VO); and consistent bleach use by IDU to clean shared injection equipment (SOC-

TABLE 9.2

Algorithm for Assigning Stage of Change for Consistent Condom Use[1]

Criterion	Stage of Change (SOC)				
	Pre-Contemplation (1)	Contemplation (2)	Preparation (3)	Action (4)	Maintenance (5)
Relative frequency of use[2]	—	—	sometimes or almost every time	every time	every time
Duration of "every time" use[3]	—	—	—	< 6 months	≥ 6 months
Immediate intention[4]	—	—	extremely/quite/slightly sure will	—	—
Future intention[5]	extremely/quite/slightly sure will	extremely/quite/slightly sure will	extremely/quite/slightly sure will	—	—

[1]Algorithm applied by starting with criteria necessary for Maintenance, then Action, etc.

[2]When you have (vaginal, anal) sex with . . . , how often do you use a condom? [every time, almost every time, sometimes, almost never, never]

[3]How long have you been using a condom (every time/almost every time) you have (vaginal/anal) sex with . . . ?

[4]How likely do you think it is that from now on you will use a condom every time . . . ? [extremely/quite/slightly sure I will, undecided, slightly/quite/extremely sure I won't]

[5]In the next six months, how likely do you think it is that you will start using condoms every time . . . ? [extremely/quite/slightly sure I will, undecided, slightly/quite/extremely sure I won't]

Bleach). In the following discussion, all analyses and figures reported include adjustments for city, target population (census tract, IDU, MSM-ngi, FST, FSP, and YHR), gender, race, ethnicity, and age.

Analysis of Covariance (ANCOVA). To determine whether the movement toward consistent condom use and consistent bleach use occurred more rapidly in the intervention areas than in comparison areas (the General Intervention Effect), time was coded as a continuous variable. Statistical significance was assessed by the Intervention-by-Time interaction term, with Intervention coded as 1 for intervention areas and 0 for Comparison areas, and Time coded as 0 for Baseline, 1 for Start-up, and 2 for Early Implementation.

Analysis of Variance Models (ANOVA). To measure the difference between intervention area respondents who reported exposure to the intervention and those who did not (the Specific Exposure Effect), time was coded as a categorical variable. Exposure to the ACDP intervention was measured by the dichotomous exposure variable ("exposed" and "nonexposed") already described. The small number of respondents reporting exposure at baseline or in comparison areas were reclassified as nonexposed. Statistical significance was assessed using this resulting dichotomous exposure term, which represents the difference after baseline between respondents in the intervention areas who report exposure and those who do not.

All mean SOC values referred to in the text and presented in graphs were calculated as population marginal means (Searle, Speed, & Milliken, 1980). These are the mean values that would have been expected if the demographics and community origins of survey respondents had been the same between intervention and comparison areas, and had remained constant across the three phases.

Although linear models are designed for interval-level outcome data, their application to ordinal-level outcomes such as the Stage of Change construct is considered a reasonable strategy if the ordinal nature of the outcome variable is due to crude measurement of an underlying continuous variable (Agresti, 1984, p. 150). Logistic analysis is designed for ordinal-level outcome variables but does not translate as succinctly as linear methods to graphics and text. However, results of analogous logistic models were very similar to those obtained from the linear models.

Results

Condom Use for Vaginal Sex with Main Partner. Overall mean SOC for condom use during vaginal intercourse with main partners (SOC-VM) is presented in Fig. 9.2. The total number of respondents represented in this

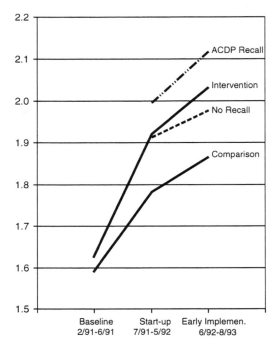

FIG. 9.2. SOC–VM. Intervention > Comparison trend (p = 0.095); ACDP recall > No recall (p = 0.029).

graph is 7,194, and the smallest number used to calculate any given mean value is 156 for treatment area respondents reporting exposure at phase 2 (start-up). The majority (n = 4,204, 58%) of respondents were female, of whom the largest proportion were FSPs (n = 1,755, 42%). Among 2,992 male respondents, the largest proportion were IDUs (n = 1,078, 36%).

At baseline, the mean SOC-VM value in the intervention area (1.63) is only slightly higher than the mean value in the comparison area (1.59). These values indicate that, on average, respondents were initially between the Precontemplation and Contemplation stages for the adoption of consistent condom use during vaginal intercourse with their main partner. As of early implementation, the mean SOC-VM of 2.03 (the Contemplation Stage, i.e., intending to start using condoms consistently in the next 6 months) among intervention area respondents was higher than the value of 1.87 (slightly below the Contemplation Stage) in the comparison areas, but this General Intervention Effect only approached statistical significance ($p < .10$).

Among intervention area respondents who reported vaginal intercourse with a main partner in the previous 30 days, 9.6% reported exposure to the ACDP during the start-up phase, and 39.3% as of Early Implementation.

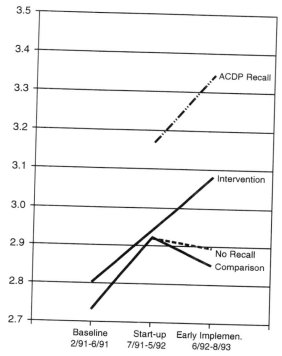

FIG. 9.3. SOC–VO. Intervention > Comparison trend ($p = 0.024$); ACDP
Recall > No Recall ($p = 0.0001$).

The Specific Exposure Effect was significant ($p < .05$), indicating that, on
average, those in the intervention area who were exposed to the intervention made significantly more progress toward consistent condom use with
their main partners (mean SOC = 2.12) than did those not exposed (mean
SOC = 1.98).

Condom Use for Vaginal Sex with Other Partners. Overall mean SOC for
condom use during vaginal intercourse with other partners (SOC-VO) is
presented in Fig. 9.3. The smallest number used to calculate any given
mean value was 112 (for treatment area respondents reporting exposure
during the start-up phase), with a total of 6,184 respondents represented
in this graph. Respondents were almost evenly split between male ($n =$
3,097, 50%) and female ($n = 3,087$, 50%). The largest proportion of male
respondents were IDU ($n = 1,142$, 37%), and the majority of women were
sex traders ($n = 2,278$, 74%).

At baseline, the mean values were similar: The mean SOC-VO was 2.80
for the intervention areas and 2.73 for the comparison areas. Note that
these means are considerably higher than those with respect to SOC-VM,

indicating that even at baseline, respondents, on average, were significantly closer to adopting consistent condom use with occasional partners or clients, than they were to adopting consistent condom use with their main partners. Indeed, whereas on average, respondents were midway between precontemplation and contemplation with respect to condom use with their main partner, they were close to being in the ready-for-action stage when it came to consistent condom use with occasional partners. One implication of this is that although intentional change may be sufficient to move people along the SOC-VM continuum, behavioral change would be required to move people with respect to SOC-VO.

As of early implementation, the mean SOC-VO had risen to 3.08 among respondents in the intervention areas, compared to the value of 2.85 in the comparison areas; this General Intervention Effect for SOC-VO was statistically significant ($p < .05$). Among intervention area respondents who reported vaginal intercourse with a nonmain partner in the previous 30 days, 7.7% reported ACDP exposure during the start-up phase, and 40.8% as of Early Implementation.

The Specific Exposure Effect was highly significant ($p < .001$). Once again, within the treatment area, community members exposed to the intervention were significantly closer to adopting consistent condom use for vaginal sex with their "other" partners (mean SOC = 3.34) than were those not exposed (mean SOC = 2.97). As already indicated, this implies that the intervention had an impact on behavior as well as on intention.

Bleach Use for Cleaning Injection Equipment. Figure 9.4 presents results for changes in the mean SOC for the use of bleach to clean injection equipment (SOC-Bleach). Respondents who reported sharing needles or works in the last 60 days were assessed for this behavior regardless of whether they were solicited as part of an IDU target community, or if they were encountered elsewhere among sex traders, MSM-ngi, street youth, or designated census tracts (by definition, FSPs did not inject). Figure 9.5 represents 3,086 such respondents, of whom 2,028 (66%) were male and 1,058 (34%) were female. As in previous examples, the smallest number of respondents used to calculate a given mean is among start-up respondents reporting exposure ($n = 53$).

The baseline mean value of 2.91 in the intervention areas was greater than the mean of 2.65 for the comparison areas. As of early implementation, the SOC-Bleach mean had increased to 3.11 among respondents in the intervention areas, but decreased to 2.53 in the comparison areas; this General Intervention Effect was statistically significant ($p < .005$). In other words, whereas respondents in the comparison areas, on average, remained between the Contemplation and Preparation stages, those in the intervention areas moved on average to a point slightly above the Preparation Stage, indicating an increase in bleach use.

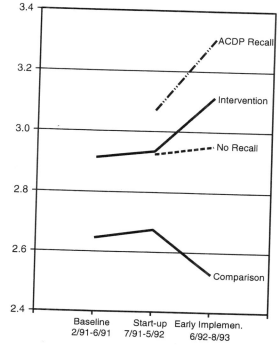

FIG. 9.4. SOC–Bleach. Intervention > Comparison trend ($p = 0.002$); ACDP Recall > No Recall ($p = 0.001$).

Among intervention area respondents who reported sharing works or needles in the previous 60 days, 6.7% reported ACDP exposure during the start-up phase, and 45.7% as of Early Implementation. Similar to the analyses for condom use, intervention area respondents who reported exposure to project materials (Early Implementation mean = 3.31) were farther along the SOC continuum toward consistent bleach use than the group not exposed (Early Implementation mean = 2.95); this Specific Exposure Effect was also significant ($p = .001$).

CONCLUSIONS

Contrary to a pervasive pessimism in public health about individuals' ability to change risk behavior (Galavotti & Beeker, 1993), these initial findings indicate that many individuals who are at high risk for sexually transmitted or needle-borne infections can be influenced to form intentions to perform, and to adopt, protective behaviors. The preliminary data presented here are encouraging.

The history of recording behavior change in HIV prevention research has typically been that of documenting dichotomous "yes" or "no" or "all-or-nothing" measures. In contrast to this practice, the Stages of Change Model indicates that behavior change takes time and often occurs in relatively small steps. By using the Stage of Change algorithm to examine these movements, it is possible to document important changes that could be overlooked if one were to rely only on assessing behavior as a dichotomous variable. The shifts that occur in a community at large can be seen more clearly as they respond to an ever-present, medium-intensity intervention (as compared with a high intensity but low frequency intervention such as an individual HIV prevention counseling session). As HIV prevention programs are shifting toward a model of comprehensive intervention strategies (which may include a variety of interventions ranging from those delivered in clinic settings to those delivered on the streets of a community), it is important to note the contribution of a community-level intervention.

The preliminary results presented in this chapter provide only a comprehensive overview of the impact of the interventions on progress toward consistent condom and bleach use. Recall that in order to promote change in these behaviors, the intervention messages focused on cognitive variables such as self-efficacy, perceptions of social norms, and attitudes toward behavioral performance. More in-depth analyses should also reveal an impact on these variables.

Furthermore, whereas the previous analyses include adjustments for demographics, city, and type of community, they represent only the comprehensive perspective of the projects. Thorough site-specific and population specific analyses will be conducted when data are available from the full intervention phase.

In summary, this chapter has described the design and methods of the CDC-sponsored AIDS Community Demonstration Projects. Preliminary results were presented for consistent condom use under two circumstances: vaginal intercourse with main partners and vaginal intercourse with other partners. Consistent bleach use for cleaning shared injection equipment was also examined. In each case, individuals in the intervention area who reported specific exposure to the ACDP intervention showed significantly more movement toward consistent protective behavior than those who did not report exposure. For SOC-VO and SOC-Bleach, the specific exposure effect was strong enough to be significant even when diluted among all intervention area respondents in contrast to comparison area respondents. These results clearly indicate that theory-based, community-level interventions using community volunteers can be an effective tool in the fight against HIV transmission.

ACKNOWLEDGMENTS

Portions of this chapter were initially published in "Community Level Prevention of HIV Infection Among High-Risk Populations: The AIDS Community Demonstration Projects," *MMWR Recommendations and Reports,* 1996, *45*, RR-6. This chapter also appears in S. Oskamp & S. C. Thompson (Eds.), *Understanding and Preventing HIV Risk Behavior: Safer Sex and Drug Use,* 1996, pp. 177–206, Thousand Oaks, CA: Sage.

REFERENCES

Agresti, A. (1984). *Analysis of ordinal categorical data.* New York: Wiley.

Ajzen, I., & Fishbein, M. (1980). *Understanding attitudes and predicting social behavior.* Englewood Cliffs, NJ: Prentice-Hall.

Bandura, A. (1986). *Social foundations of thought and action: A social cognitive theory.* Englewood Cliffs, NJ: Prentice-Hall.

Bandura, A. (1992). Exercise of personal agency through the self-efficacy mechanism. In R. Schwarzer (Ed.), *Self-efficacy: Thought control of action* (pp. 3–38). Washington, DC: Hemisphere.

Bandura, A. (1994). Social cognitive theory and exercise of control over HIV infection. In R. J. DiClemente & J. L. Peterson (Eds.), *Preventing AIDS: Theories and methods of behavioral interventions* (pp. 1–20). New York: Plenum.

Becker, M. H. (1974). The health belief model and personal health behavior. *Health Education Monographs, 2,* 324–508.

Becker, M. H. (1988). AIDS and behavior change. *Public Health Reviews, 16,* 1–11.

Campbell, D. T., & Stanley, J. C. (1966). *Experimental and quasi-experimental designs for research.* Chicago: Rand McNally.

Cook, T. D., & Campbell, D. T. (1979). *Quasi-experimentation.* Boston: Houghton-Mifflin.

Corby, N. H., Enguidanos, S. M., & Kay, L. (1996). Development and use of role-model stories in a community-level AIDS risk reduction intervention. *Public Health Reports, 111* Supplement 1, 54–58.

Fishbein, M., & Ajzen, I. (1975). *Belief, attitude, intention and behavior: An introduction to theory and research.* Redding, MA: Addison-Wesley.

Fishbein, M., Bandura, A., Triandis, H. C., Kanfer, F. H., Becker, M. H., & Middlestadt, S. E. (1992). *Factors influencing behavior and behavior change: Final report.* Rockville, MD: National Institute of Mental Health.

Fishbein, M., Middlestadt, S. E., & Hitchcock, P. J. (1991). Using information to change sexually transmitted disease-related behaviors: An analysis based on the theory of reasoned action. In J. N. Wasserheit, S. O. Aral, & K. K. Holmes (Eds.), *Research issues in human behavior and sexually transmitted diseases in the AIDS era* (pp. 243–257). Washington, DC: American Society for Microbiology.

Galavotti, C., & Beeker, C. (1993). Changing HIV risk behaviors: The case against pessimism [letter to the editor]. *American Journal of Public Health, 83,* 1791.

Goldbaum, G., Perdue, K. H., & Higgins, D. L. (1996). Non-gay identifying men who have sex with men: Formative research results from Seattle, Washington. *Public Health Reports, 111* Supplement 1, 36–40.

Guenther-Grey, C., Noroian, D., Fonseka, J., Higgins, D. L., & the AIDS Community Demonstration Projects (1996). Developing community networks to deliver HIV prevention interventions: Lessons learned from the AIDS Community Demonstration Projects. *Public Health Reports, 111* Supplement 1, 41–49.

Guenther-Grey, C., Schnell, D., & Fishbein, M. (1995). Sources of HIV/AIDS information among female sex traders. *Health Education Quarterly, 10*(3), 385–390.

Guenther-Grey, C., Tross, S., McAlister, A., Freeman, A., Cohn, D., Corby, N., Wood, R., & Fishbein, M. (1992). AIDS community demonstration projects: Implementation of volunteer networks for HIV-prevention programs—Selected sites, 1991–1992. *Morbidity & Mortality Weekly Report, 41,* 868–869, 875–876.

Harris, M. (1990). Emics and etics revisited. In N. Thomas, K. L. Pike, & M. Harris (Eds.), *Emics and etics: The insider/outsider debate* (pp. 48–61). Newbury Park, CA: Sage.

Higgins, D. L., O'Reilly, K. O., Tashima, N., Crain, C., Beeker, C., Goldbaum, G., Elifson, C. S., Galavotti, C., Guenther-Grey, C., & The AIDS Community Demonstration Projects (1996). Using formative research to lay the foundation for community-level HIV prevention efforts: An example from the AIDS Community Demonstration Projects. *Public Health Reports, 111* Supplement 1, 28–35.

McAlister, A. (1991). Population behavior change: A theory-based approach. *Journal of Public Health Policy, 12,* 345–361.

McAlister, A. (in press). Behavioral journalism: Beyond the marketing model for health communication. *American Journal of Health Promotion.*

McAlister, A., Puska, P., Koskela, K., Pallonen, U., & Maccoby, N. (1980). Mass communication and community organization for public health education. *American Psychologist, 35,* 375–379.

National Research Council (1991). *Evaluating AIDS prevention programs (expanded edition).* Washington, DC: National Academy Press.

O'Reilly, K., & Higgins, D. L. (1991). AIDS community demonstration projects for HIV prevention among hard-to-reach groups. *Public Health Reports, 106*(6), 714–720.

Prochaska, J. O., DiClemente, C. C., & Norcross, J. C. (1992). In search of how people change: Applications to addictive behaviors. *American Psychologist, 47,* 1102–1114.

Puska, P., Salonen, J. T., Koskela, K., McAlister, A., Kottke, T. E., Maccoby, W., & Farquhar, J. W. (1985). The community-based strategy to prevent coronary heart disease: Conclusions from 10 years of the North Karelia project. *Annual Review of Public Health, 6,* 147–193.

Rosenstock, I. M. (1974). The health belief model and preventive health behavior. *Health Education Monographs, 2,* 354–385.

Schnell, D. J., Galavotti, C., Fishbein, M., Chan, D., & The AIDS Community Demonstration Projects (1996). Measuring the adoption of consistent use of condoms using the stages of change model. *Public Health Reports, 111* Supplement 1, 59–68.

Searle, S. R., Speed, F. M., & Milliken, G. A. (1980). Population marginal means in the linear model: An alternative to least squares means. *The American Statistician, 34,* 216–221.

Simons, P. Z., Rietmeijer, C. A., Kane, M. S., Guenther-Grey, C., Higgins, D. L., & Cohn, D. L. (1996). Building a peer network among injecting drug users in Five Points, Denver: Implementation of a community-level HIV prevention program. *Public Health Reports, 111* Supplement 1, 50–53.

Chapter 10

Advertising Affordable Contraceptives: The Social Marketing Experience

Philip D. Harvey
DKT International, Washington, DC

The social marketing of contraceptives in developing countries has been remarkably successful in the past 30 years. Currently, 50 developing countries have contraceptive social marketing (CSM) programs in operation and these programs are providing contraceptive protection to nearly 14 million couples in Asia, Africa, and Latin America (DKT, 1996). Further, these programs are highly cost-effective, providing contraceptives at a remarkably low cost per couple served.

Social marketing has proven to be very flexible in responding to new situations. This has been most notable in Africa where government policies concerning the advertising and marketing of contraceptives changed radically and quickly in the late 1980s in response to the AIDS epidemic. Programs were soon implemented in more than a dozen African countries in response to this change in policy, with dramatic results. In 1994, more than 100 million condoms were sold through social marketing in sub-Saharan Africa, an area where this approach was virtually unknown before 1989.

The bad news is that these programs could be doing much more. Social marketing methodology is now well known. If all the world's major developing countries were host to contraceptive social marketing programs as effective as the projects in Bangladesh and Colombia (neither of which provides a particularly auspicious environment), then CSM programs would be serving 34 million couples in South Central and Southeast Asia alone (vs. today's 7 million), plus 9 million couples in Latin America (vs. today's 1.7 million), and a rapidly growing number in Africa.

147

Why then is contraceptive social marketing realizing less than a quarter of its demonstrated potential? And why has it not caught on as a means of preventing unwanted pregnancies and the transmission of HIV in the industrialized countries?

This chapter examines some of the fundamental characteristics of successful contraceptive social marketing, as well as the reasons why these programs have worked so well in certain instances, and less well in others. It also explores lessons on how social marketing can be improved and how new programs may be most effectively started.

WHAT IS CONTRACEPTIVE SOCIAL MARKETING?

Social marketing has been described to embrace everything from the spread of useful information such as that required in a metrification campaign to the subsidized sale of beneficial products such as contraceptives, oral rehydration salts, or even iodized salt. The Smoky the Bear forest fire campaign was a major effort in the United States to help mold safer behavior by people in the forests; nutritionally fortified foods have been marketed for deliberate nutritional benefit in many countries (Manoff, 1985).

The social marketing of contraceptives, somewhat ungrammatically referred to as contraceptive social marketing (CSM), has been one of the most consistent successes in the social marketing panoply. CSM, as implemented in developing countries, consists of the sale of subsidized (usually highly subsidized), branded contraceptives that are sold through widespread, established retail outlets using standard distribution and wholesaling networks. The CSM products are backed by mass media advertising. Brand-focused advertising is always a key component of such programs and it is sometimes accompanied by generic advertising about birth control and/or about specific methods.

The organizational components of a contraceptive social marketing program include a core management group dedicated to the management of the CSM activity, a distribution company or group of wholesalers, and an advertising agency. The marketing effort is usually assisted by one or more market research firms that help with brand name selection and the conduct of research that helps guide pricing and advertising decisions.

CSM programs have always involved the sale of a branded contraceptive product. These products have most often been condoms (*RAJA*, Bangladesh; *PANTHER*, Jamaica; *PRUDENCE*, West Africa and Brazil; *TRUST*, Philippines and Vietnam; *NIRODH*, India) and/or oral contraceptives (*OVACON, CHOICE, EUGYNON*), but have also included injectable contraceptives, IUDs, and spermicidal foaming tablets. More than 50 subsidized brands of condoms have been supported by social marketing budgets in more than 40 countries in the past 20 years; major international donors—the U.S. Agency for International Development (USAID), the German Kreditanstalt für Wiederaufbau (KfW), and the British Overseas Development Administration (ODA)—have supported brand advertising for these products.

The results, within limits, have been surprisingly consistent and positive. Whenever an adequately funded and reasonably energetic effort has been made to establish subsidized contraceptives through social marketing in any country, that effort has succeeded at least moderately well. There appears to be no society and no economy—even highly socialized economies—where this approach cannot be made to work. The fact that CSM has so far been largely confined to developing countries, and has not caught hold in the industrialized countries, is more a function of political barriers, lack of commitment, and the high cost of mass media than any inherent incompatibility of the approach with the more advanced economies. Further, poor program performance in LDCs has generally been the result of inappropriate management structure (e.g., management by the government as in India), or bad policy decisions (e.g., overpricing the contraceptives as in Mexico) rather than any inherent incompatibility of these projects with the economic, political, or cultural environments in which they operate.

CSM Is Highly Cost Effective

Traditional approaches to delivering family planning have cost around $18 per couple year of protection (Gillespie et al., 1989). (A couple years of protection, or CYP, consists of the supply of adequate contraceptives to fully protect one couple from pregnancy for 1 year; see Harvey & Snyder, 1987.) The cost of CSM programs, on the other hand, has traditionally fallen in the range of $2 to $8 per CYP, much less expensive than most clinic-based approaches to family planning, with the exception of sterilization, which is also highly cost-effective (Barberis & Harvey, in press; Huber & Harvey, 1989).

WHAT MAKES SOCIAL MARKETING PROGRAMS WORK, AND WHY DO THEY FAIL OR FALL SHORT?

The reasons for failure do not appear to be political, cultural, religious, or economic. Social marketing programs have demonstrated their effectiveness in a wide variety of such environments—from Catholic Colombia and the Philippines to Muslim Bangladesh to the very different cultural and economic climates of Jamaica, Egypt, and Zambia (to name just a few).

Social marketing works when there is a dedicated management team, operating in the private sector, with adequate funding to enable (and management wisdom to implement) pricing of the contraceptive products at levels that are truly affordable by the lower socioeconomic groups in the countries where these programs operate. Also essential are commercial distribution structures and mass media campaigns that reach large numbers of people with at least simple messages about the contraceptive products available.

Projects fail when they become too politicized. This often happens due to excessive government involvement (as has happened from time to time in Ghana, Egypt, and Pakistan, for example); when they are de-funded or when funds are sharply curtailed (as has happened in Mexico, Zaire, and Sri Lanka); or when program managers, by necessity or otherwise, price their contraceptives out of reach of low income people. The latter may result in small (and often shrinking) projects, as has happened in Mexico and Thailand, with condoms in Indonesia, and in Zimbabwe. Some of these problems can be avoided; some cannot.

Pricing

The issue of pricing contraceptives in developing country social marketing programs has been rigorously documented (Ciszewski & Harvey, 1994, 1995; Harvey, 1994; Lewis, 1986). The overall conclusion is that a year's supply of contraceptives should cost less than 1% of per-capita gross national product. This figure can be refined with the World Bank "Purchasing Power per-capita" (PPC) tables. Normally, a year's supply of contraceptives should cost no more than .25% of PPC. Analysis of the cost of everyday consumer items (like a cup of tea or a single cigarette), as well as coinage denominations, must also be considered.

Economies of Scale

Social marketing has clearly demonstrated that it is a more effective technique in larger markets than in smaller ones. One of CSM's secrets is that it is able to reach very large numbers of people in a very short period of time (DKT International, 1990). When the size of market is limited, particularly countries with populations of less than 5 million, cost per couple-year-of-protection is inevitably higher—often much higher—than in similar programs in larger markets. Figure 10.1 shows this fairly dramatically. The cost-efficiency of 21 social marketing programs in 1994 is plotted on the vertical axis, with lowest costs (most efficient) near the bottom. The size of market (population) of these projects is plotted on the horizontal axis, with populations ranging from a low of 3.2 million in the Central African

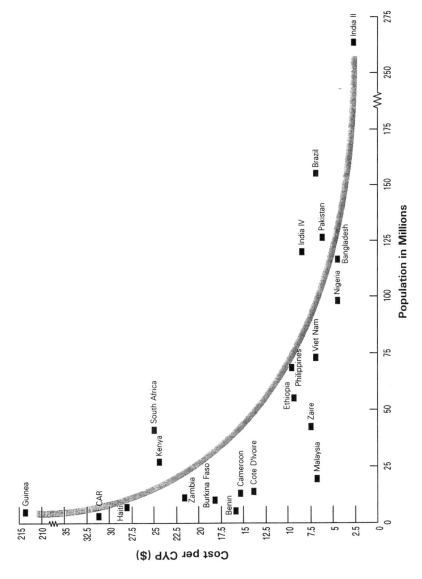

FIG. 10.1. Costs per CYP and population, selected social marketing programs, 1994.

151

Republic (CAR) to a high of 260 million (India II's North Indian market). As can be seen, there is a powerful correlation between market size (population) and cost-efficiency. The most expensive programs, with costs ranging from $15 to $200 per CYP, are all in small counties, whereas the larger countries (over 50 million) all have costs per CYP of $10 or less. Even when controlled for age of program, this correlation is strong, suggesting that social marketers should focus on large markets, other things being equal.

Elements of Social Marketing

The implementation of contraceptive social marketing programs over the past 25 years has established the following critical components of a successful CSM effort:

- A small management team operating flexibly and autonomously within the private sector.
- A distribution company or wholesaling/reselling network serving large numbers of retail outlets with branded consumer goods.
- An effective sales staff working on a commercial commission scale. When necessary project sales staff can replace to a very considerable extent distributor/wholesalers.
- An advertising agency or other company capable of designing an aggressive yet culturally sensitive campaign.
- A reasonable degree of support (or at least no objection) from the host government.
- Adequate funding to permit the contraceptives to be made available to the low income segment of the target market. This means both low pricing and aggressive distribution so that the contraceptives are convenient to buy as well as affordable.

ADVERTISING

A key to successful social marketing of contraceptives is successful advertising. The same laws that apply to the advertising of consumer-goods products anywhere apply equally to the advertising of subsidized contraceptives in developing countries. The advertiser must offer a benefit and impart useful information. In fact, contraceptives are remarkably amenable to classical advertising treatment because a product that permits people to space and plan pregnancies answers a remarkably large number of ordinary human needs. More than 50 years ago, Victor Schwab identified things people want,[1] of which a very substantial number can be satisfied to one degree or another by contraceptives. Planned pregnancies mean better control of a family budget and thus more money available to the family unit; spaced births lead to better education for a family's children; spaced pregnancies improve the health of both the children and the mother(Population Reference Bureau, 1986); and so on.

Product Advertising Versus Ideas Advertising

Social marketing programs promoting the use of a product have distinct advantages over programs attempting to change behavior through the promulgation of ideas and arguments. Perhaps the most critical of these advantages is measurability. If increased use of contraceptives (i.e., higher contraceptive prevalence) is the objective of a social marketing program, and subsidized, good quality contraceptives can be made conveniently and ubiquitously available, then the sales of project contraceptives provide an immediate and clear way of measuring the effectiveness of an advertising campaign.

It is difficult to exaggerate the importance of this point. Most programs designed to alleviate poverty or advance social aims are extremely hard to measure and the result is frequently inefficiency and even undetected failure. When a socially motivated program, on the other hand, depends on the sale of products, those sales can be quickly measured. The sales, in the case of contraceptives, can be converted into a common measurement yardstick called couple years of protection (CYPs) and the relative cost-effectiveness of various programs quickly assessed. The tabulation of CYPs from sales statistics is not sufficient for measuring everything we need to know about the impact of family planning programs. This requires follow-up surveys to determine contraceptive prevalence—that is, the rate of contraceptive use in the society as measured by surveys of scientifically selected samples of the population. But sales statistics are an excellent proxy for the family planning "bottom line" and they tell us a great deal about relative program efficiency very quickly (Harvey & Snyder, 1987). For example, Table 10.1 outlines DKT International's contraceptive social marketing program performance in 1994. The figures in this table can be usefully compared with the results of other family planning approaches as well as other CSM programs operated by other organizations. These data can also be used to analyze the relative strengths and weaknesses of each individual DKT program and, by inference, the skills and abilities of program managers and staff. The Vietnam project, for example, is highly efficient at $6.90 per

---

[1]Schwab's list: People want better health, more money, greater popularity, improved appearance, security in old age, praise from others, more comfort, more leisure, pride of accomplishment, business and social advancement, increased enjoyment (Simon, 1987).

TABLE 10.1
DKT International Costs and Results (1994)

Country	Sales		CYPs	Total Costs	Cost Per CYP
Brazil	11,568,009	condoms	115,680	$797,251	$ 6.89
Ethiopia	17,293,221	condoms	172,932	$1,608,825	$ 9.30
Bombay/India	2,272,183	condoms		$595,402	$ 8.42
	564,408	pills	70,688		
Malaysia	5,653,440	condoms	56,534	$382,544	$ 6.77
Philippines	7,836,498	condoms		$837,564	$ 9.56
	120,432	pills	87,629		
Uganda	655,088	condoms	6,551	$190,641	$29.10
Vietnam	7,202,268	condoms	72,023	$497,292	$ 6.90
HQ expenses				$394,090	
Total			582,037	$5,303,609	$ 9.11

CYP. The strength of this program is even more impressive when considering that the Vietnam program was only in its third year. Costs per couple in the first 3 or 4 years of social marketing programs tend to be high because of start-up expenses. Contrariwise, the Uganda program is very inefficient at $29 per couple per year. This efficiency ratio is one of the reasons that prompted DKT to close its Uganda operation in early 1995.

Brand Advantage

In addition to this critical aspect of measurability, there are a number of other reasons why it is easier to promote and sell branded products than to attempt to achieve similar objectives through a generic campaign. A few of these reasons are:

- Brands convey quality, build confidence.
- Brands invite (useful) comparative claims.
- Brand names, especially for condoms, can become generic and facilitate purchase.
- Promoting branded products never seems—and is not—patronizing.
- Branding permits market segmentation and image building.
- Branded products are easier to keep stocked at retail, making them more convenient.
- Brand advertising subsumes the advantages (benefits) of the entire category.
- Brands help define and focus a campaign.
- Brands may be amenable to plays on words.

First, brand advertising conveys quality. Although many individuals know intellectually that generic brands of some products are likely to be just as good as advertised brands, they still tend to believe that an advertised brand is of higher quality. In the case of condoms, for example, they are likely to think that *Trojans* or—in Bangladesh—*Raja* condoms are significantly superior to "condoms," particularly if the latter are supplied by the government or other social agency.

Second, brand advertising lends itself to comparative descriptions, which further impute quality: "Use *Trust*, the Strong Reliable Condom" sets *Trust* apart from run-of-the-mill products in the same category and creates a good spearhead for a campaign.

Third, in the case of condoms particularly, a heavily advertised brand can become generic, especially in underdeveloped economies like Vietnam and Ethiopia, with the result that embarrassment at point-of-purchase can be lessened. A successful campaign in the Philippines, for example, was built around the slogan "Don't Say Condoms, Just Say *Trust*." Similarly, the *Nirodh* in India, *Raja* in Bangladesh, and *Hiwot* in Ethiopia have reached the level of generic terminology that provides definite point-of-purchase advantages. It is less embarrassing to ask for *Trust* or *Hiwot* than for "condoms," in part because these brands *are* heavily advertised.

Brand promotions do not patronize. An important and often overlooked point about brand advertising is that it positions contraceptives in the marketplace as normal consumer products, rather than something the government (or someone else) is promoting as socially useful. Of course, good message advertising, with no product, need not be patronizing either, but it easily can be and often is, whereas brand advertising strongly discourages this tendency. Most governments tend to be patronizing anyway, and when they advocate family planning (or, of even less interest to consumers, population control) their campaigns and viewpoint are often seen by consumers as an imposition rather than a benefit. Thus, the Indian government campaign over many years relied on the slogan "Two or Three Children Are Enough." This struck many ordinary Indian citizens as being quite beside the point when it came to their own lives and reproductive habits. The same government unit has promoted *Nirodh* brand condoms as "The Safe Way to Love," a slogan that suggests a real consumer benefit. Also compare "Until You Want Another Child, Rely on *Preethi*," which was a successful brand advertising slogan for contraceptives in Sri Lanka. The latter conveys a substantial benefit to the consumer, whereas the "Two or Three Children" slogan is preachy and much less likely to have a useful impact. In summary, it is very hard to write a social marketing ad promoting a behavior ("Quit Smoking," "Buckle Up," "Have Only Two Children") without conveying to consumers the sense that they are being asked to do something that someone else thinks is good for them. The promotion of a branded product, on the other hand, easily lends itself to, indeed strongly encourages, a 100% consumer orientation.

Branding facilitates market segmentation and image building. For example, in the Bangladesh project, the *Raja* condom was well-established as Bangladesh's "mainstream" condom brand and then the *Sensation* brand was introduced at a higher price to appeal to a more upscale market. (As is frequently the case, the "upscale" characteristics also appealed to low income markets in that country.) Branding also facilitates image making. If the *Sensation* condom is associated with the good life in an urban setting (TV ads featured a well-to-do Bangladeshi man getting into a Mercedes), then this not only imparts quality to the product but, at the same time, contains the important message that even the wealthiest and best educated in society use condoms and their lives are the better for it. Similarly, some condoms may be associated with sex and sensuality (the *Panther* brand in the Philippines; the *Kama Sutra* brand in India. See Fig. 10.2). This expands the market, particularly in the context of AIDS prevention.

It is much easier to keep branded products stocked in retail outlets. One of the great advantages of social marketing as a way of providing family planning is that it makes the product convenient. In Bangladesh, for example, the *Raja* condom is available in more than 120,000 retail outlets—major pharmacies, tiny stalls, or even crate-top "stores" offering

FIG. 10.2. Some condom brands, especially in marketing campaigns for AIDS prevention, are associated with sexuality. *Panther* (Philippines) and *Kama Sutra* (India) are two such brands.

only condoms and cigarettes. The retail trade is strongly influenced by mass media advertising and it is much easier to persuade retailers to buy and stock branded products than generics, if for no other reason because this is what storekeepers expect.

Brand advertising subsumes the benefits of the entire category. When promoting a categorical benefit ("Use condoms to space your children"), copywriters do not have the luxury of particularized brand advantages ("Use *Zaroor* condoms to space your children; *Zaroor* is manufactured to ISO 4074 standards"). But there is nothing in the brand promotion to prevent taking full advantage of the generic benefit. If using condoms conveys a benefit, then using a particularly good condom conveys an even greater benefit.

A campaign dealing with brands like the *Raja* condom or *Choice* oral contraceptive helps define organizational activity and focuses that activity in such a way as to significantly increase the use of those brands. Brand names generate their own ideas and identities and facilitate the creative process.

Brand names can also be selected and described so as to impart desired qualities or attributes, which may include the use of plays on words. The *Prudence* brand in Brazil, for example, has been incorporated into slogans that make effective use of the meaning of that word ("Use *Prudence*, it may save your life.").

For these reasons, and the all-important matter of measurability, social marketing programs focused on brands have usually succeeded better than family planning campaigns built around ideas alone.

SUCCESSFUL CAMPAIGNS

The contraceptive social marketing campaigns in the Philippines and Vietnam are two interesting examples of how CSM advertising campaigns can evolve in differing market environments.

One of the lessons of these, as well as many other social marketing initiatives, is that simplicity is often more effective than complicated "creative" approaches, which often obfuscate the underlying message. But, simplicity is also difficult to maintain. Creative people (particularly in advertising agencies) have a persistent tendency to aim for award-winning campaigns and advertisements that draw attention to the advertising rather than persuading people to use products. As Ogilvy (1963) has pointed out, this is and will probably always remain one of the great sins of advertising agencies everywhere.

The Philippines

The evolution of the campaign in the Philippines for *Trust* condoms is an interesting illustration of getting back to basics. This condom was originally positioned in 1990–1991 as a safe and economical means for birth spacing, targeting lower income married couples. The campaign focused on condom use as the means to a healthier, happier life, also emphasizing financial security. Later ads depicted negative images (always risky in advertising) such as shanty towns and empty pockets representing the consequences of *not* using *Trust* (see Fig. 10.3).

Results of this early campaign were desultory. Although *Trust* sales continued to grow slowly, research revealed some confusion in the marketplace and the entire campaign was subsequently re-thought. Sales graphs (Fig. 10.4) through 1992 reveal unacceptably slow rates of growth.

For these and related reasons, a complete overhaul was undertaken in early 1993. Project managers knew from research that there were many barriers to the use of condoms and there were many more nonusers than users of condoms. The research also showed that the main characteristic looked for in a condom was one that did not break, and that could be relied on. Indeed, the general perception that condoms are prone to

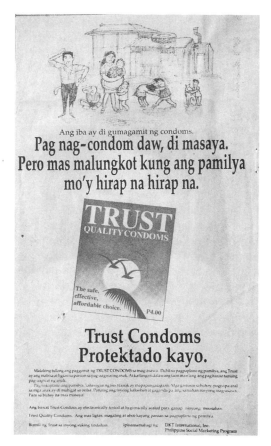

FIG. 10.3. This ad is headlined "Some people don't use condoms. . . . But there's nothing enjoyable about having a family who's hard up." Such negative images and "concept" advertising proved ineffective in this Philippine campaign.

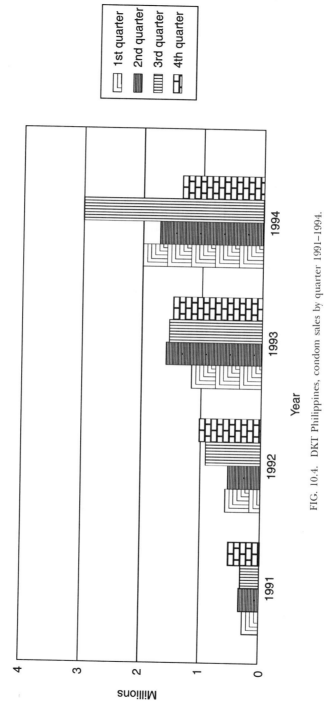

FIG. 10.4. DKT Philippines, condom sales by quarter 1991–1994.

frequent breakage was one of the main barriers to use among nonusers in the Philippines, at least as stated in focus groups. Therefore, instead of the nebulous "healthier, happier life" benefit, the new campaign promised the product to be "Strong and Reliable Protection" *(Matibay at Maaasahang Proteksiyon),* which is a much more tangible (and believable) benefit. The project has remained consistent to this message (up to mid-1995). This benefit message was repeated on the packaging, and was used in mass media and other promotional materials. This was also the first message used on the *Trust* billboard on the main thoroughfare in Manila. A glance at the sales charts reveal much healthier and steady sales growth from 1993 on, which is at least partially attributable to this much clearer, brand-focused promotional effort.

Trust advertising in 1993 also began to address some of the other major barriers to condom use. The stated advertising objective for the campaign was: "To counteract the stigma of condom use by presenting its use and purchase as commonplace and widespread, while imparting the brand's main selling points of strength, reliability and affordable price."

The campaign tackled the condom "embarrassment" barrier by producing two radio ads. The first portrayed a shy fellow at a store who cannot get up the nerve to ask for a condom from a female clerk. When the saleslady figures out what he wants, she tells him that he need not be shy because many people today ask for condoms. Anyway, if he cannot say condom, he should "Just Say *Trust.*" This ad was very well accepted, and has helped *Trust* to become synonymous with condoms in the Philippines. The second ad in the campaign opens with many people (male and female) at a neighborhood store, all clamoring for *Trust* condoms (just saying *Trust*). They show no embarrassment, implying that "everybody" buys condoms as a normal part of everyday life, albeit in an exaggerated form. (See print version, Fig. 10.5.) Also, this ad tackled the "availability" barrier, portraying the product readily available everywhere in neighborhood stores. In addition, the ad took on the male argument that condoms were "offensive" to their (regular) female partner, because females were very visibly portrayed purchasing the product. Both ads emphasized the product's strength reliability as well as the affordable price ("Still . . . only four pesos!"). These ads, in radio and print, were used from early 1993 through the first half of 1994.

In the second quarter of 1994, the project produced a commercial for cinema, which simply stated "Strong, Reliable Protection—*Trust* Quality Condoms." The background music was bold and strong, as were the visuals.

The "Just say *Trust*" radio ads also began airing over the intercom system of the Light Rail Transit commuter trains in Manila.

Project manager Craig Darden (personal communication, 1995) offered the following analysis of these campaigns:

FIG. 10.5. *Trust* condom print ad, Philippines, 1993–1994.

I believe that "getting back to basics" with clear product attributes based on consumer research is a large part of the success in 1994 and subsequently. As research has pointed out, there is an underlying reluctance to condom use or trial, simply because people are not convinced that they work. Then, all of the familiar objections (they're a bother to use, interrupt the sex act, decrease pleasure, etc.) come out to further rationalize their non-use. People need reassurance that the product works, so we told them so, and many of them believed us.

Why has the revised campaign been more successful?
I would say some of the reasons are:

1. Listening to consumers and potential consumers and applying the results of research to the advertising message definitely had a positive impact on sales.

2. Negative messages do not work. (This was also confirmed by other advertising here.) Negative messages were employed in the early campaign not in the later one.

3. A "lifestyle" approach seems to work better than a "health rationale."

4. The later campaign focused on simple, easily understood attributes of the brand—strength and reliability—that research told us was important to consumers.

Vietnam

One of the special opportunities presented to social marketers who begin programs in particularly poor countries is the chance to be among the first important advertisers in these societies. Although this poses challenges, it also presents enormous opportunities. It means advertising in an environment where there is very little clutter from other advertisers, where rates per thousand viewers/listeners/readers are usually very low, and where consumers have not been jaded by decades of competing advertising claims. The story is told of an advertising executive from France on a 2-year sabbatical to Ivory Coast in Africa, who was asked to summarize his experience on his return to Paris. The executive reported that there were two major differences between advertising in France and advertising in the Ivory Coast: "First, in the Ivory Coast they read our ads; second, they believe them!" Although this oversimplifies things, it makes an important point. Advertising in newly emerging economies has the advantage of working from a clean slate.

Contraceptive social marketing has had this characteristic most conspicuously in Bangladesh, Ethiopia, and, most recently, in Vietnam. DKT's Vietnam program manager, Andy Piller (personal communication, 1995) accordingly reported:

When *Trust* [condoms were] . . . introduced in Viet Nam in August, 1993, advertising in the mass media was still in its infancy. Most ads were very plain and were for local watch or gold shops and a few guest houses. The most "interesting" ads were for MSG. There were also a few ads for things like pens, detergents and shampoos. Most ads for other (locally made) products generally included a shot of the factory followed by shots of the management talking on the phone.

In this environment, the DKT manager recognized that brand awareness for the *Trust* condom, by itself, would probably spur significant sales growth. He therefore began with a campaign designed simply to create such awareness:

Our first ad for *Trust* was intended to make people aware of the *Trust* brand name, to mention some of the benefits of condoms/*Trust* and to show *Trust* available in different outlets. Scenes of *Trust* being purchased in a doctor's office, in a pharmacy, at a general goods store and from a street vendor, were coupled with the statements (in order) "international quality," "no side effects," "easy to use" and, "not expensive." These shots were followed by . . . [a] scene with the couple watching television and *Trust* coming out of the TV with the couple commenting, "available everywhere." Our slogan was simply, "*Trust*—International Quality."

Early feedback from this campaign suggested a further issue relating to shyness for which increased brand awareness might also be particularly helpful. As in most cultures, talking openly about sex or sex-related products is not considered "polite" in Vietnam. Having a brand name and recognizable logo allowed condoms to be promoted more openly and comfortably. This was dealt with in one of the early *Trust* ads, which approached the issue of shyness in a somewhat humorous way with the slogan (picking up from the campaign in the Philippines) "Don't say condoms, just say *Trust*." This slogan was widely repeated on television and is felt by program managers to be largely responsible for *Trust* becoming a generic term for condoms in Vietnam in a very short period of time.

Along with the lack of brand awareness of condoms and most other products, additional special opportunities presented in this "virgin market" at the time of launching *Trust* were an existing awareness about family planning; an intensive government campaign increasing awareness about AIDS; a recent drastic increase in television ownership and viewing; and favorable ad rates for TV and Radio (TV ads range in cost from US $10–$75 per 30-second spot, depending on time and station. Estimated TV viewership is 15 to 35 million people. Radio spots are around US $10 per 1-minute spot for a nationwide audience, comparable to, or larger than, the TV audience.)

Zaire

Perhaps the most successful use of advertising in a program for AIDS prevention took place in Zaire in 1988–1990.[2] The project combined a classic social marketing effort for condoms with a multimedia educational and motivational campaign. The campaign was unusually imaginative and took advantage of many special and unique communications opportunities.

First a series of TV spots, designed to undermine some destructive myths about AIDS, were produced and aired in Kinshasa, Zaire's capital and principal city. Before and after surveys revealed that the message was getting through: For example, there was a decrease of 14 points in the percent

---

[2]This description of the Zaire project is drawn largely from Julie M. Convisser's excellent article "The Zaire experience: Using mass media to battle AIDS in Africa," *Family Planning World*, September/October, 1991.

of those who responded "yes" to the question, "Can you avoid getting infected with the AIDS virus simply by avoiding contact with people who look sick?" after that issue was addressed in the TV spots.

But the campaign quickly began looking for other ways of getting the AIDS message across. Zaire boasts some of the world's most talented and highly visible musicians. The project sought to enlist this community of eloquent and persuasive performers, which had already been forced to confront AIDS. Not long before the project began, Zaire's most famous musician, Franco-Luwambo, released a song about AIDS 9 months before dying of the disease. Franco's song and startling death paved the way for the project to motivate other popular musicians to raise their voices against AIDS.

The project selected three AIDS songs after sponsoring a contest among Zaire's leading bands. The songs were released in 4-month intervals during a year and were guaranteed daily playtime through agreements with national and regional radio stations.

The public response was extremely positive. "Step by step / hand in hand / let's all fight AIDS" went the refrain of the first-released song by the well-known Empompo Loway. It could be heard on the lips of rural schoolchildren and sophisticated Kinshasa residents alike. In a Kinshasa posttest 6 months after the song's release, 65% of a target audience sampling had heard it. Of these, 90% could sing a verse or two on request. Most importantly, 93% of those who had heard the song retained its key AIDS messages and 85% of the same group said it affected their behavior.

Of the latter group, one in three said it discouraged them from having multiple partners. One in four said it encouraged abstinence, and one in six said it motivated them to be faithful to a single partner.

Buoyed by the response, the project sponsored a World AIDS Day concert in 1989, where Empompo sang his song. When a video of a performance was released just 3 weeks later, Empompo was already dead of AIDS.

Five more songs soon joined the original three—each addressing a slightly different population segment by selecting musicians with different styles and appeals. Similarly, the messages evolved over time. Due to the growing AIDS awareness, later songs veered away from the basic do's/don'ts and stressed more emotional appeals to change behavior patterns. For example, one song avoids the word "AIDS" altogether. Instead, a man and woman sing to each other of their marital trespasses and, in the face of "the dangers all around us today," renew their love and commitment to mutual fidelity.

For the 1990 World AIDS Day (December 1), the project sponsored a nationally broadcast concert featuring live renditions of six AIDS songs by the original artists. Excerpts of the moving and persuasive 5-hour performance were edited into five music videos, with cuts of musicians and other popular figures giving advice on AIDS prevention. The video clips were later broadcast on a rotating schedule on TV and cassette tapes were distributed to AIDS prevention groups throughout the country.

THE DRAMA OF AIDS

Working with Zaire's best-loved drama group, Troupe Nzoi, the project produced a four-part radio/TV series aimed at the "prospective parents" group. Its underlying behavioral messages are to avoid having multiple sex partners, practice mutual fidelity, and use a condom if you have sex in a high risk situation.

The drama, about a young woman who learns after her wedding night that her husband has AIDS, was the first mass media treatment of many socially significant and sensitive AIDS-related issues in Zairian culture. They include widespread marital infidelity and the link between the economic and social plight of women and widespread prostitution. Moreover, two specific scenes provided a first-time opportunity for an explicit televised discussion of the advantages of condom use for AIDS prevention.

The public response to the drama's realism and sensitivity was overwhelming. Follow-up research verified that presenting messages through a culturally relevant radio/TV drama effectively motivates individuals to adopt safe practices. Four "day after" surveys among a representative sample in Kinshasa showed that over two thirds of the intended audience watched each episode on TV. Of these, two thirds could recount the plot of the episodes they watched.

By the end of the project's second full year, Zaire's 13 million urban residents were receiving an average of 10 minutes a day of consistent and effective AIDS messages. Now, radio was added to cover more remote areas. Four of the country's 11 regional radio stations in high priority areas were selected to broadcast AIDS prevention messages. After several initial visits, two producers from each of the four radio stations were invited to a workshop, then asked to submit a year-long action plan for an AIDS radio campaign.

By the end of the first year of formal collaboration, the regional radio stations had produced and broadcast in over 13 local languages 28 AIDS feature programs, 22 spots, 8 AIDS radio dramas, 2 songs, and 5 AIDS-knowledge radio contests. In all, audiences in the four regions received an average of 20 minutes a day of AIDS messages via their local radio stations.

Campaign Results

The following results from the second phase of the Longitudinal Program Impact Study, conducted in August 1990, indicate the impact on the target audience in Kinshasa.

Awareness Increase Regarding Asymptotic Carriers. The ratio of people who think "you can avoid getting infected with the AIDS virus simply by avoiding sexual contact with people who look sick" dropped from 56% to 42%.

Increase in Abstinence and Mutual Fidelity for AIDS Prevention. When asked "How have you changed your behavior in the face of AIDS," 16% more people spontaneously responded "by becoming mutually faithful" in the second study than in the first (an increase from 28.9% to 45.7%).

Increase in Knowledge and Acceptance of Condoms for AIDS Prevention. Those who named condoms as their first mode of AIDS prevention increased from 5% to 13%. The ranks of those who had ever heard of condoms increased by 11 percentage points.

Increase in Condom Use for AIDS Prevention. When asked how they changed their behavior in the face of AIDS, five times the number of people responded "By using condoms" (18.8% vs. 3.6% in the first survey). Indeed, annual sales of condoms offered through the Condom Social Marketing Project increased by more than 1,000% over the 2½ years in the media campaign—from 900,000 in 1988 to 18 million in 1991.

According to an equation developed by AIDSTECH, a project of Family Health International, the 18 million condoms sold in 1991 prevented nearly 20,000 cases of AIDS in Zaire that year.

CONCLUSIONS

The power of advertising, accompanied by efficient but commonplace distribution methods, works powerful benefits. Contraceptive social marketing has contributed very substantially to the availability of contraceptives in the developing world. Nearly 14 million couples benefit from these programs, and that number is increasing rapidly. Social marketing and the advertising campaigns that drive these programs are significantly enhancing human well-being in many of the world's poorest countries. This approach to family planning and AIDS prevention demands further attention and investment: It is cost-effective, it is based on known methodologies, and it is no longer very controversial. It should be possible to at least triple the level of contraceptive social marketing in the developing world by the year 2000.

REFERENCES

Barberis, M., & Harvey, P. D. (in press). Costs of family planning programs in 14 developing countries by method of service delivery. *Journal of Biosocial Science.*
Ciszewski, R. L., & Harvey, P. D. (1994). The effect of price increases on contraceptive sales in Bangladesh. *Journal of Biosocial Science, 26*(1), 25–35.

Ciszewski, R. L., & Harvey, P. D. (1995, December). Contraceptive price changes: The impact of sales in Bangladesh. *International Family Planning Perspectives,* 150–154.

DKT International. (1990). The simple success secret in worldwide family planning: Social marketing. Washington, DC.

DKT International. (1996, August). 1995 contraceptive social marketing statistics.

Gillespie, D., et al. (1989). Financing the delivery of contraceptives: The challenge of the next twenty years. In S. Segal, A. Tsui, & S. Rogers (Eds.), *Demographic and progammatic consequences of contraceptive innovations.* New York: Plenum.

Harvey, P. D. (1994). The impact of condom prices on sales in social marketing programs. *Studies in Family Planning, 25*(1), 52–58.

Harvey, P. D., & Snyder, J. D. (1987). Charities need a bottom line too. *Harvard Business Review, 65*(1), 14.

Huber, S. C., & Harvey, P. D. (1989). Family planning programs in 10 developing countries. Cost effectiveness by mode of service delivery. *Journal of Biosocial Science, 21*(3), 267–277.

Lewis, M. A. (1986). Do contraceptive prices affect demand? *Studies in Family Planning, 17*(3), 126–135.

Manoff, R. K. (1985). *Social marketing.* New York: Praeger.

Ogilvy, D. (1963). *Confessions of an advertising man.* New York: Macmillan.

Population Reference Bureau (1986). *Family planning saves lives* (2nd ed.) [Brochure]. Washington, DC: Author.

Simon, J. (1987). *How to start and operate a mail-order business* (4th ed.). New York: McGraw-Hill.

Chapter 11

Marketing, Safer Sex, and Condom Acquisition

Darren W. Dahl
University of British Columbia

Gerald J. Gorn
Hong Kong University of Science and Technology
University of British Columbia

Charles B. Weinberg
University of British Columbia

ABSTRACT

This chapter identifies opportunities that marketing provides in a nonbusiness context. This discussion notes the importance of the concept of exchange, market segmentation, competition, and the effective implementation of an integrated set of marketing mix elements. The specific focus is on the potential application of marketing principles in the fight against AIDS. It is argued that marketing methodology can play a significant role in encouraging condom usage and in the facilitation of safer-sex practices. Utilizing the principles discussed, and drawing insights from the condom acquisition literature, a research intervention is implemented that assesses the effectiveness of a multidimensional marketing mix strategy in promoting the acquisition of condoms. More specifically, a two-phase study was run to examine the effectiveness of discount coupons distributed at different locations on the purchase of condoms.

A broad range of approaches is necessary to combat sexually transmitted diseases (STDs, including HIV). One focus is to encourage the use of safer sexual practices and to discourage risky sexual behaviors among those who are sexually active. Marketing can play a significant role in encouraging and facilitating safer sex. It can also play a role in the effective management of organizations concerned with promoting safer sex. Indeed, as Gallagher and Weinberg (1991) reported, "nonprofits are as concerned with marketing as are for-profit organizations" (p. 27). Although marketing is no panacea, a number of success stories have been reported in a variety of arts, health, and educational organizations. Despite modern marketing management's origination in the private sector, public and nonprofit marketing is no mere derivative of private sector marketing. Moreover, Drucker's (1989) article, "What Business Can Learn From Nonprofits," shows that the learning process flows in two directions.

Marketing is often misconstrued as consisting primarily of advertising and other communication efforts. Successful marketing, however, generally requires an understanding of the target population to be served and the development of a multidimensional program to meet the needs of the selected target markets.

The goal of the present study is to understand the effectiveness of marketing mix elements in promoting the acquisition of condoms. In succinct terms, if you do not have condoms, you cannot use them. More specifically, the present study examines the effectiveness of discount coupons, distributed at different locations, on the purchase of condoms.

This chapter does not attempt to document the increased prevalence of STD diseases, other than to note that by age 21, 25% of Americans are reported to have had at least one STD (DiClemente & Peterson, 1994). In addition, it is established that condoms are an effective means of decreasing the spread of AIDS and other STDs (Conant, Hardy, Sematinger, Spicer, & Levy, 1986; Morris, 1993), that a significant portion of men report never using condoms (e.g., Binson, Dolcini, Pollack, & Catania, 1993, finds that 40% of males do not use condoms with their primary and secondary partners), and that self-reports of condom use among a variety of populations rarely suggest that condoms are used as often as even half the time (Cromer & Brown, 1992; Leigh, Temple, & Trocki, 1993; MacDonald et al., 1990).

First, the chapter provides an overview of marketing as a management function in a nonbusiness context. (For more extensive discussions of marketing management in the public and nonprofit sectors see Kotler & Andreasen, 1991, and Lovelock & Weinberg, 1989.) It next reviews the literature related to barriers to condom purchase and price, in particular. It discusses discount coupons as one means to overcome price sensitivity. As there is little reported use of coupons with regard to condoms, a brief summary of findings from the literature is provided on the effect of coupons on sales of frequently purchased consumer goods. It then describes the studies conducted and presents the results. The chapter concludes with a brief discussion of implications for managers of safer-sex programs and for researchers.

NONPROFIT MARKETING MANAGEMENT

More than any other management function, marketing links the internal environment within the organization to the external environment outside the organization. The external environment of a nonprofit organization can have many constituents. Quite clearly, the first constituency is the target group whose attitudes or behaviors the organization is trying to influence. Because few nonprofits earn sufficient revenue (if any) from their primary target groups, nonprofit organizations may have sponsoring or funding groups, both government and nongovernment.[1] Marketing also helps link the organization to a range of constituencies that support or facilitate the design and delivery of its services. To choose an example from the environmental arena, an alliance of disparate environmental and animal preservation groups combined to design and coordinate campaigns to save the Spotted Owl in Washington state and the Marbled Murrelet in British Columbia. Other elements or groups in the external environment could also take an interest in the work of the organization (e.g., gay rights groups, hemophiliac groups, etc.) and the media. A broad master marketing plan is needed if the nonprofit is to develop attractive programs for people and the often wide array of organizations with whom it must interact, and if it is to be successful in changing the behavior of the target group(s). Ideally, the marketing planning process should culminate in a comprehensive marketing strategy, with tactics to achieve the target goals.

There are four concepts that lie at the heart of a marketing strategy: exchange, market segmentation, the marketing mix, and competition.

Exchange

Central to a marketing orientation is the notion of a transaction between parties. What is in it for the marketer and the customer? Clearly, in nonprofit organizations, the situation is quite complex. The concept of the "customer" is often unclear. The complexity is partly in defining the audience, as well as the fact that the customer may not identify with, or may even be against, the goal of the organization (e.g., smokers and drinkers may not want to quit or cut down). It is essential for nonprofits to be creative and aggressive in their marketing effort. In many cases, the "product" will not sell itself. Often a nonprofit is selling safety, caution, abstinence—not exactly fast moving, high demand products.

As with a private business, a nonprofit has to address the needs of the customer, as well as the cost the person is willing to incur to adopt the product or change their behavior. For the nonprofit this may be difficult, because the product may be hard to define. What exactly is the product being sold when you are telling people to engage in safer sex? What

---

[1]There are exceptions, however. A number of government and nonprofit organizations encouraged people to recycle and collected recyclable products such as plastics. In 1995, the price of plastic had risen to such an extent, that many recycling programs were actually profitable. For example, the city of Portland, Oregon, was expected to earn an estimated $160,000 from plastic recycling in 1995 (Forest, 1995).

physical products and services are involved (e.g., condoms, HIV testing)? Often, there may be no products at all (e.g., efforts to get people to obey speed limits). The benefits to the audience may be very hard to define—it may involve helping society in general (e.g., buying green products, or any other behavior related to environmental concerns). It may involve helping the person in the short term (e.g., they will cough less and generally feel better relatively soon if they stop smoking) or in the longer term (their chances of lung and other cancers will be reduced if they stop smoking). The costs to the audience may also be difficult to define. With private business, the financial payment is typically thought of as the price. However, with a nonprofit, there may be no financial payment at all. Even if there is a price, the other barriers to adopting the advocated behavior (e.g., time involved, effort required, or social stigma) may be significant. The price may mean people stop smoking or drinking.[2]

Market Segmentation

Market segmentation is the process of dividing a total market into one or more parts, each of which tends to be homogeneous in significant aspects. This concept is central to a marketing approach and can be seen as a key organizing concept for a marketing orientation. For example, you cannot decide on what type of promotion or even product will be successful until you know your customer. Not everyone will be interested in your product. Not everyone wants to be helped or informed. Of those who do, they may need to be informed, pursued, or helped in different ways.

Although the nonprofit may be trying to change large populations of people (e.g., smokers), there will still be subgroups (e.g., pregnant women) for whom this issue may be of prime importance, or for whom distinct programs need to be developed (teenagers who may become smokers vs. 20-year-olds who already smoke). A decision would have to be made as to which subgroup(s) to concentrate on initially. To not do so may mean sacrificing the needs of a critical group in an overzealous effort to help everyone in the larger target group. Clearly, marketing efforts would have to be tailored for each subgroup.

Marketing Mix

The marketing function is often perceived quite narrowly. Even in private business, it has often been perceived as, for example, tactics to make a new product or promotion successful. It would be seen as an "add-on" function,

---

[2]If anything, in certain situations, such as stopping smoking, adopting the recommended behaviors would not only involve very limited initial financial cost, but could also save the person money as well.

as in "we developed this product now let's get the salespeople to sell it." In recent years, businesses and some nonprofits (Gallagher & Weinberg, 1991) have recognized that the role of marketing should be broader and that it should begin before the product is designed.

A somewhat broader view would consider marketing in terms of the 4 *Ps*: *product, price, promotion,* and *place* (distribution). This view has more recently come into fashion in the social marketing area. It reflects a broadening of more traditional approaches, approaches that, as mentioned earlier, have typically focused on communication efforts to change people (i.e., on the promotion part of the marketing mix). The studies in this chapter focus on a different promotional element, namely, coupons. Coupons can be seen as both a promotional device and a price discount mechanism.

Ideally, of course, behavior change programs would work best, if they are enhanced by all elements of the marketing mix. In addition to the persuasive efforts to get people to use condoms, there should be a consideration of the other elements of the mix: types of condom(s) that should be developed, their price, and the location(s) where they would be available.

The 4 *Ps* have to be seen as interrelated and interactive elements. Using the metaphor of a recipe, it is not just a question of what to put into the recipe, but how these ingredients interact. In other words, the type and content of a promotion will obviously depend on the product. The method of distribution would, in turn, influence the promotion, and vice versa. This study incorporates different methods of coupon distribution to determine their relative effectiveness.

There are many interrelated elements within each of the 4 *Ps*. For example, would it be synergistic, and would more change result in the target consumer, if a TV public service announcement (PSA) message on condoms had a jingle or slogan that could also be used in a radio commercial or print ad? The success of this effort would of course depend on the nature of the subgroup, and among other things, their relative use of different media. Like industry, the elements of the marketing approach would also have to be considered in the context of competitors, as discussed later.

The elements of the 4 *Ps* are typically seen as marketer-controlled variables. However, the mandate of a nonprofit will often be more specific and not necessarily encompass all elements. An organization focusing on getting people to use condoms would have typically little control over the product or brands sold. Thus, they are advocating use of a product they do not create or sell.

Theoretically, the mandate of a nonprofit could be broad enough to potentially incorporate all elements in the mix. For example, if the goal of a nonprofit were to get people to stop smoking, it theoretically would have all of elements of the mix to work with to achieve its goal.[3] However, it typically would be limited by the resources it had available. Frequently, the resources of nonprofits are quite limited. They are not likely to be able to afford massive amounts of television time, even if this seems like the most effective strategy to adopt for the target group.[4] Thus, there are barriers to the ability of a nonprofit to control and use all of the elements of the marketing mix, and therefore to their ability to change the consumer.

Competitors

Private businesses have traditionally been concerned with competition. They need to focus keenly on the competition, as it may directly influence their profit margin. Profit is not typically the yardstick, or the only yardstick, to measure the success of a nonprofit (Drucker, 1989). Their funds have often come from government or benefactors, their employees often work for altruistic reasons for little or no pay. Funds obtained by donations or special events is at most a means to an end, and typically not the measure of a successful organization.

The nature of competition in the nonprofit arena is somewhat different than it is in private industry. First of all, in a broad sense, any nonprofit trying to raise money faces the competition of other nonprofits trying to do the same, even if the other nonprofits are trying to raise money for a different cause. A person may allocate a certain fixed amount of money for charitable donations. Hence, if they give to the Heart and Stroke Foundation, it might decrease the likelihood of them giving to an AIDS organization. Furthermore, just as there is stiff competition for people's charity dollar, there may be competitive forces trying to get the consumer to behave in a different, and often opposite, direction. A campaign to get people to stop smoking or drinking faces competitive marketing efforts (e.g., promotion) by private business to get people to smoke or drink more. (In some jurisdictions, the competition includes government owned and operated liquor stores.) In the case of safer sex, any efforts encouraging a pleasure orientation and sensuality might make initiatives to promote condom usage more difficult. After all, presumably most people would not use condoms if they did not need them for protection.

---

[3]Rather than focusing only on the 4 *Ps*, some nonprofits can also attempt to change the regulatory environment to help encourage the desired behavior. For example, antismoking groups have sought regulations to prohibit smoking in public places.

[4]As a counterexample, however, consider the case of the Transport Accident Commission in Victoria, Australia, which combined a $6 million advertising campaign, increased police enforcement of speeding laws through the use of speed cameras, and extensive use of random alcohol testing to drive down road fatalities by one half in the early 1990s (Graham, Harper, & McDougall, 1995).

There is also the competition that can come from other nonprofits whose mission might be different (e.g., an organization primarily concentrating on reducing unwanted pregnancies). Ultimately, as with industry, competition is important for nonprofits from both private business and other nonprofits.

On the other hand, there are also other nonprofit organizations with whom a nonprofit can potentially cooperate. Compared to businesses, which are typically in a competitive situation, the goals of nonprofits could often be compatible, and might at some level even be the same; presumably, the ultimate goal of all AIDS organizations is to prevent HIV infection. This research was based on a relationship with the City of Vancouver Health Department, who ran a series of campaigns to increase condom usage. Work was also done with the Man-to-Man AIDS Vancouver group to distribute coupons at one of the events they organized.

Nonprofit organizations may also cooperate with private businesses. For example, a nonprofit trying to increase condom usage may benefit from a relation with a company marketing condoms. The condom producer would clearly have expertise in the marketing of condoms and, of course, the product itself; the nonprofit would unlikely be manufacturing its own condoms. This case worked with both Ansell Canada, the manufacturer of Lifestyle condoms, and a major drug-store chain, Shoppers' Drug Mart. In conclusion, opportunities for cooperation with both other nonprofits and private business should be explored.

BARRIERS TO CONDOM PURCHASE

The prevention of STDs, such as HIV, through condom usage requires that condoms be acquired. As noted previously, if individuals do not have a condom, then they cannot use one, unless of course their partner has one. This important aspect of STD-prevention behavior has received comparatively much less attention than have the psychological processes involved in condom usage.

General theories of human behavior, like the theory of reasoned action (Ajzen & Fishbein, 1980; Fishbein, 1967), have been applied to better understand the attitudes and beliefs surrounding condom usage. Similarly, motivational models created specifically to understand health-related behaviors (e.g., Health Belief Model; Hochbaum, 1958) have also been utilized to design interventions to increase safer-sex behavior (i.e., condom use that will reduce the likelihood of STD infection). The growth in prevalence of the HIV virus has also fostered original psychological modeling specific to the disease itself. J. D. Fisher and W. A. Fisher's (1992) information–motivation–behavioral skills (IMB) model of AIDS risk reduction is an example of this innovative research stream. The extensive and growing literature that utilizes these types of models to explore STD-prevention behaviors is reviewed elsewhere (see DiClemente & Peterson, 1994; J. D. Fisher & W. A. Fisher, 1992) and, consequently, is not explored further here.

Recently, research has focused on the barriers involved in purchasing condoms. Barriers identified include embarrassment about the purchase of condoms (Helweg-Larsen & Collins, 1994), accessibility of condom selling locations (Mays et al., 1993), price levels of condoms (Harvey, 1994), and problems in selecting from condoms available for purchase (Beaulieu, Bradet, & Godin, 1994). Each of these barriers has been shown to complicate the purchase process and impede the pursuit of STD-prevention behaviors. These barriers provide good targets for behavioral interventions that will enable an easier acquisition process. Within this study, the barrier of price and the possibility of a marketing intervention that facilitates behavior is explored.

In the first published study that specifically examined the price level of condoms as a potential barrier to purchase, Lewis (1986) found that condom demand increases when prices are reduced. The study indicated that increases in price would act as a deterrent to low and moderate income individuals (but not high income). Subsequent studies of condom pricing (Ciszewski & Harvey, 1994; Harvey, 1994; Tipping, 1991) have validated these conclusions, indicating a relatively strong price sensitivity in this product class. Interestingly, each of these studies has been conducted in developing countries (e.g., Bangladesh, Kenya, Liberia). The authors identified the importance of contraception in these countries, the ability to manipulate experimental conditions, and the applicability of pricing decisions in developing countries as central reasons for pursuing research in this context.

Paralleling these studies, the importance of price sensitivity in a North American context has been confirmed in focus group studies and survey research conducted among adolescent populations. Condomania, a condom intervention program in Vancouver, Canada, found evidence of price sensitivity in the purchase of condoms. Survey research among students (Beaulieu et al., 1994) has also shown that pricing and the costs of condoms are a central obstacle to purchase. Sensitivity to condom price levels is an important element in condom acquisition that can both act as a barrier to purchase and provide an opportunity for effective intervention.

Charging a Price

While price may be a barrier to usage of a product or a service, there are a number of reasons why organizations should charge a price. Of course, unless the organization has considerable outside funding, it needs to charge a price to defray at least some of the costs of providing the service and running the organization. As Harvey (1994) pointed out, a number of family planning organizations have begun charging (or raising) prices because government support has fallen. In addition, recalling the marketing mix argument made earlier, an organization may find that it obtains greater usage of its product by increasing its marketing effort and its price, than by providing the product at the minimum possible price. For example, Ansari, Siddarth, and Weinberg (1996) found that a classical music series would attract more attenders, while covering its costs, by offering eight concerts at $13.50 per ticket, than by offering 4 concerts at $6.48 per ticket.

Price can also be used to motivate clients. For example, clients of a family planning clinic may be more likely to follow the advice given if they paid for the advice than if they obtained it for free. In a related area, Gorn, Tse, and Weinberg (1990) found that people rated the quality of services for which a price was charged higher than people who were told that the service was free.

Price can also serve to motivate retailers and others who help the organization deliver its products and services to market aggressively. For example, whereas nonprofits may be the primary organization concerned with safer sex, condoms are typically sold by retailers who are profit making. Although retailers may occasionally donate space or services to nonprofits, in the long run, retailers are only going to market condoms aggressively to the extent that the financial returns justify their efforts.

In some cases, the effect of price is to help motivate managers as well. Rather than just being concerned with controlling costs, management can also see a revenue stream over which it has some influence. This is particularly useful when the organization has a broad range of products, for example, condoms, IUDs, pills, and diaphragms. However, price can also be a misleading indicator and industry measures, such as "couple days of protection," may be a better way to measure performance.

Of course, there are a number of occasions when it is best to charge no price. Sometimes the cost of collecting fees may be greater than the price charged. Alternatively, too many people in the target group may be unable or unwilling to pay for the product, at least in the short run. The benefits to society may be so great that pricing is unreasonable. The classic example is the lighthouse. There is, however, an increasing tendency, at least in North America, to identify user constituencies and charge them for services.

COUPON REDEMPTION

Coupons are a widely (and increasingly) used marketing element in North America. For example in 1993, more than 300 billion coupons were distributed in the United States, but only 2.3% were redeemed (Deveny & Gibson, 1994). Most marketers distribute their coupons for a purpose, so the

TABLE 11.1
Factors Affecting Coupon Redemption Rates

Factor	Relationship to Redemption Rate
Face value	Positive
Distribution vehicle	Varies
Expiration date	Positive
Design of coupon	Varies
Area of country	Varies
Competitive activity	Negative
Size of coupon drop	Negative
Purchase requirements	Negative
Advertising/promotion support	Positive
Seasonality	Varies
Product class penetration	Positive
Brand market share	Positive
Brand loyalty	Positive
Brand distribution	Positive
Stage in product life cycle	Negative
Brand image	Positive
Demographics	Varies
Consumer's need for product	Positive

Note: From Blattberg & Neslin, 1990; Reibstein & Taylor, 1982.

low redemption rate suggests that much remains to be learned about the effective distribution of coupons. Nevertheless, it is known that the percentage of coupons redeemed is influenced by factors, including the size of the discount offered, the coupon distribution method, and the time of expiry (see Table 11.1 for a summary of factors that influence coupon redemption). Coupons are primarily used by marketers both for promotional purposes—as a means of calling attention to their brand—and for discounting, to provide a lower price for the product (on a temporary basis).

Some literature suggests that coupons can be used for "price discrimination" to appeal to price sensitive consumers willing to spend the time and effort required to redeem coupons (e.g., Narasimhan, 1984). Whereas some consumers will (virtually) never use coupons, increased value of the coupons and increased ease of usage of coupons are likely to increase coupon redemption rates. These are the factors investigated in the studies described here.

STUDY 1

This study focused on understanding the effects of a coupon promotion on the sales of condoms and determining if differences in the coupon discount level influenced the number of coupons redeemed. As already discussed, coupons can have an effect on purchase decisions through two elements of the marketing mix. First, they serve as a communication element because they draw consumers' attention to the product and brand being promoted. Second, they serve as a means to reduce the price of the product for the limited period of time for which the coupons are valid.

Coupons, however, are effortful to use. Narasimhan (1984) identified a variety of efforts required by consumers who choose to use coupons. These efforts include searching for the coupon (e.g., looking through magazines), clipping and organizing, storing and retrieving them, and bringing coupons to the purchase location. The efforts involved in utilizing coupons represents costs to the consumer. These costs enable a coupon promotion to act as a tool for price discrimination and serve as a measure of price sensitivity for the couponed product (Narasimhan, 1984).

Utilizing this line of reasoning, the present study varies the level of the price discount offered by the coupon promotion as a test of price sensitivity. The number of coupons redeemed for differing discount levels acts as a dependent variable in assessing the possible presence of price sensitivity for the product. The redemption level across the differing price discount levels also provides an indication of the general effect of implementing a coupon promotion in an attempt to increase condom purchase.

Sample

The sample chosen for Study 1 was 1,600 males participating in a (Gay) Pride Parade held in Vancouver, BC. Through consultation with AIDS Vancouver and the Vancouver Health Department it was determined that a majority of the men participating or attending this function were current or potential users of condoms.

Design and Procedure

The study was operationalized by issuing two separate types of condom coupons. Half of the target population (800 males) received a coupon with a 10% discount value off the price of a box of condoms. The second half of the target population (the remaining 800 males) received a coupon with a 75% discount value off the price of a box of condoms. Both types of coupons were good for one box of 12 condoms of a specific condom brand. The couponed brand was one of the four major brands, but was not the market leader. Because the coupons could not be immediately redeemed at the parade site, it was decided to make them as easy to use as possible. Consequently, the coupons were valid at any retail location offering the couponed brand and were valid for redemption any time during the 2 months after being issued.

The two levels of price discount were chosen to provide insight into the effectiveness of a coupon promotion and to discern the importance of the amount of discount in this coupon promotion. The 10% discount, although substantial, was designed primarily to represent the condition where the primary effect of the coupon was communication. That is, to draw people's attention to the product and brand. The 75% discount was considered to be a test of both the communication and pricing effect.

In determining the form of price discount, a percentage-off format was chosen instead of the more common cents-off format.[5] A cents-off format was judged to be potentially confusing to some consumers given the large price discount offered. For example, some coupon recipients may be unfamiliar with the actual price of a box of condoms and receiving a coupon for $5.00 off a box may cause the recipients to infer the true cost of the condoms to be substantially higher than it actually is. A percentage-off coupon format alleviates this concern and reflects the potential savings to the coupon recipient in a clear and concrete manner.

The coupons were distributed during a Pride Parade, which primarily attracts homosexuals, as the participants walked past a specific point in the parade route. Coupons were dispersed by four research assistants in allotments of 200 according to the discount level. An alternating procedure was followed that involved a disbursement of coupons at one discount level, a break of 2 minutes in which no coupons were distributed, and then a resumption of coupon disbursement, but at the alternate discount level. This pattern continued until the entire 1,600 coupons had been distributed. Coupons that were redeemed by the target population were returned to the investigators after being processed by the sponsoring brand.

Results

The initial reaction and acceptance of the coupon distribution was very positive. Less than 10 refusals were noted and most coupon recipients expressed thanks and positive feelings toward the couponing initiative. Typical comments included "Condoms, now that's a worthwhile coupon" and "What a great idea."

The redemption results are summarized in Table 10.2. The redemption levels for both discount conditions was very small. In the case of the 10% price discount, no coupons were redeemed. The 75% price discount condition showed a small redemption rate (.4%) with only 3 of the 800 coupons redeemed. There was no significant difference in the redemption rates

---

[5]Typically, a cents-off coupon is used because it facilitates reimbursement to the retailer. A percentage-off coupon requires the retailer to mark the list price on the coupon and therefore reimbursement to the retailer can vary.

TABLE 11.2
Coupon Redemption Results (Study 1)

Coupon Redeemed	Coupon Discount Level	
	10%	75%
Yes	0	3
No	800	797

between the price discount levels (10% vs. 75% conditions: Yates corrected $\chi^2 = 1.34$, $p > .20$).

STUDY 2

Given the initial reaction to the coupon promotion, the small number of coupons that were redeemed was somewhat of a disappointment. A second study was therefore conducted under conditions that would increase the likelihood of coupon redemption. The distribution point of the coupon promotion was moved closer to the redemption location. Previous research (Blattberg & Neslin, 1990; Reibstein & Traver, 1982) indicates that the method of distribution has a direct and significant impact on coupon redemption. Distribution methods that are close to the purchase occasion (e.g., on-package, on-shelf, in-store handout) typically result in higher redemption rates than methods that are removed from the purchase location (e.g., direct mail, newspaper insert).

Similarly, the study was interested in reducing any costs associated with the time lag between when people were given a coupon and when they might potentially redeem it. Consequently, to reduce the costs associated with any potential later redemption, immediacy of the potential purchase was reinforced through the coupon being valid only on the day it was distributed. To ensure this was understood, the persons distributing the coupons verbally made this point to the recipients. This also increased the salience of the coupons. In an effort to clarify the questions surrounding differing sensitivity to coupon discounts, two discount levels were again utilized in an attempt to test for the possibility of a divergent redemption pattern.

Sample

The sample investigated in the second study was males who were shopping in a major drugstore located in a residential area of downtown Vancouver.[6]

---

[6]Although the store was heavily frequented by gay males, it attracted non-gay shoppers as well. Thus, in comparison to the first study, the sample in the second study was broader and would have included both gay and non-gay males.

The sample size of 540 males was determined by an a priori estimate of traffic levels at the retail location.

Design and Procedure

The design and procedure of the second study was essentially the same as Study 1, with certain changes made to adjust to the new distribution location. Paralleling Study 1, half of the target population (270 males) received a coupon for 10% off a box of 12 condoms, and the other half of the population (270 males) received one for 75% off. The coupons used in the second study were identical to those used in the first study except for two distinct differences. The restriction that the coupon could be redeemed at only the drugstore where the distribution took place and only on the day the coupon was distributed was included on the coupon copy.

Other differences in the second study involved the actual distribution of the coupons. The distribution took place over two 4-hour periods on a Friday and Saturday afternoon. Coupons were distributed in front of the drugstore to males entering the store. One level of coupon was distributed for slightly less than an hour, then there was a brief break in distribution, and then distribution of the other value of coupon was resumed. The design was counterbalanced across the two days.

Results

As in Study 1, the initial reaction to the coupon promotion was predominantly positive. Comments included "I really believe in what you are doing here" and "Thanks a lot, this is really cool." Comments indicating that the coupon promotion resulted in unplanned purchase of condoms were also noted (e.g., "I didn't come into the store intending to buy condoms, but at this price, I had better").

The redemption results are summarized in Table 11.3. The redemption levels for both discount conditions were much higher than those realized in Study 1. In the case of the 10% price discount condition, 4 of the 270 coupons were redeemed for a redemption rate of 1.4%. The 75% price discount condition showed a relatively large redemption rate (7.8%) with

TABLE 11.3
Coupon Redemption Results (Study 2)

Coupon Redeemed	Coupon Discount Level	
	10%	75%
Yes	4	21
No	266	249

21 of the 270 coupons redeemed. A significant difference in the redemption rates between the price discount levels was realized (10% vs. 75% conditions: Yates corrected $\chi^2 = 10.74$, $p < .01$).

CONCLUSIONS

The studies reported here are the first step in a series of studies on using a marketing approach to encourage safer sex. As was discussed, marketing approaches provide effective methodologies to assist nonprofit organizations with achieving their goals. In a safer sex context, marketing methods can be usefully applied to overcome barriers that inhibit both condom acquisition and condom usage.

The focus of the current research project is on methods to increase the availability of condoms and stimulate actual acquisition of the product. Marketing elements involving price and promotion were utilized through a coupon intervention strategy. In the first study conducted, though initial reactions were positive, the actual redemption of coupons, across both discount levels, was negligible. In the second study, both the positive initial reactions and the redemption rates obtained indicate promotion success and provide evidence of the appropriateness of this form of intervention. The significant difference realized between the redemption levels of the two price discount conditions in the second study indicates that a price sensitivity toward condom purchase may exist. A higher redemption rate, when the discount level is greater, suggests that the price of condoms is a possible barrier to acquisition. Managers of safer sex programs need to be aware of this barrier and others that can impede the acquisition process. Clearly, the level of discount provided by a coupon for condoms has a significant impact on its redemption rate when other elements of the coupon and its distribution method are sufficiently attractive to potential users.

Intervention strategies that address pricing concerns and facilitate the purchase of condoms are beneficial to the overall goal of safer sex. Couponing and other related promotional techniques are excellent candidates for achieving this goal.

ACKNOWLEDGMENTS

We would like to thank the following people and organizations for their help and cooperation in this research: Alain Tranchemontagne and Johanne Messier (Ansell Canada), Lezlie Wagman (Vancouver Health Department), Steve Martindale (AIDS Vancouver), and Shoppers' Drug Mart.

REFERENCES

Ajzen, I., & Fishbein, M. (1980). *Understanding attitudes and predicting social behavior.* Englewood Cliffs, NJ: Prentice-Hall.

Ansari, A., Siddarth, S., & Weinberg, C. B. (1996). Pricing a bundle of products or services: The case of nonprofits. *Journal of Marketing Research, 33*(1), 86–93.

Beaulieu, D., Bradet, R., & Godin, G. (1994). Etude de l'importance des obstacles a l'achat de condoms [A study of important obstacles to condom purchase]. *Canadian Journal of Public Health, 85*(4), 231–233.

Binson, D., Dolcini, M. M., Pollack, L. M., & Catania, J. A. (1993). Multiple sexual partners among young adults in high risk cities. *Family Planning Perspectives, 25,* 268–272.

Blattberg, R. C., & Neslin, S. A. (1990). *Sales promotion concepts, methods, and strategies.* Englewood Cliffs, NJ: Prentice-Hall.

Ciszewski, R. L., & Harvey, P. D. (1994). The effect of price increases on contraceptive sales in Bangladesh. *Journal of Biosocial Science, 26,* 25–35.

Conant, M., Hardy, D., Sernatinger, J., Spicer, D., & Levy, J. A. (1986). Condoms prevent transmission of AIDS associated retrovirus. *Journal of the American Medical Association, 255,* 1706.

Cromer, B. A., & Brown, R. T. (1992). Update on pregnancy, condom use, and prevalence of selected sexually transmitted diseases in adolescents. *Current Opinion in Obstetrics and Gynecology, 4,* 855–859.

Deveny, K., & Gibson, R. (1994). Awash in coupons? Some firms try to stem the tide. *Wall Street Journal,* May 10, B1.

DiClemente, R. J., & Peterson, J. L. (1994). *Preventing AIDS.* New York: Plenum.

Drucker, P. F. (1989). What business can learn from nonprofits. *Harvard Business Review,* July–August, 88–93.

Fishbein, M. (1967). Attitude and prediction of behavior. In M. Fishbein (Ed.), *Readings in attitude theory and measurement* (pp. 477–492). New York: Wiley.

Fisher, J. D., & Fisher, W. A. (1992). Preventing AIDS-risk behavior. *Psychological Bulletin, 111*(3), 455–474.

Forest, S. A. (1995). There's gold in those hills of soda bottles. *Business Week,* September 11, 48.

Gallagher, K., & Weinberg, C. B. (1991). Coping with success: New challenges for nonprofit marketing. *Sloan Management Review,* Fall, 27–42.

Gorn, G. J., Tse, D. K., & Weinberg, C. B. (1990). The impact of free and exaggerated prices on perceived quality of services. *Marketing Letters, 2*(2), 99–110.

Graham, P., Harper, M., & McDougall, G. H. G. (1995). Transport accident commission: Drunk driving and speeding road safety advertising campaign. In McDougall & Weinberg (Eds.), *Canadian marketing cases and exercises* (pp. 122–128). Toronto: McGraw-Hill Ryerson.

Harvey, P. D. (1994). The impact of condom prices on sales in social marketing programs. *Studies in Family Planning, 25*(1), 52–58.

Helweg-Larsen, M., & Collins, B. E. (1994). The UCLA multidimensional condom attitude scale: Documenting the complex determinants of condom use in college students. *Health Psychology, 13*(3), 224–237.

Hochbaum, G. M. (1958). *Public participation in medical screening programs: A sociopsychological study* (Public Health Service, PHS Publication 572). Washington, DC: U.S. Government Printing Office.

Kotler, P., & Andreasen, A. (1991). *Strategic marketing for nonprofit organizations* (4th ed.). Englewood Cliffs, NJ: Prentice-Hall.

Leigh, B. C., Temple, M. T., & Trocki, K. F. (1993). The sexual behavior of US adults: Results from a national survey. *American Journal of Public Health, 83,* 1400–1408.

Lewis, M. A. (1986). Do contraceptive prices affect demand. *Studies in Family Planning, 17*(3), 126–135.

Lovelock, C., & Weinberg, C. B. (1989). *Public and nonprofit marketing* (2nd ed.). Redwood City, CA: The Scientific Press.

MacDonald, N. E., Wells, G. E., Fisher, W. A., Warren, W. K., King, M. A., Doherty, J. A., & Bowie, W. R. (1990). High-risk STD/HIV behavior among college students. *Journal of the American Medical Association, 263*(23), 3155–3159.

Mays, V. M., Cochran, S. D., Hamilton, E., Miller, N., Leung, L., Rothspan, S., Kolson, J., Webb, F., & Torres, M. (1993). Just cover up: Barriers to heterosexual and gay young adults' use of condoms. *Health Values, 17*(4), 41–47.

Morris, B. A. P. (1993). How safe are safes. *Canadian Family Physician, 39* (April), 819–827.

Narasimhan, C. (1984). A price discrimination theory of coupons. *Management Science, 3*(2), 128–147.

Reibstein, D. J., & Traver, P. A. (1982). Factors affecting coupon redemption rates. *Journal of Marketing, 46* (Fall), 102–113.

Tipping, S. (1991). Use of a pilot test market to determine packaging and price levels for commercial contraceptives in Liberia. *Applied Marketing Research, 31* (Spring/Summer), 43–45.

ANTISMOKING EFFORTS

Does Antismoking Advertising Combat Underage Smoking? A Review of Past Practices and Research

Cornelia Pechmann
University of California, Irvine

ABSTRACT

From 1967 to 1970, before the ban on broadcast tobacco advertising in the United States, broadcasters were required to air roughly one antismoking ad for every four cigarette ads. Smoking by youth declined markedly. Since then, the underage smoking rate has remained stable. One reason the rate has not declined further may be that, since 1970, expenditures on antismoking ads have been very low. Expenditures have increased recently, but only in three states. In 1995, Massachusetts spent $2.33 per capita, California $.40, and Michigan $.20; in contrast, the tobacco industry spent $3.76 per capita on cigarette ads. Nationally, the U.S. Centers for Disease Control and Prevention (CDC), and groups such as the American Cancer Society, distribute public service announcements (PSAs), but broadcasters tend to air the PSAs from midnight to 6 a.m. Field and lab experiments indicate that antismoking ads can reduce underage smoking. However, youth must see the ads when in grades 5–10. New ads must be created each year. The ads must be coordinated with intensive antismoking school programs. Finally, the ads must depict the short-term costs of smoking (e.g., bad breath), show youth how to refuse cigarette offers, and show that smoking is not the norm.

The U.S. surgeon general estimates that 3,000 youth begin smoking cigarettes every day in the United States and one third will die—10 or more years prematurely—of smoking-related disease (Collins, 1995). They will die of lung or throat cancer, heart disease, strokes, or other ailments directly related to their smoking, which results in substantial human, health care, and economic costs (Max & Rice, 1995). Currently, about 20% of high school seniors smoke daily, which is nearly as high as the adult smoking rate of 26%, and increasingly younger people are smoking (Lynch & Bonnie, 1994; USDHHS, 1989). Although all states have laws that prohibit cigarette sales to minors, 85% of smokers take up the habit before they turn 18 years old (Lynch & Bonnie, 1994). It may be possible, then, to combat smoking simply by enforcing existing laws and, concurrently, reducing youths' demand for cigarettes.

Antismoking advertising may help to reduce youth's demand for cigarettes. This chapter examines advertising practices and research to determine the following:

1. Do U.S. youth see sufficient antismoking advertising for it to have any impact?[1]
2. If youth saw sufficient antismoking advertising, could it reduce their smoking rates?
3. How does antismoking advertising reduce smoking rates; that is, how does it change beliefs, attitudes, and/or behavioral intent?
4. When does antismoking advertising reduce smoking rates? That is, which factors seem to enhance or detract from its impact?

YOUTH'S EXPOSURE TO ANTISMOKING ADS

This author conducted an informal telephone survey to identify groups that had disseminated antismoking ads in recent years in the United States and Canada. It was necessary to conduct a survey because no published information was available. The following groups were identified as disseminators of antismoking ads for youth:[2]

1. The Health Departments of five U.S. states: California, Massachusetts, Michigan, Minnesota, and Maryland.
2. Health Canada, a Canadian federal government organization.
3. Two organizations within the U.S. Department of Health and Human Services: the Centers for Disease Control and Prevention and the Center for Substance Abuse Prevention.
4. Three nongovernment health organizations: the American Cancer Society, the American Lung Association, and the American Heart Association.

---

[1]For parsimony, the term *antismoking advertising* (or ad) refers to advertising placed in paid media as well as to PSAs placed in donated media.

[2]Groups known to use antismoking ads were contacted and asked to identify other such groups. The final list may not be fully comprehensive, but it should be reasonably complete.

5. The R. J. Reynolds Tobacco Company.

A spokesperson from each group was interviewed and asked to provide the group's annual budgets for antismoking ads for the years 1990–1996. The budgets typically included production, media, evaluation, and public relations. When budgets were unavailable, data were obtained on the number of antismoking ads produced. The information obtained from these surveys is summarized in Table 12.1 and is discussed later.[3]

The subsequent discussion distinguishes between groups that purchase media time for their antismoking ads and those that rely on broadcasters and publishers to run the ads free of charge as PSAs. Whether a group can afford to purchase media time is perhaps the most important factor that affects whether youth will see its ads. The Federal Communications Commission no longer requires broadcasters to air specified numbers of PSAs, and broadcasters receive large numbers of PSA requests, many of which are not honored. The CDC tracked its Nic (a teen) antismoking PSA for 11 months in 1992–1993 (Arian, Lowe, Travis, & Gusick, 1993). The three networks aired the PSA 312 times (a $1.5 million value), and 147 network affiliates aired it 3,529 times (a $400,000 value); cable participation was very low. Unfortunately, 81% of the airings occurred when youth would not be watching (56% late night, 7% late fringe and 18% daytime). By purchasing media, groups can ensure its antismoking ads are placed in programs and publications that will be seen by young people.[4]

---

[3]It would have been ideal to obtain information on reach (the number of youth exposed to each ad) and frequency (the number of times youth were exposed to each ad), but that information generally was unavailable. The information reported here was obtained from the following officials and their staff assistants:

California Health Dept.	Colleen Stevens
Massachusetts Health Dept.	Greg Connolly
Michigan Health Dept.	Dianne May
Minnesota Health Dept.	Arlene Thornton
Maryland Health Dept.	Joan Stine
Centers for Disease Control	Jeff McKenna
Center for Substance Abuse Prevention	Bob Vollinger
American Cancer Society	Elizabeth Bridgers
American Lung Association	Ruth Kasloff
American Heart Association	Greg Hunicutt
Health Canada	James Mintz, Neville Layne

[4]It is beyond the scope of this chapter to examine in detail if PSAs are an effective method of exposing youth to antismoking messages. The reader can contact the U.S. Ad Council (contact: Luana Lewis) for general information on the amount of free air times PSAs receive, criteria for success, and case histories that indicate PSAs can have statistically significant attitudinal and behavioral effects. The ad council has produced and disseminated PSAs for over 50 years, but it has yet to release any antismoking PSAs.

TABLE 12.1

Recent Expenditures on Antismoking Ads Targeted at Youth (approximate amounts)

Source of Funds	1990	1991	1992	1993	1994	1995	1996
CA Health Dept.*		28.6 mil	16 mil	15 mil	12 mil		
Massachusetts Health Dept.*					16 mil	14 mil	13 mil
Michigan Health Dept.*	1.6 mil	1.6 mil	.6 mil	.5 mil	.4 mil	1.9 mil	1.9 mil
Minnesota Health Dept.*				.3 mil	.05 mil	.05 mil	
Maryland Health Dept.				Smoking Drags You Down PSAs (TV, radio, bus)			
US Health and Human Services Centers for Disease Control and Prevention	Smoking Is Out TV & print PSAs, Bug Spray print PSA, Performance Edge PSA** (.7 mil)		Nic (a teen) / Butthead print radio & TV PSAs (re-release, .2 mil)		Surgeon General's Kids Report (magazine; .4 mil)	Cartoon print PSAs, Performance Edge II**, Baseball spit tobacco TV PSAs (.9 mil)	
American Cancer Society***		Tar Lady TV PSA		Richard Marx TV PSA	Sports Celebs TV PSA	2 PSAs with MusicTV (Audition, Obsession)	
American Lung Association	The Dance TV PSA					You Smoke I Choke TV PSA	
American Heart Association				Shape Up TV & movie theater PSAs		2 Ricky Martin TV PSAs (1 Spanish, FHP)	
Health Canada****		.75 mil	.75 mil	0	1.6 mil	4.5 mil	3.6 mil

Note: PSAs (Public Service Announcements) were distributed to broadcasters to be run voluntarily, free of charge (except in Michigan; see text).
*The budgets generally covered production, media placements, evaluations, and public relations, and the moneys were used to reach several target audiences—not just youth. Michigan's budgets for 1993–1994 included other health PSAs.
**Performance Edge is cosponsored by the Center for Substance Abuse Prevention, and is primarily a video with give-away magazines.
***In addition, 4 PSAs will be distributed for the 1995 Great American Smokeout: 3 from California and Tar Lady.
****The budgets are in US $ (1 US = 1.35 Canadian). The youth ads started in 1986. Since 94/95, adults have also been targeted.

YOUTH'S EXPOSURE TO ANTISMOKING ADS (IN PAID MEDIA)

Minnesota

Minnesota was the first state to launch a multifaceted statewide program aimed at discouraging tobacco use (Murray et al., 1992). Minnesota commenced this initiative in 1986, using funds generated by a tobacco surtax. As part of its multifaceted program, it purchased media time to run antismoking ads. Minnesota spent roughly $1 million through 1989 on antismoking ads; it spent $1.6 million in both 1990 and 1991 ($.36 per capita). Since that time, though, funds have been cut due to statewide budget reductions; now, the annual budget is only $.05 million. Minnesota no longer produces antismoking ads for TV or radio. Instead, previously produced ads are occasionally broadcast free of charge as PSAs. Minnesota's pioneering efforts have had an impact beyond its state lines, however: Seventy-two entities have used Minnesota's ads to promote nonsmoking in other states and countries.

California and Massachusetts

In 1990 and 1993, respectively, California and Massachusetts began purchasing media time for antismoking ads with funds generated by tobacco surtaxes, as mandated by voter propositions. Each state has spent about $14 million a year on campaigns targeted at both youth and adults. In 1995, California spent roughly $.40 per capita, and Massachusetts $2.33. As an example of how the moneys are spent, in 1996, Massachusetts will spend $8 million on media, $3 million on production ($180,000 per TV spot), $.5 million on research, and $1.5 million on public relations.

Michigan

In the early 1990s, Michigan operated with a small annual budget of about $.45 million a year ($.05 per capita). Lacking funds to purchase media, it developed an innovative distribution plan referred to as "hybrid" PSAs. It pays the Michigan Broadcasters Association a nominal sum and is guaranteed a certain number of spots in each part of the day (e.g., in 1993, it paid $.5 million for 8 TV and 8 radio spots per station per month, 25% in each day part). In 1994, Michigan passed its own tobacco surtax, and a portion of the revenues are to be spent on health education. As a result, Michigan now spends about $1.9 million annually on antismoking ads, or $.20 per capita.

Canada

Canada's federal government has been purchasing media to run English and French antismoking ads since 1986. Initially, Canada spent only about US $.75 million a year, or US $.03 per capita. It tried to use the money prudently by focusing strictly on youth and by persuading private sector marketers with expertise in reaching youth (e.g., Musique TV and Peugeot Bicycles) to cosponsor antismoking activities. In 1994, Canada expanded its target audience to include adults, and it now spends about US $3.6 million a year or US $.12 per capita.

YOUTH'S EXPOSURE TO ANTISMOKING PSAs (IN DONATED MEDIA)

The U.S. Centers for Disease Control and Prevention (CDC)

The CDC, a unit of the federal government's Department of Health and Human Services, has produced several antismoking PSAs for youth (refer back to Table 12.1). From 1990 to 1995, the CDC spent roughly $370,000 a year producing such materials, or $.001 per capita. The CDC initially focused on disseminating PSAs to traditional media, but it was disappointed with the results. It now produces more targeted communications such as PSAs for school newspapers. It also produces educational videos and give-away magazines for schools, as in its Performance Edge program, which is cosponsored by the Center for Substance Abuse Prevention. Finally, the CDC provides a public service by cataloging and distributing other groups' antismoking ads.

Nongovernment Health Groups

The American Cancer Society, American Heart Association, and American Lung Association (as well as the state of Maryland and perhaps a few other states and entities) periodically release antismoking PSAs for youth. (Again, see Table 12.1.) These groups have become increasingly innovative in reaching youth. The American Cancer Society arranged for Music TV (MTV) to produce two antismoking PSAs, which ensured the ads would appeal to youth and would be aired in youth programs. (The CDC is now engaged in a similar joint venture with MTV.) The American Lung Association persuaded the largest chain of U.S. movie theaters, United Artists, to run a pro-health antismoking PSA for youth during an entire month in 1994.

R. J. Reynolds Tobacco Company

Finally, the R. J. Reynolds Tobacco Company disseminates antismoking wall posters to junior high and middle schools on an ongoing basis (Osmon, 1995). The color posters are designed for 12- to 15-year-olds (grades 6–9) and contain messages such as "If You Think Smoking Makes You Fit In, Think Again" and "How Can Smoking Be the Thing to Do, If Most of Your Friends Aren't Doing It?" Each semester, schools on the distribution list receive two new posters and brochures. The materials are part of school program to teach youth to make appropriate lifestyle decisions regarding smoking and drinking. The program includes teaching materials for six classes, covering decision making, responsibility, refusal skills, conflict resolution, and values.

LEVEL OF ANTISMOKING ADVERTISING NEEDED TO REDUCE UNDERAGE SMOKING

Necessary Ratio of Antismoking Ads to Cigarette Ads

To evaluate whether youth in the United States and Canada receive adequate exposure to antismoking advertising, it is necessary to first determine the minimum level needed. A useful approach is to consider the antismoking to cigarette ad ratio, because antismoking ads must have adequate "share of voice" to break through ad clutter, attract attention, and persuade (Kotler, 1991; Lavidge & Steiner, 1961). According to research by Lewit, Coate, and Grossman (1981), a ratio of one antismoking ad for every four cigarette ads may be needed. In 1967, the Federal Communications Commission (FCC) interpreted its Fairness Doctrine to require broadcasters to air one antismoking ad for every three cigarette ads and roughly a one to four ratio was attained (Schuster & Powell, 1987). Lewit et al. (1981) determined that during the Fairness Doctrine Period, the underage smoking rate was 3 percentage points smaller than in the 16-month period just prior to the Fairness Doctrine Period.[5]

---

[5]Lewit et al. (1981) analyzed cross-sectional field data (a discussion of such quasi-experiments is provided later). Specifically, Lewit et al. analyzed survey data collected by the National Center of Health Statistics who, from 1966 to 1970, contacted a random sample of 6,768 youths between the ages of 12 and 17 years old to assess health behaviors. During the 16 months prior to the Fairness Doctrine Period, 14.6% of the youth were current smokers; during the 3-year Fairness Doctrine Period, 12.4% were current smokers. A regression that controlled for price and several other factors revealed the coefficient for the experimental (Fairness Doctrine) vs. control (pre Fairness Doctrine) variable was −.03, indicating a 3% drop in smoking for the experimental vs. control group, which occurred in the first year.

In 1970, the tobacco industry agreed to a ban on cigarette ads on TV and radio that commenced on January 1, 1971. This ban eliminated the need for broadcasters to air antismoking ads, so airings declined precipitously and the drop in smoking was retarded (Lewit et al., 1981; Pollay, 1994; Schneider, Klein, & Murphy, 1981). It is unclear to what extent results from 1970 generalize to the present day. Also, it is difficult to draw conclusions about the impact of advertising on tobacco consumption based on cross-sectional data, because uncontrolled variables also may have affected consumption. Nevertheless, given the dearth of other data, a 1 to 4 ratio of antismoking ads to cigarette ads seems reasonable for present-day efforts.

Current Ratios of Antismoking to Cigarette Advertising

In 1993, the last year for which complete data are available, the U.S. tobacco industry spent $2.16 per capita on mass media cigarette ads, which included ads on billboards, buses, and kiosks and in magazines and newspapers. Overall, on cigarette ads, including point-of-purchase ads, the industry spent $3.76 per capita in 1993 (see Table 12.2). It is important to include point-of-purchase ads because these are heavily utilized. An average store that sells cigarettes in California has 26 tobacco point-of-purchase materials (posters, displays, and the like) (Hilts, 1995). It could be argued that premiums (give away items such as Marlboro t-shirts) and event sponsorships are also forms of advertising, and, including these, total U.S. cigarette advertising expenditures in 1993 amounted to $7.12 per capita.

In contrast, in the vast majority of U.S. states, expenditures on antismoking ads amount to essentially $0 per capita. Antismoking ads are prevalent in just 3 of the 50 states: California (12% of the U.S. population), Michigan (4%), and Massachusetts (2%). Further, only Massachusetts appears to have an adequate ratio of antismoking to cigarette ads, at 1 to 1.4. The ratios in Michigan (1 to 20) and even California (1 to 9.4) could be too low (again, see Table 12.2). If a 1 to 4 ratio is needed across the United States to combat underage smoking, antismoking ad expenditures clearly are insufficient.[6]

Ratio of Antismoking to Cigarette Advertising Under Clinton Proposal

In 1995, based on recommendations by the U.S. Food and Drug Administration (FDA), President Clinton proposed that the tobacco industry spend $150 million a year on antismoking education for youth (Purdum, 1995).

---

[6]When Minnesota had a large budget for antismoking ads in the late 1980s, its antismoking to cigarette ad ratio was very roughly 1:6.

TABLE 12.2

Comparison of Expenditures on Cigarette Versus Antismoking Advertising and Related Activities in United States (approximate amounts)

	Expenditures on Antismoking Advertising and Related Activities: Key States (1995)		
	Massachusetts	*California*	*Michigan*
Total	$14 million	$12 million	$1.9 million
Per Capita	$2.33	$.40	$.20

	Expenditures on Cigarette Advertising and Related Activities (1993)		
	Media Ads	*All Ads (Media + Point of Purchase)*	*Ads + Premiums + Sponsorships*
Total	$.54 billion	$.94 billion	$1.78 billion
Per Capita	$2.16	$3.76	$7.12

	Breakdown by State: Antismoking Versus Cigarette Expenditures		
	Antismoking	*Cigarette*	*Ratio: Antismoking to Cigarette*
Massachusetts	$14 million	$19 million*	1 to 1.4
California	$12 million	$113 million*	1 to 9.4
Michigan	$1.9 million	$38 million*	1 to 20

Notes: Per capita expenditures were calculated using 1990 population census figures: U.S. population = .25 billion; Massachusetts = 6 million (.02 of United States); California = 29.8 million (.12 of United States); Michigan = 9.3 million (.04 of United States).

Domestic cigarette expenditures were provided by the Federal Trade Commission; 1993 was the most recent year for which complete data were available. In total, in 1993, tobacco companies spent $6.03 billion in cigarette marketing, and $119 million on smokeless tobacco marketing (including $23 million on advertising smokeless tobacco).

Assumptions underlying calculations of cigarette expenditures by state:

(1) It is assumed the tobacco industry spent roughly the same amount on cigarette advertising in 1995 as in 1993 (1995 was used as the base to incorporate the most current data available on antismoking expenditures).

(2) It is assumed that cigarette advertising expenditures in each state are proportional to the population in that state (i.e., that per capita expenditures are constant across states).

*Based on U.S. total of $.94 billion.

If the money were spent exclusively on antismoking advertising, it would amount to $.59 per capita and the ratio of antismoking to cigarette advertising would be very roughly 1 to 6. This ratio represents a very substantial increase over current levels. Although it falls below the target of 1 to 4, it might still be adequate. During the Fairness Doctrine era when a 1 to 4 ratio of antismoking to cigarette ads reduced underage smoking (Lewit et al., 1981), the antismoking ads were not targeted solely at youth; under the Clinton proposal the ads would target youth.

However, the Clinton proposal is under attack by the tobacco industry and many advertisers (Collins, 1995). The final FDA ruling on tobacco and youth, which is expected to be issued in 1996, may be challenged in court. Thus, it is unclear when or if the tobacco industry will be required to fund antismoking education for youngsters. In the near future, therefore, antismoking advertising is likely to remain unfunded in most U.S. states.

COULD ANTISMOKING ADS WORK? WHEN AND HOW?

If youth could be exposed to sufficient antismoking advertising, could the advertising lower underage smoking rates? This section examines studies that address this question (see Table 12.3 for study descriptions). To ascertain when success is likely, conditions in which the ads worked versus did not work will be compared. Finally, this section examines why antismoking ads might reduce smoking, that is, how the ads might impact beliefs, attitudes, and/or behavioral intent. Four types of studies are reviewed:

1. Longitudinal field experiments sponsored by the U.S. National Institutes of Health (Bauman, LaPrelle, Brown, Koch, & Padgett, 1991; Flynn et al., 1992; Perry, Kelder, Murray, & Klepp, 1992).
2. Cross-sectional field tracking of adolescent smoking rates by California (the IOX, 1991 and Pierce et al. 1990–94 surveys), Minnesota (the Legislative Reports from 1987, 89, and 91), and Canada (Making a Difference I and II and Still Making a Difference Reports, 1991–93).[7]
3. Controlled laboratory experiments (Pechmann & Ratneshwar, 1994; Pechmann & Knight, 1996).
4. Qualitative studies to obtain youths' and experts' opinions of antismoking ads (Worden et al., 1988; Bauman et al., 1988; McKenna & Williams, 1993).

This review focuses on research on antismoking ads targeted at youth in the United States and Canada. Readers may want to review related studies of antismoking ads targeted at Dutch youth (Baan, 1990) and U.S. adults (Wewers, Ahijevych, & Page, 1991; Campion, Owen, McNeill, & McGuire, 1994).

---

[7]Most of the groups that use antismoking ads (listed in Table 12.1) did not evaluate or have not reported whether the ads affected adolescent smoking rates; thus, they are not listed in Table 12.3 or discussed later. Massachusetts has released data only on adult smoking rates and ad exposure levels (see Abt Independent Evaluation, 1995). Michigan's primary effort has been to track calls to its tobacco help line. The CDC and other health groups obtain, at best, very rough estimates of the media value of their PSAs.

TABLE 12.3

Recent Studies of Antismoking Ads Targeted at Youth

Study Type	Researcher(s) (Publication Yr.)	Main Study Sponsor	Sample Geo-Demographics	Sample Size (Contact Method)
Longitudinal field experiment	Flynn et al. (1992, 1994)	U.S. National Cancer Institute	5th–11th grade students in Vermont and Montana	2,086 in 6 waves (school surveys plus phone when needed)
Longitudinal field experiment	Perry et al. (1992)	U.S. National Heart, Lung & Blood Institute	6th–12th grade students in Minnesota, Dakotas	2,401 in 7 waves (school surveys)
Longitudinal field experiment	Bauman et al. (1991)	U.S. National Cancer Institute	12–16 yr. olds from 10 metro areas in SE United States	1,637 in 2 waves (home interviews)
Cross-sectional field tracking	IOX Assessments Associates (Executive Reports 1990–1991)	California (Health Dept.)	California public school students (4th–12th grade)	29,000 in 4 waves (school surveys)
Cross-sectional field tracking	Pierce et al. Evaluation (Technical Reports 1990–1993)	California (Health Dept.)	California youth (12–17 yrs old)	600,000 in 3 waves (phone surveys)
Cross-sectional field tracking	Minnesota Legislative Reports (1987, 1989, 1991)	Minnesota (Health Dept.)	Minnesota 9th graders	5 survey waves (details not provided)
Cross-sectional field tracking	Health Canada (Making a Difference Reports 1991, 1992, 1993)	Canada (Health Promotion Directorate)	Canadian youth (11–17 yrs old)	1,500+ youths/survey; 1,000+ English-speaking (home surveys distributed by Gallup in 1987; then by Creative Research)
Lab experiment	Pechmann & Ratneshwar (1994)	California (Tobacco-Related Disease Research Program)	California 7th graders	300 (school survey)
Lab experiment	Pechmann & Knight (1996)	California (Tobacco-Related Disease Research Program)	California 9th graders	700 (school survey)
Qualitative research	Worden & Flynn et al. (1988)	U.S. National Cancer Institute	5th–9th graders from 2 U.S. regions	190 (focus groups)
Qualitative research	Bauman et al. (1988)	U.S. National Cancer Institute	12–15 year olds from 15 U.S. schools	1,000 (focus groups)
Qualitative research	McKenna & Williams (1993)	U.S. Centers for Disease Control	U.S. teens (10–15 years old) in 9 cities	240 (focus groups)

National Institutes of Health Longitudinal Field Experiments

Overview of Method.   Three major studies on antismoking interventions have been funded by units within the U.S. National Institutes of Health, specifically, the National Cancer Institute (Bauman et al., 1991; Flynn et al., 1992) and the National Heart, Lung and Blood Institute (Perry et al., 1992). These studies were longitudinal in that the same youth ("cohort groups") were followed as they grew older. The studies were also true experiments: Subjects in the experimental group were exposed to mass media antismoking ads in their communities, subjects in the control group were not, and the communities were selected at random from a larger set of possible candidates. By comparing smoking rates across these groups over time, the impact of extraneous factors was removed and the impact of the antismoking ads could be ascertained.

Expected Pattern of Results.   As youngsters grow older (e.g., as they are followed from 6th to 10th grade), the percentage that smoke will almost inevitably increase, because smoking is highly correlated with age and grade (USDHHS, 1989). However, if the antismoking ads are successful, there should be a slower rate of increase in the percentage of smokers in the experimental (ad) group versus the control (no ad) group.

Flynn et al. field experiment (1992, 1994).   This experiment suggests that antismoking ads combined with special school interventions can reduce underage smoking. Approximately 2,000 students from four communities were tracked, beginning in grades 5–7, for 6 years. All students attended three or more special antismoking classes per year at their schools. However, the experimenters aired antismoking ads in only two of the four participating communities (one community in Vermont, one in Montana). Students who lived in these two communities were in the experimental group. The other students, from matched communities in the same states, constituted the control group.

Students in the experimental group saw an initial antismoking ad campaign that lasted 5 months and three annual "reminder" campaigns that lasted 1 month each (see Fig. 12.1). The ads ran on TV and radio, and media time was purchased. Several ads were used each year, and they were improved continually based on student surveys. The ads highlighted the short-term costs of smoking (e.g., smelly breath and clothes). The ads also showed youth how to refuse offers of cigarettes (Donaldson, Piccinin, Graham, & Hansen, 1995; Tanner, Hunt, & Eppright, 1991). Finally, the ads stressed that smoking is not the norm to ensure the ads did not inadvertently imply underage smoking was prevalent (Donaldson et al., 1995)

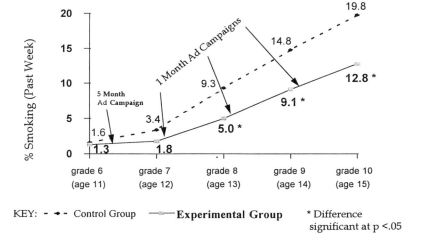

FIG. 12.1. Results of Flynn et al.'s (1992) longitudinal field experiment. Each cohort group spanned 3 grades, so the grades listed are the medians (e.g., "grade 6" represents the cohort group when in grades 5–7). Ages are approximate. A similar pattern was observed for "smoked yesterday" and "smoked recently." Flynn et al. (1994) found the effects were sustained 2 years hence (median grade = 12).

The researchers found the school program plus ad (i.e., multifaceted) intervention was far more effective than the school program alone (i.e., single faceted) intervention. Before the interventions had commenced, when the subjects' median grade was 6 (median age = 11), approximately 1% of subjects had smoked in the past week. As the subjects grew older, though smoking rates increased, rates increased significantly less in the experimental (vs. control) group. Four years later, when the ad campaign ended, 12.8% of experimental group subjects had smoked in the past week versus 19.8% of control group subjects (refer again to Fig. 12.1). Six years later (see Flynn et al., 1994), smoking rates among experimental (vs. control) subjects remained significantly lower. Additional findings suggest the ads lowered smoking rates by persuading youth that smoking is not the norm and the disadvantages outweigh the advantages, thereby lowering overall attitudes toward smoking.

Perry et al. field experiment (1992). Perry et al. (1992) evaluated a multifaceted antismoking intervention targeted at youth: an intensive school program combined with a community heart health intervention. The special school program addressed short-term negative consequences, social and advertising influences, norms, and refusal skills; it began in grade 6, lasted for 3 years, and consisted of 6 to 10 classes a year. The community

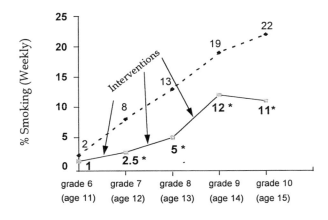

KEY: - ◆ - Control Group   ——— **Experimental Group**   * Difference
                                                           significant at p <.05

FIG. 12.2. Results of Perry et al.'s (1992) longitudinal field experiment.
The intervention depicted was a 6–10 session/year school education
program, but subjects in the experimental group were also exposed to a
multiyear community health intervention involving mass media ads. Ages
are approximate.

heart health intervention included mass media advertising, health screening and education, and numerous other community activities.

Youths in the experimental group were exposed to both the special
school intervention and the mass media/community intervention; youths
in the control group did not receive either intervention. It was found that
the experimental (vs. control) group youths were much less likely to take
up smoking. In fact, Perry et al. (1992)'s results are strikingly similar to
those reported by Flynn et al. (1992) (see Fig. 12.2).

Bauman et al. field experiment (1991).   The Bauman et al. study cautions
that antismoking ads targeted at youth may fail if short-lived, underfunded,
and divorced from special school programs. Bauman et al.'s 800+ experimental subjects saw only 6 months of antismoking ads, most ads were on
radio (vs. TV), and the ads did not start until subjects were about 13 years
old (median grade = 8). Schools did not hold special antismoking school
classes, and the antismoking ads did not show youth how to reject cigarette
offers. Before the ads commenced, 3% of the subjects had smoked in the
past week. A year and a half after the ads ended, 13% of the experimental
versus 14% of the control group subjects had smoked in the past week.
The difference between groups was insignificant (Fig. 12.3). However, the
ads lowered beliefs about the benefits of smoking.

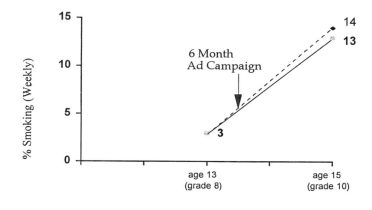

FIG. 12.3. Results of Bauman et al.'s (1991) longitudinal field experiment. Each cohort group spanned 3 years, so the ages listed are the medians (e.g., "age 13" represents the cohort group when 12–14 years old. Grades are approximate.

Stand-alone antismoking school programs, involving no advertising. Research suggests it may be possible to lower adolescent smoking rates with carefully designed school programs and no antismoking advertising (cf. Flynn et al., 1992; see Armstrong, de Klerk, Shean, Dunn, & Dolin, 1990; Best, Thomson, Santi, Smith, & Brown, 1988; Botvin, 1986; Coe, Crouse, Cohen, & Fisher, 1982; Flay, 1985; Shean, de Klerk, Armstrong, & Walker, 1994; Snow, Gilchrist, & Schnicke, 1985). However, some seemingly stand-alone programs could conceivably have been multifaceted (as in Perry et al., 1992). Program sponsors might have wanted to do all they could to combat underage smoking. Also, it is often advantageous to combine school programs with ads and community activities to reduce the amount of classroom time that must be spent on antismoking education.

Also, to be effective, school programs must meet stringent criteria such as those advocated by the National Cancer Institute (Gynn, 1989). Schools must provide several hours of antismoking instruction (perhaps 5+ hours/year) over several years starting in junior high (Bell, Ellickson, & Harrison, 1993), and they must address short-term costs, social norms and influences, and refusal skills (Bruvold, 1993; Flay, 1985; Glynn, 1989). Many programs also allow youth to create antismoking ads, and teach youth how to avoid being influenced by cigarette ads. Schools should not focus strictly on long-term health effects, because most youth think they will quit smoking before suffering health effects (USDHEW, 1979).

When Antismoking Ads Work: A Comparison of Field Experiments.   It appears
Flynn et al. (1992) were successful because they applied what they learned
from an earlier field experiment. They initially tried a brief antismoking
ad campaign that had no school component (Worden et al., 1988, p. 532).
Within 12 months, the ads had lowered youth's intent to smoke, but the
effect dissipated by the 18th month. Worden et al. (1988) speculated that
to be successful they had to structure their ad campaign as described here
and, later, they were successful with such a campaign:

1. There must be a coordinated school education program (e.g., one
   strongly endorsed by state education departments with free materials
   for schools).
2. Students must be exposed to the ads by the time they are in the
   sixth grade (11 years old).
3. The ads must be continued for several years.
4. To maintain student interest, a portfolio of ads must be used, and
   there must be a new portfolio each year.
5. The ads must stress the short-term costs of smoking, show how to refuse
   offers of cigarettes, and demonstrate that smoking is not the norm.

Cross-sectional Field Tracking

Overview of Method.   Large-scale (e.g., statewide) interventions are often
evaluated using cross-sectional field tracking. Researchers contact random
samples of youth to assess smoking rates at several points, ideally prior to, during,
and after the ad campaign. The studies are quasi-experiments because subjects
are not randomly assigned to experimental (ad) versus nonexperimental (no
ad) condition (Cook & Campbell, 1979). Thus, it is difficult to factor out the
impact of other variables that may affect smoking rates.

For instance, the interventions in California, Massachusetts, Michigan,
and Minnesota were large in scale and highly publicized. These interventions may possibly have elicited reactions from one or more tobacco manufacturers or retailers, who may have tried to counter the interventions by
increasing tobacco advertising or promotions, or by dropping prices (Hu,
Sung, & Keeler, 1995). Such retaliatory measures are costly but, when
confined to one state, could seem economically viable and important strategically.[8] These factors make it difficult to evaluate the effects of the states'
antismoking advertising.

---

[8]Cross-sectional data are difficult to interpret in other contexts as well (Kotler, 1991).
When a firm test markets a new product, for instance, competitors may reduce prices and/or
increase advertising, to undermine the success of the test market and dissuade the firm from
introducing the product nationwide.

Expected Patterns of Results. Antismoking ads may affect the underlying trend in smoking rates; for instance, smoking rates could start to drop 1% a year (26%, 25%, etc.). If rates drop steadily, public and legislative support of the ads may continue. However, because there is no control group, one cannot be sure the change in rates is due to the ads; other factors—such as general attitudes, prices, or the economy—could be involved. Likewise, if the antismoking ads result in stable smoking rates, this could be viewed as a failure, though it might be a success if rates increased elsewhere.

Alternatively, antismoking ads may result in a one time change (or "shock") in smoking rates, without affecting any underlying trend (Lewit et al., 1981). For instance, if a state commences antismoking advertising and smoking rates have been stable, rates could drop 3% and then restabilize. If effects are one-time, public and legislative support for continuing the campaign may wane. However, if the campaign were terminated, rates could jump back up. These are only a few of the complex scenarios that could arise. Thus, to reiterate, cross-sectional field data must be interpreted with caution.

California's Field Tracking (1990–1995). California's antismoking ads led very quickly to a one-time drop in underage smoking, but the underlying trend was unaffected. California's initial campaign ran in 1990–1991, and expenditures were $28.6 million (nearly $1 per capita). The campaign was evaluated by an independent educational research firm, IOX Assessment Associates (Popham et al., 1994), who repeatedly surveyed youth in grades 4–12 (approximate ages 9–17). The percent of youth that had smoked 1+ cigarettes in the past 30 days dropped significantly from 12.8% 1 month before the campaign to 10.3% 2 months after it started. The survey data indicates the ads created negative attitudes toward smoking, which then lowered youth's intent to smoke. But, for the rest of this campaign, the smoking rate remained quite stable, ending at 10.9%.

Additional campaigns have run in California, but no further decline in underage smoking rates has been documented. Pierce et al. (1994) tracked the percent of 12- to 17-year-olds who smoked "last month" concurrent with the 1990–1991 campaign, in 1991–1992 when the campaign was on hold (due to political and budget problems), and concurrent with the 1992–1993 and 1993–1994 campaigns. The data show that underage smoking in California (and in the United States as a whole; see *Consumer Reports*, 1995) has been fairly stable: 9.1% in 1990–1991, 8.7% in 1991–1992, 9.1% in 1993–1994, and 10.9% in 1994–1995. Smoking among various age groups has fluctuated moderately and sporadically; for example, from 1990–1993, smoking among 16- to 17-year-olds varied from 17.1% to 15.4% to 16.1%, and smoking among 14- to 15-year-olds varied from 7.7% to 9.8% to 9.1%

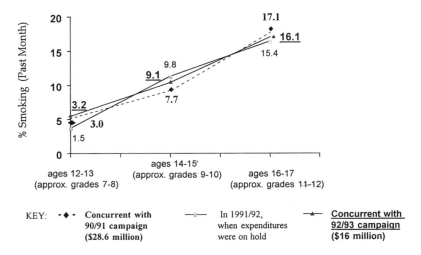

FIG. 12.4. Results from California's later field tracking (from Pierce et al.'s 1990–1993 technical reports. It was not reported if any differences were statistically significant.

(see Fig. 12.4).[9] In contrast, the smoking rate among the California adult population has been declining steadily: It was 27% in 1988, 22% in 1990, 20% in 1992, 19% in 1993, 17% in 1994, and 16% in the first half of 1995. California has experienced a steeper drop in adult smoking than the United States at large, based on surveys by the National Center for Health Statistics (CDC, 1994).

Why has California not been more successful at reducing underage smoking? It is possible that California has had limited success with youth because it has focused primarily on adults and communities. Each year, several youth ads have been aired in youth programming (e.g., MTV shows). However, most ads have been targeted at adults, because the campaign has three primary goals: to increase awareness and reduce tolerance of second-hand smoke, to increase awareness of the tobacco industry's role in promoting smoking, and to obtain support for policies that would reduce youths' access to tobacco, and for smoke-free policies. Because the media campaign has focused on adults and communities, it has not coordinated special antismoking school programs, and there have been no systematic or comprehensive changes in school programs. California has not, therefore, employed the coordinated advertising plus school education model endorsed by Flynn et al. (1992). Finally, California simply may not have spent enough money to offset tobacco marketing in that state (Hu et al., 1995).

---

[9]Pierce reported somewhat less smoking than IOX Assessments, despite focusing on older youth. The difference in findings may be attributable to the method (home vs. school surveys).

Minnesota's Field Tracking (1987–1991).   Minnesota also had limited success in reducing underage smoking with its antismoking ads (see 1991 Minnesota Legislative Report; also Murray et al., 1992). The ads ran from 1986 to 1990, and annual expenditures were about $1 million. Fifteen percent of ninth graders (roughly, 14-year-olds) smoked weekly in year one of the campaign (1986), 15% in year three (1988), and 14% in year five (1990). There was a larger drop in the percentages of ninth graders that "ever smoked," from 60% in year one to 55% in year five. But, each year in between, the "ever smoked" rate fluctuated substantially; it was 58% in year two, 56% in year three, and 58% in year four. Therefore, the drop in year five may have been sporadic rather than signaling a clear downward trend, and no statistical tests of trends were reported.

Murray et al. (1992) evaluated Minnesota's intervention using a different method and obtained similar, but slightly more promising, results. Ninth graders were surveyed in both Minnesota and Wisconsin ($n = 3,600$ students/state/year) from 1986 to 1990. Smoking was expected to be lower in the Minnesota treatment group (1988 to 1990 ninth graders) versus the Minnesota control group who had missed out on the newly instituted antismoking junior high program (1986–1988 ninth graders). Smoking was also expected to be lower in the Minnesota treatment group versus the Wisconsin control group. Instead, 13% of the treatment subjects had smoked in the past week versus 13% of the Minnesota control subjects and 16% of the Wisconsin control subjects, and the 3% interstate difference was not statistically significant. Murray et al. (1992) also tracked a separate group of Minnesota 1990 treatment subjects who had received especially intensive antismoking school instruction. Smoking among those treatment subjects (12%) was significantly lower than among Wisconsin control subjects (16%). These findings suggest Minnesota's multifaceted (ad plus school) intervention might have produced significant effects statewide if schools had provided more intensive antismoking education.

Canada's Field Tracking (1990–1993).   Canada is perhaps best compared to California, because they both have diverse populations of roughly 30 million, and manage large-scale and complex interventions. Canada spends far less than California on antismoking ads; from 1990 to 1996, Canada will spend US $11.2 million, and California will spend $86.6 million. Nevertheless, Canada has been the more successful at reducing underage smoking. From 1987 to 1990, smoking among English-speaking 11- to 13-year-olds dropped from 8% to 2%, and smoking among 14- to 17-year-olds declined from 23% to 16% (see Fig. 12.5).[10] Similar successes were obtained with

---

[10]Canadian officials believe these percentages can be directly compared. However, it should be noted that, after the 1987 survey, the research firm changed (from Gallup to Creative Research), and the question changed (from smoking "daily" to "at least occasionally"—which includes daily).

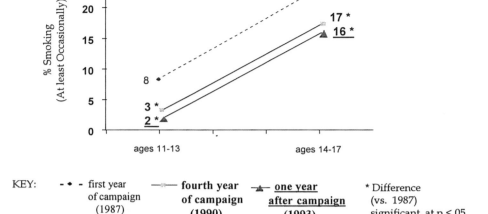

FIG. 12.5. Results from Canada's field tracking (from Health Canada's "Making a Difference" reports. The initial ad campaign ran from 1987–1992 (approximate annual expenditures = $.75 million in U.S. $). These results are for English-speaking youth (75% of population). Similar declines were observed from French-speaking youth (25% of population) who started out with higher smoking rates.

French-speaking youth, who started out with higher smoking rates. From 1990 to 1993, there were no further drops in underage smoking, but the initial drops were maintained. (Current data have yet to be released.)

To what can we attribute Canada's success with youth? A key difference between the Canadian and Californian antismoking ad campaigns is that Canada, until recently, focused strictly on youth. Not surprisingly, then, whereas the underage smoking rate was dropping in Canada from 1987 to 1990, the adult rate remained fairly stable at about 30%. The opposite pattern was attained in California, where the focus has been on adults: The adult smoking rate has been dropping, but not the youth rate. Also, Canada has adopted the Flynn et al. (1992) ad plus school program model. Federal and provincial governments have worked together to create and endorse an antismoking school program for grades 5–8+ (11- to 13+-year-olds) that has been adopted by most schools. The multisession program, frequently implemented by trained volunteers, provides peer support for nonsmoking, training in refusal skills and—since 1994–1995—training in how to resist the persuasive impact of tobacco marketing. In addition, Canada seems to have placed more focus on youth activities, such as antismoking poster and lyric contests. It has also received appreciable private sector support from marketers who are experts in reaching youth (e.g., Peugeot Bicycles and Musique Plus-TV).[11]

Two other factors must also be considered. From 1987 to 1990, Canada raised the price of cigarettes substantially, and youth may have opted not to smoke because it was too expensive (Hu et al., 1995). Also, in 1989, Canada banned ads promoting tobacco products (Turner, 1995). Thus tobacco companies were precluded from offsetting antismoking ads with cigarette ads, though they could sponsor and promote events (sports, concerts).[12] Many or all of these factors may have contributed to Canada's success.

When Antismoking Ads Work: A Comparison of Field Tracking Results. Based on field tracking, some further recommendations can be made about targeting youth: hold complementary events to promote nonsmoking, preferably co-sponsored by marketers with the resources and expertise to reach youth (e.g., MTV); and select ads and media geared strictly at youth; do not expect to reach both youth and adults with the same ads and media.

Lab Experiments

Overview of Method. In lab experiments, youth are randomly exposed either to antismoking ads (the experimental group) or to unrelated-to-smoking ads (the control group). Then, youth are asked about their attitudes and beliefs regarding smoking and/or their intent to smoke. Youth are not tracked to determine whether they subsequently smoke, because youth do not receive sufficient exposure to the antismoking ads to expect changes in smoking rates. However, any effects of the ads on smoking attitudes, beliefs, and/or intent are considered meaningful because, based on past research, these variables are leading indicators (precursors) of changes in smoking rates (Dinh, Sarason, Peterson, & Onstad, 1995). A prime advantage of lab experiments is that it is far easier to assign individuals at random to treatment versus control group, which maximizes group comparability and facilitates between-group comparisons. Also, because data collection is efficient and economical, researchers can study different groups of youth (e.g., low vs. high risk youth) as well as distinct types of antismoking ads (e.g., various themes and spokespeople).

---

[11]Canada's aggressive antismoking campaign may be motivated, in part, by its need to keep health costs down, because it provides universal health care.

[12]In 1995, the Canadian Supreme Court ruled the country's cigarette advertising ban was unconstitutional and negotiations are now underway to develop different restrictions (Turner, 1995).

Notwithstanding, very few lab experiments have examined the causal effects of antismoking ads. A few researchers have examined antismoking *warning labels.* Fischer, Richards, Berman, and Krugman (1989) found 44% of adolescents ignored the surgeon general's warning on cigarette ads, and Beltramini (1988) and Ho (1994) found people disbelieved the warning. Krugman, Fox, and Fletcher (1994) found youth paid more attention to novel warnings; similarly, Loken and Howard-Pitney (1988) reported specific warnings can reduce the attractiveness and persuasiveness of cigarette ads. Finally, Monismith, Shute, Pierre, and Alles (1981) reported 60% of youth opined antismoking ads seem effective. Relevant experiments are reported later.

Pechmann and Ratneshwar Lab Experiment (1994). This experiment helps to explain why it might be advantageous to use both antismoking ads and school programs to combat underage smoking. The study examined 300 California seventh graders who had already received antismoking health education at school and, perhaps, also at home, and therefore already believed smoking was unhealthy and unwise. These youth were, nonetheless, uncertain about whether smoking might make them look glamorous or mature, so they were still vulnerable to pro-smoking influences (e.g., cigarette ads and peer pressure). The antismoking ads were beneficial because they persuaded the youth that smoking was not only unhealthy but also unattractive and uncool. Thus, it appears the ads complemented teachers; teachers conveyed the health effects of smoking such as cancer, and the ads conveyed the social drawbacks such as smelly clothes and breath.

Pechmann and Knight Lab Experiment (1996). This experiment, conducted two years after Pechmann and Ratneshwar (1994), examined California ninth graders (though not the same students that participated in the 1994 study). The ninth graders had received antismoking schooling plus, by now, they had seen extensive antismoking ads. Thus, these youth were fairly "inoculated" against smoking: They believed it was unhealthy, unattractive, and uncool. Pechmann and Knight (1996) found that these youth were not swayed by cigarette ads alone, nor by peer smoking alone. However, when the youths were shown four cigarette ads and then a short video of peers smoking, despite the prior "inoculation," the combination caused youth to have more favorable beliefs about smokers (Pechmann & Knight, 1996). In effect, the cigarette ads and peer smoking worked synergistically: The ads showed highly attractive smoker images, and the peer smoking personalized the images, making the images seem realistic and relevant to youths' lives. Importantly, though, in this lab context, just one antismoking ad offset the effects of the cigarette ads plus the peer smoking video; that is, that one antismoking ad prevented youths from forming more favorable beliefs about smokers.

Conclusions Based on Lab Experiments. The aforementioned experiments further support the conclusions drawn from other research, namely, that antismoking ads should be used in tandem with school programs, and it is beneficial to expose youth to antismoking ads not only in junior high (e.g., sixth grade) but also in high school (e.g., ninth grade). In junior high, the ads can complement health education by showing that smoking has undesirable social, as well as health, consequences. Later, the ads can help to negate or neutralize pro-smoking influences such as cigarette ads and peer pressure.

Qualitative Research

Overview of Method. Many qualitative studies were conducted in which small groups of youth (6–10) were interviewed to obtain their ideas about smoking and their reactions to antismoking ads. Groups of ad experts also were interviewed for advice on ad content and media placement. The interviews were conducted in the formative stages of research, generally prior to implementing longitudinal field experiments (Bauman et al., 1988; Worden et al., 1988) or cross-sectional field tracking (Minnesota 1989, 1991). In addition, the CDC and others conducted qualitative research simply to develop more effective antismoking ads and PSAs (McKenna & Williams, 1993). Across the group interviews or "focus groups," there was a high degree of consensus about the components of effective antismoking ad campaigns. However, the results must be interpreted with caution, because the method is qualitative in nature. More specifically, too few people were interviewed for the data to be analyzed statistically or for the findings to be regarded as generalizable.

Conclusions Based on Qualitative Research. The following recommendations stem from past qualitative research:

1. Advice on Ad Content
   Use short messages that youth will find credible and informative. To contradict notions that smoking helps youth fit in and look grown up, stress the negative social and personal consequences of smoking.
   Discuss grooming (bad breath, smelly clothes), social issues (that smoking is not the norm and smokers do not fit in), the excessive expense, and smoking as an addiction.
   Stress that youth should make their own decisions, that they are in control.
   It is unclear whether ads that attack the tobacco industry can dissuade young people from smoking.

Focus on the negatives of smoking and smokers.

Do not try to glorify nonsmokers because most people are non-smokers, hence, generalizations about them may lack credibility. Avoid inadvertently promoting smoking by creating sympathy for smokers (e.g., by attacking smokers unjustly).

Do not focus on the long-term health effects of smoking.

This approach could backfire and suggest smoking is okay in the short run.

Also, most youth already know the long-term health effects and many do not care because they expect to quit later or they feel invincible.

Avoid showing smoking, because this might inadvertently suggest it is the norm, make smoking look exciting or attractive, or provide a smoking model for youth to emulate.

2. Advice on Ad Style (e.g., Spokesperson and Tone)

Do not present an adult viewpoint, lecture, or use exhortations (e.g., "be smoke free").

Sound conversational and casual, not overly sincere.

Do not highlight that the ad comes from the government or other authority.

Use self-confident, attractive actors that look slightly (e.g., 2 years) older than the target audience.

Do not show high risk youth in a negative light, because you may turn them off and thus fail to reach them.

Do not talk over students' heads or talk down to them.

To maintain interest, vary the spokespeople, themes, and slogans within campaigns and also for each new campaign.

3. Advice on Media Placements

Run ads on network television, after school on weekdays and during prime time (e.g., from 4 p.m. to 9 p.m.).

Place the ads in youth-oriented situation comedies and perhaps in special event youth programming (e.g., concerts, sports).

Also use cable television, such as MTV, which is far less expensive than network television.

Run complementary radio ads, avoiding school hours (e.g., run the ads from 3 p.m. to 11 p.m.).

Choose stations that youth listen to (e.g., contemporary rock).

CONCLUSIONS

Very small-scale test programs of antismoking ad campaigns and school programs have shown that these methods can reduce underage smoking (Flynn et al., 1994; Perry et al., 1992). Unfortunately, the four states (California, Massachusetts, Michigan, Minnesota) that have implemented these methods on a large scale have been less successful. Canada apparently succeeded in reducing underage smoking from 1987 to 1990 but, since then, no further reductions have been documented. Also, it is unclear to what extent Canada's apparent success from 1987 to 1990 is attributable to its antismoking ads and school programs or to its high cigarette prices and ban on cigarette ads.

One important conclusion that can be reached based on past research is that health officials should not try to rely exclusively on antismoking ads to combat underage smoking. It seems necessary to employ a multifaceted approach involving antismoking ads, special school programs and youth activities, enforcement of laws that prevent youth from purchasing cigarettes, and added restrictions that prevent youth from smoking in or around schools and popular hangouts (e.g., convenience stores, malls, and fast food restaurants). Further, policy officials should determine expenditures on antismoking advertising in a strategic manner. Expenditures should be based on, and adequate to offset, tobacco marketing. For instance, policy officials may want to strive for a 1 to 4 ratio of antismoking ads to cigarette ads (Lewit et al., 1981). Correspondingly, policy officials may want to increase antismoking ad expenditures over time to offset increases in tobacco marketing expenditures. In the past, antismoking ad expenditures have tended to decrease over time (see Table 12.1), which could be counterproductive. Finally, public health officials may need more training in implementing antismoking ad campaigns, particularly in hiring ad agencies and running strategically focused campaigns. This is the beginning of the road to stopping underage smoking with mass media antismoking advertising and a great deal still needs to be learned.

ACKNOWLEDGMENTS

The author sincerely thanks Marvin Goldberg for his advice and encouragement, and Eric Freund, John Mastrorilli, Susan Knight, and Greta Brooks for their technical assistance. She also thanks the government and nongovernment health officials and staff members who participated in interviews and sent materials about their antismoking advertising.

REFERENCES

Abt Associates, Inc. (1995). *Independent evaluation of the Massachusetts tobacco control program: First annual report, fiscal year 1994.*

Armstrong, B. K., de Klerk, N. H., Shean, R. E., Dunn, D. A., & Dolin, P. J. (1990). Influence of education and advertising on the uptake of smoking by children. *Medical Journal of Australia, 152,* 117–124.

Arian, Lowe, Travis, & Gusick (1993). Office on smoking and health: Nic (a teen) tracking report. Atlanta, GA: Department of Health and Human Services, Centers for Disease Control, Office on Smoking and Health.

Baan, B. (1990). Prevention of smoking in young children in Holland: Education and changing attitudes. New York: Springer-Verlag.

Bauman, K. E., Brown, J. D., Bryan, E. S., Fisher, L. A., Padgett, C. A., & Sweeney, J. M. (1988). Three mass media campaigns to prevent adolescent cigarette smoking. *Preventive Medicine, 17*(5), 510–530.

Bauman, K. E., LaPrelle, J., Brown, J. D., Koch, G. G., & Padgett, C. A. (1991). The influence of three mass media campaigns on variables related to adolescent smoking: Results of a field experiment. *American Journal of Public Health, 81*(5), 597–604.

Bell, R. M., Ellickson, P. L., & Harrison, E. R. (1993). Do drug prevention efforts persist into high school? How project ALERT did with ninth graders. *Preventive Medicine, 22*, 463–483.

Beltramini, R. F. (1988). Perceived believability of warning label information presented in cigarette advertising. *Journal of Advertising, 17*(1), 26–32.

Best, J. A., Thomson, S. J., Santi, S. M., Smith, E. A., & Brown, K. S. (1988). Preventing cigarette smoking among school children. *Annual Review of Public Health, 9*, 161–201.

Botvin, G. J. (1986). Substance abuse prevention research: Recent developments and future directions. *Journal of School Health, 56*, 369–374.

Bruvold, W. H. (1993). A meta-analysis of adolescent smoking prevention programs. *American Journal of Public Health, 83*(6), 872–880.

Canada Health Promotion Directorate (1991, 1992, 1993). Making a difference I, II and III: The impact of the health promotion directorate's social marketing campaigns (1987–91, 1991–92, 1992–93). Ottawa, Canada: Health Canada.

Campion, P., Owen, L., McNeill, A., & McGuire, C. (1994). Evaluation of a mass media campaign on smoking and pregnancy. *Addiction, 89*, 1245–1254.

Centers for Disease Control (1994). Surveillence for selected tobacco use behaviors: US 1900–1994. *Morbidity and Mortality Weekly Report,* CDC Surveillence Summaries, Vol. 43, SS-3, November 18, 1994.

Coe, R. M., Crouse, E., Cohen, J. D., & Fisher, E. B. (1982). Patterns of change in adolescent smoking behavior and results of a one year follow-up of a smoking prevention program. *Journal of School Health,* August, 348–353.

Consumer Reports (1995). "Hooked on tobacco: The teen epidemic," *60*(3), 142–147.

Collins, G. (1995). Companies sue to prevent control of cigarette sales. *New York Times,* August 11.

Cook, T. D., & Campbell, D. T. (1979). *Quasi-experimentation: Design and analysis issues for field settings.* Boston: Houghton Mifflin.

Dinh, K. T., Sarason, I. G., Peterson, A. V., & Onstad, L. E. (1995). Children's perceptions of smokers and nonsmokers: A longitudinal study. *Health Psychology, 14*(1), 32–40.

Donaldson, S. I., Piccinin, A. M., Graham, J. W., & Hansen, W. B. (1995). Resistance-skills training and onset of alcohol use: Evidence for beneficial and potentially harmful effects in public schools and in private catholic schools. *Health Psychology, 14*(4), 291–300.

Fischer, P. M., Richards, J. W., Berman, E. J., & Krugman, D. M. (1989). Recall and eye tracking study of adolescents viewing tobacco advertisements. *Journal of the American Medical Association, 261* (January), 84–89.

Flay, B. R. (1985). Psychosocial approaches to smoking prevention: A review of findings. *Health Psychology, 4*(5), 449–488.

Flynn, B. S., Worden, J. K., Secker-Walker, R. H., Badger, G. J., Geller, B. M., & Costanza, M. C. (1992). Prevention of cigarette smoking through mass media intervention and school programs. *American Journal of Public Health, 82*(6), 827–834.

Flynn, B. S., Worden, J. K., Secker-Walker, R. H., Pirie, P. L., Badger, G. J., Carpenter, J. H., & Geller, B. M. (1994). Mass media and school interventions for cigarette smoking prevention: Effects two years after completion. *American Journal of Public Health, 84*(7), 1148–1150.

Glynn, T. J. (1989). Essential elements of school-based smoking prevention programs. *Journal of School Health, 59*(5), 181–188.

Hilts, P. J. (1995). Study finds tobacco ads near schools. *New York Times,* August 3, A11.

Ho, R. (1994). Cigarette advertising and cigarette health warnings: What role do adolescents' motives for smoking play in their assessment. *Australian Psychologist, 29*(1), 49–56.

Hu, T.-W., Sung, H.-Y., & Keeler, T. E. (1995). The state antismoking campaign and the industry response: The effects of advertising on cigarette consumption in California. *American Economic Association Papers and Proceedings,* 85–90.

IOX Assessment Associates (1991). Evaluating the California 1990–91 tobacco education media campaign. Executive Rep. No. 1–4 (March, May, July, September 1991).

Kotler, P. (1991). *Marketing management* (7th ed.). Englewood Cliffs, NJ: Prentice-Hall.

Krugman, D. M., Fox, R. J., & Fletcher, J. E. (1994). Do adolescents attend to warnings in cigarette advertising? An eye-tracking approach. *Journal of Advertising Research,* November/December, 39–52.

Lavidge, R. J., & Steiner, G. A. (1961). A model for predictive measurements of advertising effectiveness. *Journal of Marketing, 25* (October), 59–62.

Lewit, E. M., Coate, D., & Grossman, M. (1981). The effects of government regulation on teenage smoking. *Journal of Law and Economics, 12* (December), 545–569.

Loken, B., & Howard-Pitney, B. (1988). Effectiveness of cigarette advertisements on women: An experimental study. *Journal of Applied Psychology, 73*(3), 378–382.

Lynch, B. L., & Bonnie, R. J. (1994). *Growing up tobacco free: Preventing nicotine addiction in children and youths.* Washington, DC: National Academy Press.

Max, W., & Rice, D. P. (1993). The cost of smoking in California. *Tobacco Control, 4*(Suppl. 1), S39–S46.

McKenna, J., & Williams, K. N. (1993). Crafting effective tobacco counter advertisements: Lessons from a failed campaign directed at teenagers. *Public Health Reports, 108*(Suppl. 1), 85–89.

Minnesota Department of Health (1987). *The Minnesota nonsmoking initiative June, 1985–December, 1986: A report to the 1987 legislature.* Minneapolis, MN: Department of Health.

Minnesota Department of Health (1989). *The Minnesota tobacco-use prevention initiative 1987–1989: A report to the 1989 legislature.*

Minnesota Department of Health (1991). *Minnesota tobacco-use prevention initiative: 1989–1990: A report to the 1991 legislature.*

Monismith, S. W., Shute, R. E., St. Pierre, R. W., & Alles, W. F. (1981). Opinions of seventh to twelfth graders regarding the effectiveness of pro- and anti-smoking messages. *Journal of Drug Education, 11*(3), 213–225.

Murray, D. M., Perry, C. L., Griffin, G., Harty, K. C., Jacobs, D. R., Schmid, L., Daly, K., & Pallonen, U. (1992). Results from a statewide approach to adolescent tobacco use prevention. *Preventive Medicine, 21,* 449–472.

Osmon, H. E. (1995). Right decisions, right now. [Letter and brochures sent to C. Pechmann], November 8.

Pechmann, C., & Ratneshwar, S. (1994). The effects of anti-smoking and cigarette advertising on young adolescents' perceptions of peers who smoke. *Journal of Consumer Research, 21* (September), 236–251.

Pechmann, C., & Knight, S. J. (1996). Cigarette ads, anti-smoking ads and peers: Why do underage youth start smoking cigarettes? In Kim P. Corfman and John Lynch (Eds.), *Advances in consumer research* (Vol. 23, p. 267). Provo, Utah: Association for Consumer Research.

Pierce, J. P., Evans, N., Farkas, A. J., Cavin, S. W., Berry, C., Kramer, M., Kealey, S., Rosbrook, B., Choi, W., & Kaplan, R. M. (1994). Tobacco use in California: An evaluation of the tobacco control program, 1989–1993. Unpublished report, University of California, San Diego.

Pierce, J. P., Evans, N., Farkas, A. J., Cavin, S. W., Berry, C., Kramer, M., Kealey, S., Rosbrook, B., Choi, W., & Kaplan, R. M. (1990, 1992, 1993, 1994). *California tobacco surveys: Technical reports.* Unpublished reports, University of California, San Diego.

Perry, C. L., Kelder, S. H., Murray, D. M., & Klepp, K.-I. (1992). Communitywide smoking prevention: Long-term outcomes of the Minnesota heart health program and the class of 1989 study. *American Journal of Public Health, 82*(9), 1210–1216.

Pollay, R. W. (1994). Promises, promises: Self-regulation of US cigarette broadcast advertising in the 1960s. *Tobacco Control, 3*, 134–144.

Popham, W. J., Potter, L. D., Hetrick, M. A., Muthen, L. K., Duerr, J. M., & Johnson, M. D. (1994). Effectiveness of the California 1990–1991 tobacco education media campaign. *American Journal of Preventive Medicine, 10* (November/December), 319–326.

Purdum, T. S. (1995). Clinton proposes widespread curbs on young smokers. *New York Times,* A1, A11.

Schneider, L., Klein, B., & Murphy, K. M. (1981). Government regulation of cigarette health information. *Journal of Law and Economics, 24* (December), 575–612.

Schuster, C. P., & Powell, C. P. (1987). Comparison of cigarette and alcohol advertising controversies. *Journal of Advertising, 16*(2), 26–33.

Shean, R. E., de Klerk, N. H., Armstrong, B. K., & Walker, N. R. (1994). Seven year follow-up of a smoking prevention program for children. *Australian Journal of Public Health, 18*(2), 205–208.

Snow, W. H., Gilchrist, L. D., & Schnicke, S. P. (1985). A critique of progress in adolescent smoking prevention. *Children and Youth Services Review, 7,* 1–19.

Tanner, J. F. Jr., Hunt, J. B., & Eppright, D. R. (1991). The protection motivation model: A normative model of fear appeals. *Journal of Marketing, 55*(3), 36–45.

Turner, C. (1995). Anti-smoking drive offers lessons for US. *Los Angeles Times,* September 30, A2.

U.S. Department of Health and Human Services (1989). *Reducing the health consequences of smoking: 25 years of progress. A report of the surgeon general* (DHHS Publication No. CDC 89-8411). Washington, DC: Government Printing Office.

U.S. Department of Health, Education and Welfare (1979). *Teenage smoking: Immediate and long-term patterns.* Washington, DC: US DHEW, National Institute of Education.

Wewers, M. E., Ahijevych, K., & Page, J. A. (1991). Evaluation of a mass media community smoking cessation campaign. *Addictive Behaviors, 16,* 289–294.

Worden, J. K., Flynn, B. S., Geller, B. M., Chen, M., Shelton, L. G., Secker-Walker, R. H., Solomon, D. S., Solomon, L. J., Couchy, S., & Costanza, M. C. (1988). Development of a smoking prevention mass media program using diagnostic and formative research. *Preventive Medicine, 17,* 531–558.

Chapter 13

Social Advertising and Tobacco Demand Reduction in Canada

James H. Mintz
Neville Layne
Rachel Ladouceur
Jane Hazel
Monique Desrosiers
Health Canada, Ottawa

ABSTRACT

Since 1985, social marketing has been a major component of the Canadian government's efforts to reduce tobacco use. Social advertising has been the linchpin of Health Canada's antitobacco social marketing program. Together with legislative measures and antitobacco programming that targets vulnerable segments of the population, social marketing is part of a centrally coordinated and multipronged strategy to reduce tobacco demand in Canada. This chapter describes how research is used in the design, implementation, and evaluation of antitobacco advertising. It describes ad-concept focus testing, awareness monitoring, and impact assessment, as well as two segmentation frameworks that have helped to define the target audience for new messages and evaluate the impact of advertising in changing the attitudes and behaviors of the population.

Health Canada has been in the health promotion business for 17 years. In that time, much has been learned about what works and what does not. It is apparent that raising awareness of an issue and proposing changes in behavior is not enough to actually cause people to eat nutritiously, exercise, quit smoking, or stop driving while under the influence of alcohol. Changing behavior requires a step that bridges the gap between knowing something and actually acting on it. That step is "internalizing" the knowledge and it involves examining one's values and deciding what is important. The strategy used to walk people through that step is often referred to as *social marketing*, which is defined as "the design, implementation and control of programs that seek to increase the acceptability of a social idea or cause by a target group" (Kotler & Zaltman, 1971, pp. 3–12).

For Health Canada, social marketing is more than just social advertising. A mix of traditional marketing tactics that include event marketing and corporate sponsorship is used. Resources such as pamphlets on how to talk to your kids about drugs are developed, and various programs, including television programs aimed at particular target groups, are produced. Health Canada also initiates strategic partnerships with other levels of government, as well as nongovernment and private sector organizations, who have wide access to the target audience.

THE ROLE OF RESEARCH

Health Canada's social marketing campaigns are based on careful analysis of the existing situation and trends, followed by the establishment of clear goals and measurable objectives for the initiatives, and the conception, testing, and development of marketing tools. This approach puts social marketing in the same business as that of the purveyors of breakfast cereal, toothpaste, and cars. Social marketing is different from other types of marketing in that the product of social marketing is a social climate that is conducive to health promotion, disease prevention, and positive lifestyles. Also, unlike most other types of marketing motivated by profit, the motivation behind social marketing is to reduce the incidence of deaths, illness, and health care costs, and to improve quality of life for Canadians. However, many techniques and strategies used by social marketers are similar to those of other marketing professionals, and all of the tools used are based on much market research.

The focus here is on the research that has helped shape Health Canada's antitobacco advertising campaigns. Some of this research, such as the development of psychographic profiles, helps Health Canada make choices about partnerships, special events, and the development and dissemination of its programs. Other studies, such as monitoring levels of recall and tracking changes in behavior and attitudes, are designed specifically to evaluate the reach and impact of antitobacco ads.

HISTORY OF HEALTH CANADA'S ANTITOBACCO EFFORTS

Since the 1960s, Canada has played an active role both in building the case against tobacco products and in developing policies and programs to combat the problem. In 1985, provincial and territorial health ministries and national health associations in Canada joined and launched a National

Strategy to Reduce Tobacco Use, with the ambitious vision of producing a generation of nonsmokers by the year 2000.

By the 1980s, it was evident that the tobacco problem was so complex it needed to be attacked on many fronts. The National Strategy identified seven strategic directions to achieve its goals of tobacco use prevention, cessation, and public protection. These strategic directions were legislation, providing access to information, making available services and programs, supporting citizen action, coordinating public policy across government sectors, undertaking research, and message promotion.

As part of the "message promotion" component of the National Strategy, Health Canada launched in 1985 an antitobacco social marketing campaign, "Break Free," and its French counterpart, "Fumer, c'est fini!" The goal of this campaign was to promote the benefits of being smoke-free to young Canadians between the ages of 11 and 17.

"Break Free"

When the campaign was first conceived, Canadians had barely begun to question the social acceptability of smoking. Many young Canadians were growing up in an environment where smoking was a rite of passage. Yet, research from other jurisdictions suggested that people who had not taken up the habit by age 19 were unlikely to ever start smoking. For this reason, and because of limited resources, the focus turned to prevention of tobacco use, with a primary target group of 11- to 13-year-olds.

From 1987 to 1993, the campaign used television, radio, bus and transit shelter posters, magazine ads, and targeted ublications to promote the "Break Free" message. These efforts were supplemented by special promotions and information activities, such as poster and lyric-riting contests. The campaign featured popular entertainers and sports heroes as role models for the young people, and equated not smoking with such qualities as charisma, stardom, leadership, and having a positive self-concept.

Tracking

Independent tracking and analysis, in 1987–1988, measured the campaign's impact based on six indicators. These were primary impact indicators, consisting of levels of campaign awareness among the target audience, attitudes (Were people persuaded or influenced?), current use, and trends. Secondary impact indicators included behavioral intentions (Did they intend to smoke in the future?) and interpersonal communication (Did they talk with others about smoking?).

From the beginning, the levels of awareness of the social marketing campaign were strong. Aided recall of the new stream of "Break Free" ads, for example, grew from 69% in 1987 to 80% in 1989.

TABLE 13.1
Selected Reported Reactions of Youth 11 to 17 After
Having Seen Antismoking Ads (Multiple Responses)

% Nonsmokers	Total	English Canada	French Canada
	(1,374)	(1,014)	(360)
Helped in choice not to smoke	39	35	48
Made it easier not to start	19	15	23
Has had no influence	15	16	13
% Smokers	(290)	(196)	(99)
Made it easier to cut down	15	14	15
Made it easier to quit	4	5	2
Has had no influence	36	31	47

Note: Health Canada Campaign Tracking, October 1993, Creative Research International (Toronto).

From 1993 to 1994, the last year of the antismoking campaign exclusively targeting Canadian youth, household interviews were conducted with about 2,000 youth (1,500 from English Canada and 500 from French Canada). Respondents were asked about reactions that were applicable to them after having been exposed to the ads.

For nonsmokers, the ads were reportedly successful in helping 39% not to smoke and 19% not to start smoking. Among smokers, 15% reported the ads helped them cut down the amount they smoked, whereas 4% agreed the ads made it easier to quit (see Table 13.1).

Stronger effects were reported among nonsmoking youth in French Canada and smoking youth in English Canada. Smokers were also more than twice as likely as nonsmokers to feel the ads had no influence on them (36% of smokers versus 15% of nonsmokers; see Table 13.1).

PSYCHOGRAPHICS RESEARCH

Demographic classification is quite a blunt instrument when trying to get a better fix on target markets. A more precise tool was needed with which to measure who was and was not being reached by Health Canada's messages so that efforts could be focused more productively. In 1991, work began with a research group in Toronto that had developed psychographic profiles of young people from ages 11 to 17. The youth typology was developed from young people's responses to a 30-item questionnaire on their social activities and interests. Respondents were asked about their lifestyles and personal characteristics, including leisure activities, habits, attitudes, beliefs, opinions, hopes, fears, prejudices, needs, and desires (Creative Research Group Ltd., 1989–1992a, 1989–1992b, 1989–1992c).

From the survey data, seven character types were identified. These character types and their profile summaries are:

1. Big City Independents
   Independent of spirit; not easily influenced
   Self-focused
   Outgoing and gregarious, but not likely to commit to only one person; more of a loner than a team player; not a "flag waver" in terms of belief in national pride
   Relatively free of sexual discrimination; supporter of human rights
   New products, brands, fashion hold little interest; personal appearance not important

2. Passive Luddites
   Homebody; family important; traditional family structure
   Universe is close to home
   More old-fashioned views on morality
   More tolerant of, if not involved in, substance use/abuse
   Claims some degree of independence, but is concerned about how seen by others
   Not as ready as some to support the disadvantaged
   Lacks optimism; has lower level of ambition
   Jobs are an issue
   Not comfortable with technology

3. Quiet Conformers
   A strong work ethic
   Has a social conscience
   Tends to be more placid than others; a little shy
   More of a listener; will follow rather than lead
   Against smoking and other substance abuse

4. Concerned Moralists
   Very traditional—almost old fashioned—in attitudes toward family, sex roles, sexuality, etc.
   A team player, but more of a follower than a leader
   A little less optimistic than some and not comfortable with technology; however, looks to the future and has career ambitions
   A little quiet and shy
   insecure and needs the support and approval of others
   Very conscious about how they look; interested in material things; fashion; quite brand conscious and looks to advertising for information

5. Small-town Traditionalists
   Traditional outlook—even old fashioned—on values, sex roles, sex, work ethic, family, religion
   Monogamous

Has national pride; believes in government's role

Ambitious; self-confident; tries new things

Socially active but confined to traditional value system; has a social conscience for the less fortunate, but draws the line on certain issues such as abortion, drug use, AIDS, etc. (less tolerant in these areas)

Antisubstance use/abuse—cigarettes, drugs

6. Tomorrow's Leaders

Quite ambitious with strong leadership tendencies

A participator; team person; gregarious; outgoing

Not really traditional; embraces mores of today; nevertheless has at least some faith in "the system"

The future is important; optimistic about that future

Likes to be thought of as fashionable, up-to-date, modern; fitness is important

Very antismoking

7. TGIF (Thank Goodness It's Friday)

Concern is more for today than the future

No particular work ethnic; not ambitious; not disciplined

Lacking in traditional values and without a strong social conscience; not quite a redneck, but pointed in that direction.

Culture of any sort is not a priority

Not entirely self-sufficient; needs company of others, particularly the opposite sex

Substance use/abuse is part of the TGIF lifestyle. This includes cigarettes, drugs, and alcohol.

The character types accounted for the percentages shown in Table 13.2 of the sample population.

Among these character types, smoking behaviors are very different. Within these identified groups of young people ages 11–17 (see Table 13.2),

TABLE 13.2
Psychographic Types: Percentages of
Sample Canadian Population (Age 11–17)

Psychographic Type	% of Sample Population Age 11–17
Big City Independents	18%
Tomorow's Leaders	15%
Passive Luddites	10%
Quiet Conformers	20%
Concerned Moralists	11%
Small Town Traditionalists	8%
TGIFs	18%

the percentage of those who smoke at least on occasion is as follows: Big City Independents—13%, Tomorrow's Leaders—7%, Passive Luddites—20%, Quiet Conformers—6%, Concerned Moralists—17%, Small Town Traditionalists—1%, TGIFs—49%.

The 1993 national average of smoking among youth was 17% (estimated 459,000 people), compared with 14% (360,000) in 1992 and 18% (466,000) in 1987.

The most striking result of this research was that one of the seven character types, the TGIF group, contained a dramatically higher proportion of smokers and other substance abusers than the target group as a whole. For instance, in 1993, the national average of daily smoking among youth was 17%. Among TGIFs it was a stunning 49%. These findings started new research that led to the development in 1993 of the Morphing Cigarette ad, an ad designed specifically for the TGIFers. This ad depicted an adolescent girl being transformed into a distorted, life-size cigarette as she shared a smoke in the schoolyard with her peers. In a moment of epiphany, she resumes her human form and throws away the cigarette.

THE TOBACCO DEMAND REDUCTION STRATEGY

The success of Health Canada's antitobacco efforts was being threatened on another front. The rising cost of tobacco products in Canada was being offset by a growing trade in contraband cigarettes from the United States. As a result, in February 1994, the federal and some provincial governments dramatically cut tobacco excise taxes.

The tax cuts alleviated the smuggling problem. At the same time, a strong new imperative was created to mitigate the increase in tobacco consumption that the tax cuts might cause. Therefore, the government earmarked $185 million for a comprehensive, 3-year Tobacco Demand Reduction Strategy (TDRS), financed by a surtax on tobacco manufacturers. TDRS was designed to minimize the impact of the tax reduction on tobacco consumption in Canada and buttress efforts to marginalized tobacco usage across society.

Cuts to the 1995–1996 federal budget reduced the overall budget for the Tobacco Strategy, but all of its original components have survived. The TDRSs objectives are to minimize the increase in tobacco consumption expected in those groups most likely to succumb to the opportunity presented by lower prices of tobacco, increase the priority of tobacco control as a public health measure, increase public knowledge of the dangers associated with tobacco product use, and enhance public awareness of the health risks associated with environmental tobacco smoke. To meet its objectives, the new strategy provides for programming in research, legislation, programs, and message promotion.

In the area of legislation, the federal government in 1994 proclaimed the Tobacco Sales to Young Persons Act, raising the legal age for buying tobacco from 16 to 18 and increasing the penalties to retailers for non-compliance. The government also stepped up enforcement of regulations under the Tobacco Products Control Act, which bans tobacco advertising and mandates health messages on tobacco products.

To improve access to information, the government increased its funding to the National Clearinghouse on Tobacco and Health, a national information and referral center that also serves as a resource base to support citizen action and community initiatives.

New programs and services are being developed for specific target groups, including women, youth, immigrants, aboriginals, low-income groups, high risk-takers, and groups with low education levels and literacy skills.

Besides programs at the national level, the strategy also provides funding for community-based tobacco programming and activities, both for the general population and for priority target groups.

The new tobacco control strategy targets a much wider audience than previous strategies. Consequently, Health Canada's social marketing initiatives must consist of messages that target not only teens and preteens, but also adults—both smokers and nonsmokers—particularly caregivers, young families, opinion leaders, and influencers of children and youth.

The significant declines in Canada's tobacco market since 1986 had not been uniform across the population. The data showed tobacco control measures had better results with smokers who were less addicted to tobacco, more averse to taking risks, or more amenable to quitting. Tobacco use in Canada was higher among aboriginals, youth with low literacy skills, adults of lower socioeconomic status, and some immigrant groups. These groups, along with pregnant women, therefore became secondary targets of Health Canada's newest antitobacco social marketing campaign.

CAMPAIGN OBJECTIVES

The campaign objectives are to move the issue of tobacco use from a personal choice to a public health issue, to increase pro-health choices over smoking through greater respect for nonsmokers' health and recognition of the toxic nature of tobacco products, to build and strengthen negative images of tobacco, and to increase awareness about the issue of tobacco access by minors.

Due to the strong performance of Health Canada's antitobacco media campaigns dating back to 1985, and the positive evaluations of similar campaigns in other jurisdictions, it was decided that antitobacco advertising should again form the centerpiece of the social marketing strategy.

This time, however, a different approach in advertising was necessary because attitudes toward smoking had changed significantly since the 1980s. A decade of antitobacco legislation and social marketing had transformed Canada from a society where smoking was passively accepted by nonsmokers, to a much more polarized society that pitted nonsmoker's rights against the profit motives of the tobacco industry and against the claims of smokers that tobacco use is an issue of personal choice. Antitobacco messages designed for earlier campaigns had had a positive spin. They linked nonsmoking with high self-esteem and avoided shaming tobacco users. Now that public opinion had taken a more belligerent turn, it was time to use a much more hard-hitting array of messages.

For example, research showed that 65% of respondents who said they had quit smoking in the year preceding the Health Promotion Survey of 1990 most frequently cited increased knowledge of health risks as their reason for quitting. In the Health Promotion Survey of 1990, 625 of Canadians 15 and over reported they felt adverse effects from tobacco smoke. Most Canadian smokers (81%) now believe that stopping smoking will help to improve their health and well-being.

This research indicated the tone of the messages needed to be serious and adult oriented, and focus on the public health and social consequences of smoking.

THE NEW AD CAMPAIGN

First, 16 television ad concepts were developed in four genres. Later the selection was narrowed to 13 ads of which 5 were antitobacco industry ads, 3 were health effects ads, 4 were secondhand smoke ads, and 1 was an ad that vilified retailers who sold tobacco to minors.

Instead of producing all 13, animated versions of the concepts were created and focus tested in July 1994 in 45-minute interviews with 300 randomly chosen representatives from 10 target groups.

More ads were tested in the antitobacco industry genre than in any of the others. This reflected the initial thought that a "hard-hitting" approach should focus on the tobacco industry. However, field results showed conclusively that the ads in the antitobacco industry genre were not a big hit and were soundly outperformed by the secondhand smoke and health effects ads.

All the ads were evaluated based on scores obtained from the 300 respondents responding to five criteria. These were:

Fit	Did the elements of the ad hang together?
Appeal	Did the ad make smoking much less/a little less appealing?

Credence   Was the ad's main point believable?

Enjoyableness   Did respondents enjoy watching the ad?

Thrust   Did the ad have a powerful message about smoking?

Smoking Feelings   (a) Smokers—did the ad make the respondent much
                      more or more likely to quit smoking?
                      (b) Nonsmokers—did the ad make the respondent
                      much less or less likely to take up smoking?

Ads in the *health effects* genre scored higher than any other genre in the categories of appeal, thrust, and smoking feelings. Those in the *secondhand smoke* genre scored most highly in the categories of fit and enjoyableness. The ad in the *retail* genre scored highest in the category of credence (see Table 13.3).

Meanwhile, the five ads in the *antiindustry* genre scored well below average in thrust and enjoyableness, and underperformed the other genres in the critical area of changing feelings about smoking (see Table 13.3).

Results showed there was much disparity in receptiveness to the antiindustry ads, with more negative than positive scores. There was some limited positive support from male youth and susceptible nonsmokers, but responses from adult males, French Canada, opinion leaders, and emphatic smokers were negative.

The secondhand smoke genre garnered both a high average score and positive scores in all five criteria. Target groups in support of this genre were youth of both sexes, French Canadians, as well as emphatic and susceptible nonsmokers. Only emphatic smokers rated the ads negatively, and only in the appeal category.

TABLE 13.3
Reported Scores from Test Responses to
Different Genres of Antitobacco Ads

"Facets" Responses	*Fit*	*Appeal*	*Credence*	*Enjoyableness*	*Thrust*	*Smoking Feelings*
Total	76	67	57	45	73	31
Average of antitobacco industry (ATI) ads	68	59	47	38	61	23
Average of secondhand smoke ads	81	76	62	56	83	38
Average of health effects ads	80	79	61	43	84	41
Retail ad	80	54	73	40	67	20
Average of non-ATI ads	80	74	63	50	81	37
Average of Health Canada campaign ads	82	85	69	55	89	47

The health effects ads received as many positive responses as did the secondhand smoke ads, and from similar target groups. Health effects ads also won support from adult females.

In the end, the three leading advertisements in the secondhand smoke and health effects genres were selected. The launch of these ads was accompanied by the placement of three print ads in Canadian newspapers in January 1995.

MONITORING STUDY

To measure the campaign's impact on awareness levels of the major target groups, a monitoring study consisting of two surveys was devised—a Benchmark Monitoring Wave in December 1994, immediately preceding the campaign's major media launch in January 1995, and a Post Implementation Wave in February and March 1995.

Both waves used random selection to obtain a nationally representative sample of 1,300 youth and adult respondents. Teens and French Canadians were oversampled to ensure statistically acceptable sample sizes. Data was gathered through telephone interviews.

Results from the postimplementation wave indicate that 89% of Canadians age 11 and over recalled, with prompting, the new campaign's television ads. Without prompting, the rate of recall for Health Canada's new campaign ads was 38%, compared to 20% in the Benchmark wave measuring unprompted recall of Health Canada ads from previous campaigns. Among adults, the increase in recall between the two waves doubled, from 19% to 38%. Among youth, it increased from 29% to 37% (Tandemar study; see Table 13.4).

TABLE 13.4
Rates of Recall of Health Canada's Ads

	Benchmark Wave	Postimplementation Wave	
	Without** Prompting	With* Prompting	Without Prompting
Total	20	89	38*
			49**
Adults	19	88	38*
			48**
Youth	29	96	37*
			61**

*Recognition of new Health Canada ads
**Recognition of Health Canada ads from previous campaigns

Both French and English Canada so exceeded the industry norm as to place the campaign in the top 10% of ads tracked.

CONTINUUM MODEL

As in earlier tracking studies, data will continue to be collected on smoking behavior, attitudes, and trends. However, one significant change is the adoption of a classification system, developed from studies in California, that rejects the classification of respondents as either smokers or nonsmokers, replacing it with a six-part continuum, ranging from the most committed smokers to the most emphatic nonsmokers. Changes in attitudes, beliefs, and behavior in each of the six segments of the population will be measured.

This classification system (see Table 13.5) has already proven useful in ensuring that the creative concepts chosen for the media campaign were well received by susceptible nonsmokers—those most at risk of joining the ranks of the smoking population.

Another advantage of the susceptibility analysis is that it allows researchers to project what the future profile of the population could look like in the absence of tobacco control measures.

Finally, by adding such categories as "susceptible smokers" and "quitters" to the analysis, it will be easier to evaluate how respondents' reported beliefs, attitudes, and behavioral intentions are reflected in their subsequent behaviors.

Although the monitoring study has shown the new ads are highly memorable, the results of a tracking study indicated the ads were having an effect on attitudes and behaviors of the population.

For example, the 1994–1995 tracking study showed that 67% strongly agreed with the idea that the ads successfully brought out the issue of the harmfulness of tobacco; 61% strongly agreed that the ads clearly got across

TABLE 13.5
Prevalence of Smoking Among Canadian
Youth 11–17, Smoking Continuum

	Total	11–13	14–17
Regular smokers who intend to continue	9	3	13
Regular smokers who intent to quit	3	1	5
Occasional smokers	5	3	7
Susceptible nonsmokers	16	20	13
Quitters	8	5	10
Emphatic nonsmokers	57	66	50

Note: Research Review Report, March 1995 (p. 3), Sage Research Corporation, Toronto.

the need to respect the health of nonsmokers; 85% agreed strongly that the ads made them stop and think about the harmful effects of smoking cigarettes around children and infants; 47% felt the ads had changed their own smoking behavior, and 59% felt the ads had some influence on other people's smoking behavior; and 35% had a discussion about smoking because of the ads.

CONCLUSIONS

This chapter has outlined the major research tools that have helped to shape Health Canada's antitobacco advertising campaigns during the last decade. As new research methodologies evolve, there will be better methods of influencing public behavior and evaluating advertisers' effectiveness in bringing about positive changes in tobacco use attitudes and behaviors.

REFERENCES

Kotler, P., & Zaltman, G. (1971). Social marketing: An approach to planned social change. *Journal of Marketing, 35*, 3–12.

The Creative Research Group Ltd. (1989–1992a). *Activity and interests questionaire.* Ontario: Author.

The Creative Research Group Ltd. (1989–1992b). *Campaign tracking.* Ontario: Author.

The Creative Research Group Ltd. (1989–1992c). *Youth target.* Ontario: Author.

Chapter 14

Low Yield, Light, and Ultra Light Cigarettes: Let's Understand the Product Before We Promote

Lynn T. Kozlowski
Christine T. Sweeney
The Pennsylvania State University

ABSTRACT

Low yield, light, and ultra light cigarettes have been aggressively promoted by cigarette manufacturers to help keep health-conscious smokers smoking. The industry move to lower tar cigarettes, however, has been shown to mislead consumers and promote continued smoking, rather than actually reducing risks to continuing smokers. Current consumers of low yield cigarettes need to be informed of the risks of using these products. The impressions created by advertising and marketing "safer" cigarettes needs to be met with systematic countermarketing. These campaigns and messages need to be informed by an understanding of the product. This chapter describes the Federal Trade Commission Method for testing the tar and nicotine yields of cigarettes and describes how cigarettes are constructed to produce reduced yields on smoking machines, yet high yields in the hands and mouths of smokers. Special attention will be given to issues related to ventilated-filter cigarettes. Most, if not all, cigarettes delivering less than 15 mg of tar are ventilated-filter cigarettes. This design feature allows the manufacturer to reduce tar and nicotine levels by simple manipulations (increasing filter air dilution from 0% to 80–90%). Vents can even be placed invisibly on the filters. Evidence shows that about 50% of smokers behaviorally block filter vents with their fingers or lips and thereby increase the tar and nicotine yields from these cigarettes. In the extreme, the lowest yield cigarettes (1 mg tar) can be turned into medium to high yield cigarettes (11 mg to 28 mg tar) by alterations in smoking behavior that include vent blocking. Proposals for and examples of promotions to counter the campaigns for low yield cigarettes are given.

Since the modern public health war against cigarettes began in the late 1960s, the tobacco industry has shown strong interest in the development and promotion of lower tar cigarettes (e.g., Davis, Healy, & Hawk, 1990; Kozlowski, 1981a, 1989). The so-called "tar derby" was clearly an effort to hold on to tobacco customers by offering them "less-hazardous" cigarettes (e.g., Cohen, 1992; Pollay, 1989; Warner & Slade, 1992). In one study (Kozlowski, Rickert, Pope, Robinson, & Frecker, 1982), this laboratory found, for example, that many smokers of low yield cigarettes (94% of ultra light smokers) report that they have turned to low yield cigarettes either as a "step toward quitting" or to reduce the risks of their smoking because they thought these cigarettes were "safer."

Part of the explicit rationale behind the testing of cigarettes by the Federal Trade Commission (FTC) and the reporting of these results in advertisements was to encourage smokers to smoke lower tar cigarettes (Federal Trade Commission, 1979), but at the same time the FTC provided that claims about tar and nicotine yields in advertising could not be accompanied by claims about reduced health hazards (e.g., Peeler, 1994). High profile articles in *Science* (Gori, 1976) and *Journal of the American Medical Association* (Benowitz, Jacob, & Yu, 1986; Gori & Lynch, 1978) have contributed to the support for smoking lights and ultra lights. The idea was basically, if a person must smoke, at least use a lower tar brand. Unfortunately, so-called less hazardous cigarettes often do not reduce risk, despite the consumers' fondest hopes (Gerstein & Levison, 1982; Kozlowski, 1981a, 1981b; Kozlowski, Rickert, Robinson, & Grunberg, 1980; Participants of the Fourth Scarborough Conference on Preventive Medicine, 1985).

The actual tar and nicotine yield of a cigarette primarily depends on the smoking behavior of the individual smoker. Therefore, reductions in machine-smoked standard tar and nicotine yields are often not reflected in changes in tar and nicotine exposures in smokers (Gerstein & Levison, 1982; Kozlowski, 1981a, 1981b; Kozlowski, Frecker, Khouw, & Pope, 1980; Participants of the Fourth Scarborough Conference on Preventive Medicine, 1985). Smokers can compensate easily for reduced yields by changing the way they smoke each cigarette. And, further, some smokers who would otherwise have quit have continued to smoke because they believe they have responded adequately to the disease risks of smoking by using lower tar brands (USDHHS, 1988, 1989; Warner & Slade, 1992). Compensatory smoking and decreased smoking cessation as a result of the availability of lower yield cigarettes "suggest the very real prospect that the existence of low t/n cigarettes has actually caused more smoking than would have occurred in their absence and thereby raised the morbidity and mortality associated with smoking" (Warner & Slade, 1992).

PAST RESEARCH ON THE EFFECTS
OF FILTER VENTILATION ON STANDARD TAR
AND NICOTINE YIELDS

Although a number of manufacturing changes have contributed to the development of lower tar and nicotine cigarettes, filter ventilation has been the major change behind the modern low yield cigarettes (Kozlowski, 1983). Filter vents serve to dilute smoke with air, thereby reducing standard yields of tar, nicotine, and carbon monoxide. However, simple changes in smoking behavior (i.e., blocking vents with either lips, fingers, or tape) can reduce this air dilution effect. The standard smoking-machine assay for tar and nicotine fixes puff size (35 cc), puffing rate (once every 58 sec), puff duration (2 sec), and butt length (generally filter plus overwrap plus 3 mm) to which the cigarette is smoked. Such standard assays give us so-called tar or nicotine yields by the Federal Trade Commission (FTC) Method. Many smokers mistakenly believe these reported yields indicate how much tar and nicotine is in each cigarette: Nicotine *yield*, however, is not the same as nicotine *content*. Cigarettes do not deliver fixed amounts of tar and nicotine, the way a pill delivers a fixed dose of a vitamin. Yields depend on how an individual smokes. Tar and nicotine numbers estimate the amount average smokers would get if they smoked in a standard way. Because different people smoke in different ways, there is no easy way to know how close a particular individual is to the "average" or "standard."

Although cigarette manufacturers are generally secretive about the construction of their cigarette, one can sometimes find information about unnamed "commercial cigarettes" in tobacco science journals. Parker and Montgomery, scientists for a filter manufacturer, have provided valuable data on filter ventilation (or air dilution) and tar and nicotine yields (Parker & Montgomery, 1979). (The discussion tends to focus on tar yields as the major source of carcinogens—nicotine and tar yields are generally highly correlated, above 0.9.) Their data show the strong relation between vents and yield. It also demonstrates that occluding the vents on the lowest yield cigarettes (1 mg tar) could render them high tar cigarettes. Occluding vents on a light cigarette would have proportionately less effect on yields, but it would serve to erase the apparent yield reduction from lights.

The large amount of research on compensatory smoking in self-selected smokers of various strength cigarettes does not lead to the expectation that there would be differences in average smoke exposure between smokers of light and high yield cigarettes (e.g., Gerstein and Levison, 1982; Gori & Lynch, 1983; Kozlowski, Frecker, & Lei, 1982), even if the vents on the lights were not blocked.

PAST RESEARCH ON VENT BLOCKING

Kozlowski, Frecker, Khouw, and Pope (1980) were the first to report the vent-blocking problem. Vent blocking is most easily done with the lips, although fingers can also be used to cover about half the vents at one time. Some of the research participants have actually carried rolls of tape to cover the vents. In developing this line of research on vent blocking, there have been two complementary kinds of doubt: Some critics said, "Sure, it could happen, but it doesn't happen often enough to care about." Other critics said, "If it does happen, it doesn't make very much difference to the dose of smoke to the smoker."

Prevalence

Vent blocking is far from a rare event. Four different laboratories have produced a total of eight peer-reviewed studies that have found evidence of vent blocking (Hofer, Nil, & Battig, 1991; Kozlowski, Rickert, Pope, Robinson, & Frecker, 1982; Kozlowski, Heatherton, Frecker, & Nolte, 1989; Kozlowski, Pillitteri, & Sweeney, 1994; Kozlowski, Pope, & Lux, 1988; Lombardo, Davis, & Prue, 1983; Robinson, Young, Rickert, Fey, & Kozlowski, 1983; Zacny & Stitzer, 1988).

In these studies, the prevalence of extreme vent blocking ranged from one per 1,000 to 210 per 1,000 (median = 19%) and the prevalence of "at least some blocking" ranged from 61 per 1,000 to 580 per 1,000 (median = 50%). If the brakes on an automobile failed or were compromised to any of these extents, consumers, regulators, and manufacturers would be greatly concerned.

Effects of Vent Blocking on Smoke Exposure

Smoking machine estimates of cigarette yields have been used to estimate the effects of vent blocking on smoke exposure. In one of the earliest studies, Kozlowski, Frecker, et al. (1980) demonstrated that blocking the vents of a 4 mg tar cigarette increased the yields of tar, nicotine, and carbon monoxide (CO) by 59% to 293%. In a similar study, Kozlowski, Rickert, et al. (1982) showed that completely blocking the vents of 1 mg tar cigarettes with tape increased the tar yield 15 to 39 times, nicotine yield 8 to 19 times, and CO yield 10 to 43 times. Rickert, Robinson, Young, Collishaw, and Bray (1983) demonstrated that the average yields of tar, nicotine, and CO more than doubled when 50% of the vent holes of 28 brands of ventilated-filter cigarettes were blocked with tape.

Using 1 mg tar cigarettes blocked to different degrees by the experimenter, Zacny, Stitzer, and Yingling (1986) showed that full blockage led to a doubling of CO intake. We found that two smokers of the lowest of the ultra lights (1 mg tar) who blocked vents had CO scores of 37 ppm (each) and salivary cotinine scores of 303 and 385 ng/ml: These are scores commonly found in heavy smokers of high yield cigarettes (Kozlowski, Heatherton, Frecker, & Nolte, 1989).

Benowitz and colleagues (1986) concluded that reduced tar, nicotine, and CO exposure is found while smoking ultra low but not low yield cigarettes. In effect their study supports 1 mg tar cigarettes as "less hazardous." Unfortunately, this study involved a small sample of individuals ($N = 11$) who normally smoked higher yield cigarettes and who were not assessed for vent blocking. Given the estimates of the prevalence of vent blocking, this study may well have, by chance, failed to sample enough vent blockers; it also was limited by not having selected customary ultra light smokers (Kozlowski, 1986).

The Stain Pattern Measurement Technique

It was discovered that vent blocking leaves a characteristic tar stain on conventional vented-filter cigarettes. (The specially designed filters of Barclay, Kool Ultra, and Vantage are not suitable for measurement with this technique, but the filters of the large majority of light and ultra light brands are.) When the vents on a conventional vented filter are not blocked, a characteristic "bull's eye" tar stain is produced. This is because air rather than smoke is passing through the outside edge of the filter. Vent blocking causes the tar stain to spread to the outside. Trained raters can reliably rate (reliability coefficient = .95) the stain patterns according to three categories: not-blocked, some evidence of blocking, and complete blocking (see Kozlowski et al., 1988). Independent laboratories have used the stain pattern technique and found it reliable and valid (Lombardo et al., 1983; Zacny et al., 1986). For example, Zacny et al. (1986) found that a single "blind" rater could sort butts into "no block," "partial block," and "complete block" with 91% accuracy. We have found that this can be improved upon by using the average score for a group of three trained raters, as was the case in Kozlowski et al. (1988). In a scientific community where biochemical measures are often the gold standard, we make no apologies about the value of our rater-based technique as a measurement system. We have tried repeatedly to employ higher technology (i.e., high-

contrast photography, pupilometry cameras, and high-definition, comput-
erized imagining equipment), but we keep returning to the rater system
as our own best method.

Awareness of Vents and Vent Blocking

Small, biased samples have found that most smokers who block vents are
either not aware of it or not aware of its consequences for tar and nicotine
yields. Data exist on the awareness of vent blocking from two studies (Kozlowski, Heatherton, Frecker, & Nolte, 1989; Kozlowski, Rickert, et al., 1982).
In the first, 52% reported that, when they first began smoking, they had
blocked vents with either fingers (39%), lips (20%), or tape (20%); but
only 3 of the 36 current low tar smokers (8%) said that they currently
blocked vents. Yet 38% (12 of 32) of those who later in the session claimed
not to be blocking vents did give evidence of blocking. In the second study,
12 subjects reported never blocking the vents on their filters (four of these
had no awareness of vents on the filters), and the two who said they blocked
vents gave no evidence of doing so. Overall, occurrence of vent blocking
was unrelated to awareness of it.

Smokers are rarely aware of how tar and nicotine yields are measured,
and they seem inclined to view the tar scores as if they were indicators of
tar *content* rather than *yields* under special conditions. They sometimes
reveal that the cigarettes tasted better when they block vents, but they do
not realize that taste is strongly linked to tar levels.

THE NAMES "ULTRA LIGHT" AND "LIGHT" MARKET TAR CATEGORIES

When the U.S. Federal Trade Commission (FTC) proposed a regulation
that would have required all major cigarette manufacturers to disclose the
tar and nicotine yields of cigarette brands in advertisements, the cigarette
manufacturers "voluntarily" agreed in 1971 to provide such information
(Davis et al., 1990). This agreement, however, only applies to advertising.
There is no requirement in the United States that tar and nicotine yields
be reported on cigarette packs. Therefore, unadvertised brands (e.g., many
"generics") have no requirement whatsoever to disclose their tar and nicotine yields. About 40% of brands are now "generic" (Freeman, 1994).

Information on tar and nicotine yields is in practice provided on cigarette packs for only a few brands. In their study of 160 cigarette brands,
Davis et al. (1990) found that as tar yield increased among brands, the
package was progressively less likely to show the yield. Whereas the tar
yield was not disclosed for any brand yielding 11 mg or more of tar, the

tar yield was disclosed for all brands yielding 3 mg or less of tar. Five different brands claimed to be "lowest," even though the tar yield of one (3 mg) was three times the tar yield of another (1 mg). One "ultra low tar" brand had a tar yield higher than that of several "low tar" brands. Three brands with tar yields ranging from 3 mg to 5 mg claimed to be "99% tar free," an ambiguous term suggesting the brands are virtually free of tar. Very few smokers know the tar yields of their brands (USDHHS, 1990). Cohen (1994) demonstrated that higher tar smokers have a very limited knowledge of tar numbers, and lower tar smokers do not fare much better.

The "names" of cigarettes may be much more important than advertised tar yields. Although cigarette advertising does not directly make any explicit claims concerning cigarette safety, the use of such terms as ultra light and light may indirectly communicate health reassurance. The addition of such terms to cigarette names may create a de facto categorical tar yield system as exists officially in the United Kingdom (see Davis et al., 1990, for a brief discussion). A representative of R. J. Reynolds Tobacco Co. at a recent National Cancer Institute (NCI) meeting on the FTC method (Townsend, 1994) indicated that smokers can and do gather information on broad categories of tar yields from the widespread use of the terms "ultra light," "light," and "regular" or "full flavor." Though generic brands of cigarettes are not required to disclose tar and nicotine yields, smokers can still make distinctions among various types of cigarettes by virtue of such designations. This chapter recommends that the use of such loaded terms as light and ultra light be banned.

SIGNIFICANCE

Although there is some indication that lower tar cigarettes carry a slightly lower risk of lung cancer (USDHHS, 1989), these lower levels of risk do not justify reduced efforts to encourage smoking cessation by smokers of these cigarettes. And it is important to realize that lower tar cigarettes have not been demonstrated to have any advantages over regular cigarettes with respect to cardiovascular disease (USDHHS, 1989).

In 1992, 56% of the cigarettes sold were roughly in the light range (7–15 mg tar), and 12.7% of the cigarettes sold were roughly in the ultra light range (6 mg tar or less) (Federal Trade Commission, 1994). In other words, about 4½ times more light cigarettes than ultra light cigarettes were sold. So, although the likely change in tar and nicotine yields is smaller with vent blockade of light cigarettes, the change may well influence many more smokers. If the prevalence of blocking is higher in light than ultra light cigarettes, then the public health significance would be even greater.

IMPLICATIONS FOR SOCIAL MARKETING

The design and implementation of marketing plans involves the blending of four distinct elements: product, price, place, and promotion. This discussion focuses on product and promotion.

Product

In a classic marketing sense, the product is the cigarette itself. How can the product be redesigned to reduce risks to the consumer? The first suggestion would be to make the vent holes—the design feature primarily responsible for the reduced tar and nicotine yields of low yield cigarettes—perceptible to the smoker. If smokers know where the vents are located, then they can decide to avoid blocking them. The vents could be made visually apparent and tangible using colored markings and palpable textures. These specific design changes could be accompanied by explicit written warnings on cigarette packages or package inserts instructing smokers how smoke exposures are influenced by smoking behavior.

Graphic information of tar and nicotine yields could be provided on cigarette packaging to emphasize to smokers that yields from a cigarette depend on how the cigarette is smoked. The color matching technique proposed by Kozlowski, Rickert, et al. (1982) can be used to estimate the number of puffs taken on a cigarette, and thus also tar and nicotine yields, by comparing the color intensity of the end of a spent cigarette filter to a color scale. It has been demonstrated that there is a strong relation between the "darkness" of color of the filter and the tar and nicotine yield of the cigarette. Such a color scale would allow smokers to get a sense of where they stand in relation to the standard. The previously described stain pattern technique used to indicate whether vent blocking has occurred, could also be provided to smokers. Figure 14.1 shows a modified version of both the color matching scale (upper part of figure) and the vent-blocking scale (lower part of figure) incorporated on a cigarette package. The stain pattern designated "yes" on the vent-blocking scale represents the pattern a smoker would expect to see if the filter vents were not blocked. The pattern designated "no" results when the filter vents have been completely blocked. The phrase "false light" is used to emphasize that a low yield cigarette can provide high yields when smoked in certain ways and serves as a reminder that the term "light" is symbolically very powerful and in need of special modifiers (e.g., "false") to diminish its power.

Another issue related to packaging involves the influence of pack size on smoking rates (Kozlowski, Heatherton, & Ferrence, 1989). In some Canadian markets, for example, pack sizes range from 15, 20, 25, and 30 cigarettes per pack. If consumers are carrying packs of 30 cigarettes, are they more likely to be smoking "needless" cigarettes than if they carried packs of 20

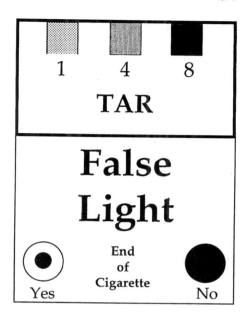

FIG. 14.1. The color matching scale and the vent-blocking scale incorporated on a cigarette package. Scale locations 1, 4, and 8 could be treated as tar yields of 1, 4, and 8 mg, which represent low, standard, and high yields, respectively. The appearance of an unblocked vented filter is shown in the bull's eye stain on the left; the uniform stain on the filter end on the right indicates extreme blocking.

cigarettes or even 10 cigarettes? Reducing the pack size of cigarettes, while keeping cigarettes expensive, might be one practical way to encourage less hazardous tobacco use (Kozlowski, 1987).

What Message Should be Promoted?[1]

Use Low Yield Cigarettes in a Way that Gives Low Yields. One alternative is to inform smokers how best to use low yield cigarettes if they are unwilling or unable to quit smoking (i.e., don't block vents, smoker fewer cigarettes per day, take fewer puffs per cigarette, leave longer butts, use feedback to know if you are oversmoking each cigarette). For those individuals who are unable or unwilling to stop smoking, such a message may aid in reducing the risks to their health of their continued tobacco use.

Even if You Use Low Yield Cigarettes, Keep Trying to Quit Smoking. The very concept of less hazardous smoking may discourage people from the only truly less hazardous course of action, which is to stop smoking entirely. Based on this notion, we might instead discourage smokers from switching to low yield cigarettes and stress that there is no "safe" level of smoking. Quitting smoking is the only means to substantially reduce risk. For example, switching to low yield cigarettes could be likened to "jumping from

[1]From some perspectives (e.g., Andreasen, 1993), the "product" for social marketing is the message you promote.

the 15th floor of a building rather than the 20th floor," or "being stabbed 15 times rather than 20 times."

A Complex Message Is Needed. It is sometimes believed that to advocate less hazardous smoking is to undermine antismoking efforts, possibly by preventing smoking cessation and encouraging recruitment to tobacco use (Kozlowski, 1984). However, it could also be argued that to exclusively promote a message of cessation is to deny that many smokers will not be persuaded to kick the habit, despite the best efforts of the antismoking campaign.

Neither message alone seems sufficient to combat the smoking problem, so it is recommended that a message including both smoking cessation and less hazardous smoking is most appropriate. Such a message would emphasize that smoking cessation is always the preferred course of action for all smokers. Those smokers who are either unwilling or unable to quit, however, should attempt to reduce their risks by switching to low yield cigarettes, but only if they can do so without compensating for the decreased yield, and only until they are ready to quit. Throughout this process, complete cessation is always the ultimate goal. Table 14.1 demonstrates the cyclical nature of this more complex "Quit/Switch" message.

Promotion Strategies

Several strategies and tactics are available for communicating the desired message to the target audience of low yield smokers. As one example, the Addiction Research Foundation in Toronto has developed an informational pamphlet entitled "Tar and Nicotine Ratings May Be Hazardous To Your Health: Information For Smokers Who Are Not Ready To Stop" (Kozlowski, 1982). Originally published in 1982, a revised version of the pamphlet was recently developed in 1993 ("Low Tar Cigarettes Are Hazardous to Your Health: Advice for Smokers") (Kozlowski, 1993). This pamphlet provides smokers with important information about low yield cigarettes, such as the presence and function of filter vents and the meaning of standard tar and nicotine yields. It is the only material of its kind of which we are aware that specifically addresses issues related to low yield

TABLE 14.1
The Need for an Interlocking "Quit/Switch" Message

1. First, quit.
2. If you can't quit, switch to lowest.
3. If you can't truly switch to lowest, quit.
4. If you can quit, quit.
5. If you can't quit, switch to lowest you can tolerate.
6. And so on.

cigarettes. The pamphlet has appeared in the Harvard Medical School Health Letter (1983), and has been translated into Swedish at the request of the Swedish government.

This pamphlet could potentially serve as an adjunct to the personalized medical advice of health professionals, such as physicians, nurses, respiratory therapists, physician assistants, chemical dependency counselors, psychologists, health educators, pharmacists, and dentists. The potential influence of health professionals on their patients' behavior should not be underestimated. One of our top priorities should therefore be to educate health professionals, as well as the smokers themselves, about the potential dangers of low yield cigarettes so they can convey this information to their patients.

The mass media sets the national agenda everyday by deciding what is considered "newsworthy." It often functions as the first step toward social awareness of an issue (Wallack, Dorfman, Jernigan, & Themba, 1993). The speed with which the media can inform the public and the vast number of people it can inform make it an effective vehicle for transmitting information. Media attention to the latest research findings regarding low yield cigarettes would legitimize this important issue. However, the mass media has a brief attention span on any particular issue and will not be as effective as an ongoing, organized campaign to counter the promotion of low yield cigarettes.

The Massachusetts Department of Health has recently developed an innovative series of promotional television advertisements geared toward educating smokers about low yield cigarettes and vent blocking. In one 30-second piece, a spokesperson demonstrates the function of filter vents using a canister vacuum cleaner. Holding the vacuum cleaner hose, he demonstrates that a turn of the nozzle exposes air vents. On a cigarette, he explains, these vents are deliberately placed where the fingers of smokers are most likely to cover them. As he empties the filled vacuum cleaner bag, he explains that when vents are covered "tar levels rise, your taste buds get more flavor, and your lungs get more of everything else." An important limitation of this otherwise informative ad is that it fails to mention lip blocking as an alternative means of covering the vents; therefore, smokers may mistakenly believe that vents are mainly blocked with fingers. Another ad featuring an animated skull and crossbones emphasizes the theme "lights are deadly." The skull and crossbones symbol is generally regarded as a trusted warning of danger. "I'm on everything that can hurt you," it says, "so why aren't I on light cigarettes?"

CONCLUSIONS

A recent economic analysis of the risks of cigarette smoking emphasizes that all models of the perception of risk crucially depend on the input of information about risk (Viscusi, 1992). If smokers do not know about the presence of and function of filter vents, then they are being deprived of information that may influence the assessment of the risks of continuing smoking. Apart from the questions of the magnitude of change in tar yields, there is a straightforward issue of smoker protection. Cigarette smokers who block vents unwittingly, or in ignorance of the consequences, are explicit victims of the failure to inform smokers about the ventilation issue. The strategies and techniques of social marketing can be effectively used to counter the aggressive promotion of low yield cigarettes by providing such crucial information to smokers.

REFERENCES

Andreasen, A. R. (1993). Presidential address: A social marketing research agenda for consumer behavior researchers. In M. Rothschild & L. McAlister (Eds.), *Advances in consumer research* (pp. 1–5). Provo, UT: Association for Consumer Research.

Benowitz, N. E., Jacob, P., & Yu, L. (1986). Reduced tar, nicotine, and carbon monoxide exposure while smoking ultra-low but not low-yield cigarettes. *Journal of the American Medical Association, 256,* 241–246.

Cohen, J. B. (1992). Research and policy issues in Ringold and Calfee's treatment of cigarette health claims. *Journal of Public Policy and Marketing, 11,* 82–86.

Cohen, J. B. (1994, December). *Consumer understanding of advertised tar numbers.* Paper presented at the National Cancer Institute Conference on the FTC Test Method, Bethesda, MD.

Davis, R. M., Healy, P., & Hawk, S. A. (1990). Information on tar and nicotine yields on cigarette packages. *American Journal of Public Health, 80,* 551–553.

Federal Trade Commission. (1979). *Report of "Tar" and Nicotine Content of the Smoke of 176 Varieties of Cigarettes.*

Federal Trade Commission. (1994). *Tar, Nicotine, and Carbon Monoxide of the Smoke of 993 Varieties of Domestic Cigarettes.*

Freeman, H. P. (1994, December). *Remarks: National Cancer Institute Conference on the FTC Test Method,* Bethesda, MD.

Gerstein, D. R., & Levison, P. K. (1982). Reduced tar and nicotine cigarettes: Smoking behavior and health. *Committee on substance abuse and habitual behavior. Commission on behavioral and social sciences and education: NRC* (pp. 1–52). Washington, DC: National Academy Press.

Gori, G. B. (1976). Low-risk cigarettes: A prescription: Low-toxicity cigarettes hold significant promise in the prevention of diseases related to smoking. *Science, 194,* 1243–1246.

Gori, G. B., & Lynch, C. J. (1978). Toward less hazardous cigarettes. *Journal of the American Medical Association, 240,* 1255–1259.

Gori, G. B., & Lynch, C. J. (1983). Smoker intake from cigarettes in the 1mg Federal Trade Commission tar class. *Regulatory Toxicology and Pharmacology, 3,* 110–120.

Hofer, I., Nil, R., & Battig, K. (1991). Ultra low-yield cigarettes and type of ventilation: The role of ventilation blocking. *Pharmacology, Biochemistry and Behavior, 40,* 907–914.

Kozlowski, L. T. (1981a). The changing cigarette: Behavioral aspects. *The health consequences of smoking: The changing cigarette. A report of the U.S. Surgeon General* (pp. 173–192). Washington, DC: U.S. Public Health Service.

Kozlowski, L. T. (1981b). Tar and nicotine delivery of cigarettes: What a difference a puff makes. *Journal of the American Medical Association, 245,* 158–159.

Kozlowski, L. T. (1982). *Tar and nicotine ratings may be hazardous to your health: Information for smokers who are not ready to stop.* Toronto: Addiction Research Foundation.

Kozlowski, L. T. (1983). Perceiving the risks of low-yield ventilated-filter cigarettes: The problem of hole-blocking. In V. Covello, W. G. Flamm, J. Rodericks, & R. Tardiff (Eds.), *Proceedings of the international workshop on the analysis of actual versus perceived risks* (pp. 175–182). New York: Polonium.

Kozlowski, L. T. (1984). Less-hazardous tobacco use as a treatment for the "smoking and health" problem. In R. G. Smart, H. D. Cappell, F. B. Glaser, Y. Israel, H. Kalant, R. E. Popham, W. Schmidt, & E. M. Sellers (Eds.), *Research advances in alcohol and drug problems* (pp. 309–328). New York: Plenum.

Kozlowski, L. T. (1986). Blocking the filter vents of cigarettes. *Journal of the American Medical Association, 256,* 3214.

Kozlowski, L. T. (1987). Less hazardous smoking and the pursuit of satisfaction. *American Journal of Public Health, 77,* 539–541.

Kozlowski, L. T. (1989). Evidence for limits on the acceptability of lowest tar cigarettes. *American Journal of Public Health, 79,* 198–199.

Kozlowski, L. T. (1993). *Low tar cigarettes are hazardous to your health: Advice for smokers.* Toronto: Addiction Research Foundation.

Kozlowski, L. T., Frecker, R. C., Khouw, V., & Pope, M. (1980). The misuse of "less-hazardous" cigarettes and its detection: Hole-blocking of ventilated filters. *American Journal of Public Health, 70,* 1202–1203.

Kozlowski, L. T., Frecker, R. C., & Lei, H. (1982). Nicotine yields of cigarettes, plasma nicotine in smokers, and public health. *Preventive Medicine, 11,* 240–244.

Kozlowski, L. T., Heatherton, T. F., & Ferrence, R. G. (1989). Pack size, reported cigarette smoking rates, and the heaviness of smoking. *Canadian Journal of Public Health, 80,* 266–270.

Kozlowski, L. T., Heatherton, T. F., Frecker, R. C., & Nolte, H. E. (1989). Self-selected blocking of vents on low-yield cigarettes. *Pharmacology, Biochemistry and Behavior, 33,* 815–819.

Kozlowski, L. T., Pillitteri, J. L., & Sweeney, C. T. (1994). Misuse of "Light" cigarettes means of vent blocking. *Journal of Substance Abuse, 6,* 333–336.

Kozlowski, L. T., Pope, M. A., & Lux, J. E. (1988). Prevalence of the misuse of ultra-low-tar cigarettes by blocking filter vents. *American Journal of Public Health, 78,* 694–695.

Kozlowski, L. T., Rickert, W. S., Pope, M. A., Robinson, J. C., & Frecker, R. C. (1982). Estimating the yield to smokers of tar, nicotine, and carbon monoxide from the "lowest yield" ventilated-filter cigarettes. *British Journal of Addiction, 77,* 159–165.

Kozlowski, L. T., Rickert, W. S., Robinson, J. C., & Grunberg, N. E. (1980). Have tar and nicotine yields of cigarettes changed? *Science, 209,* 1550–1551.

Lombardo, T., Davis, C. J., & Prue, D. M. (1983). When low tar cigarettes yield high tar: Cigarette filter ventilation hole blocking and its detection. *Addictive Behaviors, 8,* 67–69.

Low-tar cigarettes: How to use them (if you must). (1983, July). *Harvard Medical School Health Letter, 8,* 1–2.

Parker, J. A., & Montgomery, R. T. (1979). Design criteria for ventilated filters. *Beiträge zur Tabakforschung International, 10,* 1–6.

Participants of the Fourth Scarborough Conference on Preventive Medicine. (1985). Is there a future for lower-tar-yield cigarettes? *Lancet, 2,* 1111–1114.

Peeler, C. L. (1994, December). Remarks: Before the National Cancer Institute Conference on the FTC Test Method, Bethesda, MD.

Pollay, R. W. (1989). Filters, flavor . . . flim-flam, too! On "health information" and policy implications in cigarette advertising. *Journal of Public Policy and Marketing, 8,* 30–39.

Rickert, W. S., Robinson, J. C., Young, J. C., Collishaw, N. E., & Bray, D. F. (1983). A comparison of the yields of tar, nicotine, and carbon monoxide of 36 brands of Canadian cigarettes tested under three conditions. *Preventive Medicine, 12,* 682–694.

Robinson, J. C., Young, J. C., Rickert, W. S., Fey, G., & Kozlowski, L. T. (1983). A comparative study of the amount of smoke absorbed from low yield ("less hazardous") cigarettes Part 2: Invasive measures. *British Journal of Addiction, 78,* 79–87.

Townsend, D. (1994, December). Remarks: Before the National Cancer Institute Conference on the FTC Test Method, Bethesda, MD.

U.S. Department of Health and Human Services. (1988). *The health consequences of smoking: Nicotine addiction. A report of the surgeon general.* Washington, DC: U.S. Government Printing Office.

U.S. Department of Health and Human Services. (1989). *Reducing the health consequences of smoking: A report of the Surgeon General.* Rockville, MD: U.S. Department of Health and Human Services.

U.S. Department of Health and Human Services. (1990). *The health benefits of smoking cessation: A report of the Surgeon General.* Rockville, MD: U.S. Department of Health and Human Services.

Viscusi, W. K. (1992). *Smoking: Making the risky decision.* New York: Oxford.

Wallack, L., Dorfman, L., Jernigan, D., & Themba, M. (1993). *Media advocacy and public health.* Newbury Park, CA: Sage.

Warner, K. E., & Slade, J. (1992). Low tar, high toll. *American Journal of Public Health, 82,* 17–18.

Zacny, J. P., & Stitzer, M. L. (1988). Cigarette brand-switching: Effects on smoke exposure and smoking behavior. *Journal of Pharmacology and Experimental Therapeutics, 246,* 619–627.

Zacny, J. P., Stitzer, M. L., & Yingling, J. E. (1986). Cigarette filter vent blocking: Effects on smoking topography and carbon monoxide exposure. *Pharmacology, Biochemistry and Behavior, 25,* 1245–1252.

Chapter 15

The Dangers of Advertising Low Tar Cigarettes: Let's Understand What Consumers Understand

Joel B. Cohen
University of Florida

ABSTRACT

Survey data presented in this chapter raises concerns about smokers' understanding and use of advertised tar numbers resulting from the Federal Trade Commission (FTC) testing method. These results are presented against the historical background of government policy to reduce the overall tar level of cigarettes offered for sale, the cigarette industry's targeting of health concerned smokers via low tar cigarettes, and growing misgivings about the value of this information to smokers.

The notion that "tar" might be of some concern to smokers was first brought to widespread attention in the early 1940s when several tobacco companies associated lower tar with less throat irritation in their advertising. The FTC brought several suits against such advertising, and tar and nicotine claims in advertising subsided until *Consumer Reports* published tar and nicotine ratings by brand in the early 1950s.[1] The FTC again brought suit against advertising claims linked to tar and nicotine levels, and in 1955 published cigarette advertising guidelines prohibiting relative tar and nicotine claims in the absence of competent scientific proof that the claim was true, and the differences among cigarettes were significant. The latter reflected the FTC's view that tar and nicotine claims were, in fact, implied health claims. Indeed, in 1959 all cigarette companies were informed that any representation of low or reduced tar or nicotine would be construed as a health claim by the agency.

---

[1]See Calfee (1985) and Peeler (1996) for valuable perspectives on FTC policies and actions over the years.

As information regarding the possible involvement of tar in lung cancer diffused through the population following magazine and newspaper articles (e.g., several reports suggested that a feasible 40% reduction in tar and nicotine would likely reduce the risk of cancer) and laboratory testing and reporting of cigarette brands' tar and nicotine levels intensified, a so-called "tar derby" in advertised tar numbers ensued. In 1960, the FTC obtained industry-wide agreement to refrain from placing tar and nicotine information in advertising. However, a number of prominent health organizations and spokespeople registered their opposition to this policy. With the dramatic impact of the 1964 surgeon general's report listing smoking as a cause of lung cancer, the FTC, in 1966, reversed its position. Cigarette manufacturers were encouraged to provide consumers with comparative information on tar and nicotine levels. The restriction against claims of reduced health hazards remained in effect.

THE VOLUNTARY DISCLOSURE PROGRAM
AND SMOKERS' RESPONSE

In 1970, the FTC proposed a trade regulation rule that would have required disclosure of tar and nicotine ratings in all advertising. The rulemaking was suspended when the industry agreed voluntarily to include FTC tar and nicotine ratings in their advertising (the lone dissenter agreeing to do so as part of a consent agreement a year later). This voluntary agreement remains in effect today. The FTC established a laboratory to analyze cigarette smoke, adapting the Cambridge Filter Method, typically referred to as the "FTC method" for this purpose. The FTC method utilizes a multiport smoking machine, careful nationwide sampling of cigarettes available for sale, and standardized conditions. One 35 mL puff of 2 seconds' duration is taken every minute until a specified butt length is reached. Despite the method's inability to determine the amount of tar and nicotine inhaled by a particular smoker—or even an average smoker—there seemed to be widespread agreement that the method did permit valid comparisons across cigarettes, and reductions in yields were associated with a lessening of health risks (Peeler, 1996; U.S. Department of Health and Human Services, 1981). This issue is discussed further shortly, because it is at the heart of current controversies over the value of this information for low tar cigarette smokers. The FTC testing protocol was extended to carbon monoxide in 1980, and the FTC laboratory was discontinued in 1987, with subsequent testing conducted by an industry laboratory using the same method and subject to FTC monitoring.

The combined impact of the greater salience of tar (as a surrogate for what is unhealthy in cigarettes) and the industry's promotion of low tar cigarettes has been dramatic. U.S. smokers have exhibited a substantial shift from high tar (i.e., total particulate matter, subtracting moisture and excluding nicotine) cigarettes, averaging 37 mg of tar in the 1950s, to low tar alternatives. The market share of cigarettes yielding 15 mg of tar or less went from essentially 0 in 1960 to over 68% in 1992 (Federal Trade Commission, 1994). The shift is especially pronounced for women and college-educated smokers, 85% of whom smoke such cigarettes (NHIS–CCES, 1992). This "second revolution" in cigarette smoking behavior followed on the heels of the massive shift to filtered cigarettes: from less than 1% of the domestic market in 1950 to 58% in 1963 and to 97% in 1992 (Federal Trade Commission, 1994). Propelled by dramatic advertising appeals—such as Carlton's promotion of a very low tar cigarette (via a display of 13 rings of ventilation holes) in the mid-1960s and the rapid development of a category of "super Hi-Fi" brands such as True, Doral, and Vantage—smokers were presented with what appeared to be a set of less harmful cigarettes. The tar competition eventually produced a category of cigarettes described as "ultra low tar" and "ultra light" (containing 6 mg of tar or less), and these achieved almost a 13% share by 1992 (Federal Trade Commission, 1994). Smokers of "ultra light" cigarettes have been disproportionately female, college-educated, or over 60 years of age (NHIS–CCES, 1992).

Advocates of required disclosure of tar and nicotine content could not have anticipated the major shifts in cigarette marketing that have taken place since the mid-1970s, or they might not have settled for the voluntary program. First, discount brands that are sold with much less advertising support (or none at all) have grown to over 30% of the 507 billion cigarettes consumed in 1992 (down from a high of 637 billion cigarettes in 1981). Smokers have much less opportunity to learn about the tar and nicotine levels of these cigarettes. Second, whereas cigarette companies spent over 60% of their advertising and promotional budget on a combination of outdoor, magazine, and newspaper advertising in the early to mid-1970s, that was cut in half by the mid-1980s. By 1992, cigarette advertising and promotional expenditures totaled $5.2 billion; however, only 11% of this was spent in the same three media. Increasing percentages of the overall budget are going to promotional allowances to middlemen and retailers (29%) and coupons, value-added offers, and specialty items (48%; Federal Trade Commission, 1994). Because only the lowest tar cigarette brands go out of their way to ensure that people see their ratings (e.g., on cigarette packages), it is likely that many smokers are exposed to less tar and nicotine information than might be imagined.

DESIGNING CIGARETTES TO GENERATE LOWER MACHINE-ESTIMATED YIELDS

Lower tar yields via the FTC method are achieved by modifying tobacco composition (e.g., reconstituted tobacco, expanded or puffed tobacco) and by reducing the diameter or smoking length of cigarettes as well as increasing cigarette burn rates. Advances in filtration over the years have succeeded in reducing particulate matter and some harmful smoke constituents. In addition, a significant mechanism for moving down to "ultra low tar" levels is dilution of mainstream smoke by means of ventilated filters and more porous paper. The smoking machine parameters, established between 25 and 40 years ago, were based on at best informal observation, when cigarettes were substantially different than today's lower tar products (Pillsbury, 1996). Even leaving aside explicitly compensatory smoking behavior (discussed later), the appropriateness of these parameters for today's cigarettes is questionable. For example, many of today's "milder" filtered cigarettes draw harder and require more effort, so it is reasonable for smokers to puff more frequently or with greater intensity (Mueller, 1996). As inflation adjusted cigarette prices increase, many smokers may also increase the number of puffs per cigarette, thereby smoking the cigarette closer to the filter and drawing in higher levels of tar.

Some cigarette design features, such as placement of ventilation holes in a manner likely to lead to either inadvertent or deliberate (i.e., compensation-based) blocking, would obviously produce machine-based yields quite different from actual tar deliveries. Indeed, in 1981, competitors helped convince the FTC that Brown and Williamson's Barclay cigarettes were not entitled to their advantageous 1 mg tar rating. An investigation indicated that smokers' lips would compress the channels used to bring air into smokers' mouths. A successful FTC lawsuit enjoined Brown and Williamson from advertising any tar number not specifically approved by the FTC.

Cigarette industry officials have argued that the machine-estimated yields still provide valuable *relative* information, despite both over-time and across-individual variance in smoking behavior (Covington & Burling, 1994; Philip Morris, 1994; R. J. Reynolds, 1994). There are two key assumptions in this defense of the existing smoking-machine methodology. The first is that the numerical rating system is, in fact, reliable. However, if the true distribution of delivered tar contains substantial individual variance, there should be a meaningful overlap in deliveries across cigarettes receiving different ratings. Thus, a single tar number may be misleading, even for ordinal judgments (i.e., ranking cigarettes). Further, actual between-cigarette differences might be very small and of little practical importance. The second key assumption is that consumers will use the tar numbers strictly to make relative choices. The main part of this chapter examines consumers' understanding of these numbers and their use.

Compensatory Smoking Behavior for Very Low Tar Cigarettes

A number of studies have identified smokers' compensatory mechanisms associated with nicotine intake (Food and Drug Administration, 1995a; Mueller, 1994; U.S. Department of Health and Human Services, 1988).

Henningfield, Kozlowski, and Benowitz (1994) indicated that all marketed cigarettes contain approximately 6 mg to 11 mg of nicotine, from which smokers obtain on average 1 mg of nicotine (regardless of whether the FTC estimated yield is .1 mg or 2 mg). In order to obtain the "desired" nicotine delivery from a very low tar and nicotine yield cigarette, smokers may compensate by changing their puffing patterns or depth of inhaling. A considerable amount of evidence has now been accumulated on the compensation issue. Although there are a number of important methodological factors that have led to different study conclusions (e.g., the time given to subjects to adapt to different yield levels), there is considerable evidence that a decrease in nicotine yields is associated with increases in mean puff volume, total duration and volume, and flow rate (Bridges et al., 1990). Thus, there is substantial reason to question the existing FTC method from the standpoint of both the accuracy and meaningfulness of the tar and nicotine yield numbers.[2]

THE VALUE OF ADVERTISED TAR AND NICOTINE LEVELS REVISITED

In conjunction with the FTC's investigation of Barclay cigarettes, comments were invited from interested parties concerning the validity of the FTC testing method. Whereas the FTC, with concurrence by a federal district court, took the position that the testing method remained a viable way to determine "how much relative tar and nicotine a smoker would get in his mouth were he to smoke two cigarettes in the same manner" and that no better method was currently available, comments from groups such as the American Heart Association, American Lung Association, and American Cancer Society were far less supportive (Peeler, 1994). Serious concerns were raised about compensatory smoking behavior and the potential for advertising built around low tar and nicotine ratings to mislead consumers as to the relative safety of particular brands. However, the FTC, relying on the best available evidence associating lower tar levels with a reduction in lung cancer deaths, decided not to abandon the only existing method for making comparative tar information available to smokers.

---

[2]An ad hoc committee of the President's Cancer Panel (National Cancer Institute) said the following in the statement it distributed to the press on December 6, 1994: "The FTC test protocol was based on cursory observations of human smoking behavior. Actual human smoking behavior is characterized by wide variations in smoking patterns which result in wide variations in tar and nicotine exposure. Smokers who switch to lower tar and nicotine cigarettes frequently change their smoking behavior, which may negate potential health benefits."

By mid-1994, enough doubts had been raised about both the accuracy of advertised tar and nicotine yields and their potential to mislead smokers, that the chairperson of the House of Representatives Subcommittee on Health and the Environment and the FTC chairman independently requested the National Cancer Institute to convene a scientific conference to make recommendations as to the appropriateness of continuing the current rating system (Steiger, 1994; Waxman, 1994). The FTC expressed a particular concern regarding how consumers interpreted these numbers and incorporated the information into decisions about cigarettes.

SMOKERS' UNDERSTANDING OF TAR NUMBERS

There is little published evidence on smokers' understanding and use of advertised tar numbers. Documents made available during litigation make it clear that cigarette companies have considerable data on such issues. For example, one field study systematically manipulated tar and nicotine ratings on packages to observe their influence on taste and preference evaluations (Dunn, 1970). Another study carried out several years after the voluntary agreement was put in place (when such advertising might have captured more attention that it does now) concluded that, "There is very little knowledge of the actual tar and nicotine deliveries of leading brands of cigarettes." The report added, "The judgments of relative tar and nicotine deliveries almost exactly parallel the judgments of taste delivery" (Philip Morris, 1973).[3]

Chapman, Wilson, and Wakefield's (1986) study of 498 Australian smokers indicated only a 2% correct recall of their cigarette's tar level (from its pack labeling). About 70% of Australian smokers underestimated their cigarette's tar level. Gori (1990) used telephone interviewing to solicit open-ended responses from 400 smokers and 77 ex-smokers in the United States (as well as a 150-person sample in each of five European countries) to two very general questions: "What, in your opinion, is the meaning of the tar value of cigarettes?", and "Is a 10 mg tar cigarette more relevant to health than a 5 mg one, and, if so, how much more?" About one quarter of U.S. smokers answered "don't know" to the first question. Another 20% provided ambiguous responses that essentially played back the question (i.e., "amount of tar in cigarettes"). Another 20% answered in terms of such things as taste, flavor, amount of nicotine, amount of junk. Thirty-five percent of the sample referred to some health risk or disease. The lack

---

[3]Interestingly, the study noted the failure of Lucky Ten (the second lowest tar cigarette in the study) to capitalize on the "evident purpose" of its name because of its incorrect identification with Lucky Strike Regular, a high tar cigarette.

of probing or follow-up questions makes it difficult to know what such responses imply about smokers' knowledge and health-related inferences.

The wording of the second question is somewhat curious, both because of the ambiguity of the term *relevant* and the fact that it might make more sense to phrase the comparison in the opposite direction. Most of those answering "yes" to the greater relevance to health of a 10 mg tar cigarette responded to the follow-up (i.e., "how much more?") by providing answers categorized in terms of percentage differences in health relevance.[4] It is interesting to note that 49% of current smokers' answers could be categorized as "100% more": Hence, the 10 mg tar cigarette was thought to have twice the impact on health. The author indicated that such responses imply that smokers believe published tar yields correspond to quantitative assessments of smoke intake, and he expressed concern over such an "unwarranted" belief (in part because of substantial interindividual variance in smoke intake and compensatory behavior focused on nicotine intake).

DO SMOKERS EQUATE LOW TAR WITH "SAFER"?

From the outset, the FTC found itself in the uncomfortable position of trying to differentiate between possibly useful comparative information about tar and nicotine levels and tar and nicotine-based health claims, because there was little basis for knowing when such information might suggest absolute levels of safety (or even a "safe cigarette"). The difficulty became still greater as medical research began to shed more light on relations between components of cigarette smoke other than "tar" (e.g., nicotine, carbon monoxide, nitrosamines, hydrogen cyanide, acrolein, catechols) and various health hazards. These substances pose a particular problem if their potential risk does not diminish as a linear function of FTC tar numbers, but smokers associate lower tar levels with generally reduced health risks. This is a major concern for heart disease, where the risk seems to be largely independent of cigarette tar level (Palmer, Rosenberg, & Shapiro, 1993; U.S. Department of Health and Human Services, 1989).

Cigarette advertising, certainly in the post-1970s voluntary agreement era, contains few if any explicit claims concerning cigarette safety (Ringold & Calfee, 1989). However, many of these advertisements communicate health reassurance somewhat more indirectly, by stressing "mildness" and effective filtration (Cohen, 1992). Research carried out for cigarette companies has made it clear that "milder products translate into somewhat

---

[4]No indication is given of the number of people answering "no" or "don't know" to the first part of the question, and because the table percentages are based on an unstated number of "yes" answers, there is no way to determine the number of respondents giving each answer.

safer smoking alternatives, and safety (low tar and nicotine levels) provides solid rational appeals" (see discussions in Ringold & Calfee, 1989, and Cohen, 1992). This judgment was supported by a 1980 Roper survey in which 36% thought that their low tar cigarette did not significantly increase a person's risk of disease over that of nonsmokers and another 31% who were not sure if this were the case.

Earlier FTC concerns regarding the health implications of promoting low tar cigarettes seemed to have been well-founded. For example, R. J. Reynolds' Canadian affiliate, RJR–Macdonald, positioned Vantage for the "concerned smoker" via the appeal, "Vantage provides the psychological benefits of low 'tar' and the physiological benefits of full flavor" (RJR–Macdonald, Inc., 1989a). Vantage research indicated that the brand was viewed as a way of "cutting down on harmful elements while not eliminating smoking." It could hardly be put more explicitly than in a 1981 marketing plan for Matinee cigarettes by Imperial Tobacco Company (British American Tobacco's Canadian affiliate): "Due to continuous anti-smoking publicity, the public continues to be aware of and concerned with the suggested hazards of cigarette smoking. Matinee, then, is in an ideal position to take advantage of this situation with its low tar and nicotine and 'safer for health' proposition" (RJR–Macdonald, Inc., 1989b). Roy Brown, Imperial Tobacco's vice president of marketing put it bluntly when asked about smokers' interpretation of the word "milder": "They interpret it to mean lower tar and, yes, they would then interpret lower tar as safer" (RJR–Macdonald, Inc., 1989c, p. 1159). He indicated that this opinion was based on "a history of research from consumers" (RJR–Macdonald, Inc., 1989d, p. 1192).

The 1987 National Health Interview survey reported that about 46% of those smoking cigarettes with 6 mg or less tar believed that low tar cigarettes posed reduced cancer risk, compared to about 30% for those smoking higher tar cigarettes. A 1993 Gallup survey reports that 56% of smokers believed that cigarette advertising using terms like low tar, low nicotine, or lower yield was trying to communicate that the brand was safer, healthier, or less harmful (Coalition on Smoking OR Health, 1993).

Industry-sponsored research, as discussed earlier, indicates there is a general perception of relative safety associated with low tar cigarettes. Indeed, many such studies report a "decline in the levels of anxiety" among smokers switching to brands whose copy strategy is addressed to the "concerned smoker" (Cohen, 1992; Ringold & Calfee, 1989). A particularly ominous implication of such smoker perceptions is that those who have found it difficult to quit might be tempted to rationalize their shift to an ultra low tar brand. Once again, cigarette industry documents speak to this issue: "We have evidence of virtually no quitting among smokers of those brands, and there are indications that the advent of ultra low tar cigarettes has actually retained some potential quitters in the cigarette market by offering them a viable alternative" (RJR–Macdonald, Inc., 1989e, p. 2).

This is supported by data from the 1986 Adult Use of Tobacco Survey. Whereas 58% of those smoking cigarettes whose tar yields were 16 mg or higher had stopped smoking for some period of time, only 34% of those smoking cigarettes with tar yields of 6 mg or less had done so. This relationship is even more startling given the substantially lower prevalence of *perceived* health risks among those smoking these higher yield cigarettes (i.e., 68% concerned about health effects compared to 84% among low yield cigarette smokers). Moreover, those who never switched to reduce tar and nicotine levels were more likely to have stopped smoking than those who had switched for the same purpose (50% vs. 37%; Giovino et al., 1996).

The present study was designed to focus on smokers' awareness, interpretation, and use of the numerical tar ratings appearing in cigarette advertising. The research has implications for the FTC's continued endorsement of the existing rating system and its support for the 1970 voluntary agreement among cigarette companies that provides the basis for including these numbers in cigarette advertising.

SMOKERS' UNDERSTANDING AND USE
OF ADVERTISED TAR NUMBERS

A telephone survey among a national probability sample of 1,005 adults (502 men and 503 women) 18 years of age and older was conducted between November 17 and 20, 1994. Data were weighted by age, sex, geographic region, and race so that each respondent was assigned a single weight based on the relation between the actual population proportions on the listed characteristics and the comparable sample proportions.

The sample's estimate of everyday smoking (23%) matches current assessments of adult U.S. smoking prevalence (22%). When everyday and some-days smokers were combined, the current smoking percentage (28.7%) was slightly higher than the Centers for Disease Control and Prevention (CDC) comparable estimate of 26.5% for 1992. This sample reported somewhat higher current smoking percentages for females (29%) than did the 1992 CDC surveys (24.6%). Total smoking reported by Whites (29%) was slightly higher than in the 1992 CDC surveys (27.2%), whereas total smoking reported by African Americans in this sample (27%) was virtually identical (27.8%). A high percentage of those who report having attended but not graduated from college are some-days smokers. When added to everyday smokers, this total was substantially higher (36%) than that reported in the CDC surveys (24%) and was closer to the latter's estimate for high school graduates (31%). College graduates in this sample

TABLE 15.1
Tar Level of Cigarette Last Smoked

	Very Low Tar 1–5	Low Tar 6–10	Medium Tar 11–15	High Tar 16+	Can't Determine
Current smokers					
Some-days smokers (56)	9%	34%	9%	23%	25%
Everyday smokers (232)	8%	22%	21%	40%	10%
Recent (2–3 years) quitters (36)	11%	11%	25%	28%	25%
Those smoking in the past 2–3 years					
All smokers (325)	9%	22%	19%	35%	14%
Male (152)	5%	24%	13%	42%	17%
Female (174)	12%	21%	25%	29%	12%
White (268)	10%	23%	21%	31%	15%
African American (28)	0	14%	18%	64%	4%
Hispanic (26)	4%	15%	4%	58%	19%
High school or less education (107)	6%	15%	21%	41%	18%
At least some college education (146)	12%	32%	23%	30%	12%
Smokers of regular size cigarettes (145)	5%	28%	11%	40%	16%
Smokers of king-size or longer cigarettes (173)	12%	19%	27%	32%	11%
Smokers of soft pack cigarettes (180)	13%	17%	22%	33%	16%
Smokers of hard pack cigarettes (133)	3%	29%	17%	41%	9%
Smokers of plain cigarettes (223)	9%	24%	18%	35%	15%
Smokers of menthol cigarettes (101)	8%	20%	23%	38%	12%

were also somewhat more likely to smoke (19% compared with 15.5% reported in CDC surveys). Age breakdowns were not entirely comparable among the surveys, but the present sample reported a higher incidence of smoking among 18- to 24-year-olds (32% compared with 26.4%).

Table 15.1 reports the tar levels of cigarettes last smoked, determined by asking the brand, size, and other characteristics of the cigarette. These data are provided, first, by current smokers and, second, by those smoking during the past 2 to 3 years. The latter will become the base for subsequent analyses. Tar level responses were compared with actual FTC tar ratings (Federal Trade Commission, 1994). In 15% of the cases, respondents could not provide sufficiently detailed product information to make this comparison ("Can't Determine" respondents). These respondents are likely to come disproportionately from lower tar categories, because there is greater within-brand differentiation among lower tar cigarettes.[5] A four-category designation of tar levels was selected. It allowed for somewhat greater differentiation among lower tar users, has an equal number of rating scale

---

[5]Tar yields vary within the same brand as a function of length (e.g., king size, 100 mm, 120 mm) and descriptors (e.g., light, special light, ultra light).

points in each of the low tar categories, and was consistent with a recently proposed four-category nicotine and tar rating system (Henningfield et al., 1994). Cell sizes for the five tar categories (including "Can't Determine") were small: 28, 75, 70, 116, and 48 for those smoking cigarettes in the past 2 to 3 years.

Fifty-eight percent of current smokers (i.e., everyday smokers plus somedays smokers) smoked a cigarette with 15 mg tar or less, and 9% smoked a cigarette with 1 mg to 5 mg tar. Recent quitters tended to come disproportionately from relatively higher tar categories, consistent with evidence suggesting that switching to the lowest tar cigarettes is often a substitute for, rather than a stepping stone to, quitting. High tar cigarette use was more frequent among males, African Americans, and Hispanics and decreased markedly with educational attainment.

Smokers' Awareness of Advertised Tar Numbers

The 325 people who reported smoking cigarettes in the past 2 to 3 years were asked to tell the interviewer the tar number of their most recently smoked cigarette. Seventy-nine percent indicated they did not know. This increased to about 90% for those having less than a high school education, smokers ages 55 and older, and African American smokers. Respondents answering "don't know" then were asked to come as close as they could, and interviewers were to probe for their "best guess." Fifty-eight percent still reported not knowing.

Initial responses were slightly more likely to be underestimates (9%) than correct answers (defined as plus or minus 1 from the actual tar level) or overestimates (6% in both of the latter two cases). When probed responses were included in the analysis, there was a substantial increase in responses that underestimated tar levels (from 9% to 20%) with very small changes in correct answers or overestimates. Such underestimates may result from inferences based on names such as "Light" and "Mild" that cigarette companies know imply low tar delivery (Tindall, 1973; R. J. Reynolds, Inc., 1989c). When actual tar numbers were regressed against respondents' initial and probed answers, the relations were quite weak (r = .26 and .20, respectively).

Smokers of very low tar cigarettes had a much greater awareness of their cigarettes' tar numbers. Thirty-nine percent of those who smoked 1 mg to 5 mg tar cigarettes were correct initially, increasing to 50% with probing. These figures stand in marked contrast to responses of those who smoked cigarettes considered to be low tar (6 mg–10 mg), whose comparable percentages correct were 4% and 9%, respectively,

It may be argued that smokers may be familiar with their cigarettes' tar *levels* without necessarily being able to recall specific tar *numbers*. Consumers routinely convert numerical information to descriptive or categorical information (e.g., good gas mileage, long-lasting medicine). Still, if that accounts for smokers' dismal performance in recalling their cigarettes' tar numbers, it is also a challenge to those favoring a continuation of the current test protocol and policy. This issue is discussed further later.

To further evaluate smokers' "operational" knowledge of cigarette tar levels, half of the sample were asked whether a 16 mg (or, for the other half, a 5 mg) tar cigarette is lower in tar than most other cigarettes on the market. The correct answers are "no" for the 16 mg tar cigarette, and "yes" for the 5 mg tar cigarette. Table 15.2 shows respondents' answers cross-tabulated by the tar level of their most recently smoked cigarette. Whereas 35% of the smokers of 1 mg to 5 mg tar cigarettes did not know that a 16 mg tar cigarette was not lower in tar, between 55% and 66% of all other smokers either did not know or gave incorrect responses to this question. For those smoking cigarettes having upward of 5 mg tar, between 56% and 74% either did not know that a 5 mg tar cigarette was lower in tar than most other cigarettes or said that it was not lower (with 10% to 20% incorrect).

Though the performance of very low tar smokers was considerably better than other smokers on the 16 mg tar question, it was by no means good, and the 15% correct response, for the 5 mg tar cigarette represents the lowest score of any tar level group in the study. There are several reasons why very low tar smokers—for whom tar numbers are more salient and better recalled—might do worse than expected on these questions. First, they probably do not care very much about where a 16 mg tar cigarette falls relative to most cigarettes: Their focus is on cigarettes with very low

TABLE 15.2
Knowledge of FTC Tar Numbers Corresponding to Lower Tar Levels

	Very Low Tar 1–5	Low Tar 6–10	Medium Tar 11–15	High Tar 16+	Can't Determine
Believe that a 16 mg tar cigarette is lower in tar than most other cigarettes (N = 179)	(14)	(36)	(40)	(64)	(25)
% Correct	65	45	44	34	32
% Incorrect	0	10	10	16	12
% Don't know	35	45	46	50	56
Believe that a 5 mg tar cigarette is lower in tar than most other cigarettes (N = 158)	(14)	(39)	(30)	(52)	(23)
% Correct	15	34	44	27	25
% Incorrect	13	10	14	19	16
% Don't know	73	56	42	55	59

tar levels. Second, this narrow focus probably contributes to the perception that there is a much higher proportion of cigarettes having less than 5 mg of tar than is, in fact, the case.

Inferences Based on Tar Numbers

Several approaches were used to better understand how smokers interpreted the advertised tar numbers. In the first, half the sample were asked whether pack-a-day smokers could significantly lower their health risks due to smoking by switching from a 20 mg tar cigarette to a 5 mg tar cigarette (for the other half, the switch was to a 16 mg tar cigarette). In total, 56% of smokers thought that a switch to a 5 mg tar cigarette would significantly lower health risks, whereas 28% thought that a switch to a 16 mg tar cigarette would significantly lower health risks.

Table 15.3 cross-tabulates answers to these questions against the actual tar levels of smokers' cigarettes. For the dramatic shift to a 5 mg cigarette, low to heavy tar cigarette smokers are evenly divided between believing there would be a significant reduction in health risks and either believing this would not be the case or being unsure about this. Presumably, one of the major goals of the 25-year program of providing tar numbers was to encourage such major reductions for those not willing or able to quit smoking. That message does not appear to have gotten through to large numbers of smokers. Whereas over 60% of smokers did not think switching to a 16 mg tar cigarette would lead to a significant reduction in health risks due to smoking, a sizable proportion of low to heavy tar cigarette smokers either thought it would or did not know. Such responses suggest that smokers simply do not know how to interpret these abstract tar numbers, particularly given the absence of a meaningful baseline.

The interpretation of data in Table 15.3 is complicated by almost certainly differing beliefs of smokers in the four tar categories regarding the risks of smoking a 20 mg tar cigarette, and hence about the gain from any reduction in tar level. Because this belief is likely to be invariant across the two versions of this question, it is useful to examine relative judgments about reduced health risks (i.e., perceived benefits when switching to the 5 mg tar alternative compared to the 16 mg alternative) shown in the last row of the table. Once again, the evidence points to a clear difference between smokers of cigarettes with 1 mg to 5 mg tar and all other smokers. These very low tar smokers believe that it takes a substantial reduction in tar yields to significantly reduce health risk, whereas this belief does not appear to be held by a substantial number of smokers in other categories. Unfortunately, this belief also may support a judgment that a substantial reduction in tar levels may be a reasonable substitute for quitting.

The study next examined smokers' understanding of the distinction between tar yield and delivery, together with their willingness to treat the

TABLE 15.3
Inferences About Health Risks as a Result
of Switching to Lower Tar Cigarettes

	Very Low Tar 1–5	Low Tar 6–10	Medium Tar 11–15	High Tar 16+	Can't Determine
Switching from a 20 mg to a 5 mg tar cigarette would significantly reduce health risks	83%	49%	49%	55%	60%
Switching from a 20 mg to a 5 mg tar cigarette would not significantly reduce health risks	13%	32%	35%	25%	29%
Don't know	4%	19%	15%	20%	12%
Switching from a 20 mg to a 16 mg tar cigarette would significantly reduce health risks	18%	35%	28%	25%	33%
Switching from a 20 mg to a 16 mg tar cigarette would not significantly reduce health risks	68%	61%	61%	61%	37%
Don't know	14%	4%	10%	14%	31%
Relative difference in health risks between switching to a 5 mg and a 16 mg tar cigarette	65%	14%	21%	30%	27%

numerical information as if it had ratio scale properties rather than merely ordinal properties. Many of those supporting the dissemination of tar numbers have assumed that consumers would use these numbers in an ordinal fashion, essentially to rank-order cigarettes. Ordinal scales do not possess the property that each numerical interval is of the same magnitude (i.e., the difference between 1 and 2 being precisely equal to the difference between 10 and 11). The FTC method may produce tar ratings that have this interval scale property for tar yields, but it cannot be said to do so for actual deliveries of tar, because smokers' inhalation intensifies as we move lower on the scale. A ratio scale has the further property of having a genuine zero point, such that it is proper to regard a scale score of 10 as being twice as high as a scale score of 5.

FTC concerns about this precise issue led the agency to challenge Carlton advertising containing statements such as "Ten packs of Carlton have less tar than one pack of these brands" (picturing single packs of five other brands). Though no evidence was formally presented to support this message "takeaway," the FTC complaint alleged that such ads represented that consumers could possibly smoke 10 packs of 1 mg Carltons without taking in more tar than from 1 pack of these other brands (rated at 12 mg–17 mg tar). The FTC's willingness to prosecute and American Tobacco's willingness to refrain from making such verbal and pictorial rep-

TABLE 15.4
Inferences About Trade-Offs Between Tar
Deliveries and Number of Cigarettes Smoked

	Very Low Tar 1–5	Low Tar 6–10	Medium Tar 11–15	High Tar 16+	Can't Determine
The person probably could smoke more than one, but these numbers can't tell you how much less tar the person would take in from the 1 mg tar cigarette.	28%	33%	31%	40%	39%
The person could smoke more than 1 or 2, but less than 9 or 10 of the 1 mg tar cigarettes without taking in more tar.	18%	33%	22%	25%	22%
The person could smoke about 10 of the 1 mg tar cigarettes without taking in more tar.	44%	25%	31%	21%	21%
None of these/don't know	10%	10%	16%	14%	18%

resentations in the future suggests that both are sensitive to concerns that smokers might be making inappropriate (i.e., ratio scale) inferences about tar deliveries.

Consumers' understanding of this matter was examined by asking respondents to assume that a person switched from a 10 mg tar cigarette to a 1 mg tar cigarette. The three statements shown in Table 15.4 were then read twice and respondents were asked to decide which of these came closest to their opinion. Primacy and recency effects were controlled by rotating the order of the first and third statements. The first answer is the correct choice, whereas the second answer suggests some reluctance to rely on the absolute numerical values when thinking about such tradeoffs.

The most general conclusion to be drawn from these data is that at least one quarter of smokers (i.e., those selecting the third interpretation) clearly are misinformed about the meaning of the tar yield numbers. Interestingly, this increases to 44% for smokers of very low tar cigarettes. In line with other evidence presented here, this increases concern about the safety reassurances that such very low tar cigarettes appear to provide. By comparison, FTC and private party lawsuits alleging misleading/deceptive advertising are routinely validated by evidence that 20% to 25% of the relevant public has been misled.

Finally, smokers' self-reports of having used these tar numbers to make judgments about the relative safety of different brands of cigarettes were examined. Whereas only 14% of the sample indicated doing so, once again, smokers of 1 mg to 5 mg tar cigarettes were different: Fifty-six percent reported using advertised tar numbers to make judgments about the relative safety of various cigarettes.

CONCLUSIONS

Over the past 30 years, the cigarette industry has fought a skillful "holding action" against the ever-increasing amount of information detailing the health risks of smoking. Although many smokers have quit, and many fewer start smoking, the low tar and nicotine cigarette has been one of the principal means of retaining health-concerned smokers: "We target at people who are looking for milder brands and we are well aware that the primary reason many of them are looking for milder brands is because they believe that a milder brand is better for their health" (RJR–Macdonald, Inc., 1989e). The health community in general and the FTC in particular have found themselves, in the words of the classic song lyric, "between the devil and the deep blue sea." The predominant message to the public has always been: "Don't smoke; there is no safe cigarette." The reality is that many smokers have a difficult time quitting (only 8% are successful, according to a 1993 study by the Centers for Disease Control), and so a secondary message has been: "If you have to smoke, smoke as little as possible and smoke low tar and nicotine cigarettes."

From the consumer standpoint, tar numbers "must" have some health significance, or they wouldn't seemingly be "required" in cigarette advertisements; nor would cigarette brands build advertising appeals and product descriptions around them. The cigarette industry continues to argue that advertised tar ratings give consumers useful comparative information, which they define as information about yields, perhaps assuming that consumers understand both that these are not the same as the actual amount ingested and they are only valid for cigarettes smoked in exactly the same way. Because there has been a substantial reduction in sales-weighted average tar and nicotine yields (approximately 60% since 1955, but whose rate of decrease has slowed considerably since 1981), one could also say that there has been a desirable, but small, reduction in smoking-attributable mortality despite widespread confusion over the meaning and health significance of these tar numbers. In essence, the existing policy has facilitated the development and promotion of low yield cigarettes, while leaving individuals confused about the relative risks they incur by smoking cigarettes having different tar yields.

The dangers of communicating this implied "safer cigarette" message have troubled health professionals from the start. The current analysis of these issues—spurred by a congressional and FTC-initiated scientific conference sponsored by the National Cancer Institute in December 1994—is likely to focus on improving the accuracy of tar yield numbers and putting this information into more of a consumer-friendly format such as a graphic representation, possibly to appear on cigarette packages as well as in advertisements (in part to overcome the lack of advertising for discount brands).

Although information format issues comprise a more tractable agenda, these are secondary to an analysis of the wisdom of continuing to provide governmental support for publicly perceived relative safety ratings. Consider the following conclusion from the Ad Hoc Committee of the President's Cancer Panel (as distributed to the press on December 6, 1994): "The smoking of cigarettes with lower *machine-measured* yields has a small effect in reducing the risk of cancer caused by smoking, no effect on the risk of cardiovascular diseases, and an uncertain effect on the risk of pulmonary disease. A reduction in *machime-measured* tar yields from 15 mg tar to 1 mg tar does not reduce relative risk from 15 to 1" (Jenks, 1995, p. 15; emphasis in original). Despite this conclusion, the Committee still recommended providing numerical information on tar, nicotine, and carbon monoxide yields to smokers.

Such a decision should be made with full recognition of the fact that many smokers, trying to make sense of such information and why it has been presented, will interpret it in terms of meaningful differences in overall harmfulness. Hoping for a substantial public education program to properly qualify the meaning of cigarette yield information may be unrealistic at this time. So, if the health community is not prepared to say that "lower is less harmful" for machine-measured yields (and perhaps not even for tar *deliveries*), it should not appear to be doing so through the use of a numerical scale. However, it might be feasible to require a single statement on all cigarette packages to the effect that, "Cigarettes with reduced tar have a slightly lower cancer risk, but do not reduce the risk of heart attack, stroke, or other lung disease."

A wide range of policy options should also be considered. At the extreme, this might include banning production of cigarettes that exceed certain levels of identified constituents or requiring special warnings on them. Such options should also be reviewed for their potential role as incentives for the tobacco industry, including the ability to promote meaningful reductions in harmful elements. This would not prevent the health community from recommending appropriate (perhaps multifactor) standards for assessing cigarettes, analogous to some of the Food and Drug Administration's requirements for health-related terms in food advertising. A multifactor rating system may be a useful way of dealing with compounds whose meaning and significance is not widely appreciated by smokers and for which a massive public education program is not feasible.

Current suggestions for revising the format for FTC-yield assessments and conveying these to consumers begin with developing more realistic puffing parameters that incorporate both compensation and inadvertent lessening of aeration. One proposal likely to receive serious consideration would generate a range of outcomes rather than a single tar number for each cigarette as a function of variability in the above factors (Food and Drug Administration, 1995b). There would be a certain arbitrariness to whatever range in conditions might be adopted for such a test protocol. Further, communicating the meaning of this range to consumers, as evidenced by the results of the study reported here, would be a difficult enterprise.

It might be worthwhile to consider a somewhat different approach in which ratings better reflected smoking profiles of more "intense" smokers as well as easily defeated methods of aeration (e.g., placing air holes where they could be covered by one's lips or fingers). It is difficult to make a public health case for supplying tar information based on a "best case" set of conditions, because smokers have no real basis to know whether those conditions should apply to them. Further, smokers are more likely to want to believe the more optimistic assessment. Accordingly, basing the standardized test parameters on observations of smoking behavior of, say, the upper 25% (in terms of smoking intensity) might be an appropriately conservative procedure, especially if tar yields would then be linked to nicotine levels (i.e., in order for the cigarette to achieve a particular rating).

Data from the survey also raises concerns about the absolute level of the FTC tar numbers. One to 5 mg tar numbers are not only lower, they are low! Unless we are willing to have consumers develop the belief that such cigarettes are, for all intents and purposes, free of harmful elements and hence safe, there is some value in adopting a rating system that does not convey a virtual absence of what many smokers presume to be the primary harmful element.

As the study demonstrated, there are inherent difficulties in communicating this type of information by means of numerical ratings. This gives added support to proposals that might convert appropriately arrived at numerical ratings to category-descriptive labels. Above all, we should think about the FTC testing methodology as a means to an end, rather than a system that might require technical modifications to accurately report variability. The system was put in place to provide a standardized basis for information thought to be helpful to consumers. Whatever changes are made should be responsive to what is known about consumers' understanding and use of this and related types of information.

ACKNOWLEDGMENTS

Appreciation is expressed to Donald Shopland at the National Cancer Institute and John Pinney at the Corporate Health Policies Group, who made it possible to carry out the survey, and to the American Cancer

Society and the Coalition on Smoking OR Health, for providing financial support necessary to carry out the survey. Particular thanks are due to Joe Gitchell at the Corporate Health Policies Group for his considerable help with project coordination and coding of data. A preliminary report of the survey data was presented to the National Cancer Institute Conference on the FTC Test Method, Bethesda, Maryland, December 5–6, 1994.

REFERENCES

Bridges, R. D., Combs, J. G., Humble, J. W., Turbek, J. A., Rehm, S. R., & Haley, N. J. (1990). Puffing topography as a determinant of smoke exposure. *Pharmacology, Biochemistry, and Behavior, 37,* 29–39.
Calfee, J. E. (1985). Cigarette advertising, health information and regulation before 1970 (Working Paper No. 134). Washington, DC: Federal Trade Commission, Bureau of Economics.
Chapman, S., Wilson, D., & Wakefield, M. (1986). Smokers' understandings of cigarette yield labels. *Medical Journal of Australia, 145*(8), 376–379.
Coalition on Smoking OR Health (1993). *Gallup poll survey on the public's attitude towards the regulation and advertising of cigarettes.* Washington, DC, April 1993.
Cohen, J. B. (1992). Research and policy issues in Ringold and Calfee's treatment of cigarette health claims. *Journal of Public Policy and Marketing, 11*(1), 82–86.
Covington, & Burling (1994, December). The FTC's test method provides useful and reliable information about the relative "tar" and nicotine yields of cigarettes (for American Tobacco, Brown & Williamson, Liggett, and Lorillard). Written submission presented to National Cancer Institute Conference on the FTC Cigarette Test Method, Bethesda, MD.
Dunn, W. L., Jr. (1970). [Memo to Dr. H. Wakeham], August 17.
Federal Trade Commission Report to Congress for 1992 (1994). Washington, DC: Federal Trade Commission.
Federal Trade Commission (1994). Tar, nicotine, and carbon monoxide of the smoke of 933 varieties of domestic cigarettes. Washington, DC: Federal Trade Commission.
Food and Drug Administration, Department of Health and Human Services (1995a). Analysis regarding the food and drug administration's jurisdiction over nicotine-containing cigarettes and smokeless tobacco products. *Federal Register, 60*(155), 198–205.
Food and Drug Administration, Department of Health and Human Services (1995b). Regulation restricting the sale and distribution of cigarettes and smokeless tobacco products to protect children and adolescents. *Federal Register, 60*(155), 41339.
Giovino, G. A., Tomar, S. L., Reddy, M. N., Peddicord, J. P., Zhu, B. P., Escobedo, L. G., & Eriksen, M. P. (1996). Trends in attitudes, knowledge, and beliefs about low-yield cigarettes among adolescents and adults. In *The federal trade commission test method for determining tar, nicotine, and carbon monoxide levels in cigarettes* (Smoking and Tobacco Control Monograph No. 8). Bethesda, MD: Department of Health and Human Services, Public Health Service, National Institutes of Health, National Cancer Institute.
Gori, G. B. (1990). Consumer perception of cigarette yields: Is the message relevant? *Regulatory Toxicology and Pharmacology, 12*(1), 64–68.
Henningfield, J. E., Kozlowski, L. T., & Benowitz, N. L. (1994). A proposal to develop meaningful labeling for cigarettes. *Journal of the American Medical Association, 272,* 4.
Jenks, S. (1995). Low-tar cigarettes pose hidden health threat, panel says. *Journal of the National Cancer Institute, 87*(1), 15.

Mueller, M. (1996). Overview of 1980–1994 research findings relating to the standard FTC test method for cigarette smoking. In *The Federal Trade Commission test method for determining tar, nicotine, and carbon monoxide levels in cigarettes* (Smoking and Tobacco Control Monograph No. 8). Bethesda, MD: Department of Health and Human Services, Public Health Service, National Institute of Health, National Cancer Institute.

NHIS-CCES (1992). *National health interview survey—cancer control and epidemiology supplements.* Hyattsville, MD: U.S. Department of Health and Human Services.

Palmer, J. R., Rosenberg, L., & Shapiro, S. (1993). Low yield cigarettes and the risk of non-fatal myocardial infarction in women. *New England Journal of Medicine, 320,* 1569–1573.

Peeler, C. L. (1996). Remarks of C. Lee Peeler. In *The Federal Trade Commission test method for determining tar, nicotine, and carbon monoxide levels in cigarettes* (Smoking and Tobacco Control Monograph No. 8). Bethesda, MD: Department of Health and Human Services, Public Health Service, National Institutes of Health, National Cancer Institute.

Philip Morris, Inc. (1973). Consumer knowledge and opinions of "tar" and taste levels of cigarettes. Unpublished report of Marketing Research Department, New York.

Philip Morris, Inc. (1994, December). *Written submission presented to National Cancer Institute Conference on the FTC cigarette test method.* Bethesda, MD.

Pillsbury, H. C. (1996). Remarks of Harold C. Pillsbury. In *The Federal Trade Commission test method for determining tar, nicotine, and carbon monoxide levels in cigarettes* (Smoking and Tobacco Control Monograph No. 8). Bethesda, MD: Department of Health and Human Services, Public Health Service, National Institutes of Health, National Cancer Institute.

RJR–Macdonald, Inc. (1989a). Trial Document AG-14, 1978 Annual Business Plan, RJR–Macdonald and Imperial Tobacco Limitée c. Procurer Général du Canada.

RJR–Macdonald, Inc. (1989b). Trial Document AG-35, 1971 Matinee Marketing Plans, RJR-Macdonald and Imperial Tobacco Limitée c. Procurer Général du Canada.

RJR–Macdonald, Inc. (1989c). RJR–Macdonald and Imperial Tobacco Limitée c. Procurer Général du Canada, *8,* 1159.

RJR–Macdonald, Inc. (1989d). RJR–Macdonald and Imperial Tobacco Limitée c. Procurer Général du Canada, *9,* 1192.

RJR–Macdonald, Inc. (1989e). Trial Document AG-41, "Response of the Market and of Imperial Tobacco to the Smoking and Health Environment," RJR–Macdonald and Imperial Tobacco Limitée c. Procurer Général du Canada.

R. J. Reynolds, Inc. (1994, December). The FTC test method should be retained. Written submission presented to National Cancer Institute Conference on the FTC Cigarette Test Method, Bethesda, MD.

Ringold, D. J., & Calfee, J. E. (1989). The informational content of cigarette advertising. *Journal of Public Policy and Marketing, 8,* 1–23.

Steiger, J. (1994). [Letter from FTC chairman Janet D. Steiger to Dr. Samuel Broder, National Cancer Institute], July 20.

Tindall, J. E. (1973). *A new low delivery segment.* Philip Morris, Inc. Research Center.

U.S. Department of Health and Human Services (1981). *The health consequences of smoking: The changing cigarette* (Pub. No. PHS 8150156). A report of the Surgeon General. Washington, DC: DHEW.

U.S. Department of Health and Human Services (1988). *The health consequences of smoking: Nicotine addiction* (Pub. No. CDC 88-8406). A report of the Surgeon General. Washington, DC: DHHS.

U.S. Department of Health and Human Services (1989). *Reducing the health consequences of smoking: Twenty-five years of progress* (Pub. No. CDC 89-8411). A report of the Surgeon General. Rockville, MD: DHHS.

Waxman, H. (1994). [Letter from Representative Henry A. Waxman to Dr. Samuel Broder, National Cancer Institute], June 7.

Part V

THREE DIFFERING INSTITUTIONAL APPROACHES: GOVERNMENT, NONGOVERNMENT ORGANIZATIONS, PRIVATE CORPORATIONS

Chapter 16

Marketing Public Health: The CDC Experience

Fred Kroger
Jeffrey W. McKenna
Melissa Shepherd
Elizabeth H. Howze
Dorothy S. Knight
Centers for Disease Control and Prevention

ABSTRACT

In 1992, the Centers for Disease Control and Prevention (CDC) adopted a 5-year plan to make health communications an integral component of all its programs to promote health, foster healthful environments, and improve the quality of life. This chapter presents a sampler of current CDC activities that employ marketing strategies for making health communications more effective. These activities, as presented at the *1995 Society for Consumer Psychology Conference*, include programs to reduce tobacco consumption, promote HIV prevention behaviors, improve nutrition and physical activity, increase use of health information services, and improve public understanding about essential public health services.

INTRODUCTION
Fred Kroger

Peters and Waterman (1984) described eight functions that contribute to, or are essential to success. If seven of these were eliminated, then it would be marketing that remains. It is the one that focuses on the end result. "Marketing is not peripheral to success, but central" (Peters, 1984, p. 17).

Andreasen, in his opening remarks at this conference, noted that some parts of CDC have adopted marketing principles to their programs to a significant degree. Perhaps the word "adapted" should be used here for

267

the time being, because none of the CDC's prevention programs have embraced marketing principles to the degree Peters suggested. But, a number of programs have borrowed from the tools of marketing to enhance the effectiveness of consumer education efforts.

This chapter provides a sampler of CDC programs that have been applying marketing notions and methods to improve consumer prevention practices. Although nowhere near exhaustive, they represent a mixture of old and new programs, and of those that market specific health behaviors (e.g., smoking cessation) versus more general public health services (e.g., health information on the Internet). They also reflect a wide range of "scholarliness." They were prepared by people whose main work is to do health marketing on a daily basis, not necessarily to write or speak about their own work or that of others. Some of the authors are scientists; others are not. Some would be comfortable in academia; others would not.

A good topic for a future conference might be a case study of CDC's strategic efforts to translate the very real threat of emerging infections, as underscored by the recent outbreak of Ebola fever in equatorial Africa, into financial support for the hemorrhaging infrastructure of the U.S. public health system, from a Congress that has been openly hostile to funding increases for "social" programs. Yet, that would be a story of intuitive marketing, as has been the practice of public health leaders for decades. What follows, then, are representative efforts of public health people who have been engaged in the intentional practice of marketing health enhancing behaviors.

First consider CDC's most mature marketing program. Jeffrey McKenna highlights some of the progress that has been made in the 30-year effort to control tobacco use in this country. One only needs to know that tobacco claims more lives annually in the United States (400,000) than any other single cause of death, to appreciate the importance of this work. Fred Kroger describes preliminary research on a broad-based effort to improve public understanding and appreciation for what public health does. It is this context that offers a glimpse into the future of public health in regard to the practice of social marketing. Dorothy Knight addresses CDC's efforts to market prevention information services via the burgeoning new array of communication technologies and roadways. Elizabeth Howze, representing one of CDC's newest marketing projects, presents some preliminary consumer data that is being used to target a campaign to improve eating and physical activity habits, two of the risk factors most directly associated with America's "epidemic" of obesity. Next, Melissa Shepherd describes the largest marketing effort in which CDC is engaged, the Prevention Marketing Initiative of the HIV Prevention program. From out of nowhere, in a decade and a half, AIDS has become the leading cause of death among all persons between the ages of 19 and 45.

USING ALL 4 *P*s IN TOBACCO CONTROL PROGRAMS
Jeffrey W. McKenna

According to Wallack, Dorfman, Jernigan, and Themba (1993):

> Social Marketing tends to reduce serious health problems to individual risk factors and ignore the proven importance of the social and economic environment as major determinants of health. In the long run, this risk factor approach that forms the basis for social marketing may contribute relatively little to reducing the incidence of disease in a population. (p. 23)

With that as prologue, this section attempts to do four things: First, using two data points from recent U.S. tobacco control experience, it offers a rough assessment of the merits of Wallack's critique. Second, it proposes a perspective shift in how the consumer is viewed and the four *p*s in tobacco control marketing (product, price, place, and promotion). Third, it examines how exchange theory from marketing can be applied with as much fidelity to policy change as to individual behavior change. Last, it considers how advertising can support the "de-marketing" of tobacco.

Regarding the first objective, what about Wallack's premise that, after all is said and done, social marketing has little power to improve public health? The search for answers begins with a look at the results of the Community Intervention Trial for Smoking Cessation (COMMIT), which were published earlier this year. There are numerous data already reported from COMMIT that could be summarized here, and many more that will be reported in coming years. This chapter highlights only a few (COMMIT Research Group, 1995).

In COMMIT, the National Cancer Institute spent $45 million to reduce smoking prevalence in 11 small-to-midsize North American communities. The communities implemented a set of mandated smoking cessation activities: media events, health professional counseling, worksite programs, and community cessation services. Compared to matched comparison communities, COMMIT produced only a modest effect on smoking prevalence in the intervention communities, and had no measurable effect on the prevalence of heavy smoking—the key target of COMMIT.

Additional data from other sources present a comparable picture as they relate to teen smoking rates. According to data published by the National Institute on Drug Abuse (1994), the percentage of high school seniors who reported themselves to be daily smokers actually increased from 18.7% to 19.4% in the decade between 1984 and 1994—in spite of the fact that tobacco prevention programs of some type were included in virtually every school in America.

Consider, now, the classic marketing model and the four *p*s. A look at COMMIT or other tobacco control interventions over the past 30 years reveals that a vast portfolio of tobacco control *products* have been developed, pretested, and evaluated; these products have been offered at no charge or at minimal *price*; made available at countless *places*; and persistently *promoted* to various consumers, primarily individual teenagers and adults.

Based on these examples, it appears that Wallack deserves a nod. Admittedly, most tobacco control programs, including COMMIT, were not developed as "social marketing" initiatives and have never claimed to be such. However, their individual behavior change orientation seems to have done relatively little in recent years to reduce tobacco use, especially among young people, and the concomitant incidence of tobacco-related disease.

To address the second objective, the focus of the consumer and of the four marketing *p*s is shifted:

Let the consumer be *policymakers*, not potential or current tobacco users.

Let the four *p*s relate to countering the marketing practices of the tobacco companies, not to marketing individual behavior change interventions.

With such a refocusing, the product now becomes regulations that require full disclosure of ingredient information about cigarettes and chewing tobacco. Addiction is the concept. About 90% of smokers begin as teenagers, who do not internalize the health hazards of tobacco and never expect their smoking behavior to be longstanding (USDHHS, 1994).

The new focus on place seeks to restrict tobacco sales to minors. Vending machines and over-the-counter sales provide kids with wide-open access to tobacco products. Even though it is illegal to sell tobacco to anyone under age 18 in every state, these laws are rarely enforced (USDHHS, 1994).

Promotion efforts are shifted to focus on restricting and countering the advertising and promotion campaigns of the tobacco industry. In 1993, cigarette companies spent a record $6.03 billion on advertising and promotion (Federal Trade Commission, 1995), which works out to an hourly expenditure of $700,000—the same amount that CDC's Office on Smoking and Health spends on its national counteradvertising and education efforts in an entire year.

This perspective moves tobacco control marketing away from a focus on individual behaviors toward that of responsible corporate behaviors, which, for better or worse, can be most immediately influenced by strong public policy. It also answers Wallack's call to pay heed to the social and economic environments that powerfully effect health behaviors.

Moving to the third objective, does this tobacco "de-marketing" approach violate the essence of exchange theory, in which consumers voluntarily comply with pro-health messages in exchange for some overriding benefit? Or, as some might argue, isn't this simply an attempt to regulate, legislate, and mandate behavior?

The answer is not if the consumer population in this alternate model is policymakers. A city council member will support licensing and penalty systems for local tobacco retailers, a state senator will vote for an increase in the tobacco tax, and a U.S. Congressperson will endorse a bill to eliminate the tax deductibility of tobacco advertising, that is, *if* the perceived political benefits of their vote outweigh the political costs.

In some cases, workers in tobacco control can facilitate that exchange process by direct lobbying and advocacy. A powerful, indirect influence is to inform and energize other opinion leaders and the citizenry at large, to whom policymakers must ultimately report. If the money and messages of the tobacco industry dominate, the costs of supporting tobacco control may exceed the benefits, thereby short-circuiting the pro-health policy exchange.

Finally, the fourth objective, how can advertising support tobacco "de-marketing"? Here are examples from three different states' program efforts:

1. The following script from a Massachusetts Department of Health television counteradvertisement repositions the concept of product. It stands in sharp contrast to other ads that label cigarettes, rather than cigarette companies as the villain:

SUPER: The Truth.

ANNCR: Do you know what's in a cigarette? No. Because the last thing the tobacco companies want is for you to know how many poisonous chemicals there are in cigarettes. So they just don't tell you. Not on the pack. Not in their ads. I'm Patrick Reynolds, the grandson of R.J. Reynolds. My family's name is printed on the side of 7 billion packs of cigarettes every year. Why am I telling you this? Because I want my family to be on the right side for a change.

2. This California Department of Health Services TV spot repositions place by raising public concern about youth access:

KID 1: I'd like the filter lights, please.

KID 2: The 100's. Soft pack.

KID 3: The thin ones. In a box.

KID 4: The menthol kings. Yeah. The green guys.

ANNCR: Every day a half million American kids buy their cigarettes from a friendly neighborhood pusher.

KID 2: The 100's. Soft pack.

KID 3: I'd like the filter lights, please.

KID 5:   Hey, two packs. Wouldn't want to run out.

ANNCR: Vending machines don't know any better. But what about the rest of us?

3. And this ad from the Minnesota Health Department repositions promotion by exposing the real intent of tobacco advertising:

(BILLBOARD: "WOMEN ARE MAKING THE RUSH TO RICH FLAVOR.")

VOICE: Cigarette companies spend a lot of money advertising to women. And on the surface, they make it all look so good.

(WIND BEGINS TO BLOW AWAY SOME PANELS OF BILLBOARD HEADLINE.)

VOICE: But you have to ask yourself: What are their real intentions?

(BILLBOARD NOW READS: "WOMEN ARE MAKING US RICH.")

Notably, these three advertising examples were from state-funded paid media campaigns, allowing the states to control both the content and placement of these messages for maximum audience impact. Campaigns that rely solely on public service announcements (PSAs) can rarely achieve comparable impact. Media gatekeepers may reject hard-hitting tobacco counteradvertisements as too controversial for placement as PSAs, and tobacco control PSAs must compete with a host of other worthwhile health and social issues for donated time or space (McKenna, 1994).

Clearly, it is impossible to ignore behavioral interventions in tobacco control. More and better school programs are needed. Better media strategies can use social influence theory to deglamorize and denormalize teen smoking. And, we need better pharmacologic and clinical approaches to help addicted smokers quit.

But, as long as tobacco is addictive and affordable, and promoted and sold with virtually no restraints, environmental change must be advanced as vigorously as health education. Marketing can help do that.

MARKETING THE MERITS OF ESSENTIAL PUBLIC HEALTH SERVICES
Fred Kroger

Winston Churchill said, "Nothing in life is so exhilarating as to be shot at without result." To some extent, that is what public health is all about. Public health creates systems and circumstances, such that when the viral, bacteriological, environmental, occupational, chemical, and even gun powder propelled shots that cause disease, disability, or premature death are whizzing about, they do so, most often, without result.

Individuals involved in public health believe that public health is a good thing. They try to keep bad things from happening to people. But somehow, even the greatest prevention successes fail to produce anything resembling Churchill's exhilaration within the body politic.

Of the 30 years that have been added to life expectancy since the turn of the century, 25 can be attributed to population-based, public health measures, compared to the 5 years added by advances in clinical medicine. Between 1981 and 1993, total U.S. health expenditures increased by more than 210%; but, during that same period of time, funding for public health strategies as a proportion of the health care budget declined by 25% (PHS, 1995).

One problem may be that successes in prevention are often measured by an absence of impact, and in effect become non-news. Smallpox is gone forever. Polio has been virtually eliminated. Fluoridated community water supplies have produced dramatic reductions in tooth decay. Childhood blood lead levels are way down. Yet, prevention failures, which are faithfully tracked and described—AIDS outbreaks, reemergent tuberculosis, the Ebola scare, increased prevalence of obesity, persistent teenage smoking rates, and urban immunization rates below that of third world countries— are more likely to capture the nation's headlines than are prevention successes. (When was the last time you saw a television newscast that led with an apartment building or abandoned warehouse that *did not* catch on fire?)

As noted by the Institute of Medicine (IOM) in its report on "The Future of Public Health" (1988), which clearly documented the deterioration of the nation's public health infrastructure, public health has faced the paradox of having a terrific, life-enhancing product. Yet, few outside of the public health fraternity know it or care. When colleagues at the state and local levels try to sell their city councils, their boards of supervisors, or their state legislators on the merits of public health, folks are not buying. Some in public health have even admitted publicly that public health has done a singularly poor job of marketing!

This failure to effectively market public health became more painfully evident when the Clinton administration's initial proposals on health care reform surfaced. Public health found itself all but absent from the planning process, and consequently from the plans themselves.

With this as a wake up call, CDC, in collaboration with a number of public health partners, has initiated a long-term effort to better tell the public health story. One of the initial steps was to task Macro International Inc. (1994) and Westat Inc., contractors for health communications evaluation, to gauge the public's understanding of public health's role, to identify misconceptions, and to identify potential strategies for strengthening the marketing abilities of these public health partners.

Core Public Health Functions

The IOM (1988) report identified three core public health functions that served as a foundation for this research: assessment, policy development, and assurance. Though helpful to internal understanding, this language was viewed by communications professionals as being "serious eye-glaze material" for most laypersons, legislative types included.

Subsequently, a working level group appointed by the Core Public Health Functions Steering Committee (agency heads of the seven Public Health Service agencies and the presidents of eight partner associations, and chaired by Philip R. Lee, the Assistant Secretary for Health) developed terminology that translates the three Core Functions into 10 Essential Services (PHS, 1994; e.g., "Monitor the health status of the population," and, "Prevent epidemics").

Focus Group Research

Focus group discussions were held in six communities among persons who were convened in two separate groups: community leaders and elected officials. The former were recruited from a broad range of advocacy, civic, and professional organizations. The latter included local county commissioners, members of boards of health, and state legislators.

The focus group participants confirmed the belief that public health is largely invisible, except for a few specific services. But, they also revealed a readily stimulated reservoir of appreciation for the services of public health, within the public in general and among elected officials in particular.

Favorable findings included:

Public health functions, once pointed out, are appreciated.

Personal benefits can be seen, even by persons who do not use public health services directly.

Local examples and issues were the most compelling.

Regulatory roles are reassuring and protective.

Public health is uniquely qualified/willing to address communitywide issues.

Public health's focus on prevention and on providing community health education distinguishes it from other parts of the health care system.

Among the misconceptions or negative findings were:

Limited awareness of public health's scope or significance.

Strong, erroneous belief that public health is exclusively in the business of delivering services for the poor.

Misplaced confidence that public health functions are being and would be carried out by others.

Conflicting values among some church and civic groups with positions taken by public health (e.g., condom promotion).

Resentment over public health's regulatory role; the intrusiveness of some lifestyle messages.

Generic antigovernment sentiment; presumption that tax dollars are being wasted.

The focus group participants resonated favorably with some of the message concepts that the contractors tested, including such concepts as:

"Public health and prevention work."

"Public health protects you and your family."

"Only public health is responsible for your *community's* health."

"Public health is vigilant and indispensable."

"Public health is there for you; it is objective, protective, and responsive."

"Public health is a network or a system of services."

Recommendations

Based on these findings, the contractors have recommended that CDC and its partners adopt the following strategies:

1. Increase awareness of public health as a system. This could be accomplished through a variety of communication materials and opportunities, including support for National Public Health Week.

2. Build understanding of essential services. This, too, can be accomplished through a variety of opportunities. Using breaking news stories to illustrate the role that various services play in protecting the local community's health is one such example.

3. Build community partnerships. Involving and training lay leaders to assist the public health system in its planning and policy-making roles can expand the cadre of informed, supportive citizens willing to go to bat for public health programs.

4. Increase appreciation of public health by elected officials. Conscious, systematic, and carefully focused efforts to develop relationships with key legislators can create bidirectional communication channels that could be mutually beneficial.

Conclusions

In its 50-year history, the Centers for Disease Control and Prevention has made significant contributions to the health of many. These contributions have most often been carried out in collaboration with state, local, or other national public health partners.

Public health has employed many different tools to intervene in the course of preventable disease and disability. Along with tools from the medicine kit (vaccines, antibiotics, and microscopes) have been the tools of communications (brochures, training lectures, and press releases.) Even though communicable diseases remain prominent on the list of major health concerns, they have been largely replaced as leading causes of death in this century by chronic diseases (heart disease, cancer, diabetes), injuries, and violence. These health problems, along with the newest major communicable disease killer, HIV infection, are rooted in culturally supported lifestyle behaviors, which in turn are notoriously impervious to change.

As the 20th century proceeds into the 21st, a relative newcomer, marketing, enters the public health arena, offering hope for the public health practitioner of the future. Can marketing make a difference? Can a federal agency such as CDC apply the tools of marketers to uproot harmful, population-based behaviors, as successfully as a surgeon's knife is able to excise a fulminating cancer? Or, can new, health enhancing actions be added to a population's repertoire of practices as spendidly as a cherry tree shoot can be grafted onto a pear tree? Will the public health community be able to translate the findings and recommendations that have sprung from this market-place research into programs and actions that will strengthen legislative support for essential public health measures? Can the same marketing methods on which manufaturerers have spent billions to put cigarettes and fatty foods into our nation's mouths, be deployed as adeptly toward their removal?

These and many related questions remain to be answered. The agency's experiences with tobacco control measures and with HIV prevention, as discussed earlier, offer some assurances that hard-won victories in prolonging life and improving health may be rewarded with continued progress against the health threats facing future generations.

What is true for the carpenter and is true for the surgeon, is that the value of any tool is discovered best when it has been placed in the hands of a skilled artisan. Hopefully, the ranks of professional marketeurs will find those persons whose skills and whose hearts are in tune with their own. Together, we can make a difference. Does life offer the marketing or the public health professional a nobler purpose than this?

BROKERING AND DISSEMINATING PUBLIC HEALTH INFORMATION
Dorothy S. Knight

This is an era of shrinking federal budgets. For better or worse, the fact of diminishing resources has been a principal driving force in the use of technology to help meet CDC's objectives related to health information. One of those objectives, and one that is shared with all of the Public Health Service's agencies, is to provide U.S. citizens with easy access to accurate and meaningful health information—to make preventive health information ubiquitous. Even though bold and ambitious, it is an achievable objective, one that is tied to a futures vision of communication. But, to succeed in meeting this objective, the approach must be aggressive. This is a highly competitive communications environment. Other messengers continue to promote conflicting, antihealth messages that are often backed by "big bucks."

Because information is a tangible product, to which standard marketing principles can be applied, there are additional reasons for optimism. Within the marketplace of exchange, the benefits that offered to people who buy into the "product," and who adopt changes in health related behaviors, are improvements in health itself—tangible and valued rewards that make the incentives of other marketers pale in comparison.

Figure 16.1 illustrates CDC's information dissemination strategy. The two groups of people who will participate most extensively in the electronic exchange of information are represented in the columns on the far left and on the far right of the diagram. The people labeled "CIOs" carry such governmental acronyms as NCID, NCEH, NIOSH and EPO, which stand for the Centers (National Center for Infectious Diseases and National Center for Environmental Health), Institute (National Institute for Occupational Health and Safety), and program Offices (Epidemiology Program Office) of CDC.

On the far right of Fig. 16.1 are the constituent groups of CDC, who serve as both the source and the audience for much of the information that CDC processes. Practitioners in public and private health and policy makers or legislators have been among the traditional constituents. More recently, CDC has been called on to speak directly with a broader range of publics, and through a more diverse set of intermediaries.

Data from a variety of sources throughout the world are gathered by CDC scientists, statisticians, and program heads. These, in turn, are used to formulate policies and program recommendations that are aimed at influencing the health practices of individuals, communities, the United States, and the global community. Once formulated, the product line of ideas are crafted into communication formats and translated into the lan-

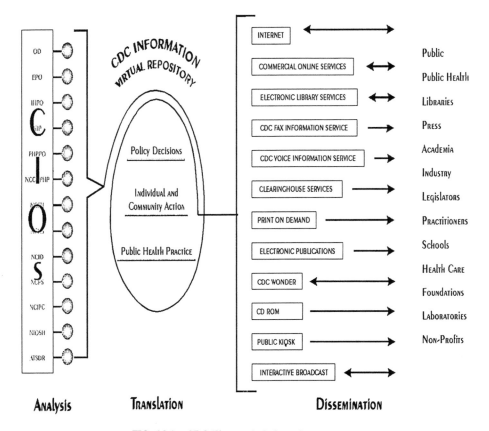

FIG. 16.1.   CDC Electronic infomation strategy.

guages of diverse audiences—the scientific and lay audiences—and disseminated through a variety of communication vehicles. The figure shows some of the electronic tools that are currently used to disseminate health information. The two-way arrows indicate that some of these tools are interactive and that information flow can be bidirectional.

There are three major points for communicating information and how they relate to CDC's information dissemination strategy: guarantee equal access; same message, different delivery; and use of dynamic technology implementation. To provide equal access, the population is defined in broader terms than are typically used to target markets. Audiences include:

Seekers. Seekers are people who know what they need and where to turn to find the information. For this population, more traditional methods of delivery usually will suffice.

Needers at risk. Needers are those who need information because of their personal risk status, but who may be unaware of their need and of the availability of relevant information. This audience includes, but is not limited to racial and ethnic minority populations, persons for whom English is a second language, or those whom we might refer to euphemistically as "literacy challenged."

This latter population is often uninformed on health issues or unmotivated to seek the information. It is a population that public health workers describe as being hard to reach, at least through traditional methods.

Two questions that may come to mind are: "How do you propose to reach these audiences?", and, "Says who?" Starting with the second question first, says me. I am a communication technologist with a 20-year marketing background. It is my job to talk to, listen to, anticipate and respond to the information demands of the public. It is my job to make technology work for us in practical applications. CDC manages systems that respond to more than 5 million inquiries a year. In addition, "consumers" communicate through public comment opportunities related to congressional action and to procurement notices, and on a daily basis with each outbreak of disease and illness, whether caused by a new or emerging organism like Ebola, or by old standbys like syphilis or measles.

But, what could I possibly know about persons who don't seek information? What I know comes partly from the fact that I am one of them! Or at least one kind of them.

I am a "redneck" from south Georgia. I speak with four syllables in one syllable words. My home town still uses rotary phones. I have worked in tobacco fields, know what it is like to have my body covered in tar, and understand the economics of the tobacco market in a small town. My world was one where reproduction begins around the age of 14 or 15, where infant mortality rates remain well above the national averages. (I have only learned some of these facts since beginning work at CDC, though their reality was evident at my 20th high school reunion. I had just had my first child while most of my friends were becoming grandmothers.)

Through these experiences, I can put faces and technology together to create the type of systems that truly communicate and inform. Maybe your experiences have been different than mine, but I believe that we all agree that marketers and communicators have to understand the people, their behavior, their environment, and their culture in order to be effective. To meet the needs of audiences like this, passive methodologies, along with those that are aggressively applied through the use of interactive technologies in clinics, libraries, and school curriculums, combined with concentrated community programs, will provide a comprehensive, full circle approach for educating and informing.

The point is this educating people about their need for health information is a major aspect of marketing health information services. Before
risk behaviors can be changed, consumers must be taught how to be successful information seekers. Technology can be an important ally in our
efforts to reach those that don't seek.

Success in marketing of information requires that the message be succinct and consistent. It cannot present too many different messages at one
time. It must be consistent with the needs of intended users, and be
delivered in ways that allow and encourage them to receive it.

Very recently, my son had been working on a major social studies project.
I sat down with him for about 15 minutes, and explained in detail what
he should do. Once I had finished, he fed back his interpretation of what
I had said, and it could not have been more opposite from what I thought
I had told him than up is from down. Now, this is a child that can hear
a song once and tell you every word, or see a movie once and repeat entire
portions of the dialogue. (I have decided that the best way for me to
communicate important information to my son, will require that I quickly
learn how to sing.) Messages must be clear and delivered in the way a
person or an audience will best receive it.

Messages should speak to a person's needs and should create a need
to change. This may be far different from the kinds of messages that make
us as "public health people" feel good about how much we know or how
many technical terms we can throw around. It is, as we all know, not
enough to "talk at" people, when our goal is to truly communicate.

For the contemporary provider of information, a new and cardinal rule
is that the information should be easy to manage and maintain, and it
should be "outputable" to multiple formats, almost instantaneously. Digital
or electronic technology now provides the best mechanism for multiformat,
rapid response. This technology allows for the continuous management
of the content, while offering the ability to automatically and concurrently
update multiple forms of delivery. Once the initial programs are in place,
this process requires minimal human intervention other than in the crea-
tion or translation of the information.

To disseminate information in a timely manner, providers will have to
incorporate the creative use of technology and interactive communication
for delivery to those who seek it; in passive methodologies and located
close to the point of need; packaged in ways it will attract the attention
of the target population; and, finally, to be more responsive in the absolute
numbers it can serve.

Figure 16.1 illustrates information translation at the point of origination
of data. The data is interpreted into salient messages that communicate to
the general or other target populations. Once those messages are created,
the information will be maintained in one database, the "virtual repository"

of CDC information, so that changes can be easily recorded and automatically disseminated through the electronic or digital avenues of choice.

There are many benefits to this approach: information can be standardized, and the number of separate documents can be reduced; portions of a given item can be easily and instantly updated, at far less cost than for printed materials, offering consumers information that can be entirely current; dissemination to multiple formats can be automated, based on file access and updates, reducing the human labor factor, and allowing the agency to do more with less; and, the information database acts as a feeder to the multiple avenues of dissemination so that the consumer may be more likely to be reached in the manner or mode that is the most "user friendly."

Through the use of this model, CDC will be able to respond faster, more efficiently, and with increased potential for positive health impact as the CDC strives to meet the health information needs of the people it serves.

FORMATIVE RESEARCH UNDERTAKEN FOR THE NUTRITION AND PHYSICAL ACTIVITY COMMUNICATIONS PROJECT
Elizabeth H. Howze

Sedentary lifestyles and unhealthy diets account for more than 300,000 deaths in the United States each year (McGinnis & Foege, 1993) and contribute to the development of serious chronic diseases and conditions such as heart disease, cancer, diabetes, osteoporosis, and obesity (Pate et al., 1995). For example, physical inactivity has been recognized as a major risk factor for coronary heart disease; the relative increased risk associated with physical inactivity ranges from 1.5 to 2.4 (to 1), which is comparable to the risks associated with cigarette smoking, elevated serum cholesterol, and elevated blood pressure (Pate et al., 1995).

In 1994, the National Center for Chronic Disease Prevention and Health Promotion of the Centers for Disease Control and Prevention initiated the Nutrition and Physical Activity Communications (NuPAC) project, a health communications effort that simultaneously addresses diet and physical activity. The campaign's mission is to promote moderate physical activity (30 minutes of moderate activity $\geq$ 5 days per week), low fat eating ($\leq$ 30% of daily caloric intake), and increased fruit and vegetable consumption ($\geq$ 5 servings a day).

This section briefly describes the steps taken in the formative research process that lay the foundation for selecting the initial target audience and developing campaign strategy and message concepts for NuPAC. The Health Communications Wheel (Roper, 1993), diffusion theory (Rogers, 1983), stages of change model (Marcus et al., 1992), and social marketing approach

(Winett, 1995) have provided the central practical and theoretical frameworks for developing the campaign. Thorough formative research is critical to developing a strategy and implementing activities in any successful social marketing-driven project. According to Winett (1995), "a program designed without a firm conceptual base is suspect, and a framework that stresses implementation but lacks a strong research base is equally suspect" (p. 348).

Methods

Literature Review. The review of the literature encompassed epidemiological studies, surveillance reports, research on behavioral determinants, intervention and marketing studies, and published and unpublished reports by national and governmental organizations on physical activity and nutrition.

Analysis of Target Market and Initial Segmentation. Considerations for selecting an initial target audience included having the largest possible impact with limited resources in the shortest time. The initial target audience was therefore limited to White and Black adults from age 29 to 54 who were contemplating or preparing to make a change in physical activity, dietary fat intake, or consumption of fruits and vegetables. Additional criteria included having a moderate level of education (from high school to some graduate school), a moderate annual income (from low moderate to high moderate), and children in the home. By applying to these criteria, attitudinal and behavioral measures related to nutrition, physical activity, general health, media use patterns, and stage of change from a large national consumer database ($N = 5,174$), profiles were developed of potential target audience segments.

Focus Group Research. NuPAC focus groups in four metropolitan areas were comprised of people from the initial target audience. Each focus group examined questions that evolved from the literature review, data analysis, theory, and personal experience. Table 16.1 lists some of the themes and considerations for developing message concepts that emerged from the focus groups.

Next Steps and Some Observations

The next steps before launch of the NuPAC campaign are further segmenting the target audience, developing and testing message concepts developing a strategic communications plan, establishing an evaluation plan, and collecting baseline data. Formative research to lay the groundwork for the campaign has uncovered a number of things. Existing public

TABLE 16.1
Themes and Concepts Emerging from NuPAC Focus Group
Discussions about Physical Activity and Healthy Eating

Primary Themes
  Family is a priority.
  Life is busy and stressful.
  Life transitions influence behavior.
  Spiritual, mental, and physical health are connected.

Secondary Themes
  Chief barriers are perceived lack of time and internal motivation.
  Chief motivators are children and other people important in one's life.
  Supportive, encouraging messages are persuasive, particularly for women.

Considerations for Developing Message Concepts
  Tailor by gender or lifestage rather than by race or region.
  Focus on family responsibility and love of family.
  Emphasize that a healthy lifestyle can enable one to meet responsibilities and enjoy life.
  Reassure that health benefits can accrue from incremental, manageable changes.
  Emphasize holistic health.
  Remember that the target audience is experienced with attempting to change nutrition
    and physical activity behaviors.
  Position changes as lifelong rather than short term.
  Use positive, encouraging messages and social support.
  Address misconceptions about healthy eating and physical activity.

health data sources, such as the Behavioral Risk Factor Surveillance System, which are useful for surveillance and monitoring of trends in physical activity and behavior, have little utility for psychographic profiling, determining communication channels, or tracking the influence of a health communications campaign. Private, proprietary market research data also presents significant limitations for designing and tracking health communications campaigns in physical activity and nutrition. Not only are such data sources expensive, but they also may phrase health-related questions differently from questions on public health instruments. This creates problems for appropriate segmentation and profiling, as well as for tracking and comparison with variables from other public surveillance systems. There is a need, therefore, to incorporate the positive attributes of both private and public data systems into a comprehensive, affordable surveillance and tracking mechanism.

One of the values of formative, consumer-based research, such as NuPAC, is that it can protect against inappropriate labeling of audience segments or the development of communications based on a social construction of those segments by researchers that is not grounded in the reality of people's lives. Consumer-based research can provide a rich tapestry of information about individuals and their lifestyles in the context of larger and powerful system influences on behavior—family, work, community, the environment, and public policy. Knowledge of contexts can help shift the focus from chronic disease largely as "a personal problem to health as a social issue" (Wallack et al., 1993, p. 5), thereby opening numerous avenues by which "conditions in which people can be healthy"—the mission of public health (Institute of Medicine, 1988)—can be created.

PREVENTION MARKETING: A FRAMEWORK INTEGRATING SOCIAL MARKETING AND MEDIA ADVOCACY
Melissa Shepherd

Social marketing often employs communications approaches intended to effect individuals and their behaviors, and media advocacy is a communications approach intended to effect policies, laws, and/or institutions (Wallack, 1989). Some may erroneously view social marketing and media advocacy in a competitive sense. However, more and more communications practitioners are recognizing the importance of policy communications as an individual-level behavior change strategy and are including media advocacy, or communications intended to effect policy and institutional constructs, as an integral part of social marketing and other behavior change methodologies.

The Division of HIV/AIDS Prevention at the Centers for Disease Control and Prevention (CDC) created a framework, called *Prevention Marketing*, which employs strategies intended to impact at the individual, network, community, and institutional levels to prevent the transmission of HIV, the virus that causes AIDS. The Prevention Marketing Initiative (PMI), a program based on this framework, is designed to prevent sexual transmission of HIV and other sexually transmitted diseases among people younger than 25. PMI intervenes at various levels, with specific, audience-centered communication goals for each level (Fig. 16.2). Media advocacy strategies are integrated with social marketing activities to create a synergistic effect intensified by consistent or complementary messages, appropriately timed, and delivered through strategic channels.

The strategic activities that CDC has undertaken, through PMI, to affect public perceptions regarding condom effectiveness, are an example of an application of this approach.

Condom Promotion

By 1994, public health professionals were concerned that many people held misperceptions about the effectiveness of condoms as barriers to HIV and other sexually transmitted diseases. Surveys had documented a decline

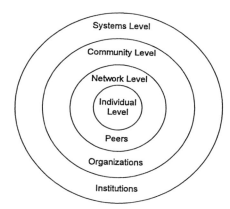

FIG. 16.2. Communication levels for HIV/AIDS prevention marketing initiative, Centers for Disease Control and Prevention.

in individual-level beliefs about condom effectiveness (NCHS, 1992). A key determinant of condom use is the belief that they will work, so this decline was alarming. In addition, older Americans were much more likely than were younger people to believe that condoms were not effective. This was considered important because it is these individuals who are most likely to influence organizational and institutional policies related to HIV prevention and condom promotion activities.

Communication approaches were, therefore, designed and implemented to mobilize social systems, organizations, and networks that could serve as channels for information about condom effectiveness. These included the media, state and local health departments, state and local departments of education, national organizations, and community-based organizations. Six months prior to beginning social marketing activities, CDC released new scientific evidence demonstrating that latex condoms are highly effective as a barrier to HIV when used consistently and correctly. This information was released in CDC's Morbidity and Mortality Weekly Report (CDC, 1993) in an article co-authored by CDC, the Food and Drug Administration (FDA), and the National Institutes of Health (NIH).

News media outreach was conducted to ensure that messages about this new scientific evidence were widely distributed through the media. Information kits were sent to 250 health and science reporters. Message training was conducted with media spokespersons from CDC, FDA, and NIH. Interviews were conducted with the Associated Press, Cable News Network, and all four major television networks. In addition, satellite interviews were conducted in 30 media markets and a joint press conference was conducted by CDC and FDA at a science writer's conference. A matte article on the science of condom effectiveness was produced and distributed to more than 500 minority-focused newspapers and community-based organizations. All of this activity generated more than 285 media reports, with estimated audience impressions exceeding 80 million. A content analysis documented that 90%

of the media stories focused exclusively on CDC's intended messages and were 100% accurate. The remaining 10% contained some inaccuracies or contradictory information about condom effectiveness.

This initial media advocacy activity provided the scientific foundation for many other communication activities targeting social systems and organizations. Up to four meetings were held with executives of each major television network. The CDC and FDA jointly conducted the first round of meetings, which focused on communicating the science of condom effectiveness. The other rounds of meetings were held to advocate for less restrictive network policies regarding condom public service announcements and to secure commitment for donated air time for CDC's prevention marketing messages (which promote both abstinence and condom use).

A letter was sent from CDC director David Satcher to general managers of all radio and television stations advocating less restrictive policies regarding condom public service announcements and recommending, in light of the new science, that the stations review any restrictive policies they still had regarding condom advertising.

In addition, CDC exhibited at 10 major media conferences and sponsored media forums in 12 communities across the country. CDC also hosted one meeting of cable community affairs and public service directors in New York and another meeting of television public service directors in Atlanta. (These meetings resulted in an increase in donated public service air time for HIV prevention messages of 361% when compared to donated air time in these markets prior to the meetings.)

To further encourage the media's participation in HIV prevention activities, Secretary of the Department of Health and Human Services, Donna Shalala, appeared in a satellite discussion sponsored by the National Association of Broadcasters (NAB) about the important role that the media plays in HIV prevention.

To disseminate information about the science of condom effectiveness to state departments of health and education, CDC sponsored a video workshop on the topic. Information kits were sent to more than 60 downlink sites across the United States, and the workshop was attended by 226 individuals representing these important constituencies. In addition, a slide presentation and video on the science of condom effectiveness were produced and marketed to state departments of health and education. As a result, more than 1,050 sets of these materials were distributed.

To disseminate this information on a community level, the American Red Cross and the CDC co-sponsored a video workshop targeting community-based organizations. This workshop was attended by over 300 individuals representing community-based organizations across the United States. Information kits on the science of condom effectiveness were produced and marketed to these same organizations. Over 100,000 kits were requested and distributed. A CDC exhibit on the science of condom effectiveness was produced and displayed at 15 conferences attended by national and community-based organizations. Individuals in these organizations were encouraged to activate their personal and professional social networks.

In the midst of this media advocacy, Secretary Shalala released a series of CDC-sponsored public service announcements promoting abstinence and/or condom use targeting individuals 18 to 25 years of age. CDC used the release of these materials to gain the media's attention about HIV prevention, the importance of abstinence messages, and, once again, to focus attention on the condom effectiveness message. The news conference releasing the PSAs was well attended by the press and by more than 200 individuals representing state health and education departments, national organizations, and community-based organizations. More than 400 additional individuals participated in the news conference via satellite at more than 50 locations across the United States. The release of the PSAs garnered more than 4,600 media placements with total audience impressions exceeding 2 billion.

Organizations and individuals across the country conducted local press conferences, visited their local television stations, wrote letters, and participated in various ways to generate media attention. CDC received and answered over 3,000 letters regarding the PSAs and/or the science of condom effectiveness in the first 90 days after the release of the PSAs. In addition, CDC authored and placed a response on the science of condom effectiveness in an Ann Landers column and has placed over 25 letters to the editor in publications throughout the United States regarding the science of condom effectiveness.

Various other social marketing activities were conducted throughout 1994, including entertainment programming, classroom instruction, and outreach to college campuses.

Results

Although cause and effect cannot be demonstrated, there is some indication that the public's perception about condom effectiveness and its willingness to support HIV prevention and condom messages have increased. Public opinion polls, commissioned by CDC, were conducted in 1994 and again in 1995. This research was simply intended to detect possible trends and was not as rigorous as national probability surveys would have been. However, the polls picked up significant movement in perceptions, especially among individuals 55 to 64 years of age, the age group from which

TABLE 16.2
Percent of Population Who Answered "Yes" to the Question:
"Do You Think AIDS Prevention Information Should Be on Television?"

	Year	
Population	1994	1995
18 years of age and over	86%	89%
55–64 years of age	80%	91%

TABLE 16.3
Percent of Population Who Answered "Yes" to the Question:
"Do You Think Information About Condoms for
AIDS Prevention Should Be Aired on Television?"

	Year	
Population	1994	1995
18 years of age and over	73%	75%
55–64 years of age	61%	77%

TABLE 16.4
Percent of Population That Answered "Very" or "Somewhat" (Eff)
to the Question: "In Your Opinion, How Effective Are Latex
Condoms at Preventing Transmission of the AIDS Virus?"

	Years			
	1994		1995	
Population	Eff	DK	Eff	DK
18 years of age and over	69%	(20%)	77%	(10%)
55–64 years of age	58%	(28%)	72%	(9%)

Note: Percentages of those who answered "Don't Know"(DK) in parentheses.

many of the policy makers in this country are drawn. Perceptions about condom effectiveness increased from 58% to 72% for this age group, with a reduction of 19% in the number of individuals who answered "don't know" to the condom effectiveness question (see Tables 16.2–16.4).

It is still too early to determine whether or not actual policy or institutional-level changes have resulted from these activities. Individual-level change may never be able to be attributed directly to these activities because of their widespread scope and reach. But, there is every reason to believe that impact is occurring, and, assuming consistent and sustained activity targeting individual, network, community, and institution levels, this approach of combining social marketing and media advocacy certainly appears promising.

REFERENCES

Centers for Disease Control and Prevention. (1993). Barrier protection against HIV infection and other sexually transmitted diseases. *MMWR, 42*, 626–628.
COMMIT Research Group. (1995). Community Intervention Trial for Smoking Cessation (COMMIT): I. Cohort results from a four-year community intervention. *American Journal of Public Health*, 183–192.
Federal Trade Commission Report to congress for 1993. (1995). *Pursuant to the federal cigarette labeling and advertising act.* Washington, DC: Federal Trade Commission.
Institute of Medicine. (1988). *The future of public health.* Washington, DC: National Academy Press.
Macro International, Inc. (1994). *Marketing Core Public Health Functions: Summary of Focus Group Findings and Implications for Message Concepts* (Draft Report). Atlanta, GA: Centers for Disease Control and Prevention.
Marcus, B. H., Banspach, S. W., Lefebvre, R. C., Rossi, J. S., Carleton, R. C., & Abrams, D. B. (1992). Using the stages of change model to increase the adoption of physical activity among community participants. *American Journal of Health Promotion, 6*, 424–429.
McGinnis, J. M., & Foege, W. H. (1993). Actual causes of death in the United States. *Journal of the American Medical Association, 270*, 2207–2212.
McKenna, J. (1994). Editorial: The promise of advertising and media advocacy for tobacco control. *American Journal of Preventative Medicine, 10*, 378–379.
National Center for Health Statistics. HIV/AIDS Supplement. *National Household Interview Survey.* Centers for Disease Control and Prevention, Atlanta, GA, March 14, 1990 (#183); December 18, 1990 (#195); July 1, 1991 (204); January 6, 1993 (#225).
National Institute on Drug Abuse. (1994). *Monitoring the future study, 1975–1994: National High School Senior Drug Abuse Survey.* Rockville, MD: National Institute on Drug Abuse.
Office of Disease Prevention and Health Promotion (1994). Core public health functions steering committee. *Prevention Reports.* August/September, 3.
Pate, R. R., Pratt, M., Blair, S. N., et al. (1995). Physical activity and public health. *Journal of the American Medical Association, 273*, 402–406.
Peters, T., & Waterman, R. (1984). *In search of excellence.* New York: Warner Books.
Rogers, E. M. (1983). *Diffusion of innovations* (3rd ed.). New York: The Free Press.
Roper, W. L. (1993). Health communications takes on new dimensions at CDC. *Public Health Reports, 10*, 179–183.
Tobacco Institute. (1994). *The tax burden on tobacco.* Washington, DC: Tobacco Institute.
U.S. Department of Health and Human Services. (1994). *Preventing tobacco use among young people: A report of the surgeon general.* Atlanta, GA: Centers for Disease Control and Prevention.
U.S. Public Health Service (1995). *For a Healthy Nation: Returns on Investment in Public Health.* Washington, DC: Department of Health and Human Services.
Wallack, L. (1989). *Social marketing and media advocacy: Two approaches to health promotion.* U.C. Berkeley, June 1989.
Wallack, L., Dorfman, L., Jernigan, D., & Themba, M. (1993). *Media advocacy and public health: Power for prevention.* Newbury Park, CA: Sage.
Winett, R. A. (1995). A framework for health promotion and disease prevention programs. *American Psychologist, 50*, 341–350.

Chapter 17

Community Involvement in Health Planning: Lessons Learned From Practicing Social Marketing in a Context of Community Control, Participation, and Ownership

Susan E. Middlestadt
Carol Schechter
Jackson Peyton
Brian Tjugum
Academy for Educational Development, Washington, DC

Social marketing is one method of developing interventions to facilitate social and behavior change. Although the principles of social marketing are essentially neutral as to the context in which they are applied, social marketing has most commonly been practiced by external agents in more of a top-down manner. Increasingly, social marketers are being asked to design and implement programs under conditions where local control, community ownership, and community participation are the norm. Whether directed from the political right as an attempt to reduce federal control and budgets, or from the political left, as a strategy to increase the role of affected populations in determining the shape of programs that serve them, the outcome is the same: Program control is shifting from the national or central to the local or community level. To be successful, social marketers must meet the challenges of developing methodologically sound programs in a context defined by community participants, leaders, and advocates.

This is not the first time that social marketers have found themselves working in an environment where the rules and parameters are defined by individuals trained in other disciplines. The challenges of designing social marketing programs within a health or medical environment have been addressed by a number of commentators on social marketing methods. Schwartz (1996) discussed special issues in adapting principles of social marketing to the context of state and federal health programs. Balch and Sutton (1995) wrote about the challenges of designing appropriate social marketing evaluations when the accepted medical evaluation standards are declines in morbidity or mortality—criteria clearly inappropriate for measuring social marketing interventions. Smith (1995) commented on the dangers of applying a "vaccine approach" to social marketing intervention design. Smith noted that the application of a medical model to community interventions assumes that the host environment is stable, and it is possible to identify an intervention that can "inoculate" a community. And so, it is a continuing challenge to educate health and medical planners to look beyond finding a single solution that works for all, by identifying what works with different audiences under specific conditions.

Similar challenges confront the social marketer designing programs in a context of community participation and control. McKee (1992) considered the related models of social mobilization and social marketing in the developing country context. Social mobilization models draw heavily on the principles of community control, participation, and action. McKee discussed the history of the development and use of the models and presented a cogent discussion of some of the conceptual issues involved. This chapter addresses some lessons learned from a practical point of view as social marketing is applied in an era of increasing community participation in health planning.

The Academy for Educational Development (AED) has a long history of developing social marketing programs in partnership with local communities, both domestically and internationally in developing countries. Committed to addressing education, health, and social development needs, AED has 30 years of experience managing projects that provide consultation, training, and technical assistance and integrate behavioral theory, communication science, and social marketing methodologies within applied program settings. The following sections present some of the challenges and lessons learned from these program experiences. These experiences are drawn from four specific projects:

AIDS Communication Support Project—This project provides technical support services to the Centers for Disease Control and Prevention (CDC) and its project areas throughout the United States to enable national, regional, state, and local organizations to use health communication, behavioral science, and social marketing strategies effectively for HIV prevention.

AIDSCOM—AED's AIDS Technical Support Project, under contract with the U.S. Agency for International Development (AID), helped local health planners in over 20 countries in Africa, Latin America, and Asia devise HIV prevention interventions targeted to reach populations engaging in high-risk behaviors.

BASICS—The BASIC Support for Institutionalizing Child Survival Project, under AID, assists ministries of health worldwide to design, implement, and evaluate behavior change strategies to reduce child morbidity and mortality and to promote child survival in developing countries.

GreenCOM—AED's Environmental Education and Communication project, again under contract with AID, supports program design, field work, and applied research at the request of missions and bureaus to help individuals, groups, organizations, and countries make environmentally sustainable development a reality.

These projects and the programs developed by these projects vary in the degree to which community partners share decision-making in programs. One can envision a continuum of participation from no participation at one extreme to full decision-making authority at the other. Steps of increasing participation would move from no participation through working with the community: to provide advice when asked, to assist in the identification and specification of needs, to design the intervention, to implement some or all components, to manage the intervention, and to exercise full decision-making authority for the entire program from beginning to end. Social marketing projects typically function at the second level; they seek input from a target audience as part of consumer research. Programs highlighted in this chapter encompass increasing participation of the community, not only including consumers as part of the research, but working with community individuals, groups, and organizations in planning, implementing, and evaluating programs.

Sharing decision making with the community presents many challenges for the social marketer. This chapter focuses on the challenges of practicing social marketing in a context of community control, ownership, and participation, as well as on the recommendations for meeting them. The first section provides a more detailed discussion of social marketing and community mobilization. It lays out the differences in definition and perspective between these two orientations to program and intervention design. The second section focuses in more detail on the role that behavioral research can play in bridging the gap between these two disciplines and their underlying cultures. The last section discusses the lessons learned about providing technical assistance in social marketing to community partners. And, finally, the summary presents recommendations for social marketers for successfully working in partnership with community organizations.

THE INTERFACE BETWEEN SOCIAL MARKETING
AND COMMUNITY MOBILIZATION

As previously described, social marketing programs to promote health and
to prevent disease are increasingly being designed in a context in which
community participation is expected. Viewed in one way, social marketing
and community mobilization represent two different approaches or
orientations to social change. This section examines the differing
perspectives and expectations of social marketers and community mobilizers with particular attention to how members of both groups approach
the design of programs to promote health and prevent disease.

Differing Definitions

Definitions provide a useful, beginning platform for examining the differences between social marketing and community mobilization as two approaches to social change. Andreasen (1995) proposed the following
definition of social marketing: "The adaption of commercial marketing
technologies to programs designed to influence the voluntary behavior of
target audiences to improve their personal welfare and that of the society
of which they are a part" (p. 110).

Community mobilization, as defined in the community organizing literature, is commonly defined as empowering individuals to find their own
solutions, whether or not the problem is solved. The goal of community
mobilization is for individuals to develop skills and power applicable in a
context beyond that of the presenting problem. Chavis' definition of community development (Chavis & Florin, 1990) outlines four additional components to the definition of community participation, the components of
citizen action, cooperation, empowerment, and holism. More specifically,

> "community development has traditionally been defined as the process of
> voluntary cooperation and self-help and mutual aid among residents of a
> locale aimed at the creation of improved physical, social, and economic
> conditions. [First,] community development refers to a process of citizen
> action in which citizens initiate and control activities. Second, the community
> development process involves voluntary participation, cooperation, and col-
> laborative problem-solving. Third, the process goal is empowerment—to
> build the community's capacity to manage and control change in order to
> influence conditions affecting community residents' lives. Fourth, the im-
> pacts sought are holistic and are concerned with the development of all of
> a community's human, economic, and environmental resources." (p. 2)

Differing Perspectives

Thus, social marketing and community mobilization differ fundamentally
in definition. Beyond definitions, what are the differences in how these

two orientations are practiced? Five points can be used to articulate the differing perspectives and expectations of social marketers and community participants: How is the problem defined, who is the primary decision maker, what are the strategies for creating change, what is the role of data, and what is the potential for program ownership and sustainability?

Definition of the Problem. Both social marketers and community participants recognize that available funding places constraints on problem definition. However, within the parameters established by funding considerations, there is a fundamental difference in the way that problem is defined by social marketers and community participants. When defining a problem, a social marketer poses the question: "Whose behavior do we need to influence and how?"

A community participant would view problem definition through a different lens: "How should we, as community members, address this issue given the overall context of our community?"

Clearly, social marketers and community participants have differing expectations about who will define the problem and how it will be defined. This difference in expectation needs to be addressed if the two groups are to work together effectively.

Primary Decision Makers. The locus of control in making decisions may also be a major issue that confronts social marketers and community participants working together. Social marketers assume, by virtue of their expertise, that they will have the ultimate decision-making authority, as exemplified: "We'll conduct our research and consult with the target audience and then make our decisions based on our professional analysis and interpretation."

Community participants, while respectful of the social marketer's expertise, believe that control resides with those most directly affected by decisions: "We need to be involved at every step of the process. Our involvement is inherent to the development of an effective intervention. We need to be involved in, in fact, in control of, all parts of a program."

Strategies for Creating Change. There is an essential difference in the way that social marketers and community participants view strategies for behavior change. Social marketers tend to focus primarily on the individual and individual behavior change, whereas community participants more often view an intervention as an opportunity to change the community context in support of behavior change. This can lead to conflict over planning and resource allocation when social marketers and community participants attempt to work together.

A social marketer's strategy rests on the following principles:

Audience-Centered. Interventions should be built on a solid base of formative research to understand the target audience.

Voluntary Behavior Change. Interventions are noncoercive and nonmanipulative.

Beneficial Exchange. Persons will do something (e.g., change their behavior) in exchange for a clearly offered benefit they desire or need. Successful interventions effectively identify and convey an exchange.

Four Ps. Interventions can be addressed to influence and integrate the four *p*s of product, price, place, and promotion.

A community participation model emphasizes the centrality of the community to the behavior change process. Some of the basic principles underlying this approach are:

Audience-Directed. Community participation goes beyond "audience-centered" and requires that the target audience control the development and delivery of the program.

Voluntary Behavior Change. Interventions may also look at nonvoluntary methods of changing behavior such as advocating for legislation or changing policies.

Mutuality. The "doer" is changed by contributing to the process.

Conceptual Tools. Any of a number of program management tools, one of which might be social marketing, may be used to design interventions.

In summary, social marketers maintain it is careful attention to the four *p*s and their proper balance that ensure the development of a successful intervention: "It doesn't matter so much who is doing the work as long as they are qualified and the methodology is OK. All the well-intentioned people in the world don't make an effective program unless a sound methodology is followed."

On the other hand, community participants maintain they are in the best position to define, design, and deliver programs for their community: "It makes all the difference who is doing the work. My community's participation is what makes a program effective and acceptable because it incorporates community values and perspectives."

The Role of Data. The use of data to establish behavioral objectives may also be an area of dispute for social marketers and community participants. Social marketers rely heavily on data to guide them in program development and use these data to establish measurable behavioral objectives: "We have to use good data to establish a clear set of behavioral objectives."

Community participants often believe they have an intuitive knowledge of their communities that allows them to truncate the formative research process and cut directly to program development: "Data are OK, as far as it goes, but the conclusions based on data must match my intuitive knowledge of my community."

In addition, community participants may want to establish objectives addressing issues other than those addressing behavior change. For example, in the case of HIV prevention, the objective might be to create an environment where safer sex messages could be disseminated without undue controversy.

Potential for Ownership and Sustainability. Social marketers and community participants may also differ on the relative importance of the potential for community ownership and sustainability of programs. Professional social marketers traditionally focus more on program outcomes without giving necessary attention to maintaining programs over the long haul. Community participants argue that community ownership is essential, not only because of the inherent value of working with a program, but because if the program is to be sustained over time and behavior change maintained, the community must own, adapt, and readapt the program. A community participant might state this as follows: "Community ownership and sustainability are primary goals. We have had to deal with these problems long before the experts came and will have to deal with them long after they leave. Besides, involving the community in solving its own problems is very cost effective."

Implications

These differences in definition and perspective have a number of implications for social marketers working in collaboration with community participants to develop social change programs. Social marketers may appear to jealously guard their professional domain and to discount the skills that community participants bring to the process: "They don't recognize my expertise. They are slowing the process down at every step."

Community participants may seem to want control over every decision: "They think I have no expertise. They are trying to railroad me."

Suspicion is a natural by-product of the differing perspectives. Both social marketers and community participants may become suspicious of each other, with negative consequences for program planning. Above all, these differences in definition and in perspective need to be recognized and taken into consideration to prevent the negative consequences for program design and to potentially lead to more effective interventions.

THE ROLE OF THE BEHAVIORAL SCIENTIST
ON THE INTERVENTION DESIGN TEAM

As described earlier, designing social marketing programs in the context of community participation can mean designing interventions with a team of designers, a multidisciplinary team whose members can include social marketers and community participants who may differ fundamentally in the definitions and perspectives on the program design process. This section discusses and illustrates two major contributions behavioral scientists can make to the development of social programs in real-life field settings with particular attention to the challenges of integrating social marketing and participatory approaches.

More specifically, the theories and methods of the several behavioral sciences can help teams developing interventions in two ways. First, a behavioral science orientation can help the design team define interventions in terms of behavioral objectives. Second, a behavioral science orientation can help design interventions aimed at influencing behavioral determinants. The emphasis here is on how a behavioral science orientation can assist in keeping a program design team on track for programs developed in collaboration with people and organizations at various points on the participation continuum. That is, these two principles can help program designers with a range of differing and complementing expertise, whether they are health and medical practitioners, professional social marketers, or community participants.

Contribution 1: Begin with Behavior

A behavioral science orientation can help the design team define and clearly articulate the objectives of the intervention by encouraging them to *begin with behavior*. Stated another way, a behavioral science orientation can help designers plan interventions in terms of behavioral objectives. All too often, social marketers are called in to develop programs to inform people, to make them aware, or to involve them emotionally. They are asked to develop programs to educate people about the sexual practices that put them at risk for HIV infection, to raise their awareness about the deteriorating state of their environment, or to teach mothers and fathers about what they should do to take care of the health of their children. The underlying assumption is that once educated or informed, people will do what is best or reasonable. Social marketing is reduced to social communication.

Social marketers now know that information is not always enough and are not surprised when raising awareness is not sufficient to influence behavior. However, these intervention design practices are so natural and ingrained that they often find themselves developing a program that informs, teaches, or moves. Social marketing becomes "what message to deliver." The all-too-critical "call to action" is forgotten.

One key role for a behavioral scientist during the intervention definition process is to keep reminding program managers to define the intervention objectives in behavioral terms: What is it that you want people to do? This sounds easy. In fact, it is easy for the behavioral scientist to think in terms of behavior. However, the epidemiologist, the doctor, and the environmental scientist are all focused on the health or state of the individual, the child, or the environment. They think in terms of morbidity and mortality, or of the quality of the air, the water, and the ecosystem. Applied behavioral scientists on the teams designing interventions or assisting institutions, organizations, and communities in the practice of social marketing often find themselves in the position of facilitating a productive dialogue among program planners, other behavioral scientists, representatives of affected communities, and the health or environmental scientists, in order to arrive at specific and behavioral objectives.

One illustration of this comes from AED's work on the environment. In Ecuador, staff of the GreenCOM project were called in to assist with the task of selecting behaviors to promote the sustainable use of land resources in the buffer zones surrounding the Cotacachi-Cayapas Ecological Reserve (Booth, 1996). From a long list of over 30 potential behaviors (e.g., use natural pesticides, use organic fertilizers, cultivate at least two species that are ecologically compatible in each plot, rotate crops, cultivate existing agricultural fallow land, and plant crops on the contour), the task was to prioritize or choose those behaviors that were environmentally sound from a technical point as well as were feasible from the point of view of the community.

Participatory social marketing principles were used with a team that included national natural resource managers, extensionists working in the field, representatives of nongovernmental organizations, and community groups and individuals. The team was intentionally constructed to be multidisciplinary, multisectoral, and multilevel with equal representation of men and women to ensure that different gender issues and inputs were explored. The team worked together to complete the basic steps of identifying the "ideal" behaviors, conducting research with "doers" and "nondoers," selecting and negotiating the target behaviors and developing strategies.

The theme of beginning with behavior helped the team members work together to develop a strategy that would be expected to be effective from the environmental point of view with the community involvement necessary for its successful and sustainable implementation. So, for example, formative research conducted collaboratively by the team members revealed that no farmers owned land on slopes of less than 45 degrees and thus the behavior of "cultivating on slopes of less than 45 degrees" was not feasible and was changed to "planting trees as windbreaks to prevent erosion." As another example, the farmers recommended that the behavior of "controlled burning" be more specifically defined as "opening fire breaks" and "burning against or into the wind." It is important to note that use of a participatory process can have benefits beyond helping complete the technical task of selecting the behaviors to be addressed. Here, use of a participatory approach helped motivate and reengage the team members, thus helped revitalize the project.

A second illustration of the importance of beginning with behavior comes from work with medical staff and field operations staff to address child survival in developing countries on the BASICS project funded by AID to promote child survival. Here the first task was to help medical and field staff state health problems in behavioral terms: $x\%$ of children die of dehydration in a country and caretakers could prevent this by mixing and administering enough oral rehydration salts or other fluids to prevent dehydration during diarrhea.

Put another way, behavioral scientists assisted staff in stating program objectives as behavioral objectives. The program objective of improving diarrhea case management in the home needed to be restated in behavioral terms of increasing caretakers' correct mixing and administration of oral rehydration salts during diarrhea. The behavioral staff assisted with the process of discussing, reaching consensus, and articulating a set of projectwide emphasis behaviors. The caretaker behaviors were divided into the four areas of breastfeeding, immunization, home health care practices, and care seeking. And specific behaviors were defined for each area: breastfeeding (e.g., initiate breastfeeding immediately after birth and breastfeed exclusively for 4 to 6 months); immunization (e.g., take child for measles immunization at 9 months and seek tetanus toxoid vaccine at appropriate times); home health care practices (e.g., wash hands at appropriate times and mix and administer oral rehydration salts correctly); and care seeking (e.g., seek appropriate care if infant is not feeding or develops fever). Stated in this final fashion, the task of stating program objectives in terms of specific behaviors looks like it was easy. However, it is important to note that this simple step took a collaborative process that occurred with multiple players, representing multiple viewpoints, over 12 to 18 months to reach agreement as to the project's ideal caretaker behaviors. The applied behavioral scientists on the team worked carefully to develop emphasis behaviors that were in fact behaviors and to keep the team on track.

In this example, there is a second challenge to beginning with behavior; a second challenge with two aspects. Program planners need to think beyond mothers and to be concerned with other health professionals. And, when thinking beyond mothers, when considering health care workers, once again one needs to consider what people should do. Stated another way, the behavioral focus needs to apply to all interventions, not just to education and communication interventions addressed to mothers, but to the training, organization, and other interventions aimed at other parts of health care delivery.

One needs to think not just about mothers but all people in the loop, including health care workers, community groups, policymakers, and private physicians. And, in designing interventions for each of these people in the health system, the process should begin with behavior. That is, think about what these people should do. When thinking of health care workers, do not think about what message they should deliver in working with mothers and other caretakers, but what they should do with mothers when they interact with them. To be more specific, in designing an intervention to train health care professionals on how to deliver services and education about child survival, training objectives need to be stated in behavioral terms: greet mother in appropriate way, give recommendations, and ask her to repeat the recommendations.

Thus, beginning with behavior can assist in the definition of the objectives of an intervention in behavioral terms both initially during program design and continually through each step in the process of designing a program of interventions.

Contribution 2: Design with Determinants

A second role for a behavioral science orientation during intervention planning is to help the program planning team design interventions that attempt to influence critical factors that are determinants of behavior according to the major theories of behavior. No matter how many times people call on social marketers, they usually think of social marketers as communication specialists. People come to them for a well-designed poster, an effective brochure, or an innovative and exciting public service announcement. They want an effective message that has been pretested according to established practices and will reach the right people. Of course, sophisticated practitioners have expanded their repertoire of communication channels; they now ask for street outreach, individual counseling, or training.

A second key role for a behavioral scientist is to provide a different logic to the intervention design process, one in which theory-based formative research in the relevant populations is used to identify the internal and/or external determinants of behavior and interventions are designed that address these critical factors. An intervention becomes a simple and elegant hypothesis: The intervention influences a behavioral determinant, which in turn influences the behavior, which in turn influences the desired outcome.

Intervention —> Determinant —> Behavior —> Outcome

If this intervention is delivered to these people, this behavioral determinant will be changed, the likelihood that this behavior will be performed is increased, ever so slightly, and there is some resultant improvement in an outcome.

Here are three examples:

An intervention of street outreach by peers can be designed to influence the determinant of perceived norms from potential partners to increase the likelihood of the behavior of correct and consistent condom use to reduce the risk of HIV infection.

A training intervention that helps health workers talk to mothers will increase their skills at communicating with mothers, which will help mothers follow recommended health care practices and children will suffer less morbidity and mortality from childhood diseases.

An intervention that mobilizes a community group to create containers for different kinds of garbage, to place them in convenient places, and to regularly take the contents of these cans to recycling industries will increase the likelihood that people will effectively separate and recycle their garbage and thus reduce the amount of solid waste produced in the community.

In its work in a variety of health, education, and social domains, AED uses a simple set of behavioral determinants that are loosely grouped into external and internal determinants. In the work on HIV infection, external determinants can include aspects of demographics, technologies, policies, access to services, culture, skills, and epidemiology; and internal ones can include knowledge, attitudes toward behaviors, intentions, perceived consequences, self-efficacy, and perceived risk (Smith, Helquist, Jimerson, Carovano, & Middlestadt, 1993). Note these determinants come from the major theories of health and social behaviors.

A *design with determinants* approach has a number of advantages. It helps increase the range of interventions considered from just communications to interventions that address place, product, policies, and price. It helps design an intervention that addresses determinants rather than making assumptions about what needs to be said. It helps design interventions that are more widely generalizable. It helps communicate the content of the intervention to other program planners. It helps in the evaluation of the impact of programs. And, in all these ways, thinking about determinants can help the design team keep on track.

The determinants approach to intervention design can be illustrated from AED's international program for HIV prevention, the AIDSCOM project (Middlestadt, Hernandez, & Smith, 1993). As one example, in the Dominican Republic, a multidisciplinary team of researchers, intervention designers, and representatives of the affected community worked together to design and test the effectiveness of the intervention to reduce exposure to HIV infection. Based on the STD and HIV epidemiology and the behavioral studies in the country, the team selected very sexually active men working in Haina, the port city, as an important population for correct and consistent condom use interventions. In behavioral terms, the goal was to encourage the adult men working in this city to use condoms, correctly at all times and with all partners, including their steady partners.

Given behavioral research in the region and the views of local program planners, there was reason to be concerned with three basic determinants: social norms perceived from partners, condom skills, and perceptions of risk or susceptibility to HIV infection. The team designed and pretested three interventions, one for each of these determinants. Each was in comic book form using the main character, Mario, which was presented in flip chart form with an accompanying text from tape recorder. One was intended to let the men know their partners wanted them to use a condom; Mario is shown overhearing his steady partner talk to her girlfriend about how she would like Mario to use a condom but does not know how. Another was intended to demonstrate correct condom use; the setting was a bar and Mario shows the correct way to put on a condom using a Coke bottle to demonstrate. A third was intended to let the men know that men in the Dominican Republic were at risk; a doctor is presenting statistics from the DR.

To evaluate the impact of this intervention an experimental, longitudinal study was designed and implemented by the team. The sample of 300 men was randomly selected from a list of workers and was randomly assigned to one of five experimental conditions, one control (no intervention) and four intervention groups: intervention to change perceived social norms, intervention to change condom skills, intervention to change perceived susceptibility, and double intervention group (perceived norms and skills). All participants were exposed to the intervention (that is, the flip chart plus an audio tape reading the text) twice. Then, they immediately completed a posttest assessing knowledge, attitudes, intentions, and behaviors. The participants came back 6 weeks later and completed a delayed posttest.

The evaluation analyses examined the impact of the different versions of the intervention on each of the key determinants of the behavior of using a condom with my steady partner (i.e., beliefs, attitudes, norms perceived from partners, perceived susceptibility or risk, intentions, actual, and perceived skill in using a condom with a steady partner) and on behavior as reported in the delayed posttest. Briefly, the skills alone and skills plus perceived norm interventions had the most impact on intention to use condoms. The skills alone intervention had the largest impact on actual skill at using a condom assessed by observing the participant place a condom on an artificial penis and scoring with an observational measure. The skills (both alone and in combination with the norm) interventions seemed to be effective at changing self-efficacy or perceived skill at using a condom under any circumstance. The percent of condom protected sex acts from pretest to posttest improved the most for the skills intervention. In sum, almost across the board, the skills intervention (whether alone or in combination with norms) was most effective at changing determinants and behaviors.

The main point of this work on encouraging condom use among heterosexuals in the Dominican Republic goes beyond the demonstrated effectiveness of the intervention. Throughout the process of designing and testing the intervention, the determinants approach helped keep the team on target and facilitated their communication about what they were trying to achieve and what they did achieve. Designing with determinants continually informed the team's logic of intervention design and evaluation.

In sum, the theories and methods of the several behavioral sciences can help people developing interventions in two ways. First, a behavioral science orientation can help program planners design interventions in terms of behavioral objectives. Second, a behavioral science orientation can help design interventions aimed at influencing behavioral determinants.

PROVIDING TECHNICAL ASSISTANCE IN SOCIAL MARKETING: PUTTING THEORY AND METHOD INTO THE HANDS OF COMMUNITY PARTNERS

This section explores some of the challenges social marketers have faced and the lessons they have learned as they provide technical assistance in a climate that places increasing significance on community ownership, participation, and development. Whereas the previous section emphasizes the contributions that behavioral science theory and methodology can make, the focus here is on what works and what does not work in conveying these theories and methods to community partners.

In every social marketing project AED has managed, it has collaborated with partners in the field. These partners have ranged from health-related institutions at national, regional, and local levels, nongovernmental organizations (NGOs) and community-based organizations (CBOs), private firms, and community coalitions and committees. This collaboration has occurred on various points along the continuum of participation discussed previously and labeled under headings such as technology transfer, capacity building, community involvement, or community participation.

In this age of community planning for health, social marketers are confronted with a new test of faith in their ability to provide social marketing technical assistance in a partnership context, because it is the community that holds ultimate decision-making authority. Part of the challenge of ensuring that the programs are derived from good, responsible, theory- and method-based decisions comes from content, that is, what concepts and principles get conveyed. Another part of the challenge is the delivery, or how should one go about blending skills as social marketers and technical assistance providers with the skills and experiences of community persons while applying and fostering the skills necessary to benefit the projects.

AED has learned several lessons in this regard, many of them coming from two of the activities of its AIDS Communication Support Project. Under this contract with the Centers for Disease Control and Prevention (CDC), AED provides support to the five community demonstration sites of CDC's Prevention Marketing Initiative (AED, 1995; Ogden, Shepherd, & Smith, 1996) as these sites apply the principles of social marketing to the development of HIV prevention programs for those under 25. In addition, as one of the national technical assistance providing organizations, AED works with the over 200 HIV Prevention Community Planning Groups (AED, 1994a) throughout the United States.

In preface, it is important to acknowledge that the politics of HIV are passionate. In working in HIV prevention, individuals must recognize the issues important to the many, different HIV-affected populations, as well as contend with conservative forces that may oppose prevention efforts. The fact that the disease strikes most frequently in disenfranchised populations and the relative lack of prompt and effective response by government and other public health organizations have spurred the mobilization of highly active people infected with and affected by HIV. Individuals and groups of individuals have become involved in every aspect of prevention, care, and treatment. Many of these individuals and groups are overtly or quietly distrustful of traditional means of addressing public health issues. This distrust encompasses social marketing, despite the excellent record the discipline has in effecting positive health behavior change.

It is essential to overcome that distrust. Today, without the support and commitment of a community, a social marketer can never implement a successful HIV prevention program. Moreover, by engaging the community in the process, difficult though it may be, the outcome is usually better because the process was enriched by the involvement of community members.

Lesson 1: Begin with Behavior

One lesson social marketers have learned about delivering and building support for social marketing concepts in the field is that program planners should *begin with behavior*. Beyond the benefits to good intervention design, the introduction of behavioral science theory and method at the beginning of program planning may serve as a doorway to the acceptance of a social marketing methodology. It helps the community planner to think in terms of the end result—behavior change. Achieving a behavioral goal involves first identifying and then setting out to accomplish objectives along the way. Thus, social marketing can be offered as a roadmap to help the community-based program planner set the course (objectives) toward his destination (behavioral goal). In this manner, a social marketing method-ology is applied within a behavioral context, and social marketers can avoid the negative connotation the word "marketing" has in many communities. And, in instances where the community planner is actually a committee of 20 or 30 community-based service providers, prevention professionals, academics, and activists, the social marketing framework, within a behav-ioral context, can help build consensus for decision making. Again, the focus is on behavior: All 20 or 30 members are reminded that they are working toward the same end result—behavior change. The more this point is emphasized, the less chance there is of encountering conflict.

Lesson 2: Sell the Ingredients of a Social Marketing Recipe Not the Label

A conflict often encountered is the suspicion or skepticism among commu-nity partners of what social marketing claims to do. This suspicion can result in resistance to efforts to provide social marketing technical assistance. Good social marketers offer a product, that is, social marketing technical assist-ance, to community partners in a way that exhibits a clear benefit to its use for program planning. AED has found it is better to sell the ingredients of social marketing rather than the label. Although community persons may reject the notion of a methodology borrowed from the commercial section for their programs, they are intrigued by its individual components. A social marketing program planner must decide which ingredients are important to include without sacrificing the integrity of the process. AED has identified four key ingredients that community persons find palatable: formative research, segmentation, exchange, and monitoring.

Formative Research. One of the ingredients that communities often re-spond to is research and the notion that social marketing programs are theory based and data informed. Formative research excites people. Information such as community inventories, key informant interviews, well-run focus groups, condom market audits, and secondary data on the target audience's media habits raises people's interest levels and helps to engage them in the process.

Segmentation. Another key ingredient is understanding the principles and techniques of target audience segmentation, how social marketers divide populations in groups not always based on traditional demographics such as race and ethnicity. In the beginning, it is difficult to move communities beyond the idea that segmentation leaves people out, a difficult dilemma for groups concerned with inclusion. However, communities often find nontraditional segmentation approaches appealing. In one of the Prevention Marketing Initiative (PMI) demonstration sites, for example, the target audience identified by the planning committee consists of young people who access youth service agencies. By segmenting a population by access, the debate among committee members was depoliticized because young persons who are Hispanic, African American, and Caucasian, from all areas of Newark and different socioeconomic and educational backgrounds, are included.

Exchange. The next appealing ingredient is the concept of exchange and the corresponding consideration of costs, benefits, and competition. Even people who are hard-set against marketing concepts buy into the notion that to effect behavior change, the price that people pay to change their behavior and the offering of a clear benefit of doing so must be considered.

Monitoring. The final ingredient is the monitoring aspect of the planning wheel. Whereas community persons may be accustomed to program evaluation, they generally view evaluation from the perspective of showing impact to their funder so that their programs can continue. Continual monitoring of a program, and using the new data to revise programs, is often slighted by community planners. A social marketing framework helps ensure that program monitoring is not neglected.

Lesson 3: Train Managers Rather than Doers

A third major lesson in putting social marketing theories and methods into the hands of community-based persons concerns the role of community members. Stated simply, in providing technical assistance, there is a risk of creating a whole community of social marketers, of doers. Community participants are hard-working individuals responsible for program management, and though some may be skeptical, they often are starving for some sort of assistance. They see help in a set of planning tools and they seize upon it. A clinician wants to become a more effective focus group moderator; physician wants to launch a communications campaign; and community activist wants to learn how to write more appealing copy for his poster. These community partners, who are more used to doing the work than managing a process, are likely to jump immediately into applying principles learned during technical assistance visits. For example, a training on the purpose of formative research might stimulate some to develop a focus group discussion guide based on the behavioral determinants they best remember.

There is an important distinction that needs to be made clearly from the outset. Technical assistance providers need to distinguish between training community members to be doers and training them to be good "consumers" of social marketing technical assistance and to be good "clients" of an advertising agency and of service providers carrying out the planned interventions. Considering community members as consumers and clients helps them develop an appreciation for the professional skill level required to do work associated with program planning. Community members are already used to doing the work; they need to be reoriented. Instead of training them how to conduct focus groups, social marketing technical assistance should teach them to buy formative research (AED, 1994b, 1995), that is, to write scopes of work for a research vendor, to interpret focus group results, to hold initial meetings with the research firms to lay the ground rules and set timelines, and to review reports and products together. All of this helps to demonstrate for the community person how the research phase is "managed" instead of "done."

Social marketers need to emphasize again and again that social marketing is not just about social advertising or health promotion or public service announcements, but rather it is a program management tool for strategic problem solving that uses a set of general principles, theories, and methods. By encouraging a community planner to be a *manager of the process* or a *consumer of services*, social marketing gives community planners the freedom to step back and view the program in terms of the objectives they must accomplish to reach their goal. The community planners can move away from focusing on quick-fix solutions, on materials development, on a single channel for message delivery, or on a single method of data collection for audience research. The better a program manager is equipped to act as a consumer, client, or manager of research firms, ad agencies, graphic designers, and service providers, the better chance there is that the program will be successful.

Lesson 4: Do the Best You Can

The fourth and final major lesson about providing social marketing technical assistance in an era of increased community participation is that it can be a challenging and sometimes frustrating effort. It is difficult to remain a purist in the real-world application of social marketing. Social marketers have to give up some control. In order to be successful, social marketing must be seen by community partners as a flexible and inclusive process. In order to have an impact on program planning, technical assistance can be integrated at different stages of program development.

When community partners define the ground rules, the social marketer encounters tremendous compromise to the traditional, familiar social marketing methodology. The reality is that you do the best you can, but you must acknowledge having less control over the process. You may find it difficult to say that the resultant target audience was not identified based on the data, or the product might be difficult to sell or the promotional strategy may be flawed because those decisions were made by the community. In these instances, social marketers who find themselves in conflict with the community planner must learn how to compromise. Instead, what a social marketer can do is suggest options to consider, convey behavioral science core elements, and share the key ingredients of a social marketing framework. This can be a frustrating dilemma for those who are used to overseeing and directing the entire process.

The challenges underlying the development and implementation of social marketing programs in a community planning environment are not insurmountable. It is helpful to remember to respect each other's roles, to recognize that there will be differences of opinions and approaches, and to be willing to identify the disagreements and work through conflicts. Above all, remember that social marketing is about the business of helping people.

CONCLUSIONS

AED's domestic and international experience has demonstrated that programs can be enriched when social marketing professionals work in partnership with community-based organizations and when the perspectives of social marketers and community mobilizers are represented in the intervention design process. The following lessons summarize the recommendations to help ensure the success of these partnerships:

Recognize that participation may mean different things to different people. These difference in definitions, perspectives, and parameters for participation may need to be explicitly discussed by all of those involved.

Allow plenty of time and be patient with the process. Almost certainly, joint efforts between professional social marketers and community participants will take longer to produce results than would a more traditional approach.

Identify community strengths and work with them. Allowing indigenous skills and talents to emerge can result in a richer program.

Be willing to give up some control. Have confidence in the collective wisdom of the process.

Begin with behavior and design with determinants. It is likely that introducing these two contributions of behavioral science may serve as a doorway to the community acceptance of social marketing as a tool for program management and helping keep the partners focused on the end result—behavior change.

Sell the ingredients and not the label. Community persons seem to respond more positively to the concepts of social marketing when they are introduced as elements of program planning. To avoid resistance to social marketing, focus on those key ingredients, rather than the term *social marketing*.

Train "managers and clients" instead of "doers." Training and technical assistance enable community partners to become skilled consumers in planning, procuring, reviewing, and assessing professional expert assistance. And a good program manager has a better chance of running a successful program.

Be flexible. Begin where the community is, get out of their way when assistance is not needed, and be available at the moment they do need it.

REFERENCES

Academy for Educational Development (AED). (1994a). *Handbook for HIV prevention community planning*. Washington, DC: Academy for Educational Development for the Centers for Disease Control and Prevention.

Academy for Educational Development (AED). (1994b). *The second Prevention Marketing Initiative (PMI) community demonstration sites workshop*. Washington, DC: Author.

Academy for Educational Development (AED). (1995). *Lessons learned from the Prevention Marketing Initiative (PMI): Year 1*. Washington, DC: Academy for Educational Development for the Centers for Disease Control and Prevention.

Andreasen, A. (1995). *Marketing social change: Changing behavior to promote health, social development, and the environment*. San Francisco: Jossey-Bass.

Balch, G., & Sutton, S. (1995, May). *Keep me posted: A plea for practical evaluation*. Paper presented at Society for Consumer Psychology Conference, Atlanta, GA.

Booth, E. M. (1996). *Starting with behavior: A participatory process for selecting target behaviors in environmental programs*. Washington, DC: Academy for Educational Development.

Chavis, D., & Florin. (1990). *Community development, community participation and substance abuse prevention*. Santa Clara, CA: Prevention Office, Bureau of Drug Abuse Services, Department of Health.

McKee, N. (1992). *Social mobilization and social marketing in developing countries: Lessons for communicators.* Penang, Malaysia: Southbound.

Middlestadt, S. E., Hernandez, O., & Smith, W. A. (1993). Beginning with behavior: Research to reduce risk. In W. A. Smith, M. J. Helquist, A. B. Jimerson, K. Carovano, & S. E. Middlestadt (Eds.), *A world against AIDS: Communication for behavior change* (pp. 37–66). Washington, DC: Academy for Educational Development.

Ogden, L., Shepherd, M., & Smith, W. A. (1996). *The Prevention Marketing Initiative (PMI): Applying prevention marketing.* Washington, DC: Academy for Educational Development for the Centers for Disease Control and Prevention.

Schwartz, B. (1996). Working within the system: Adapting the social marketing approach to the implementation of state and federal health programs. *Social Marketing Quarterly, 3*(1), 64–70.

Smith, W. A. (1995, March). *The science of community planning: Standards of practice.* Paper presented at the prevention summit: HIV prevention community planning co-chairs meeting, Atlanta, GA.

Smith, W. A., Helquist, M. J., Jimerson, A. B., Carovano, K., & Middlestadt, S. E. (Eds.). (1993). *A world against AIDS: Communication for behavior change.* Washington, DC: Academy for Educational Development.

Chapter 18

The Benefits of Corporate Social Marketing Initiatives

Paul N. Bloom
University of North Carolina

Pattie Yu Hussein
Fleishman Hillard, Inc.

Lisa R. Szykman
University of North Carolina

ABSTRACT

Corporate social marketing programs are defined as corporate initiatives that have a primary goal of persuading people to engage in socially beneficial behaviors. These programs are different from other corporate initiatives such as philanthropic efforts (giving money to a charitable cause) and cause-related marketing efforts (giving money to a charitable cause every time a purchase is made). This chapter argues that these programs can be classified as social marketing programs, even though the corporations may reap benefits (such as increased sales or an improved image) from such efforts. Advantages and drawbacks of having corporations involved in social marketing programs are discussed; and several case studies are presented to demonstrate characteristics of successful corporate social marketing programs.

When corporations invest resources in marketing activities,[1] they usually are seeking a return on their investment in the form of increased sales of their products or services. As long as a corporation is not selling a dangerous or harmful product, an investment in marketing that produces more increased sales than expenses should not only benefit the firm's

---

[1]The term *corporation* refers to both privately and publicly held companies that are in business to make a profit. In some cases, individual corporations form an association (such as the Dairy Council) in order to undertake marketing campaigns that will benefit an entire industry. These associations are included in the discussions of corporate initiatives and programs.

shareholders and employees, but also provide benefits to society. Successful marketing of products and services can help society by lowering prices, accelerating innovation, adding variety, creating employment opportunities, and basically providing wanted products and services. In a sense, many corporations do social marketing through the normal marketing of their products and services.

However, there are some corporations that have gone beyond this passive or incidental type of social marketing. They have invested substantial resources in marketing activities (including public relations programs) designed to achieve certain positive social outcomes, and they have not always done this solely for enhancing their image or improving their sales. They have engaged in what can be considered *corporate social marketing programs*, defined here as a corporate initiative where significant amounts of the time and know-how of the marketing personnel who work for the corporation or one of its agents are applied toward achieving a primary goal of ultimately persuading people to engage in a socially beneficial behavior.

This definition differentiates corporate social marketing programs from several other types of corporate initiatives, including corporate philanthropic efforts, corporate cause-related marketing efforts, and corporate social responsibility efforts. The differences in these efforts are summarized here:

> *Corporate philanthropic efforts* involve merely the giving of money or other gifts to a charitable cause. The marketing talent of the company or its agents (e.g., advertising agencies, public relations firms, or trade associations) is not asked to devote significant energy or time to promoting a socially beneficial behavior.
>
> *Corporate cause-related marketing efforts* are efforts that involve giving money or gifts to a charitable cause every time a purchase is made of one of a company's products or services (Varadarajan & Menon, 1988).
>
> *Corporate social responsibility efforts* involve a variety of attempts to be a good corporate citizen, deploying talent from human resources, operations, finance, or other disciplines. These can be proactive efforts designed to put a company on the forefront of a social issue (e.g., environmental protection), or they can be reactive efforts designed to rebuild a company's reputation tarnished by past corporate actions (e.g., spills, accidents, deceptive acts). Social marketing programs can be viewed as a particular type of social responsibility program or can be a part of a larger social responsibility effort.

The most distinguishing aspect of a corporate social marketing program is its focus on persuading people to engage in a socially beneficial behavior. As long as this is a primary goal, and some members or agents of a corporation are working toward achieving this goal, a program will fit the definition—even if a consequence of the program is an increase in sales of the company's products or services or an improvement in its corporate image.

Thus, programs that encourage people to eat healthy, exercise, engage in safe sex, drive carefully, and so forth can be considered social marketing programs, in spite of the fact that they end up boosting the sales of a company's products. These behaviors are considered socially beneficial because they produce important benefits for more than just the people performing them. For instance, if individuals eat a healthier diet, then society benefits through lower health care and insurance costs. If people begin to drive more carefully, then the roads become a safer place for everyone, also lowering health care and insurance costs.

It should be noted that other authors have looked with disfavor on using the social marketing label for programs seeking increases in socially beneficial behaviors as well as private benefits for organizations. For example, Andreasen (1994) made the following comment in an attempt to define the domain of the field of social marketing:

> It can be argued that private sector firms engage in "social marketing," for example, when the insurance industry encourages seat belt usage or the beer industry promotes "responsible drinking." Again, Rangun and Karim (1991) would argue that such efforts should not fall within the domain of social marketing because social change is a secondary purpose of the campaign from the private sector firm's standpoint. (p. 109)

Andreasen confirmed his agreement with this viewpoint by noting

> that the definition of social marketing omits cases in which the beneficiary is the social marketing organization. This is a major distinction between private sector and social marketing and, as Rangun and Karim (1991) argue, it prevents us from including efforts of private sector organizations to achieve social ends, as in the insurance industry's seat belt campaign. (p. 112)

Basically, this chapter disagrees with this point of view and feels it is appropriate to label corporate programs with a primary goal of increasing socially beneficial behaviors as corporate social marketing programs, no matter what the effect on corporate sales.

Just because a corporation may enjoy peripheral benefits from a social marketing campaign does not seem to be sufficient grounds for labeling the program as something other than social marketing. Corporations are made up of people, many of whom are concerned with the state of society and want to be involved in improving the lives of those around them. Whereas it may be easy to discount the motives of a faceless corporate entity, it is more difficult to question the true motives or sincerity of the people within the corporation. Social marketing programs are no different than any other marketing program in that corporate managers probably evaluate the potential effects that social marketing campaigns will have before undertaking them. Like any other marketing campaign, only those expected to have a positive effect on the business will be pursued. But, this fact alone is not enough to discount the sincerity of the individuals involved in the decision. Just because the managers do not want to harm their corporations does not make them any less sincere in their desire to contribute to a social cause.

Moreover, many successful social marketing programs have been supported by partnerships or teams consisting of corporations, nonprofit, and government agencies. Just because a corporation is involved with a joint program does not automatically mean the program is any different from a social marketing program that does not have a corporate partner. Remember that nonprofit organizations may have very limited resources, and may be unable to undertake a social marketing campaign without the assistance of a corporation. Perhaps adding the term *corporate* to the label used here will disclose a reference to a different type of program than those run by purely nonprofit social change organizations.

However, whether you "brand" the program social marketing or corporate social marketing, the emphasis is the same—a focus on the consumer and the application of the marketing framework to bring about social change. That social goal might be to generate a behavior, stop a behavior, or switch a behavior. This chapter attempts to provide some initial support for the notion that society obtains substantial benefits from corporate social marketing programs. It first presents a few theoretical ideas about how society can benefit from these programs. It also outlines some of the drawbacks of certain programs. Finally, it presents several case studies of programs that we feel have produced important benefits for society.

BENEFITS AND DRAWBACKS IN THEORY

There are a host of problems in the United States (and elsewhere) that can be ameliorated to some extent by persuading people to engage in certain socially beneficial behaviors. The incidence of many health problems could be reduced if people ate better, exercised regularly, and had more preventive health check-ups. Environmental pollution could be reduced if people recycled and reused materials more frequently. Poverty could be reduced if young people stayed in school and practiced birth control more effectively. To the extent that social marketing programs are successful in persuading people to perform socially beneficial behaviors, they provide benefits to society. However, the benefits provided by a particular program have to be weighed against the costs. Some social marketing programs may be able to achieve benefits very efficiently, whereas others may end up being too expensive for what they accomplish. Indeed, some may not have the level of commitment and resources needed to raise awareness, stimulate action, or encourage repeated behavior in any significant ways.

Clearly, corporate social marketing programs have created benefits for society. But it is not obvious that these benefits have been provided efficiently. It may be that society would be better off if the programs that corporations have conducted were instead run by government agencies or nonprofit organizations, perhaps using only financial support provided by corporations and not any of their marketing talent. Indeed, corporations may have less ability than others to either change behavior or control costs. A corporation may have less credibility with a target audience than the government or a nonprofit, hurting the persuasive ability of its messages. Audiences may be cynical about the true motives of the messages. Furthermore, a corporation may not receive the tax breaks or other concessions that government agencies and nonprofits receive, giving it a more substantial cost structure.

In theory, corporations should be able to conduct social marketing programs that produce important benefits with as much efficiency as government agencies or nonprofits. Although some corporations may have low credibility or an inability to keep program costs down, many corporations may have the following comparative advantages in managing social marketing programs.

Corporate marketers may have done extensive consumer research, providing an understanding of consumer behavior in a certain context or market that may make them better able to design and place persuasive messages about socially beneficial behaviors for a particular target audience. For example, a food manufacturer may have knowledge of consumer eating habits that can help in determining the best way to promote healthier diets.

Corporate marketers may have more experience putting together the kind of multifaceted, comprehensive marketing programs that are needed to achieve significant changes in behavior. Many government and nonprofit programs have limited resources at their disposal, restricting the number of marketing tools that can be deployed for each campaign (e.g., using only public service announcements or pamphlets). Increased repetition of the social message using a variety of techniques would probably lead to more change in behavior, thereby making the campaign more successful. Corporate marketers, with more resources at their disposal, may be more skilled and capable of developing mutually supportive product, price, distribution, and integrated communications strategies.

Corporate marketers may have substantial credibility on certain topics, creating more of an opportunity for persuasion to occur. For example, a company such as Johnson & Johnson has credibility on health care issues.

Corporate marketers may not have to be as political in running programs as some government agencies and nonprofits. The need to answer legislators, advisory committees, or nonprofit board members about issues such as "wasting money on marketing" may inhibit the success of the latter's programs. Additionally, corporate marketers may not to have to pay as much attention to having campaigns that are relevant to all minority segments and special interest groups. Efforts that try to be everything to everybody become diluted—and therefore ineffective. A corporate social marketing campaign can more specifically target the audience, define the promise, and deliver the message.

However, although the nonprofit organizations may have limited resources, they also have their own comparative advantages. First of all, society already has trust and confidence in the nonprofit organizations. Because most nonprofits exist for the sole benefit of society, and not to make money, most people do not question the nonprofit's motives. Therefore, when delivering messages to the public, nonprofit organizations may be viewed as more credible than their corporate counterparts.

Also, nonprofits have more experience in their own cause than the corporations. Because they have been providing services to society for some period of time, nonprofits may already have an established network of agencies set up to help people in need. For instance, the American Red Cross already has a national network of offices across the country that can quickly meet the needs of their communities.

Finally, experts in the field may be more willing to share crucial information with nonprofit organizations than corporations. Like the general public, field experts may question the motives of the corporations, especially if the company's bottom line is directly tied to their social marketing campaign. Therefore, experts may not be as forthright in sharing their latest findings, delaying the communication of potentially crucial information to the general public.

Corporations and nonprofits have their own unique strengths, so theoretically, society would benefit the most if the corporations and nonprofits became partners. By working together, both partners would benefit—the nonprofits would have access to more communication networks and highly skilled marketing professionals who may more efficiently get their message to the public. Moreover, as the federal government cuts back on funding for certain issues and causes, it would provide the nonprofits with a new source of income. The corporations would be able to tie their product or company to a cause or issue that matters to their customer base and their employees. In addition, it would give the corporation an opportunity to make a difference to society, perhaps making it a better place to do business.

Whereas on the surface this appears as an ideal situation, these partnerships have their own drawbacks for society, the corporation, and the nonprofits. The drawbacks for society are summarized here.

If a company does not commit to a social marketing program for the long haul, then society loses the continuity and reinforcement of an education campaign. Changing behavior takes time, and without a long-term commitment from the corporation, there is little chance than many people will actually change their behavior.

Issues and causes that are not politically correct or do not have marketing appeal may be at a disadvantage because corporations may be reluctant to take up their cause. Although their message may be just as important to improving society, their negative image may deter potential corporate partners. Corporations may not want to link their organizations to an issue that would give them a negative public image. In essence, Corporate America will be helping to determine which causes get funding and which do not.

As corporations and nonprofits enter into longer term relationships, the nonprofits may become too dependent on the funding and assistance of the corporations. Over time, the nonprofits may begin to consider the needs of the corporations over the needs of society, adversely affecting the long-term direction of the cause. There is a danger that corporate profitability, and not the needs of society, may become the driving force behind the strategic decisions of the nonprofit organizations.

Corporations also have to be aware of the potential pitfalls they may encounter when partnering with a nonprofit organization. By getting involved in social issues, corporations may be setting themselves up for public criticism. Instead of praising the corporations for being socially conscientious, the media may criticize the corporation for doing too little. As corporations try to respond to the criticism, they may begin to lose sight of their corporate mission while focusing on the social issue. This may lead to adverse effects on the corporation's bottom line.

What does the corporation do when their corporate goals conflict with the goals of the nonprofit organization? As corporations enter into long-term partnerships with nonprofits, they increase the probability that their future goals may conflict. Then, the corporation must decide whether to drop the partnership (which could damage their corporate image), try to influence the nonprofits' goals (which may cause ethical concerns), or change their corporate goals to fall in line with the nonprofit organization (which may alarm the stock holders).

Corporations may become involved with nonprofit organizations that have internal problems, administrative conflicts, or distribution difficulties.

When the nonprofit suffers from adverse publicity, the corporation may also suffer. In addition, when entering into long-term commitments, the corporation gambles on the issue/cause remaining "marketable" over the long term. If the issue/cause falls from public grace during the partnership, the corporation's public image may be also be damaged (Barnes, 1991, p. 26).

Finally, the partnerships have potential drawbacks for the nonprofit organization as well. When a corporate partner suffers from bad publicity, the nonprofit may also suffer adverse consequences because of their association with the corporation. In the long run, this may harm the flow of funding from other sources, making the nonprofit even more dependent on the corporation with the bad publicity. In addition, nonprofits may be compromising their integrity by partnering with a corporation (Barnes, 1991, p. 26). To some in society, it may appear that the nonprofit may be selling out or selling themselves to the highest bidder. And, the media may become more critical of the nonprofit organization that is closely aligned with a corporate sponsor. Routine decisions may be scrutinized for evidence of impropriety by members of the media. As a result, decision-makers may take longer to reach decisions, may be less willing to take risks, and may become overly sensitive to the impressions they are making to the media.

CASE STUDIES

Consider a review of several corporate social marketing programs, some of which are a part of a partnership between nonprofit organizations and corporations and others represent independent programs of corporations. The sense is that most of the described programs represent effective and efficient initiatives. Programs can be described in this way if the following two questions are answered positively about them: Is society better off because of this program? And, could this program have performed better if corporate involvement had not existed and only a nonprofit and/or government agency ran it? Unfortunately, there is no strong empirical evidence to address these questions for any programs. Rigorous evaluations of the effects of corporate social marketing programs have not typically been done. In a few cases, there is evidence that the program was associated with a change in socially beneficial behaviors, but there is no strong causal evidence. In other cases, there is only anecdotal support for positive program effects, because about the only hard data available is on the scope and reach of the programs and not on behavior changes. Nevertheless, experience in this area over the last 20 years suggests that the reviewed programs are worthy examples of beneficial corporate social marketing efforts.

Programs possessing a range of different attributes are discussed here. Corporate social marketing programs differ based on a number of factors, including the type of social problem addressed, the type of sponsorship structure (i.e., solo to partner to team), the strength of the tie between the behavior sought and the purchase of the company's product (weak to strong), and the amount of direct personal benefits received by a person engaging in the sought behavior (few to many). This chapter is particularly concerned with presenting examples of programs that demonstrate diversity on the last two attributes.

Figure 18.1 shows an attempt to present examples that come from all locations in the two-dimensional space created by "strength of tie" and "amount of personal benefits." In this view, the examples in the upper right-hand quadrant of Fig. 18.1 represent programs with the greatest likelihood of achieving desired effects in the short-run, whereas programs in the bottom left-hand quadrant represent those least likely to achieve such effects. At the same time, the upper right-hand quadrant programs

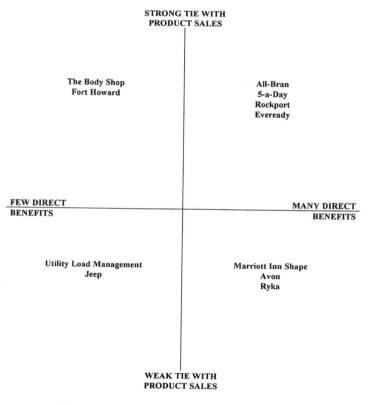

FIG 18.1. Examples of social marketing programs.

are probably easiest to evaluate, whereas the bottom left-hand ones are probably hardest to evaluate.

Social marketing programs that have a strong tie with product sales (programs in the top two quadrants)—such as the classic All-Bran cereal campaign—are more likely to achieve desired short-term effects. First of all, the companies should have somewhat more motivation to find the most efficient and effective marketing strategies, recognizing that the program can have a direct, short-term positive impact on their bottom line. Secondly, the company will have more incentive to change behavior, because product sales are tied directly to the new behavior. Moreover, corporations may be more likely to stick with the campaign for the long run, given that their sales are increasing as the "preferred" behavior becomes more common.

When programs and product sales are not strongly tied together, the corporations see no direct short-term impact to the bottom line. Indeed, investors and lenders might actually pressure managers not to allocate resources to activities that lack an immediate payoff/payout. However, this does not mean these programs have no benefits to the corporations that undertake them. First, these companies can experience an improved corporate image, which may lead to an increase in product sales over time. According to the Cone/Roper Benchmark Survey on Cause-Related Marketing, 78% of the 2,000 Americans surveyed stated they were more likely to buy a product associated with a cause they care about. Sixty-six percent stated they would switch brands to support a cause they care about, and 62% stated they were impressed with a company that commits to a cause for more than a year (Arnott, 1994, p. 71). Secondly, if the employees care about the cause/issue of the social marketing program, then they may feel better about working for the company. Eventually, this may lead to higher employee morale, higher productivity, and lower turnover. In fact, in some cases, these indirect benefits may have a more lasting effect of the corporation's bottom line than those programs with direct product ties.

Social marketing programs that provide many direct personal benefits to targeted consumers are also likely to be more effective, primarily because they provide consumers with greater incentives to engage in the requested socially beneficial behaviors. Programs that ask people to engage in behaviors that provide personal benefits in a less direct fashion—such as those requesting pro-environmental or conservation behaviors—are more prone to fall victim to "free riding," where people assume they can get the benefits of everybody else engaging in the behavior without doing it themselves.

Evaluating social marketing programs of any type is problematical (Bloom, 1980). Being able to measure something like a change in product sales to obtain an indicator of program effectiveness makes the evaluation task less complex and more feasible. Looking for evidence of a program creating direct personal benefits for consumers is also easier than looking for evidence of a program creating indirect benefits. Fewer alternative explanations for any discovered effects typically must be ruled out when looking at direct personal benefits. Nevertheless, it must be recognized that many companies see little value in conducting evaluations of their social marketing programs, especially if they have a program that is not tied to product sales. Approaching the evaluation problem from a corporate perspective, one can see that it often represents a Catch-22 situation for them. If they evaluate and find no results, then they can be accused of wasting corporate funds by investors and lenders (on both the program and the evaluation) or of conducting a meaningless, self-serving public relations effort. And, if they evaluate and find positive results, then they may put themselves under pressure by social critics to do even more of the campaign in the future.

The discussion that follows presents short descriptions of programs from the upper right-hand quadrant of Fig. 18.1. As suggested, these programs have stronger evidence of effectiveness. The discussion then moves to the upper-left, bottom-right, and bottom-left of the figure.

All-Bran Cereal Fiber Campaign

One of the most widely publicized and extensively examined corporate social marketing programs—based on this chapter's definition of such a program—is the All-Bran cereal campaign conducted by Kellogg Company in collaboration with the National Cancer Institute. Started in the mid-1980s, this campaign encouraged the eating of a high fiber, low fat diet (in part by consuming All-Bran) as a means of reducing the risks of some types of cancer. Print ads, television spots, mailings to health professionals, and public speaking engagements were used to deliver this basic message. The toll-free telephone number of the National Cancer Institute's Cancer Information Service was placed on the back panel of the All-Bran box (Freimuth, Hammond, & Stein, 1988).

As a first attempt to incorporate a very strong, credible, preventive health message in an advertisement for a commercial product, this campaign attracted considerable comment and review. Several evaluation studies were conducted that looked at the campaign's impact on consumer knowledge, attitudes, and behavior. Commenting on several of the studies, Freimuth et al. (1988) stated:

> All of these studies confirm that the Kellogg campaign had significant impact on consumers' knowledge, attitudes, and practices regarding consumption of fiber. Although it is not possible to attribute these changes to the Kellogg campaign directly, given the extensive exposure of the campaign, it seems reasonable to assume the campaign was quite influential. The Cancer Infor-

mation Service data provide an opportunity to directly link the campaign to the consumer reaction. Nearly 20,000 calls were made to the CIS in the first year after the campaign by individuals who specifically identified either the cereal box or the TV commercial as the motivation for their call. (p. 559)

Additionally, it was reported that the campaign was associated with a substantial increase in All-Bran's sales, as well as an increase in sales and share of all Kellogg cereals (Freimuth et al., 1988).

The results achieved by this campaign are generally recognized to be something that could not have been achieved by the National Cancer Institute or any other nonprofit group acting by itself (Freimuth et al., 1988; Ippolito & Mathios, 1991). The finding and know-how provided by the Kellogg marketing people, coupled with the credibility provided by the National Cancer Institute, created positive outcomes for both Kellogg and society.

5-a-Day for Better Health Campaign

A second program with a strong tie between the desired social behavior and product sales, along with offering direct personal benefits to consumers, is one conducted since 1991 by the Produce for Better Health Foundation[2] in conjunction with the National Cancer Institute (NCI). Titled "5-a-Day for Better Health," this program was designed to increase the awareness of the health benefits associated with consuming five servings of fruit and vegetables a day.

The target audience for the 5-a-Day message was identified as adults already eating fruits and vegetables, but who still fall short of the recommended five daily servings. Members of the foundation actively participate in the 5-a-Day program, which is the largest public/private nutrition education program. It is also the first nationwide health promotion focusing on the importance of fruits and vegetables in the American diet. The goal of the 5-a-Day program is to increase the average daily consumption of fruits and vegetables to 5 daily servings by the year 2000.

The 5-a-Day program has proved to be a highly effective vehicle in communicating the need to eat healthy. The first National 5-a-Day Week was held September 10–16, 1993 to call attention to the 5-a-Day message and urge all Americans to take the 5-a-Day Challenge. As part of the celebration, all 50 of the nation's governors proclaimed September 10–16 "5-a-Day Week" in their respective states.

---

[2]The Produce for Better Health Foundation is a 501C3 nonprofit organization established to serve as the official sponsor for the produce industry. Today, more than 800 organizations, representing all facets of the fruit and vegetable industry (including 30,000 grocery store outlets), are members of the foundation.

According to a recent NCI study, the percentage of Americans who acknowledge that they should eat at least five servings daily of fruits and vegetables nearly tripled in 2 years. In addition, only 1 in 10 Americans believes that a person needs to eat only one or fewer daily servings. This is a dramatic drop from 1991, when one in three believed one serving to be sufficient.

Rockport's Benefits of Walking Campaign

A good example of a social marketing campaign that has many direct benefits and has strong ties to the product is Rockport's campaign to educate Americans on the health benefits of walking. In 1982, Rockport began the campaign to give "a corporate soul for its comparatively pedestrian walking shoe business" (Oldenburg, 1992, p. 23).

As part of the campaign, Rockport distributed over 2 million brochures and founded the Rockport Walking Institute, dedicated to studying and promoting fitness walking (Oldenburg, 1992, p. 23).

Today, Rockport's campaign is credited with increasing the number of people that participate in fitness walking. In addition, present sales reflect a twentyfold increase over the sales of 1982, and many consumers relate the Rockport brand name with walking for good health (Oldenburg, 1992, p. 23).

Eveready's: "Change Your Clock, Change Your Battery"

The roots of "Change Your Clock, Change Your Battery" began with a simple yet highly compelling finding that no other group had addressed. One third of all smoke alarms in place today are not working because their batteries are worn or missing. This situation, according to the International Association of Fire Chiefs (IAFC), is to blame for the majority of deaths, serious injuries, and property damage caused by fire every year.

With this information, Eveready, the leader in the 9-volt battery category (used by most smoke detectors), launched a first-of-its-kind public education campaign to encourage Americans to change their smoke detector batteries once a year when they change their clocks from daylight-savings time in the Fall. Thus, the "Change Your Clock, Change Your Battery" concept was born. As of 1995, the successful program has been running for 8 years.

To strengthen the program's credibility, the IAFC was recruited as co-sponsors. In its first year, fire chiefs in 37 target cities were actively recruited to carry out the program in their communities. A multitiered publicity campaign created extensive exposure, including placements on networks and nationally syndicated talk shows, at both the national and local levels.

Since then, more than 4,000 fire departments across the country adopted the program and the number continues to grow.

The campaign generated 1 billion media impressions with an advertising equivalency of $20.9 million. Coverage highlights included six national wire placements, two placements in *USA Today*, "Dear Abby," "Today Show," "Good Morning America," "Larry King Live," "Regis & Kathie Lee," "CNN Headline News," "CBS Weekend News," *Parade Magazine*, UPI Radio, National Public Radio, Mutual Broadcasting Network, 1,772 local newspaper placements, more than 500 local television, and 1,000 radio placements.

During the promotion, overall category sales increased by 8% in the first year alone. Eveready, as the clear category leader, garnered most of these sales.

From a qualitative standpoint, "Change Your Clock, Change Your Battery" has received outstanding coverage treatment and proved itself as an important news story. More important, response to the program indicates Eveready Battery Co. and "Change" are well on their way toward institutionalizing a new home safety habit.

The Body Shop's Once Is Not Enough Program

A program with a strong tie between requested social behavior and sales of the company's products, but that does not provide consumers with direct personal benefits from engaging in the social behavior, is the "Once is Not Enough" program of The Body Shop. This chain of franchised stores sells a line of naturally based cosmetics and personal care products and has been urging customers to bring in their empty cosmetic containers for recycling or reuse. They pay 5 cents a piece for containers to be recycled and 25 cents a piece for containers that customers ask them to refill. Shop owners feel the program is successful, seeing that they hand out thousands of dollars in rebates each year. However, it would be impossible to determine how much social impact this campaign has had in reducing solid waste.

The Fort Howard Forever Green Campaign

Another program with a pro-environmental orientation is the "Forever Green" campaign of the Fort Howard Corporation, which was started in 1990. In part, it was meant to promote their new line of "Green Forest" paper towels and bath tissues. This program involved several activities, including the distribution of "Housegreening Tips" booklets at point-of-purchase displays in retail stores, the use of video news releases, and the placement of speakers at community schools. The program has apparently reached many consumers with its message, without provoking much criticism from environmental groups—as many "green" programs have done.

More than 25 million media impressions have resulted during the test markets. Green Forest was recognized as one of the 1990s "friendly products" in the *Chicago Tribune* and other newspapers covering the Food Marketing Institute trade show. An article in the *Wall Street Journal* noted Fort Howard's request to Green Bay, Wisconsin, residents to donate their old Yellow Pages for recycling. More than 13,000 directories were donated in less than 2 months. Although there is no hard evidence that this campaign has created more pro-environmental behaviors by consumers, studies show—and corporate America is responding to—that green consumers are growing the demand for major consumer product companies to repackage, reposition, and reformulate their products.

The Inn Shape with Residence Inn Program

An example of a program that is not tied to product sales but does urge people to engage in behaviors that provide direct personal benefits to themselves is the "Inn Shape with Residence Inn" program run by this chain of extended-stay Marriott Hotels. Using media stories and brochures, this chain has been urging people to eat better and exercise more, both at the hotel and elsewhere. Working with the American Heart Association to develop recipes (for in-room cooking) and exercises (for in-room workouts), the chain has obtained considerable publicity and distribution of materials. However, it is not known whether they have motivated changes in the diets or exercise habits of their guests.

Avon's Breast Cancer Crusade

This campaign is an example of a social marketing campaign that is not directly tied to the company's product, but does have direct benefits. In 1993, Avon began the Breast Cancer Crusade, a 5-year marketing campaign designed to educate women about breast cancer and to encourage women to follow the guidelines for early detection.

As part of the campaign, Avon is utilizing their sales representatives extensively. First of all, they are selling enamel pink, breast cancer awareness ribbons, modeled after the red AIDS awareness ribbons, with the proceeds going to fund local education programs and early-detection programs for low income and minority women. Second, they are distributing brochures and information about the benefits of early detection. Finally, because many of the interactions between sales representatives and customers are on a one-on-one basis, the sales representatives are trained to offer support and guidance about breast cancer (Arnott, 1994, pp. 70–79).

Avon is also using its catalog and advertising to promote the crusade. For instance, Avon produced a 30-second commercial that aired during a 1-hour

ABC special on breast cancer. The commercial included a toll-free number that viewers could call for more information about breast cancer.

In October 1993, Avon underwrote a 1-hour PBS program entitled, "The Breast Cancer Test." In conjunction with this special, Avon's sales representatives distributed more than 15 million educational fliers discussing the 10 most asked questions about breast cancer (Miller, 1993b, p. 13).

Ryka and Violence Against Women

Ryka, a manufacturer of women's athletic shoes, has aligned itself closely to the issue of ending violence against women. Sheri Poe, the founder and owner of the company, was a victim of date rape during her freshman year in college, and she has made ending violence against women her personal and corporate mission (Stodghill, 1993, p. 82).

For starters, Ryka contributes 7% of its pretax earnings to the ROSE (Regaining One's Self-Esteem) foundation, which was developed to build awareness to end violence against women and assist victims of violence.

Although their campaign to end violence against women does not have direct ties to their athletic shoes, Ryka's product advertising directly links the cause with the product. For example, in their print campaign, one Ryka ad juxtaposes the image of a woman working out with a woman that has been victimized. The copy of the ad reads: "Sometimes the only way to work it out, is to work it out." Other print ads describe the company's support for women's psychological as well as physical wellness through their support of the ROSE foundation (Miller, 1993a, p. 13).

Ryka has also tied the issue and their product together in the stores by replacing traditional hangtags with wallet-size cards that include safety tips for women along with a toll-free number for the National Victim Center (Miller, 1993a, p. 13).

Finally, Ryka has partnered with Lady Foot Locker in their fight to end violence against women. As partner, Lady Foot Locker has donated funds to Rape Crisis Centers and shelters for battered women, undertaken an in-store signage and literature campaign, and has educated their entire sales force so that they can answer questions and provide information to their customers (Arnott, 1994, p. 70).

Utility Load Management Programs

Since the early 1980s, many electric utilities have promoted "load management" programs to reduce how much electricity they need to generate during peak periods. Most of these programs have involved encouraging customers to put load management devices on their water heaters and air conditioning systems, which allow the utilities to shut them off remotely at certain times of the day, or switch to paying "time-of-day" rates, where they pay more for electricity used during peak periods. These programs have also typically urged energy conservation on people. Thus, these programs have essentially asked people to buy less of the product of the utilities for indirect personal benefits (except for the savings achieved). A wide variety of marketing approaches have been used in these programs, ranging from door-to-door selling to media advertising to heavy use of incentives (Burby et al., 1985). Many have achieved considerable success in terms of numbers of participants, even without providing financial incentives, but it is less clear how much conservation has been achieved.

Jeep's *Tread Lightly!* and Use Common Sense Campaign

Jeep, a company that prides itself on making a long-standing effort to be environmentally responsible, was a founding member of the nonprofit organization, *Tread Lightly!*. *Tread Lightly!* was started by the U.S. Forest Service and Bureau of Land Management to protect the environment by encouraging the ethical and responsible use of off-road practices. In other words, *Tread Lightly!* encourages off-roaders to consider the potential impact that their actions may have on the environment. *Tread Lightly!*'s pledge can be easily summarized in a few main points:

Never venture off established trails.

Respect the rights of hikers, skiers, and campers to enjoy their activities undisturbed.

Educate yourself by obtaining travel maps and regulations from public agencies, complying with signs and barriers and asking owners permission to cross private property.

Avoid streams, lakeshores, meadows, muddy roads and trails, steep hillsides, wildlife, and livestock.

Drive responsibly to protect the environment and preserve opportunities to enjoy your vehicle on wildlands.

Jeep reinforces the *Tread Lightly!* message in several different ways. First of all, in its advertising all vehicles are shown only on approved roads or trails. Secondly, Jeep organizes several off-road trips each year. These Jeep Jamborees bring together Jeep owners and experts for several days of off-road adventure and education. Finally, Jeep includes the *Tread Lightly!* message in their new product brochures and videos that each new Jeep owner receives with their vehicles.

CONCLUSIONS

Although hard empirical evidence about the effects of corporate social marketing programs is difficult to acquire, there are numerous examples of programs that companies describe as successful ventures in terms of the benefits they have provided to both the companies and society. Moreover, experience working in this area suggests that many of these programs have achieved changes in socially beneficial behaviors that could not have been achieved by nonprofit organizations or government agencies working on their own. The corporate involvement has made a difference, not only because of the extra funding provided, but also because of the experience, information, and skills the corporate marketers have been able to deploy to attack social problems.

In the future, more serious attempts should be made to conduct rigorous evaluations of corporate social marketing programs. Whereas there are persuasive reasons not to pursue evaluations, only through this type of research can the effectiveness of the strategies and tactics used in social marketing efforts be systematically improved.

REFERENCES

Andreasen, A. R. (1994). Social marketing: Its definition and domain. *Journal of Public Policy and Marketing, 13*(1), 108–114.

Arnott, N. (1994). Marketing with a passion. *Sales and Marketing Management, 146*(1, January), 64–71.

Barnes, N. G. (1991). Joint venture marketing: A strategy for the 1990's. *Health Marketing Quarterly, 19*(1/2), 23–36.

Bloom, P. N. (1980). Evaluating social marketing programs: Problems and prospects. In R. Bagozzi, K. L. Bernhardt, P. S. Busch, D. W. Cravens, J. F. Hair, Jr., & C. A. Scott (Eds.), *Marketing in the 1980's: Changes and challenges* (pp. 460–463). Chicago: American Marketing Association.

Burby, R. J., Didow, N. M., Jr., Marsden, M., Hanna, C., Bunn, M., & Johnston, S. (1985). *Electric utility load management: Marketing strategies and tactics.* Totowa, NJ: Rowman & Allanheld.

Freimuth, V. S., Hammond, S. L., & Stein, J. A. (1988). Health advertising: Prevention for profit. *American Journal of Public Health, 78*(5, May), 5561–5570.

Ippolito, P. M., & Mathios, A. D. (1991). Health claims in food marketing: Evidence on knowledge and behavior in the cereal market. *Journal of Public Policy and Marketing, 10*(1), 15–32.

Miller, C. (1993a). Pitch for sneakers is also campaign to end violence. *Marketing News, 27*(25), 13, 15.

Miller, C. (1993b). Tapping into women's issues is potent way to reach market. *Marketing News, 27*(25), 1, 13.

Oldenburg, D. (1992). Big companies plug big causes for big gains. *Business and Society Review* (Issue No. 83, Fall), 22–23.

Rangun, V. K., & Karim, S. (1991). *Teaching note: Focusing the concept of social marketing.* Cambridge, MA: Harvard Business School.

Stodghill, R., II (1993). What makes Ryka run? "Sheri Poe and her story." *Business Week* (No. 3323, June), 82–84.

Varadarajan, P. R., & Menon, A. (1988). Cause-related marketing: A coalignment of marketing strategy and corporate philanthropy. *Journal of Marketing, 52* (July), 58–74.

Part VI

THE BROAD POTENTIAL
OF SOCIAL MARKETING

Chapter 19

Reducing the Level of Violence in Hockey

Marvin E. Goldberg
Pennsylvania State University

Ozlem Sandikci
Pennsylvania State University

David Litvack
University of Ottawa

ABSTRACT

This chapter aims to provide a basic understanding of the sources and causes of violence in hockey and offers possible ways to reduce it. First, the relation between violence in society and violence in sports is examined and its implications for the case of hockey are discussed. Various determinants of hockey violence are reviewed. The remaining section focuses on the question of how the level of violence in hockey can be reduced and offers a three-prong strategy that draws mainly from social learning theory (Bandura, 1973, 1986) and dyadic processes leading to behavior change. Examples are drawn from an ongoing "Fair Play" campaign in Canada that is intended to reduce violence in hockey and in sports in general. Although player and spectator violence are interrelated components of violence in sports, this chapter focuses on player violence.

There is not much question that violence has become a central concern in late 20th-century America. Interestingly, however, violence in sports traditionally has been invested with an aura of legitimacy and has tended to be viewed as something other than "real" violence. Social norms and laws specifying what constitutes acceptable conduct in society are temporarily suspended under the umbrella of sport (Russell, 1993; Smith, 1975, 1983). This seems to be true even for "extreme fighting"—a combination of boxing, wrestling, and martial arts—which, with very few rules to control the use of excessive violence, often devolves into "free-for-all bloody brawls" (Barry, 1995, p. B3). Responsibility for enforcing rules and sanctions rests with the governing body of a given sport and are generally restricted to penalties and, at most, suspension from the game. However, sports may be viewed as a microcosm of society at large (Eitzen & Sage, 1986; Russell, 1981) and in past years, with the increase of violent activity both on the part of participants (Atyeo, 1979; Russell, 1993) and spectators (Cellozzi, Kazelskis, & Gutsch, 1981), violence in sports has become an important and worrisome social issue. This chapter examines the possible relation between violence in the broader society and in sports. It then considers violence in hockey, where the issue is seen as particularly problematic. Finally, it proposes a three-prong intervention to reduce the level of violence in hockey.

VIOLENCE, SOCIETY, AND SPORTS

A number of arguments have been made for the proposition that sports mirror the fundamental beliefs and values of a culture. In an archival study of 10 warlike (e.g., Tibetan, Aztec) and 10 relatively peaceful (e.g., Copper Eskimo, Kung Bushman) societies, Sipes (1973) found a positive correlation between the degree to which past societies were involved in conflicts and the extent to which combatant sports were featured in these same societies; that is, the more violent the societies, the greater the tendency to engage in and prefer aggressive or combative sports. Sipes (1973) also tested the relation between war and combative sports in a single society over a period of time—the United States between 1920 and 1970. Popular American sports were divided into combative (e.g., football) versus noncombative (e.g., baseball) categories. Interestingly, combative sports such as football rose sharply in popularity (i.e., attendance increased) during periods of major conflicts, whereas attendance at noncombative sports declined. Although interpretation of these results are difficult and causality cannot be inferred from this association, the pattern of results supports the hypothesis that combative sports are components of a broader cultural pattern.

In the so-called harbinger hypothesis, Snyder and Spreitzer (1979) proposed that any major changes occurring in a society will be reflected in corresponding changes in sports. They argue that, in particular, those sports enjoying mass participation and spectator appeal may provide the earliest and most valid signals of social change. Hence, one might expect to see the first signs of an upturn or downturn in the level of violence in a society within the subculture of sports. Russell's (1991) analysis of the games played in the National Hockey League (NHL) during the past 50 years leads to results supportive of this view. Russell started with recording the number of penalty minutes per season in the NHL at 5-year intervals from 1930 to 1988. He then superimposed the national homicide rate for each of these years. The findings indicate a significant correlation between the homicide rate and the level of hockey aggression (penalties) in the United States. Furthermore, when the hockey data which leads (occurs prior to) the homicide data is advanced 10 years, the correlation improves and therefore supports the harbinger hypothesis. Russell speculated that the corresponding increases in both variables may be indicative of the changes in basic values and norms in our culture.

Although there is no evidence that the relation between violence at the societal level and violence in sports is a causal one, Jones, Ferguson, and Stewart's (1993) comparative study between American and Canadian hockey fans further suggests the merits of such a hypothesis. The Jones et al. (1993) study starts with the premise that American society is considerably more violent than Canadian society, and postulates that American fans ought to be more attracted to violent hockey than Canadian fans. "Major" (more serious) penalties are taken as proxy measures of "serious" aggression. The researchers then examine the relation between the cumulative level of such major penalties as a season progresses and the level of future attendance that season. Factors such as the team's rank in the league, the degree of uncertainty of the game outcome, and playoff drive are treated as covariates. The results indicate that the level of such major penalties was predictive of future attendance in U.S. cities but not in Canadian cities. To the extent this differential fan response is indicative of broader differences in violence-related norms and attitudes between the two societies, the results support the thesis of a broader link between levels of violence in society and in sports.

VIOLENCE AS PART OF THE SPORTS SUBCULTURE

Apart from the studies investigating a possible link between violence at the societal level and violence in sports, a number of studies look at the subculture of sports and try to identify the factors that motivate pro-violent attitudes. Drawing on research on delinquency, crime, lower social class structures, values, and ethnographic studies of traditionally violent cultures, Wolfgang and Ferracuti (1967) proposed that violence is the product of subcultural normative standards. In what they called the "subculture of violence," physical assault is the expected response to a perceived challenge or insult. Conformity to this code is essential in acquiring and maintaining honor, especially for young, lower class males, and especially when such challenges are associated with one's masculinity. Following the violent societal subculture hypothesis, several sociological investigations of amateur and professional hockey (e.g., Faulkner, 1974; Smith, 1979a; Vaz, 1976) suggest that the game has an occupational subculture based on a theme of violence, that is, players purposefully adhere to a set of pro-violent values and norms derived from the occupation of professional hockey. These studies suggest a strong masculinity theme in the use of violence as an occupational tool in hockey. That is, players seem to approve violence to the extent that it "works" as an occupational tool and to the extent it expresses masculine "character"—a willingness to stand up and be counted in tough situations. Although not the only way of establishing a positive identity, displays of toughness, courage, and willingness to fight are important means of doing so. Allowing oneself to be intimidated, on the other hand, results not only in coming to be regarded as of doubtful moral worth but in being rendered relatively useless to the team.

SOCIAL DETERMINANTS OF HOCKEY VIOLENCE

Social determinants such as parents, peers, and mass media each play an important role in desensitizing and making an individual more tolerant toward violence. An extensive body of research on family violence and child abuse indicates that children learn much about the uses and justification of violence from their parents (e.g., Feshbach, 1979; Sears, Maccoby, & Lewin, 1957; Straus, Gelles, & Steinmetz, 1980). Several studies reveal that both fathers and mothers are inclined to encourage their sons' aggression especially when attacked, threatened, or dominated by other boys and tend to approve of some forms of athletic assault (Bandura & Walters, 1959; Becker, 1964; Kagan, 1964; Mussen, 1971; Smith, 1983). This approval usually comes under the heading of "teaching boys to be men." Smith's (1979b) study based on 12- to 21-year-old hockey players in Toronto reveals interesting findings about players' perceptions of their parents' approval of fighting in hockey. Smith asked players if they thought their father and mother would approve of a minor league hockey player punching another player in each of four situations: if ridiculed, if threatened, if shoved, or if punched by the other player. An index of Parents' Approval of Hockey Fighting was then constructed by summing the "yes" responses across these four situations. Whereas a majority of players (60%) thought their father would not approve of one player punching another in any of the four situations, perceived approval increased considerably with age and level of competition. Although mothers were consistently perceived as less approving than fathers, the same pattern held for them too. The same study noted a substantial correlation between players' scores on the Parents' Approval Index and the number of self-reported hockey fights. Although not necessarily causal, the pattern would seem to be indicative of a general parental influence.

Teammates and nonplaying peers are other important reference groups influential in legitimizing violence and reproducing "machismo" values within the player community. After interviewing professional hockey players in the United States, Faulkner (1971, 1973) reported that players regard violence as essential in gaining and maintaining the respect of opponents and teammates who see violent encounters as "character contests." Other studies (Smith, 1975; Vaz, 1982; Vaz & Thomas, 1974) have pointed out similar attitudes at the amateur and high school level, where players perceive their teammates as considerably more approving of fighting than their coaches and parents, and perceive their nonplaying peers as eager to see violence in any form. In fact, the actual level of expressed approval of violence is relatively high among players (33%), but not as high as the level that individuals attribute to their teammates collectively (64%; Smith 1979b).

The reasons for players' aggression also vary. Buss (1961) made a distinction between *hostile* and *instrumental* aggression. Hostile aggression refers to actions intended to harm and injure another person and usually represents an emotional response to an individual perceived as a threatening enemy or a frustrating rival. Instrumental aggression on the other hand is defined as an aggressive act with the goal of attaining a particular reward. In a sports context, rewards may include winning, recognition, or popularity. It has generally been argued that sports violence is more instrumentally motivated (Bredemeier, 1975; Russell, 1993). Coach-sanctioned intimidation of opponents or the threat of violence for instrumental purposes is an established practice (Faulkner, 1973; Russell, 1993; Smith, 1975; Vaz, 1982). Coaches, especially in certain sports like hockey, routinely designate one or more players whose major function is to defend weaker teammates and/or attack opposing players. Smith's (1979b) study suggests that hockey coaches, like many hockey fathers, encourage physically aggressive play, including fighting and other assaultive acts, both for what it symbolizes and for its utility in winning games and enhancing players' potential careers in the sport. Players' perceptions of coaches' approval of assaultive play do seem to have an impact on their attitudes and behavior at all levels of hockey. Vaz and Thomas (1974) reported statistically significant associations in all age groups between players' perceptions of how much their coaches emphasized "playing rough and being aggressive" and players' approval of "taking out an opposing player any way you can in order to save a goal even though you risk injuring the opposing player" (p. 45). The more coaches approve of fighting, the more players fight and the more penalties they receive (Vaz & Thomas, 1974).

Three decades of research has suggested a causal link between the exposure of children to violent images on television and their subsequent violent behavior (e.g., Huesman, 1986; Huesman & Eron, 1984; Turner, Hess, & Peterson-Lewis, 1986; Wood, Wong, & Chachere, 1991). Consistent with these findings, the results of a study conducted by Smith (1978) among young hockey players in Canada suggests that viewing aggressive hockey models (mostly on TV) may have a long-term impact on the behavior of amateur players of different ages. When the young hockey players were first asked whether they had learned how to hit another player illegally by watching professional hockey, 56% replied affirmatively, with only slight variations by age and level of competition. Notwithstanding the somewhat biased nature of this question, players' responses regarding their actual behavior that season seemed to verify their initial answer: When asked how many times during the season they had actually hit another player illegally, 37% said at least twice and 15% said more than five times. Official game records verified these verbal responses; players who said they performed such acts received significantly more major and minor penalties than those who indicated they did not. Regardless of the actual level of violence in a game, the media also plays a significant role in shaping viewers perceptions of the game. In one experiment (Comisky, Bryant, & Zillmann, 1977), moderators who portrayed a hockey game on video as tougher than it actually was, succeeded in altering perceptions of the level to which the game was seen as violent and the degree to which viewers reported enjoying it.

Finally, the sports equipment itself (e.g., hockey and lacrosse sticks, bats, etc.) may elicit aggressive behavior. In a series of experiments, it has been demonstrated that simply having a weapon in view of a frustrated individual typically heightened their aggressive response to the target stimulus (e.g., Berkowitz & LePage, 1967; Boyanowsky & Griffiths, 1982; Turner, Simons, Berkowitz, & Frodi, 1977). Weapons in general are presumed to be rife with aggressive cues as a result of their long-standing associations with injury and killing. From the perspective of classical conditioning theory, initially neutral objects like hockey sticks may gradually acquire aggressive cue value thorough repeated pairing with anger arousal and violent images. The stick in the hockey game may come to be perceived as a dangerous weapon and during the course of the game when competition is heightened, the possession of the stick may motivate aggression and violent behavior. Of late, stick-related penalties appear to have increased in the National Hockey League.

STRATEGIES FOR REDUCING THE LEVEL OF VIOLENCE IN HOCKEY

With the level of participation in hockey by young players in the United States showing explosive growth (West, 1995), the concern for the level of violence associated with the game increases. How can we successfully intervene to moderate the level of hockey violence? As in other social marketing campaigns (e.g., the effort to reduce drinking and driving, smoking, alcohol use, etc.), success typically requires a long-term approach employing cognitive, affective, and behavioral strategies. The following is an outline of a three-prong strategy for reducing the level of violence in hockey:

1. Public education aimed at generating awareness and insight about the problem.
2. Restructuring the regulatory environment in professional hockey to motivate behavioral change.
3. Facilitating positive role models to achieve internalized attitudinal change.

Public Education Aimed at Generating Insight About the Problem

Any strategy aimed at behavioral change initially requires creating an awareness of the problem. Over the past decade, violence in hockey has seemingly become more salient, generating greater concern, at least in Canada. An Angus Reid poll taken in 1986 revealed that 67% of Canadians surveyed felt that hockey was too violent. However, the results also showed that a significant minority—48% of men and 24% of women from age 18 to 34—thought hockey was not that violent and that fighting is just part of the game (The Reid Report, 1986). Moreover, there is evidence that it may be misleading to interpret a general survey response as suggesting real "awareness" of the problem; for one thing, there are significant differences between what individuals generally say and what they would specifically do about violence (Berger & Luckman, 1966; Ingham & Loy, 1973; Smith, 1975). Whereas social norms and values lead people to describe fighting as an undesirable behavior, they also legitimize and encourage standing up for yourself. Additionally, the perceived provocations and threats associated with most, if not all, violent incidents, result in fighting being perceived as justifiable. Thus, especially in the context of sports, when people are asked their opinion about "motherhood" statements, such as whether "violence is wrong" or "hockey is far too violent," they may agree without giving much thought to it. However, these reactive responses may easily be offset by the tendency to regard violence as part of the game and by justifications on the basis of standing up for yourself. In fact, as discussed in the previous section, these types of justifications appear to be a common practice both among players and parents. Therefore, simply creating a basic level of understanding and true awareness of the scope and consequences of violence in hockey may represent a real challenge.

Prochaska, DiClemente, and Norcross (1992) distinguished between two levels of awareness in their behavioral change model. In the *precontemplation stage*, individuals are unaware or underaware of their problems and have no intention to change. On the contrary, in the *contemplation stage* people become aware that a problem exists and seriously think about overcoming it. To date, the efforts of the Canadian Amateur Hockey Association (CAHA), in conjunction with the Canadian government, focus on creating an awareness about the violence in hockey and, thus, moving people from precontemplation to contemplation. Referred to as "Fair Play Canada" (Fair Play Commission, 1994, Canada; now identified as Canadian Centre for Ethics in Sports), the campaign relies mainly on cognitive exhortation. It promotes fair play as an attitude that can be taught and learned and aims to communicate both the consequences of excessive violence and the importance of fair play in sports through various educational materials. It is targeted to all the parties involved (i.e., owners and managers, coaches, players, spectators, parents and school teachers; see Fig. 19.1 for an example of "Fair Play Code for Athletes").

This cognitive exhortation approach ("you should be less violent") may move the general public (and young players) from unawareness to a general and perhaps specific awareness of violence as a problem. However, although it may be a necessary strategy, it is unlikely to be sufficient to result in widescale and lasting internalization of norms encouraging the reduction of hockey violence. Providing information about the extent and consequences of violence in hockey and telling players and other involved parties to refrain from using excessive violence during the course of a game are attempts based mainly on persuasion. Yet social marketing efforts to use mass media persuasion to produce long-lasting change in complex behaviors have met with minimal success (e.g., Berkowitz, 1965; Berkowitz & Geen, 1966). The results may be due in part to the fact that subjects have not integrated new information into their own belief systems (Kelman, 1958) or have not taken it as the basis for making an attribution about themselves (Kelley, 1967). Moreover, recall that as discussed earlier, violent and aggressive behaviors in hockey are regarded as an established occupational tool; practiced and justified on the basis of winning a game or standing up for yourself. Under these circumstances, antiviolence-based persuasive arguments are likely to be counterargued by those who have strong, pro-violent initial beliefs, limiting the effects of persuasive efforts (Wood, 1982).

Restructuring the Regulatory Environment in Professional Hockey

It has been argued that at the professional level, violence is deliberately fostered by leagues and teams to increase attendance and profits (Carlsen, 1991; Jones, 1984; Jones & Ferguson, 1988; McMurtry, 1974). The argument is that violence helps teams win games; a winning record generally results in increased attendance and ticket sales, and thus greater revenues. Greater revenues serve both the interests of the owners and players as both profits and salaries increase. Consequently, when one or more clubs use excessive

FIG. 19.1. Fair play code for athletes.

violence to win, other clubs also resort to the use of excessive violence in order to remain competitive. Because most teams have financial incentives to win, no club would be likely to choose a nonviolent approach unless a collective decision is made by the owners in the professional league or as a result of some type of government intervention/regulation. The best hope for a collective decision by team owners' lies in the league's desire to expand beyond its traditional base of Canada and the U.S. Northeast.

It has been observed that fans in these areas may be accustomed to and desire a certain level of violence. However, as the league expands into the South and Southwest, "a certain level of suburban (non-violent) comfort-zone must be packaged and sold" (Lipsyte, 1995, p. B12).

For the moment, however, very limited financial disincentives exist to discourage the use of excessive violence. In sports in general, civil suits, criminal penalties, or internal league sanctions in the form of fines and suspensions have had a limited effect (Carlsen, 1991). Although game officials have the power to impose penalties and eject players during games, the infrequency and nominal nature of disciplinary measures, the lack of effective standards for discipline, and the lack of an impartial decision-maker makes internal league sanctions less than successful in deterring excessive violence among athletes (Carlsen, 1991). Thus, employees, coaches, or players who encourage or engage in excessively violent conduct and who cause injury or create a risk of injury are rarely required to bear the costs of their conduct.

Unless the league in its desire to expand operates very differently in the future, the imposition of government-sanctioned regulations may be the only viable strategy to reduce violence. An arbitration board might be established that would structure more severe penalties and less tolerance for violent acts. The board would be empowered to impose fines on players and clubs and would hold clubs financially liable for the excessively violent acts of the players. It would also serve to broaden the range of behaviors defined as violent (Carlsen, 1991). Holding not only the player but also the employer liable for the acts of its employees may induce management to control the use of excessive violence. Another possible option is the structuring of tax incentives that would link the level of advertising-related tax deductions to the level of penalties incurred across a year by the team in question. Whereas it is difficult to think of such rewards and penalties leading to truly internalized change on the part of the players, over time, that might be the case. (This argument parallels that of the logic behind civil rights legislation put into effect to curb racial discrimination and hostile attitudes toward African Americans.)

Research and research findings can help provide the impetus for legis-lative or regulatory actions. For example, it appears that the now generally accepted link between TV violence and children's aggressive behaviors (for a meta-analysis of this research see Paik & Comstock, 1994) has contributed to the recently revived government interest in curbing violence on TV. The aim with regard to hockey violence is similar: to use research to call attention to the negative consequences of hockey violence on TV, for one, by illustrating how young players imitate such violent behavior.

Social Learning Theory (Bandura 1973, 1986) offers an explanatory framework for understanding the potential effects of watching sports events that feature aggression and violence exhibited by spectators and television audiences. The theory posits that individuals can acquire aggressive responses as a result of observing others. In a now classical series of experiments (Bandura, 1973), a group of nursery school children watched an adult model beating up a life-size, inflated plastic Bobo doll, while control groups watched either no one or an adult model playing nonaggressively with the Bobo doll. In some cases, the violent model was praised and offered a reward for this behavior. In other cases, the violent model was roundly criticized and even mock spanked. In still other cases, neither reward nor punishment followed the assault on the Bobo doll. The studies showed a reliable result: When the children were given the opportunity to play with the Bobo doll, those who watched a violent model were more violent toward the doll than those who observed either no model or a model who played nonaggressively with it. The most violent children were those who saw the violent model go unpunished. Even when the model was punished, the children still learned that although Bobo bashing was not acceptable in that setting, violence might be performed in another setting in which they would feel safe from punishment yet able to get the same "enjoyment" the model had.

Children and youngsters see violent models every day on television. A long history of research on the effects of television violence on aggressive behavior suggests a positive and significant correlation between exposure to television violence and subsequent aggressive behavior (Paik & Comstock, 1994). Moreover, research has documented that prolonged exposure to episodes of violence in general tends to desensitize the viewer toward such acts (Bjorkqvist, 1985; Cline, Craft, & Courrier, 1973; Thomas, Horton, Lippincott, & Drabman, 1977). In the context of hockey violence, extended viewing of the NHL games may well increase younger players' tendencies toward aggression following exposure to a role model's violent and aggressive acts and related success. As noted earlier, Smith's (1978) study, where over half of young hockey players indicate that they have "learned how to hit another player illegally by watching TV" seems to support this view.

This study aims to develop an intervention that would causally demonstrate how exposure to violent hockey scenes encourages violence among young players. Immediately prior to a game, sets of opposing middle and high school hockey teams will be shown either a 20-minute videotape of the "best of hockey fighting" or a 20-minute videotape of the "best goals/passes." Control groups will be shown an irrelevant film. Paralleling the Bobo doll experiment, it is expected that there would be an increase in violence, as measured in part, by the number of minor and major penalties in the games that immediately follow exposure to the violent hockey scenes. As already noted, a demonstration of such a causal link along with reminders of the actual physical toll of hockey violence is intended to encourage public officials to take some action to address the problem.

Documenting that viewing violence in professional hockey on TV encourages violence among young hockey players may also encourage parents to prohibit children from viewing these games. Such parental control may be facilitated by a "V-Chip," which is to be installed in all TVs (Mifflin, 1996). Programs are coded as to their level of violence, with the information encoded and carried electronically by the program. The V-Chip will be capable of reading this information. Parents will then be able to electronically block a subset of programs they deemed violent so that their children could not see them (Purdum, 1995). To the extent parents viewed hockey as violent, and the consequences of the violence as negative, it would be expected that they would block out these games. The anticipation of such a motive might influence the league and team owners to reduce the level of violence.

**Facilitating Positive Role Models
to Achieve Internalized Change**

There is evidence that at the high school level, behavior modification techniques such as more rigorous application of penalties for aggressive play can lead to a decrease in the level of hockey violence (Smith, 1975). As such, this is a strategy that needs to be more widely adopted. But, as noted with regard to professional teams, such sanctions standing alone are unlikely to lead to an internalization of antiviolence norms.

Similarly, if conducted long and extensively enough, the Canadian Fair Play Program's public education effort at generating a national dialogue about hockey violence, should contribute toward an awareness of the problem and an understanding of its consequences. However, its primarily didactic approach is likely to limit its ability to lead to an internalization of antiviolence norms.

In order to achieve truly internalized and lasting change, it is necessary to involve young players in a systematic and programmatic way. It is with this in mind that we propose a "Big Brother/Little Brother" relationship between an older and a younger team. Both the rationale for such a system and the rough outline of how such a system would work are provided here.

As discussed in the previous section, when applied to sports violence, Social Learning Theory (Bandura, 1973, 1986) predicts an increase in younger players' tendencies toward aggression following exposure to a role model's violent and aggressive acts and the related success of such acts. Equally, one might anticipate that it would be possible to change younger players' attitudes and behaviors in a nonviolent direction by providing them with role models that promote fair play and reduced violence. Interestingly, research is available to suggest that changes in attitudes and behavior may occur not just among the younger players, but also among the role model older players, as they come to realize that they represent role models.

One such application of this approach is found in education and is commonly referred to as *peer tutoring*. The system of young tutors and tutees working together to the advantage of both has been well documented (e.g., Cohen, J. A. Kulik, & C. L. Kulik, 1982; Cook, Scrugs, Mastropieri, & Casto, 1986; Goodland & Hirst, 1989; Malamuth & Fitz-Gibbon, 1978). The peer tutoring schemes use a role model theory framework for the conceptual analysis of tutoring (Allen, 1976). According to role model theory, individuals inhabiting specific roles will feel themselves constrained by the expectations of other people to behave in particular ways. For example, if a child is temporarily given the role of teacher, and put into interaction with younger children, the older child's behavior will be constrained by the expectations of the younger children. The older children will, thereby, come to sympathize with the role of teacher and perhaps develop a deeper respect for learning. Many peer tutoring programs draw on this model and report significant improvements for both participants of this dyad in math or reading skills (Fitz-Gibbon, 1985; Kelly, 1972; Kenemuth, 1974; Webb, 1982), learning science (Allen & Feldman, 1973), and self-concepts (Dobbs, 1975; Robertson, 1971; Scruggs & Osguthorpe, 1986).

Role model theory also suggests that pupils will learn better from tutors who are their peers, or who are similar in general culture and background, than from teachers who may be perceived as belonging to an alien world (Barnes & Todd, 1977; Collier, 1983; Slavin, 1981). Tutees benefit most from having tutors somewhat advanced in age and achievement, who could bring a wider range of knowledge and experience to bear on the tutoring. Many studies suggest that cross-age tutoring—17-year-olds with 13-year-olds being the most effective—is more promising than same-age tutoring (e.g., Cohen, 1986; Fitz-Gibbon, 1980; Linton, 1972; A. Sharpley, Irvine, & C. Sharpley, 1983). This gap in age appears to maximize the feelings of responsibility on the part of the tutors.

The same role modeling system has been used to alter the smoking behavior of younger and older participants in similarly structured dyads (Goldberg & Gorn, 1982). In this study, older teens who smoked were told that their help was needed to encourage younger teens not to smoke. They were further told that they would be in contact in a month or so with a younger teen who smoked, and it would be their task to convince this younger person not to smoke. The researchers suggested that whereas the older teens were probably too old to have their smoking behavior changed, they could be far more effective than adults in persuading young people not to smoke. For the first month they were to be given antismoking information in written and video form that could be used in talking to the younger teen. Giving these older teens the sense that they were the change agents resulted in their being highly receptive to this information, as opposed to their adopting a more typical reactive stance vis-à-vis information coming from adults. In fact, the primary focus of the Goldberg and Gorn (1982) study was on the older teens, and the evidence suggested that a significant percentage of the older teens who smoked stopped smoking as a result of the experience. It appeared that the recognition that they were a role model and bore some responsibility for the younger teens led them to think twice about their own behavior.

As already noted, the felt responsibility on the part of the older participant in the dyad is the key to getting them to change. Given information at odds with their actual behavior ("smoking is bad for you" directed at a smoker), and faced with the responsibility of influencing an impressionable junior, the evidence suggests that older teens are influenced to change their own behavior. This intervention can be described as an "induced compliance" situation, which leads to dissonance and a possible change in attitude to reduce this dissonance. According to a newer formulation of dissonance theory (Cooper & Fazio, 1984), the inconsistency between attitude and behavior causes dissonance in such induced compliance settings only when the individual feels true responsibility for the counterattitudinal views they come to express, exactly the purpose of structuring the big brother role.

The process described is what this study seeks to replicate in the Canadian field experiment with regard to hockey violence. A Big Brother/Little Brother interaction will be structured where players in younger and older teams will interact throughout a season. Such a system, properly developed, might serve to change the attitudes and behaviors of both the younger and older members of the structure. An older (17- to 19-year-old) and a younger (11- to 12-year-old) hockey team will be matched over the playing season, with some practices held in common and other occasions for interaction developed. The Canadian Fair Play materials would be reviewed with the older players, who would be encouraged to discuss the issue of fair play and avoiding violence, with the younger players. Paralleling the cigarette study discussed, the goal would be to avoid reactance on the part of the older team players by suggesting they were too old to be influenced and they really were there to help with the younger players. One measure of success would be the degree to which penalties for both these teams would be reduced, relative to control teams where no equivalent intervention was introduced.

CONCLUSIONS

It has been suggested that there may be a link between violence in the broader society and in sports in general and in hockey in particular. To the extent this is the case, any effort to ameliorate the level of violence in hockey will be constrained by the level of violence in the broader society. Nevertheless, three strategies have been suggested to directly address the issue of violence in hockey per se. First, a public education campaign already energetically pursued in Canada is suggested. With the explosive growth of amateur hockey in the United States, a similar strategy ought to be followed in this country. Additionally, it has been suggested that much more aggressive steps to be taken to curb the level of violence at both the professional and amateur levels. These include regulatory oversight of violence in professional hockey and a Big Brother/Little Brother system of influence in amateur hockey. Ultimately, the goal of such steps is to reduce the level of violence so that both fans and participants can enjoy it as a true sport.

REFERENCES

Allen, V. L. (1976). *Children as teachers.* London: Academic Press.
Allen, V. L., & Feldman, R. S. (1973). Learning through tutoring: Low achieving children as tutors. *Journal of Experimental Research, 46*(3), 355–385.
Atyeo, D. (1979). *Blood and guts: Violence in sports.* New York: Paddington.
Bandura, A. (1973). *Aggression: A social learning analysis.* Englewood Cliffs, NJ: Prentice-Hall.
Bandura, A. (1986). *Social foundations of thought and action.* Englewood Cliffs, NJ: Prentice-Hall.
Bandura, A., & Walters, R. H. (1959). *Adolescent aggression.* New York: Ronald.
Barnes, D., & Todd, F. (1977). *Communication and learning in small groups.* London: Routledge & Kegan Paul.
Barry, D. (1995, November 16). State halts armory lease for "extreme" fight event. *New York Times,* p. B3.
Becker, W. C. (1964). Consequences of different kinds of parental discipline. In M. L. Hoffman & L. W. Hoffman (Eds.), *Review of child development research* (Vol. 2, pp. 137–167). New York: Russell Sage Foundation.
Berger, P. L., & Luckman, T. (1966). *The social construction of reality.* Garden City, NY: Anchor Doubleday.
Berkowitz, L. (1965). Some aspects of observed aggression. *Journal of Personality and Social Psychology, 2,* 359–369.
Berkowitz, L., & Geen, R. G. (1966). Film violence and the cue properties of available targets. *Journal of Personality and Social Psychology, 7,* 202–207.
Berkowitz, L., & LePage, A. (1967). Weapons as aggression-eliciting stimuli. *Journal of Personality and Social Psychology, 7,* 202–207.
Bjorkqvist, K. (1985). Desensitization to film violence in aggressive and nonaggressive boys. In K. Bjorkqvist (Ed.), *Violent films, anxiety and aggression* (pp. 45–50). Helsinki, Finland: Societas Scientiarum Fennica.
Boyanowsky, E. O., & Griffiths, C. T. (1982). Weapons and eye contact as instigators or inhibitors of aggressive arousal in police–citizen interaction. *Journal of Applied Social Psychology, 12,* 398–407.
Bredemeier, B. J. (1975). The assessment of reactive and instrumental athletic aggression. In D. M. Landers (Ed.), *Psychology of sport and motor behavior* (pp. 71–83). State College, PA: Pennsylvania State University.
Buss, A. H. (1961). *The psychology of aggression.* New York: Wiley.

Carlsen, C. J. (1991). Violence in professional sports. In G. A. Uberstine (Ed.), *Law of professional and amateur sports* (pp. 16.1–16.33). New York: C. Boardman Co.

Cellozzi, M. J., Kazelskis, R., & Gutsch, K. U. (1981). The relationship between viewing televised violence. In ice hockey and subsequent levels of personal aggression. *Journal of Sport Behavior, 4,* 157–162.

Cline, V. R., Craft, R. G., & Courrier, S. (1973). Desensitization of children to television violence. *Journal of Personality and Social Psychology, 27*(3), 360–365.

Cohen, J. (1986). Theoretical considerations of peer tutoring. *Psychology in the Schools, 23*(2), 175–186.

Cohen, P. A., Kulik, J. A., & Kulik, C. L. (1982). Educational outcomes of tutoring: A meta analysis of findings. *American Educational Research Journal, 19,* 237–248.

Collier, K. G. (1983). *The management of peer group learning: Syndicate Methods in Higher Education.* Guildford, UK: Society for Research into Higher Education.

Comisky, P., Bryant, J., & Zillmann, D. (1977). Commentary as a substitute for action. *Journal of Communication, 27,* 150–152.

Cook, S. B., Scrugs, T. E., Mastropieri, M. A., & Casto, G. C. (1986). Handicapped students as tutors. *Journal of Special Education, 19*(4), 483–492.

Cooper, J., & Fazio, R. H. (1984). A new look at dissonance theory. *Advances in Experimental Social Psychology, 17,* 229–266.

Dobbs, M. E. (1975). A study of certain effects of cross-age tutoring. *Dissertation Abstracts International, 35,* 12, pt. 1.7783A. (University Microfilms No. 75-13, 669)

Eitzen, D. S., & Sage, G. H. (1986). *Sociology of North American sport.* Dubuque, IA: Brown.

Fair Play Canada (1994). Dollco Printing (currently identified as Canadian Centre for Ethics and Sports, Gloucester, Ontario).

Faulkner, R. R. (1974). Making violence by doing work: Selves, situations, and the world of professional hockey. *Sociology of Work and Occupations, 1,* 288–312.

Faulkner, R. R. (1973). On respect and retribution: Toward an ethnography of violence. *Sociological Symposium, 9,* 17–36.

Faulkner, R. R. (1971, December). *Violence, camaraderie and occupational character in hockey.* Paper presented at the Conference on Sport and Social Deviancy, New York State University at Brockport.

Feshbach, N. D. (1979). The effects of violence in childhood. In D. Gil (Ed.), *Child abuse and violence* (pp. 575–585). New York: AMS Press.

Fitz-Gibbon, C. T. (1985). Peer tutoring projects: Social education improves achievement. *Noise, 4*(2), 4–10.

Fitz-Gibbon, C. T. (1980). *Measuring time use and evaluating peer tutoring in urban secondary schools* (SSRC End of Grant Report 6570/2). London: Social Science Research Council.

Goldberg, M. E., & Gorn, G. J. (1982). Increasing the involvement of teenage cigarette smokers in antismoking campaigns. *Journal of Communication, 32*(1), 75–86.

Goodland, S., & Hirst, B. (1989). *Peer tutoring: A guide to learning by teaching.* London: Kogan Page.

Huesman, L. R. (1986). Psychological processes promoting the relation between exposure to media violence and aggressive behavior by the viewer. *Journal of Social Issues, 42,* 125–139.

Huesman, L. R., & Eron, L. D. (1984). Cognitive processes and the persistence of aggressive behavior. *Aggressive Behavior, 10,* 243–251.

Ingham, A. G., & Loy, J. W. (1973). The social system of sport: A humanistic perspective. *Quest, 19,* 3–23.

Jones, J. C. H. (1984). Winners, losers and hosers: Demand and survival in the National Hockey League. *Atlantic Economic Journal, 12,* 1–10.

Jones, J. C. H., & Ferguson, D. G. (1988). Locational and survival in the National Hockey League. *Journal of Industrial Economics, 36,* 443–457.

Jones, J. C. H., Ferguson, D. G., & Stewart, K. G. (1993). Blood sports and cherry pie: Some economics of violence in the National Hockey League. *American Journal of Economics and Sociology, 52*(1), 63–78.

Kagan, J. (1964). Acquisition and significance of sex typing and sex role identity. In M. L. Hoffman & L. W. Hoffman (Eds.), *Review of child development research* (Vol. 2, pp. 137–167). New York: Russell Sage Foundation.

Kelley, H. H. (1967). Attribution theory in social psychology. *Nebraska Symposium on Motivation, 14*, 192–238.

Kelly, M. R. (1972). Pupil tutoring in reading of low-achieving, second-grade pupils by low-achieving, fourth-grade pupils. *Dissertation Abstracts International, 32*, (9A) 4881. (University Microfilms, No. 72-99399)

Kelman, H. C. (1958). Compliance, identification and internalization: Three processes of opinion change. *Journal of Conflict Resolution, 2*, 51–60.

Kenemuth, G. L. (1974). An experimental study of the effects on achievement and self-concept of sixth-grade pupils as a result of tutoring younger elementary pupils in selective activities. *Dissertation Abstracts International, 35*, 11, 7043A. (University Microfilms No. 75-9793)

Linton, T. (1972). The effects of grade displacement between student tutors and students tutored. *Dissertation Abstracts International, 33*, (8-A) 4091. (University Microfilms No. 72-32, 034)

Lipsyte, R. (1995). Hot under the collar for the "coolest game." *New York Times*, November 10, B12.

Malamuth, N. M., & Fitz-Gibbon, C. T. (1978). *Tutoring and social psychology: A theoretical analysis* (CSE Rep. No. 116). Los Angeles: Center for the Study of Evaluation, UCLA.

McMurtry, W. R. (1974). *Investigation and inquiry into violence in amateur hockey.* Toronto: Ministry of Community and Social Services.

Mifflin, L. (1996). $ network plan a rating system for their shows. *New York Times*, February 15, A-1.

Mussen, P. H. (1971). Early sex-role development. In N. Reeves (Ed.), *Womankind: Beyond the stereotypes* (pp. 398–418). Chicago: Aldine-Atherton.

Paik, H., & Comstock, G. (1994). The effects of television violence on antisocial behavior: A meta analysis. *Communication Research, 21*(4), 516–546.

Prochaska, J. O., DiClemente, C. C., & Norcross, J. C. (1992). In search of how people change. *American Psychologist, 47*(9, September), 1102–1114.

Purdum, T. (1995, July 11). Clinton Takes on Violence on TV. *The New York Times*, p. A1.

The Reid Report (1986, April). *Sports poll—Hockey violence.* Vancouver: Angus Reid.

Robertson, D. J. (1971, April). *The effects of an intergrade tutoring experience on tutor self-concept.* Paper presented at the Annual Conference of the California Educational Research Association. (ERIC Document Reproduction Service No. ED 059 769)

Russell, G. W. (1993). *The social psychology of sport.* New York: Springer-Verlag.

Russell, G. W. (1991). Athletes as targets of aggression. In R. Baenninger (Ed.), *Targets of violence and aggression* (pp. 211–252). North Holland: Elsevier.

Russell, G. W. (1981). Aggression in sport. In P. F. Brain & D. Banton (Eds.), *A multidisciplinary approach to aggression research* (pp. 431–446). North Holland: Elsevier.

Scruggs, T. E., & Osguthorpe, R. T. (1986). Tutoring interventions within special educational settings: A comparison of cross-age and peer-tutoring. *Psychology in the Schools*, April, 23.

Sears, R. R., Maccoby, E., & Lewin, M. (1957). *Patterns of child rearing.* Evanston, IL: Southern Illinois University Press.

Sharpley, A., Irvine, J., & Sharpley, C. (1983). An examination of the effectiveness of a cross-age tutoring program in mathematics for elementary school children. *American Educational Research Journal, 20*, 1.

Sipes, R. G. (1973). War, sports and aggression: An empirical test of two rival theories. *American Anthropologist, 75*, 64–86.

Slavin, R. E. (1981). Synthesis of research on cooperative learning. *Educational Leadership*, May.

Smith, M. D. (1983). *Violence and sport.* Toronto: Butterworths.

Smith, M. D. (1979a). Hockey violence: A test of the violent subculture thesis. *Social Problems, 27*, 235–247.

Smith, M. D. (1979b). Towards an explanation of hockey violence. *Canadian Journal of Sociology, 4*, 105–124.

Smith, M. D. (1978). From professional to youth hockey violence: The role of mass media. In M. A. B. Gammon (Ed.), *Violence in Canada* (pp. 269–281). Toronto: Methuen.

Smith, M. D. (1975). The legitimization of violence: Hockey players' perceptions of their reference groups' sanctions for assault. *Canadian Review of Sociology and Anthropology, 12*(1), 72–80.

Snyder, E. E., & Spreitzer, E. (1979). Structural strains in the coaching role and alignment actions. *Review of Sport and Leisure, 4*, 97–109.

Straus, M. A., Gelles, R. J., & Steinmetz, S. K. (1980). *Behind closed doors: Violence in the American family.* Garden City, NY: Anchor.

Thomas, M. H., Horton, R. W., Lippincott, E. C., & Drabman, R. S. (1977). Desensitization to portrayals of real-life aggression as a function of exposure to television violence. *Journal of Personality and Social Psychology, 35*, 450–458.

Turner, C. W., Hesse, B. W., & Peterson-Lewis, S. (1986). Naturalistic studies of the long-term effects of television violence. *Journal of Social Issues, 42*, 51–73.

Turner, C. W., Simons, L. S., Berkowitz, L., & Frodi, A. (1977). The stimulating and inhibiting effects of weapons on aggressive behavior. *Aggressive Behavior, 3*, 335–378.

Vaz, E. W. (1982). *The professionalization of young hockey players.* Lincoln, NE: University of Nebraska Press.

Vaz, E. W. (1976). The culture of young hockey players: Some initial observations. In A. Yiannakis, T. D. McIntyre, M. J. Melnick, & D. P. Hart (Eds.), *Sport sociology: Contemporary themes* (pp. 211–216). Iowa: Kendall Hunt.

Vaz, E. W., & Thomas, D. (1974). *What price victory: An analysis of minor hockey league players' attitudes toward winning.* Unpublished manuscript, University of Waterloo, Ontario.

Webb, N. M. (1982). Peer interaction and learning in co-operative small groups. *Journal of Educational Psychology, 5*(74), 642–655.

West, D. (1995). Young hockey players bring new ice age, prompting need for more rinks. *New York Times*, July 31, B-1.

Wolfgang, M. E., & Ferrracuti, F. (1967). *The subculture of violence.* London: Tavistock.

Wood, W., Wong, F. Y., & Chachere, J. G. (1991). Effects of media violence on viewer's aggression in unconstrained social interaction. *Psychological Bulletin, 109*, 371–383.

Wood, W. (1982). Retrieval of attitude-relevant information from memory: Effects on susceptibility to persuasion and on intrinsic motivation. *Journal of Personality and Social Psychology, 42*, 798–810.

Chapter 20

Effective Health Promotion Among Communities of Color: The Potential of Social Marketing

June A. Flora
Caroline Schooler
Stanford University School of Medicine

Rosalind M. Pierson
The California Wellness Foundation

ABSTRACT

There is a general assumption on the part of many health communication planners that culture matters. This chapter identifies and articulates how social marketing principles can effectively guide the development, implementation, and evaluation of culturally appropriate and relevant health promotion programs. The emphasis on audience in social marketing provides a conceptual framework for incorporating culture in health promotion programs. It discusses how to incorporate issues of cultural appropriateness and relevance to three essential social marketing principles: audience orientation, tailoring, and exchange theory. Identifying and understanding how racial and ethnic cultures differ and how this variance affects the health behavior change process can lead to more effective health promotion campaigns.[1]

The health status of African Americans, Latino Americans, Asian Americans, and other people of color in this country remains unconscionably low when contrasted with that of many Anglo Americans. This disparity is not new, reflecting a historical trend that is evident across the leading causes of death and disease (Braithwaite & Lythcott, 1989). The dispro-

---

[1]Various terms are used to refer to members of underrepresented ethnic and racial groups. The term *people of color* is used to describe persons who do not belong to the Anglo majority. A variety of words are used to denote persons who belong to diverse cultural, ethnic, and racial groups.

portionate morbidity and mortality experienced by members of underrepresented racial and ethnic groups in this country underscore the need for more effective health promotion efforts.

People of color differ greatly in social, political, and economic history, current socioeconomic status, extent of acculturation, and cultural norms. Although members of some racial or ethnic groups may be similar with regard to their relative social position and power, these groups are not monolithic in their composition. Research demonstrates that for many psychosocial attributes, there is as much or more variation within groups designated as races or ethnicities than between such groups (USDHHS, 1986; Vega, Zimmerman, Warheit, Apospori, & Gil, 1993; Williams, 1992; Zuckerman, 1990). For example, Manfredi, Lacey, Warnecke, and Buis (1992) demonstrated differences in smoking behavior and attitudes both between African-American and Anglo young women and between two groups of African-American young women. This kind of research contributes to growing sophistication in the scientific and health delivery communities in acknowledging the heterogeneity in lifestyles, beliefs, behaviors, and culture that underlie observable racial and ethnic distinctions (Anderson & Jackson, 1987; Cooper, 1991).

Many health communication planners believe that culture matters. What is lacking, however, is theory and research articulating a process that guides the development, implementation, and evaluation of health promotion programs directed toward people of color. This chapter argues that health professionals should increasingly turn to social marketing for guidance in improving health programs.

SOCIAL MARKETING

Social marketing involves increasing the acceptability of ideas or practices in a target group (Kotler, 1975; Kotler & Zaltman, 1971). As such, it is a process for developing effective communication strategies (Manoff, 1985; Novelli, 1984). Social marketing concepts and methods draw strongly from the commercial marketing literature. Social marketing, however, is distinguished by its emphasis on the introduction and dissemination of ideas, issues, and lifestyle changes rather than on the more tangible products and services that are the focus of marketing in the business, health care, and nonprofit service sectors.

According to Lefebvre and Flora (1988), social marketing is especially well-suited to the task of translating necessarily complex educational messages and behavior change techniques into concepts and products that will be received and acted on by a large segment of the population. Clearly, social marketing campaigns alone cannot be expected to lead to substantial cognitive and/or behavior changes. The strategic and continuous application of social marketing principles, however, contributes importantly to effective health promotion efforts. It is particularly salient today to consider how to best utilize these strategies to improve the health status of those who suffer the most health problems.

Culture and Social Marketing

The idea that health promotion efforts must be aware of and responsive to audience needs is fundamental to social marketing (Lefebvre & Flora, 1988). The emphasis on audience in social marketing provides a framework for incorporating culture in health promotion programs. *Culture* refers to a set of shared behaviors and ideas (Nobles, 1985); in other words, a framework of language, customs, knowledge, ideas, and values that provides people with guidelines for interpreting reality and living (Airhihenbuwa, DiClemente, Wingood, & Lowe, 1992; Servaes, 1989).

A "lens" metaphor is often used by those who study culture. This metaphor describes how individual members of a culture view the world (Michal-Johnson & Bowen, 1992). According to this comparison, the lens functions as a filter or screen and reflects the "sum total" of people's experience that is projected onto a situation. The filter is developed by membership and participation in a particular racial or ethnic group and forms a mechanism through which history, tradition, and norms influence thoughts, feelings, and behavior. Some mores are common across all cultures, such as the idea of maternal love. The manifestations and norms of such mores, however, differ substantially in various cultures. Moreover, appeals to such seemingly universal values and ideals must still be embedded in a specific cultural context to be relevant and appropriate for audience members.

A substantial number of studies in cross-cultural psychology and in anthropology have shown not only that members of various cultures differ in their perceptions of the world, but also that these differential world views influence behavior (Marin & Marin, 1991). Cultural values include such things as preference for time perspectives (Hall, 1983), sense of control (Kluckhohn & Strodbeck, 1961), level of group centeredness (Hofstede, 1980), and social and personal space (Hall, 1969), among others. Among African Americans, for instance, prominent cultural themes include historical facts such as abuse and oppression; economic constraints; values such as the church, the family, and community; and a shared language (Airhihenbuwa et al., 1992; Bowen & Michael-Johnson, 1990; Duh, 1991; Mays, 1989). Other culturally specific values include social scripts, or the set of behavioral patterns that are expected in certain social situations; for example, *simpatía* (the value given to fluid and positive interpersonal relations) is a cultural script specific to Latinos and *amae* (passive dependence) is a script characteristic of many Japanese (Doi, 1973; Feldman, 1968; Triandis, 1972; Triandis et al., 1984). Disentangling cultural attributes is very difficult, yet these characteristics contribute to patterns of social existence. As Earls (1993) illustrated, being 16 years old, male, Dominican, Catholic, and poor in the Bronx constitutes a cultural pattern that is likely to be distinctly different from that of an African-American Baptist, of the same age and sex, whose parents migrated from the South to New York and are also poor.

Cultures vary in distinct ways that have important implications for health. People's habits and lifestyles, attitudes, and even their knowledge regarding health issues are significantly influenced by their cultural heritage (Earls, 1993). There are three elements of social marketing that help health program designers plan and implement culturally appropriate and relevant campaigns: audience orientation, tailoring, and exchange theory.

Audience Orientation

A fundamental tenet of social marketing is that health promotion programs must be designed in response to audience needs, implemented to meet those needs, effective in satisfying those needs, and monitored both to ensure the program continues to meet these needs and to discover new or changing needs. Because a group's history, language, values, and beliefs influence group members' health-related knowledge, attitudes, and behavior (Singer, 1991), the values of a culture must be used as the foundation or building blocks of health promotion programs (Marin & Marin, 1991). Interventions or strategies that do not conform to cultural values (e.g., emphasizing long-term gains to a culture that prefers a present orientation) or worse, that actually challenge a group's values (e.g., assertive techniques in a society that values cooperative and fluid social relations) can be expected to fail.

Social marketing underscores the importance of defining the focus of a health campaign from the perspective of the audience. A racial or ethnic group's history often plays a critical role in influencing lay theories about health problems. For example, in the African-American community, the legacy of Tuskegee doubtless continues to inspire distrust of government-sponsored health campaigns, especially those in the arena of sexually trans-mitted diseases (such as current efforts regarding AIDS; Thomas & Quinn, 1991). Another way history plays a role in influencing how people think about the causes of health problems involves past experience with disease. For example, the myth that AIDS is spread by mosquitoes is quite wide-spread in the Chinese and Southeast Asian language press in the United States, perhaps because malaria, which is endemic to many Asian countries, is transmitted this way (Aoki, Ngin, Mo, & Ja, 1989). In addition, ethnicity and race cannot be interpreted independently from their environmental context, such as poverty (Wilkinson & King, 1987). Mays (1989) explained that for the very poor, a lot of health promotion advice is confusing or does not make sense. For example, "Just Say No" antidrug messages probably do not have much persuasive impact on a welfare mother whose 13-year-old son makes $13,000 a month selling drugs (Christon, 1988).

Program goals must incorporate culturally specific ways of viewing health issues. Goals include defining the intended audience, specifying the advocated health behavior change, planning how various messages or products will be disseminated, and designing how the campaign will be implemented. Advocated actions that do not conform to cultural precepts about appropriate thoughts, attitudes, or behaviors will doubtless not be initiated or maintained. Barriers to change that may be culturally based must also be recognized. Health, in general, and any disease, in particular, may not be high priorities for low income populations or some cultural groups (Kerner, Dusenbury, & Mandelblatt, 1993). When unemployment, inferior or inadequate housing, violence, crime, and other major community problems are very salient, long-term health risks such as those associated with smoking pale in comparison.

Effective health promotion programs involve comprehensive, well-integrated messages delivered through a variety of channels such as influential community leaders, mass electronic and print media, and organizations and institutions such as schools, churches, and worksites (Schooler, Flora, & Farquhar, 1993). People's habitual media use habits, as well as their reasons for using various media, are influenced by culture. Communication channels differ according to such characteristics as cost, how many people are reached, preservability or the extent to which people can save and reuse or reread, level of receiver control that refers to whether audience members can determine how quickly or slowly they read or view, and interactivity—to name a few. Traditional channel considerations such as these, although clearly germane to health promotion efforts with people of color, are not sufficient. Thorough analysis and selection of communication channels requires a good understanding of what channels the intended audience comes into contact with on a regular basis and perceives as being more influential and important (Lefebvre & Flora, 1988).

Perceptions of a channel's effectiveness, credibility, or personal relevance are influenced by culture (Flora, Schooler, Mays, & Cochran, 1996). For example, a number of health campaigns directed toward Latinos have been based on *fotonovelas* (a set of captioned photographs that depict a story in comic book format). The rationale is that fotonovelas are common in Latin America and thus are a culturally appropriate channel. G. Marin and B. V. Marin (1990) found, however, that Latino Americans perceive fotonovelas as the least credible channel of information for health information, ranking below posters and television and radio commercials. The study indicated that books, pamphlets, and newspaper articles were perceived to be the most credible.

Tailoring

Another important tenet of social marketing is the idea that campaigns and products must be tailored to the intended audience. This emphasis on tailoring a program to be relevant and appropriate for the consumer has important implications for health promotion efforts among people of color. Messages, products, and services that are tailored to be sensitive and appropriate to a particular group's culture will be more informative, persuasive, and ultimately effective (Airhihenbuwa et al., 1992; Bowen & Michal-Johnson, 1990; Kalichman, Kelly, Hunter, Murphy, & Tyler, 1993; Mays, 1989; Michal-Johnson & Bowen, 1992; Nickens, 1990). In order to tailor messages to focal audience groups, audience members are often segmented into meaningful subgroups. The intent of audience segmentation is to define homogenous subgroups for channel selection, message, and product design purposes.

People of color have often been viewed by health program planners as homogenous, belonging to lower socioeconomic strata, and having similar preferences, styles, and behaviors (Freimuth & Mettger, 1990). In fact, not only do ethnic and racial groups differ from each other, but intragroup differences have important implications for health promotion efforts (Williams, 1992). The importance of considering both intergroup and intragroup differences is illustrated by the variance among Native Americans, Alaskan Natives, and Native Hawaiians who constitute the largest number of cultural groups and perhaps the widest degree of cultural diversity among all underrepresented racial and ethnic groups in the United States. Some 300 tribes, 278 reservations, and 209 native villages are recognized by the federal government (U.S. Bureau of the Census, 1984a, 1984b). Disaggregation of an audience allows the planner to obtain detailed information about subgroups, which is necessary to develop and position messages with regard to the attributes of the segment.

Research indicates program planners often rely on variables that have traditionally been used to segment Anglo majority audiences such as geography (region, county, census tract), demography (age, gender, family size, occupation, ethnic or racial background, socioeconomic status), social structure (worksites, churches, voluntary agencies, families, legislative bodies), and psychographics (lifestyle, personality, level of readiness for change) (Kotler, 1975; Murphy, 1984; Novelli, 1984; A. Weinstein, 1987). These may not capture the diversity among underrepresented ethnic and racial groups. It is important to consider variables for intragroup comparison, as well as some segmentation criteria like education, which may have different meanings in various cultures.

There are several important segmentation variables when working with people of color.

Immigration Status. Ogbu (1985) asserted that an essential distinction among members of racial and ethnic groups rests in the circumstances under which they emigrated to the United States. For some people of color, immigration has been voluntary; examples include many of the immigrants from the Far East, Southeast Asia, Latin America, and the Caribbean. Persons choosing to emigrate probably do not represent a random sample of the population. Although few generalizations can be made regarding the combination of factors that contribute to decisions to come to the United States, it is generally accepted that the first wave of immigrants is highly motivated to succeed (Beiser, 1988). Involuntary emigrant people of color, on the other hand, have often ruptured bonds with their places of origin and with their traditions. For African Americans, the transition from slavery to racial segregation maintained Blacks in a position of powerlessness and contributed to the enduring fragility of the family.

Family Structure. The concept of family varies both between and within cultures. The majority culture in this country has accorded the greatest legitimacy to the nuclear family, consisting of two biological parents and their children. In such families, parent–child relationships are often close, with an emphasis on educational achievement and maximizing individual success in mainstream society (Modell, 1989). In extended families, however, there is greater emphasis on group sharing and less focus on competitiveness and individual achievement (Slaughter & Epps, 1987). Because extended families have more generations and larger numbers of children, the traditional culture can be transmitted with greater intensity (Wilson, 1986). The family unit becomes more powerful as an institution and often effectively transfers the values of cooperation and group sharing (Earls, 1993). Davis (1992) described an example of research based on cultural misconceptions: analyses of single-parent African-American families. The demographics of African-American households, as defined by parental status, can best be observed and understood not in juxtaposition to those of traditional nuclear families but in relation to the extended-family structures of nonnuclear households (Farley & Allen, 1987; Hunter & Ensiminger, 1992).

Degree of Assimilation or Accommodation to the Majority Culture. *Assimilation* and *accommodation* represent two major strategies by which a cultural minority adapts to life within a structure governed by a cultural majority (Earls, 1993). Individuals can assimilate into another culture, relinquishing minority cultural attributes in the process. Portes and Zhou (1994) explained that assimilation can take two forms: One form of adaptation is acculturation into the majority White middle-class culture; a second form leads to linkages with underclass culture. An example of this is second generation Haitian youth in Miami who assimilate not to white mainstream society (where Haitians face racial discrimination) but to the values and norms of innercity native-born African-American classmates (Portes & Zhou, 1994).

In the second strategy, accommodation, the individual learns the rules, values, and habits of the dominant culture, while making a conscientious effort to preserve the original culture as well (Ogbu, 1988). This can lead to the pursuit of economic advancement with deliberate preservation of and solidarity with the immigrant community's values (Portes & Zhou, 1994). Olmeda and Padilla (1978) explained that people can assimilate or accommodate across a variety of domains: language, religion, health beliefs, and educational aspirations. As an underrepresented racial or ethnic group becomes more highly assimilated into the mainstream of American values and customs, changes in health-related attitudes and behaviors may also occur. For example, first generation Mexican-Americans experience lower rates of infant mortality and low birthweight than other groups (Bautista-Hayes, 1990). Later generations, however, appear to lose this advantage, which may be a consequence of adopting the lifestyle and habits (e.g., dietary changes, more sedentary lifestyle, higher rates of smoking among women) of the dominant culture (Andersen, Lewis, Giachello, Aday, & Chiu, 1981; Earls, 1993; Wells, Golding, Hough, Burnam, & Karno, 1989).

Language Use. Although, for many years, bilingualism was thought to be associated with educational disadvantage (Hakuta, 1986), research demonstrates that bilingualism can expand the range of expressive capacities without restricting or inhibiting mastery of the majority language (Diaz, 1983). In addition, not only is it important to understand the appropriate sounds and grammatical structures, or language, of a culture, but also a culture's particular communication *style*. Style refers to the way a speaker, "puts sound and grammatical structure together to communicate meaning in a larger context" (Smitherman-Donaldson, 1977, p. 16). Although it is common to integrate obvious language changes (e.g., translating English to Spanish), often more subtle stylistic changes that differentiate how racial and ethnic groups communicate (e.g., variations in the type of Spanish spoken, or the use of Black dialect rather than "standard" English) are overlooked. As Marin, Marin, Perez-Stable, Sabogal, and Otero-Sabogal (1990) explained, translating a booklet originally created for middle-class non-Hispanic Whites into Spanish; or changing the context of the storyline to reflect a Latin barrio in New York, Los Angeles, Miami, or San Antonio; or calling the actors José and Maria instead of Johnny and Mary, leads to interventions that are cultural hybrids but still fall short of being culturally sensitive or relevant for Latinos.

Health Beliefs and Practices. Due to a long history of distrust of the medical community, many racial and ethnic groups use traditional healing techniques and home remedies in order to ensure the survival of their communities. Many in the majority culture believe that the use of traditional medicine and folkways is unfortunate and possibly harmful (Earls, 1993). The availability of multiple systems through which to pursue health, however, is more likely to be an advantage than a disadvantage (Neighbors & Jackson, 1984; Snow, 1978). For health promotion to be most effective in cultures using traditional or non-Western medical systems, interventions need to more clearly articulate the benefits of Western medicine in an effort to develop hybrid models and strategies in which multiple health beliefs can reinforce healthful behavior.

Tailoring a health promotion program to a specific audience also entails directing attention to examination of how potential audience groups perceive their needs. A traditional approach to audience needs analysis is reliance on archival information (e.g., census data, Chamber of Commerce reports) and secondary reference material (e.g., U.S. food consumption patterns, marketing surveys, national polls). Such data can provide information regarding the relative extent of violent behavior, intentional and unintentional injury, substance abuse, teenage pregnancy, and other diseases and disorders in various subgroups. These data, however, are limited. They seldom provide information about health-sustaining behaviors. In addition, they do not guide an understanding of what the communities themselves would define as their most pressing health-related problems. Furthermore, the validity and reliability of these types of data are questionable, especially for inner-city communities, recent immigrants, and the economically disadvantaged.

Audience needs analysis is vitally important if health promotion campaigns are to provide what the intended audience desires and requires for healthful behavior change. In addition, examination of the specific barriers audience members experience is critical if people are to adopt new behaviors. Many interventions are designed on the belief that certain groups lack information about the causes of a given health problem and that behavior change would take place once the members of the group learn the required information. This is not necessarily the case. For example, Trotter's (1990) study of Mexican Americans in the lower Rio Grande Valley of Texas found that a lead oxide glazing compound was common in two types of traditional earthenware pots. Trotter found that virtually everyone was aware that the pots were a potential source of lead poisoning and used a variety of techniques to test the safety of their pots: tapping the pot and listening for a dull sound, smelling the pot, looking for bubbles in the glaze, and filling the pot with vinegar and letting it stand for a day or two. Supporting the continued use of these pots was a strong shared belief that food cooked in them tasted much better than food cooked in modern pots and pans. An intervention to reduce lead poisoning in this community would not need to educate people; community members already knew about the risks of lead in cookware. The goal should be to change attitudes about modern cookware and promote use of lead-free cooking utensils.

Exchange Theory

Another important element in social marketing is the use of exchange theory to conceptualize service delivery and program participation. *Exchange theory* is based on the premise that something of value must be transferred or traded between parties who each benefit. Marketing, as distinguished from other forms of persuasion, is oriented toward satisfying consumer interests through the utilization of techniques that facilitate voluntary exchanges between the consumer and the producer. Exchange provides an avenue for audience participation and input. Planners should not merely recognize what the health agency has to offer audience members, campaign designers should also acknowledge and utilize the expertise and assistance of audience members. This process renders health promotion efforts more interactive and helps move away from unidirectional, distanced communication. In other words, by expressly providing for meaningful trade or transfer of value between both the health agency and audience members, the health program meets the needs of both sender and receiver.

Central to exchange theory is the idea of *value*. The parties engaged in a transaction must share an understanding of what the other considers valuable. Perceptions of value, or worth, are importantly influenced by culture. Moreover, health topics are extremely personal. Many people respond to health promotion messages, especially those warning of the dire consequences of unhealthful behavior, in less than objective manners. Subjective interpretation of messages concerning health means that sociocultural factors may strongly affect an audience member's response (Markova & Power, 1992). The way individuals view themselves in relation to at-risk groups also affects the way they respond to health promotion messages because of issues relating to guilt, stigma, and prejudice (Valdiserri, Lyter, Leviton, Callahan, Kingsley, & Rinaldo, 1987). For example, many African Americans reacted to early efforts at AIDS education with feelings of suspicion and mistrust (Airhihenbuwa et al., 1992; Dalton, 1989), perhaps because of feelings that AIDS was a white gay men's disease (Mays, 1989) and because of distrust of the predominantly white institutions who were conducting the education programs (Dalton, 1989; Mays & Cochran, 1988; Thomas & Quinn, 1991).

According to Lefebvre and Flora (1988), the core of designing and implementing marketing plans involves the blending of four distinct elements: product, place, promotion, and price. Culture plays an important role in how each aspect of a social marketing program should be construed and implemented.

Product. A product is typically conceived of as something tangible: a physical entity or service that can be exchanged with a target market. Social marketing, however, extends the concept of products to include ideas, social causes, and behavior changes (e.g., use contraceptives, eat more fiber). Under this rubric, the message is the product. Curricula, promotional print pieces, self-help kits, group programs, screenings, public service announcements, and so forth are the products in a health promotion program. The features, quality, styling, brand name, and packaging of each of these products can have a far-reaching impact on public perceptions of the health campaign and whether or not the intended audience is motivated to adopt the advocacy (Kotler, 1975).

A culturally relevant intervention requires that the actual intervention strategies fit within the behavioral repertoire of the intended audience (Marin and Marin, 1990). In this sense, the components of the intervention must reflect patterns of use of the possible intervention channels (e.g., whether electronic or printed media are used more frequently), the credibility and perceived usefulness of the strategies among the group's members, as well as the actual preferences of the members of the audience for certain strategies. For example, certain groups may prefer group-based activities over individualized interventions such as self-help kits. In another example, research by Marin and Marin (1991) about smoking cessation demonstrated that setting a target date, a technique widely used in cessation approaches directed at non-Hispanic Whites, was not effective with Latinos who perceived it as cheating oneself into never thinking seriously about quitting.

Place. Place refers to how health messages are disseminated. This refers both to who delivers a message and ways in which the message is spread. Placement considerations relate to the number and location of distribution points the health effort can reasonably manage, including the use and motivation of intermediaries such as volunteers, opinion leaders, and gatekeepers (such as newspaper editors and journalists). Distribution systems need to incorporate strategies the intended audience will actually use (e.g., tear-off coupons on promotional flyers for stores audience members shop at or for products audience members desire).

Some of the key issues in presenting culture-specific health promotion messages are how the information is delivered and by whom (Michal-Johnson & Bowen, 1992). The cultural context of messages, therefore, shapes how they are perceived by audience members. For example, a recent study demonstrated that young urban African Americans of the "hip-hop generation" reject African American mainstream culture and its messengers (e.g., the Rev. Jesse Jackson, Bill Cosby) as thoroughly as they reject white mainstream culture (Tucker, 1992). This demonstrates that within an ethnic or racial group, there are diverse subgroups whose members may respond very differently to health education messages.

Moreover, it is important to understand the cultural context in which people of color live and the influences this might have of perceptions of health promotion efforts. Religion, for example, plays a central role in the lives of many. In the African American community, it is important to examine how different religions shape attitudes and behaviors concerning health. In the arena of AIDS, for example, methods of education or intervention involving fundamentalist Christians, such as The Church of God and Christ (or Pentecostal) should differ from those targeting more liberal Episcopalians. It has been estimated that approximately 90% of fundamentalists and Baptists believe in an afterlife (Mays, 1989). For many, the afterlife is a place of reward or punishment for actions on earth. One strategy for addressing groups with this orientation is that of asking them not to judge, but to leave God to judge the actions of individuals. Instead, they can focus on the role they can play in ministering to and helping those suffering from AIDS through house visits, food drives, and providing child care or respite care to families. This service, regardless of the sin of the person served, will be rewarded by God. The language and the method of intervention used in working with fundamentalists become appropriate in the context of their belief system.

Promotion. No decision about the promotion of a health product should be made without a clear outline of the objects of the promotion: who the intended audience is, what effect is sought, and what the optimal reach and frequency should be. Advertising, publicity, personal contact, and attention to creating an environment designed to produce specific cognitive and/or emotional effects (e.g., atmosphere) among audience members are specific ways by which promotion goals can be met (Kotler, 1975; Kotler & Zaltman, 1971). Promotion strategies must be clearly tied to the product, its price, the channels of distribution (placement), and the intended audience. All too often, according to Lefebvre and Flora (1988), program promotion is poorly integrated with other parts of a health promotion effort. Promotion is more than awareness development or public relations. Used properly, promotion can be a major tool to make health promotion messages more acceptable to the audience and enhance their effectiveness.

Price. Prices can be thought of in a variety of ways. In addition to economic considerations, there are social, behavioral, psychological, temporal, structural, geographic, and physical reasons for adopting or not adopting new health-related behaviors. The costs, or barriers, to consumer use of health promotion products receive the most attention. For example, the cost in terms of effort and inconvenience for rural or poor women to take their children to be immunized is the enemy of many immunization programs (Ling, Franklin, Lindsteadt, & Gearon, 1992).

Prices are inherently culture specific. What one group of people perceive as a benefit may be considered irrelevant or even negative by another group. Incongruence with culture, in fact, is a price of many health innovations. In addition, the situation in which people live can also affect their perceptions of the costs and benefits associated with an advocated behavior change. Interventions aimed at altering patterns of sexual behavior among poor women, many of whom are of color, demonstrate this point. N. Weinstein (1987) described three possible functions of sexual behavior: procreation, recreation, and an expression of emotional connectedness. One additional component of sexuality, however, is survival. Women who work in the sex industry understand this function of sexual behavior (Alexander, 1987). But women do not need to be paid for sex directly to reap economic or social status benefits from sexual involvements with men. Research reveals that in poorer African American communities there is a greater likelihood of sexual activities for survival or in exchange or barter for needed resources (Mays & Cochran, 1988, 1989). In such situations, for a woman to insist that her sexual partner use condoms when other readily available partners may not could adversely affect her and her children's safety and welfare. Thus, in these women's lives, the cost of their immediate survival outweighs, and may even threaten, the long-term benefits of practicing safer sexual behaviors.

Evaluation

It is important to conduct both process and summative evaluation of health promotion programs. Process evaluation tracks the ongoing activities of the program, providing data for assessing program delivery and utilization. Over the course of a health marketing program, process tracking data can provide a good overview of activities, identify program elements that are either not offered often enough or are underutilized by the target groups, and help establish priorities in program planning and implementation.

Evaluation should consider what it is about society, the environment, and human interaction that makes cultural group an important variable for the health program being examined (Ponterotto, 1988). Traditionally, there has been a willingness on the part of program evaluators to use race or ethnicity as a proxy variable for actual causal variables, such as poverty, unemployment, and family structure. According to Davis (1992), evaluators must be more inclined to investigate the economically disadvantaged and the social conditions and cultural responses to poverty, not just racial and ethnic categorizations that often provide merely superficial analyses. Evaluations of programs for culturally diverse populations should be sensitive to the nature of the social construction of the programs (Richardson, 1990). In addition, evaluation should incorporate intragroup differences into research designs. It is important to consider how some variables such as socioeconomic status may have different meanings among people of color (Gordon, 1973), which means that such variables ought to be categorized from a culturally specific viewpoint.

Evaluation, moreover, always involves judgments regarding success. Interpretations of success may vary greatly depending on culture. Acknowledgment of the way success is construed and openness to other definitions are critical for evaluation of health promotion programs in diverse communities. Evaluators must cultivate a multi-ethnocultural perspective by which they can recognize and incorporate the experiential differences between and among individuals and groups (Davis, 1992).

Despite the importance of culture in evaluation, it is also necessary not to "overculturalize" (Ponterotto, 1988). Culture, although an important influence on human behavior, is not the only variable that shapes people's thought, feelings, and actions. Culture-transcendent factors that all people experience and that have important implications for health—economic deprivation, uncertainties about the future, loss of significant others, a traumatic illness, and rapidly changing world events—play a role in program effectiveness and need to be considered in evaluation of health programs (cf. Casas, 1984; Lonner & Sundberg, 1985).

FUTURE CHALLENGES OF SOCIAL MARKETING AND PEOPLE OF COLOR

This chapter has sought to identify and articulate how social marketing principles guide the development, implementation, and evaluation of culturally appropriate and relevant health promotion programs for communities of color. Several ideas have been suggested for how health promotion efforts can meet the challenges posed by the increasing diversity of the United States.

First, move beyond the individual level of analysis. This has implications for problem definition, intervention strategies, message and product design, and evaluation. For example, in a youth violence prevention program, conflict resolution curricula in the schools may not be an effective program because of high drop-out rates and feelings of disenchantment with the educational system. Instead, health program designers might benefit by considering mobilizing the community to participate in policy advocacy efforts to change school discipline practices to enhance student retention, and to encourage community members to work together for economic development and new jobs.

Second, construe audience needs more broadly. Audiences for health promotion effects can be defined by the sender, typically a health agency. In addition, audiences can be self-defined, such as members of various groups or organizations. Furthermore, audiences can be defined by shared psychosocial attributes such as involvement in an issue, shared experiences such as losing a loved one to AIDS, and habitual media use. An African American woman, for example, may feel most strongly allied with women's causes, with civil rights issues, or with her African heritage and traditions. Another dimension of audience to consider is its potential function. These include audience as consumer, or potential customer, which is the traditional view articulated by social marketing; audience as client, or the beneficiary of communication, which is based on the precept that the health professional knows what is best for the audience; audience as dialog partner, which proposes that communications are conceptualized as the dynamic interaction of equal partners working toward mutual understanding and negotiated problem solving; and audience as communicators, which recognizes the importance of audience members as participating in the health promotion effort as opinion leaders, role models, and resources for the community.

Third, develop awareness of the underlying assumptions made about audiences and the role of the health educator (Windahl & Signitzer with Olsen, 1992). In other words, health promotion efforts can stem from a paternalistic orientation wherein program planners view their role as educating and informing the audience whose subjective needs, interests, and likes are not of much concern. Another set of assumptions could be termed *overprofessionalism*, which connotes that program planners believe that only trained health professionals think they are competent to decide on message content, knowing better than audience members what it should be. Thirdly, program planners can inhibit the effectiveness of their programs via overreliance on tried and true methods. In this manner, program planners seek to avoid complex and controversial issues and techniques. Clearly, this orientation limits how innovative, tailored, and far-reaching health efforts can be.

Fourth, increase sensitivity to the modes of behavior and patterns of change that are most appropriate to the intended audience. Cultural groups vary according to how comfortable they are with rapid social change, especially change that comes from the outside. Therefore, thorough consideration of the mores and style of audience members should be integrated into all aspects of program planning.

Fifth, enhance cooperation toward health improvement. Essentially, this viewpoint calls for communication strategies to build mutual trust and reduce tension between people and groups (Windahl et al., 1992). The end result of such efforts is the facilitation of group processes that are critical to achieving long-term health benefits. Institutionalization of health programs can only occur when community members believe in and share the vision and strategies that comprise the health promotion effort. According to this viewpoint, beneficial change is not achieved quickly by outside agencies, but instead is the product of consistent and repeated interaction over time.

Shweder and Sullivan (1993) stated that "the 1990s is the decade of ethnicity" (p. 517). It is critical, therefore, that health program planners recognize and consider the importance of culture and the diversity both within and across racial and ethnic groups, and strategically integrate this knowledge throughout the entire health promotion process. Central to this task is acknowledging that racial and ethnic prejudice, and economic discrimination clearly persist. These forms of bias sustain the depreciation and devaluation of people and communities of color, creating both external and internal barriers to healthful lifestyles, and economic and social success (Earls, 1993). Because assumptions of personal control and investment in one's future are fundamental to health promotion, these barriers must ultimately be removed if people of color are to optimize their level of fitness and survival.

Social marketing provides a useful framework for developing, implementing, and evaluating health promotion programs directed toward people of color. However, it does not provide a theoretical explanation to guide behavior change strategies. Instead, it is a useful planning tool that can incorporate theoretical perspectives such as social learning theory (Bandura, 1986), the theory of reasoned action (1975), or stages of change (Prochaska & DeClemente, 1983). For example, Winett (1995) discussed how various principles of behavior change can be integrated into social marketing strategies.

To optimize the potential for social marketing efforts, however, more research is needed. Future studies should examine which segmentation variables are most important both within and between various racial and ethnic groups for diverse health issues. Although studies indicate that tailoring messages enhances program effectiveness (e.g., S. R. Rossi et al., 1994; Skinner, Strecher, & Hospers, 1994), more research is needed to determine how to best design behavior change strategies for people of color. Another area for research is how various audience groups construe the exchange implicit in health promotion programs. This includes examination of perceptions of costs versus benefits, how senders and receivers define value, and incorporating ideas of exchange into evaluation as well as implementation. To guide this research and develop effective health promotion programs among communities of color, a focus on audience orientation, tailoring, and exchange theory is encouraged.

ACKNOWLEDGMENTS

Preparation of this manuscript was supported by the Institute of Medicine's Health Promotion and Disease Prevention Board and the Commission on Behavior, Social Science, and Education's Board on Children and Families.

REFERENCES

Airhihenbuwa, C. O., DiClemente, R. J., Wingood, G. M., & Lowe, A. (1992). HIV/AIDS education and prevention among African-Americans: A focus on culture. *AIDS Education and Prevention, 4,* 267–276.

Alexander, P. (1987). Prostitutes are being scapegoated for heterosexual AIDS. In F. Delacoste & P. Alexander (Eds.), *Sex work: Writings by women in the sex industry* (pp. 248–263). Pittsburgh, PA: Cleis.

Andersen, R., Lewis, A. L., Giachello, A. L., Aday, L., & Chiu, G. (1981). Access to medical care among the Hispanic population of the Southwestern United States. *Journal of Health and Social Behavior, 22,* 78–79.

Anderson, N. B., & Jackson, J. S. (1987). Race, ethnicity and health psychology. In G. C. Stone, S. M. Weiss, J. D. Matarazzo, N. E. Miller, J. Rodin, C. D. Belar, M. J. Follick, & J. E. Singer (Eds.), *Health psychology: A discipline and a profession* (pp. 265–283). Chicago: University of Chicago Press.

Aoki, B., Ngin, C. P., Mo, B., & Ja, D. Y. (1989). AIDS prevention models in Asian-American communities. In V. M. Mays, G. W. Albee, & S. F. Schneider (Eds.), *Primary prevention of AIDS: Psychological approaches* (pp. 290–308). Newbury Park: Sage.

Bandura, A. (1986). *Social foundations of thought and action: A social cognitive theory.* Englewood Cliffs, NJ: Prentice-Hall.

Bautista-Hayes, D. E. (1990). *Latino health indicators and the underclass model: From paradox to new policy models.* Unpublished manuscript, Chicano Studies Research Center, UCLA.

Beiser, M. (1988). Influences of time, ethnicity and attachment on depression in Southeast Asian refugees. *American Journal of Psychiatry, 45,* 46–51.

Bowen, S. P., & Michal-Johnson, P. (1990). A rhetorical perspective for HIV education with Black urban adolescents. *Communication Research, 17,* 848–866.

Braithwaite, R. L., & Lythcott, N. (1989). Community empowerment as a strategy for health promotion for Black and other minority populations. *Journal of the American Medical Association, 261*(2), 282–283.

Casas, J. M. (1984). Policy, training and research in counseling psychology: The racial/ethnic minority perspective. In S. Brown & R. Lent (Eds.), *Handbook of counseling psychology* (pp. 785–831). New York: Wiley.

Christon, L. (1988, July 9). Whoopi puts truths on the laugh track. *Los Angeles Times,* part 6, pp. 1, 10.

Cooper, R. S. (1991). Celebrate diversity: Or should we?. *Ethnicity and Disease, 1,* 3–7.

Dalton, H. L. (1989, Spring). AIDS in black face. *Daedalus,* 205–227.

Davis, J. E. (1992). Reconsidering the use of race as an explanatory variable in program evaluation. In A. Madison (Ed.), *Minority issues in program evaluation* (pp. 55–67). San Francisco: Jossey-Bass.

Diaz, R. M. (1983). Thought and two languages: The impact of bilingualism on cognitive development. *Review of Research in Education, 10,* 23–54.

Doi, T. L. (1973). *The anatomy of dependence.* Tokyo: Kodasha International.

Duh, S. V. (1991). *Blacks and AIDS: Causes and origins.* Newbury Park, CA: Sage.

Earls, F. (1993). Health promotion for minority adolescents: cultural considerations. In S. G. Millstein, A. C. Petersen, & E. O. Nightingale (Eds.), *Promoting the health of adolescents* (pp. 58–72). New York: Oxford University Press.

Farley, R., & Allen, W. (1987). *The color line and the quality of American life.* New York: Russell Sage Foundation.

Feldman, R. E. (1968). Response to compatriot and foreigner who seek assistance. *Journal of Personality and Social Psychology, 10,* 202–214.

Flora, J. A., Schooler, C., Mays, V., & Cochran, S. (1996). Symbolic social communication: The case of Magic Johnson. *International Journal of Health Psychology, 1*(3), 353–366.

Freimuth, V. S., & Mettger, W. (1990). Is there a heard-to-reach audience? *Public Health Reports, 105,* 232–238.

Gordon, T. (1973). Notes on White and Black psychology. *Journal of Social Issues, 29*(1), 87–95.

Hakuta, K. (1986). *Mirror of language: The debate on bilingualism.* New York: Basic Books.

Hall, E. T. (1969). *The hidden dimension.* Garden City, NY: Doubleday.

Hall, E. T. (1983). *The dance of life.* Garden City, NY: Anchor Books.

Hofstede, G. (1980). *Culture's consequences.* Beverly Hills, CA: Sage.

Hunter, A. G., & Ensiminger, M. (1992). The diversity and fluidity of children's living arrangements: Life course and faily transitions in an urban Afro-American community. *Journal of Marriage and the Family, 54,* 239–248.

Kalichman, S. C., Kelly, J. S., Hunter, T. L., Murphy, D. A., & Tyler, R. (1993). Culturally tailored HIV/AIDS risk reduction messages targeted to African-American urban women: Impact on risk sensitization and risk reduction. *Journal of Consulting and Clinical Psychology, 61,* 887–891.

Kerner, J. F., Dusenbury, L., & Mandelblatt, J. S. (1993). Poverty and cultural diversity: Challenges for health promotion among the medically underserved. *Annual Review of Public Health, 14,* 355–377.

Kluckhohn, C., & Strodbeck, F. L. (1961). *Variations in value orientations.* Westport, CT: Greenwood Press.

Kotler, P. (1975). *Marketing for nonprofit organizations.* Englewood Cliffs: Prentice Hall.

Kotler, P., & Zaltman, G. (1971). Social marketing: An approach to planned social change. *Journal of Marketing, 35,* 3–12.

Lefebvre, R. C., & Flora, J. A. (1988). Social marketing and public health intervention. *Health Education Quarterly, 15*(3), 299–315.

Ling, J. C., Franklin, B. A. K., Lindsteadt, J. F., & Gearon, A. N. (1992). Social marketing: Its place in public health. *Annual Review of Public Health, 13,* 341–362.

Lonner, W. J., & Sundberg, N. D. (1985). Assessment in cross-cultural counseling and therapy. In P. Pedersen (Ed.), *Handbook of cross-cultural counseling and therapy* (pp. 199–205). Westport, CT: Greenwood Press.

Manfredi, C., Lacey, L., Warnecke, R., & Buis, M. (1992). Smoking-related behavior, beliefs, and social environment of young Black women in subsidized public housing in Chicago. *American Journal of Public Health, 82*(2), 267–272.

Manoff, R. K. (1985). *Social marketing: New imperative for public health.* New York: Praeger.

Marin, G., & Marin, B. V. (1990). Perceived credibility of chanels and sources of AIDS information among Hispanics. *AIDS Education and Prevention, 2*(2), 156–163.

Marin, G., & Marin, B. V. (1991). *Research with Hispanic populations.* Newbury Park, CA: Sage.

Marin, G., Marin, B. V., Perez-Stable, E. J., Sabogal, R., & Otero-Sabogal, R. (1990). Changes in information as a function of a culturally appropriate smoking cessation community intervention for Hispanics. *American Journal of Community Psychology, 18*(6), 847–864.

Markova, L., & Power, K. (1992). Audience response to health messages about AIDS. In T. Edgar, M. A. Fitzpatrick, & V. S. Freimuth (Eds.), *AIDS: A communication perspective* (pp. 111–130). Hillsdale, NJ: Lawrence Erlbaum Associates.

Mays, V. M. (1989). AIDS prevention in Black populations: Methods of a safer kind. In V. M. Mays, G. W. Albee, & S. F. Schneider (Eds.), *Primary prevention of AIDS: Psychological approaches* (pp. 264–79). Newbury Park: Sage.

Mays, V. M., & Cochran, S. D. (1988). Interpretation of AIDS risk and risk reduction activities by Black and Hispanic women. *American Psychologist, 43*, 949–957.

Mays, V. M., & Cochran, S. D. (1989). Methodological issues in the assessment and prediction of AIDS risk-related sexual behavior among Black Americans. In B. Voeller, M. Gottlieb, & J. Reinisch (Eds.), *AIDS and sex: An integrated biomedical and biobehavioral approach.* New York: Oxford University Press.

Michal-Johnson, P., & Bowen, S. P. (1992). The place of culture in HIV education. In T. Edgar, M. A. Fitzpatrick, & V. S. Freimuth (Eds.), *AIDS: A communication perspective* (pp. 147–172). Hillsdale, NJ: Lawrence Erlbaum Associates.

Modell, J. (1989). *Into one's own: From youth to adulthood in the United States 1920–1975.* Berkeley: University of California Press.

Murphy, P. E. (1984). Analyzing markets. In L. W. Fredrickson, L. J. Solomon, & K. A. Brehony (Eds.), *Marketing health behavior: Principles, techniques and applications.* New York: Plenum.

Neighbors, H. W., & Jackson, J. S. (1984). The use of informal help: Four patterns of illness behavior in the Black community. *American Journal of Community Psychology, 12*, 629–644.

Nickens, H. W. (1990). *Health promotion and disease prevention among minorities.* Health Affairs, Summer, 133–143.

Nobles, W. W. (1985). Back to the roots: African culture as a basis for understanding Black families. In W. W. Nobles (Ed.), *Africanity and the Black family: The development of a theoretical model.* Berkeley, CA: The Institute for the Advanced Study of Black Family Life and Culture.

Novelli, W. D. (1984). Developing marketing programs. In L. W. Frederiksen, L. J. Solomon, & K. A. Brehony (Eds.), *Marketing health behavior: Principles, techniques and applications* (pp. 59–89). New York: Plenum.

Ogbu, J. U. (1985). A cultural ecology of competence among inner-city Blacks. In M. B. Spencer, G. K. Brookins, & W. R. Allen (Eds.), *Beginnings: The social and affective development of Black children* (pp. 45–66). Hillsdale, NJ: Lawrence Erlbaum Associates.

Ogbu, J. U. (1988, May). *Minority youths' school success.* Invited presentation at a Conference on School/College Collaboration, Johns Hopkins University, Baltimore, MD.

Olmeda, E. L., & Padilla, A. M. (1978). Measure of acculturation for Chicano adolescents. *Psychological Reports, 42*, 159–170.

Ponterotto, J. G. (1988). Racial/ethnic minority research in the *Journal of Counseling Psychology*: A content analysis and methodological critique. *Journal of Counseling Psychology, 35*(4), 410–418.

Portes, A., & Zhou, M. (1994). *The new second generation: Segmented assimilation and its variants among post-1965 immigrant youth.* Baltimore, MD: Johns Hopkins University Press.

Prochaska, J. O., & DiClemente, C. C. (1983). States and processes of self-change of smoking: Toward an integrative model of change. *Journal of Consulting and Clinical Psychology, 51*, 390–395.

Richardson, V. (1990). At-risk programs: Evaluation and critical inquiry. In K. Sirotnik (Ed.), *Evaluation and social justice: Issues in public education* (pp. 61–75). New Directions for Program Evaluation No. 45. San Francisco: Jossey-Bass.

Rossi, S. R., Rossie, J. S., Rossi-DelPrete, L. M., Prochaska, J. O., Banspach, S. W., & Carleton, R. A. (1994). A processes of change model for weight control for participants in community-based weight loss programs. *International Journal of the Addictions, 29*, 161–177.

Schooler, C., Flora, J. A., & Farquhar, J. W. (1993). Moving toward syngery: Media supplementation in the Stanford Five-City Project. *Communication Research, 20*, 587–610.

Servaes, J. (1989). Cultural identity and modes of communication. In J. A. Anderson (Ed.), *Communication yearbook* (Vol. 12, pp. 386–434). Newbury Park, CA: Sage.

Shweder, R. A., & Sullivan, M. A. (1993). Cultural psychology: Who needs it? *Annual Review of Psychology, 44,* 497–523.

Singer, M. (1991). Confronting the AIDS epidemic among IV drug users: Does ethnic culture matter? *AIDS Education and Prevention, 3,* 258–283.

Skinner, C. S., Strecher, V. J., & Hospers, H. (1994). Physicians' recommendations for mammography: Do tailored messages make a difference? *American Journal of Public Health, 84,* 43–49.

Slaughter, D. T., & Epps, E. G. (1987). The home environment and academic achievement of Black American children and youth: An overview. *Journal of Negro Education, 56,* 3–20.

Smitherman-Donaldson, G. (1977). *Talkin and Testifyin: The language of Black America.* Boston: Houghton Mifflin.

Snow, L. F. (1978). Sorcerers, saints and charlatans: Black folk healers in urban America. *Culture, Medicine and Psychiatry, 2,* 69–106.

Thomas, S. B., & Quinn, S. C. (1991). The Tuskagee syphilis study, 1932–1972: Implications for HIV education and AIDS risk education programs in the Black community. *American Journal of Public Health, 81*(11), 1498–1505.

Triandis, H. C. (1972). *The analysis of subjective culture.* New York: Wiley.

Triandis, H. C., Marin, G., Lisansky, J., & Betancourt, H. (1984). Simpatia as a cultural script of Hispanics. *Journal of Personality and Social Psychology, 47,* 1363–1375.

Trotter, R. T. II (1990). The cultural parameters of lead poisoning: A medical anthropologist's view of intervention in environmental lead exposure. *Environmental Health Perspective, 89,* 79–84.

Tucker, C. (1992). Can America salvage the hip-hop generation? *San Francisco Chronicle,* June 12, A29.

U.S. Bureau of the Census. (1984a). *American Indian areas and Alaska native villages, 1980* (Supplementary Report PC 80-51-13). Washington, DC: U.S. Government Printing Office.

U.S. Bureau of the Census. (1984b). *A statistical profile of the American Indian population: 1980 census.* Washington, DC: U.S. Government Printing Office.

U.S. Department of Health and Human Services (1986). *Report of the Secretary's task force on Black and minority health* (Vol. 4, Pt. 1). Washington, DC: Government Printing Office.

Valdiserri, R. O., Lyter, D. W., Leviton, L. C., Callahan, C. M., Kingsley, L. A., & Rinaldo, C. R. (1989). AIDS prevention in homosexual and bisexual men: Results of a randomized trial evaluating two risk reduction interventions. *Current Science, 3,* 21–26.

Vega, W. A., Zimmerman, R. S., Warheit, G. J., Apospori, E., & Gil, A. G. (1993). Risk factors for early adolescent drug use in four ethnic and racial groups. *American Journal of Public Health, 83*(2), 185–189.

Weinstein, A. (1987). *Market segmentation: Using demographics, psychographics and other segmentation techniques to uncover and exploit new markets.* Chicago: Probus.

Weinstein, N. (1987, October). *Perceptions of risk.* Paper presented at the Centers for Disease Control Conference on Behavioral Aspects of High Risk Sexual Behavior, Atlanta.

Wells, K. B., Golding, J. M., Hough, R. L., Burnam, M. A., & Karno, M. (1989). Acculturation and the probability of use of health services by Mexican Americans. *Health Services Research, 24,* 237–256.

Wilkinson, D. Y., & King, G. (1987). Conceptual and methodological issues in the use of race as a variable: Policy implications. *Milbank Quarterly, 65,* 57–71.

Williams, J. E. (1992). Using social marketing to understand racially, ethnically, and culturally diverse audiences for public health interventions. In D. M. Becker, D. R. Hill, J. S. Jackson, D. M. Levine, F. A. Stillman, & S. M. Weiss (Eds.), *Health behavior research in minority populations: Access, design, and implementation* (pp. 122–129). Washington, DC: National Institutes of Health.

Wilson, M. N. (1986). The Black extended family. *Developmental Psychology, 22,* 246–258.

Windahl, S., & Signitzer, B., with Olsen, J. (1992). *Using communication theory: An introduction to planned communication.* Newbury Park, CA: Sage.

Winett, R. A. (1995). A framework for health promotion and disease prevention programs. *American Psychologist, 50,* 341–350.

Zuckerman, M. (1990). Some dubious premises in research and theory on racial differences: Scientific, social, and ethical issues. *American Psychologist, 45*(12), 1297–1303.

Chapter 21

Advertising and Its Role in Organ Donation

Jeffrey Prottas
Brandeis University

BACKGROUND

American law—in fact, the law in all Western nations—forbids the buying and selling of human organs and tissue (although there are limited exceptions in the United States for certain blood products). In addition, federal and state laws require that families of potential tissue and organ donors be given the option to donate when the deceased is medically suitable. This is called *required request.*

In combination, these laws make organ and tissue donation ideal candidates for social marketing and advertising. The supply of transplantable tissue is a function of the number of families asked to donate and the number of those asked who agree. Required request laws are a partial answer to the problem of ensuring that all suitable families are asked. Although practice falls far short of theory, these laws, and the intensive efforts of organ procurement organizations (OPOs) to motivate medical professionals, aim to increase the number of families asked.

But there remains the issue of motivating families to answer affirmatively. The families cannot be offered any material incentive whatsoever. Appeals to them must be on an ethical and social plane. This is a natural environment for social marketing.

It is also important to understand that it is the donor's family that must be persuaded. Here practice departs from law. In law, individuals may determine how their organs are to be disposed of after death by completing a simple organ donor card (Uniform Anatomical Gift Act). In most states, these cards are routinely distributed along with driver's licenses. However, the universal practice is not to act based on these cards. Next of kin are invariably asked to allow a donation. Pro-donation advertising, therefore, should be aimed at survivors in a family.

Therefore, it appears that advertising's place in the organ and tissue procurement process is clear and, perhaps, central. Every family contains a potential donor—with the partial exception of the old. A fatal accident, a stroke, or other unpredictable medical catastrophe is the sin qua non of donation and this could happen to anyone at any time. Therefore, if the families of potential donors are to be contacted prior to entering the hospital, virtually every family qualifies and mass media advertising is the obvious and traditional method of communicating under these circumstances.

There is also a strong justification for contacting families before the tragedy. The horrible stress and pain that comes with the sudden death of a family member is not the best time to introduce a new idea regarding ways to utilize parts of the human body. Prior knowledge and preparation can be a kindness to the family and an aid to the procurement process.

Yet, despite these favorable circumstances, there are serious problems facing pro-donation advertising. These problems only emerge when more specific and less generic issues are raised. Advertising ought to have a productive role in organ donation. But, when examining the characteristics of the populations meant to be influenced, the nature of the message being sent, and the cost-effectiveness balance, it is not quite so clear that it can contribute as much as might be expected.

GOALS OF ADVERTISING

The problem starts with the confusion regarding the purposes of advertising (although some might argue that the lack of agreement and clarity as to goals embolizes rather than underlies the problem). In the organ procurement community, advertising and related social marketing efforts are routinely referred to as "public education." This reflects a widespread belief that the goal of these efforts is, in fact, to inform the public about organ transplantation and organ donation. The rationale is that the public, under the law, has a right to decide to donate or to refuse and that individuals ought to be given enough information to make that decision. The expectation is, of course, that when provided with information about the benefits of transplantation, most people would agree to donate.

With this as the goal, the measure of both the need for, and the success of, advertising is the amount and distribution of accurate information about transplantation and donation.

The competing view is that advertising ought to persuade rather than inform. This somewhat more focused and utilitarian approach suggests that the need for advertising is a function of the percentage of families that refuse to permit an organ donation. It also suggests that success ought to be demonstrated by, at the least, an increase in permission rates and, possibly, by an actual increase in donor supply.

In practice, organ donation advertising has lighted on a rather odd and somewhat self-serving compromise. In content it seeks to persuade. Ads convey a strong message that donation is morally and socially good. In terms of formal goals and evaluation criteria, it adheres more closely to the public education model, although among the more sophisticated, one important modification has occurred. Increasingly, family discussion has become an important formal goal of public education. This takes the public education model beyond its core (and retained) aim of merely informing. However, it stops short of expecting advertising to improve organ supply.

Organ donors are dead, so it is too late to ascertain individual preferences once the body is at the hospital. There is data (Prottas & Batten, 1991; Partnership for Organ Donation, 1993) to support the belief that when family members know the deceased wished to donate they are more likely to grant permission. This fact has made encouraging family discussion of organ donation a central goal of current advertising.

It also provides a useful bridge between a purely educational and a persuasive orientation. It is within the public education paradigm in that its goal is to encourage discussion and therefore spread knowledge within the family of attitudes and facts. On the other hand, it goes further toward inducing action—or, at least, talk—rather then simply to imparting knowledge. This action has some reasonable connection to donation decisions themselves but avoids the expectation that advertising actually be evaluated in terms of donation or permission rates.

From the point of view of public institutions, it is impossible to justify informing the American people about transplantation as an end in itself. Advertising in organ procurement is overwhelmingly funded via organ procurement organizations and the United Network for Organ Sharing. These organizations are supported primarily by federal money allocated under the End-Stage Renal Disease Program (ESRD). The ESRD program treats those with renal failure and supports transplantation as a method of doing so. It has no mandate to educate, enlighten, or otherwise improve the American public; it spends its organ procurement money to obtain transplantable organs. The public benefit of more knowledge regarding transplantation is negligible unless it leads to more transplants. Therefore, a serious evaluation of the role of advertising must be in terms of its impact on donation rates.

STATE OF THE "MARKET" FOR ORGAN DONATION

A great deal is known about what the American people feel and know about organ donation. If advertising is to have a positive impact on permissions and donation, this information must be incorporated into its message and media strategies. Much of these data is encouraging. The public is supportive of donation and transplantation and sees organ donation as socially desirable and as a help to the families of donors themselves. This is fertile ground for persuasion; indeed, there may be certain excess of riches here.

General Attitudes and Willingness

The American public hardly needs to be persuaded that organ donation is a good thing. About 85% of the public strongly supports organ donation. And, about as many people as support organ donation overall believe that organ donation helps a family deal with grief (Prottas & Batten, 1991). These figures reflect the two motifs of public support for organ donation. One is "simple" altruism. Donation is seen as morally positive because it helps others. Even people who would not permit a donation agree that organ donation is morally good (Prottas & Batten, 1991). At the same time, the public believes that organ donation is of some help to the donor family itself. Between 60% and 80% of those surveyed respond that they think donation helps a family with its grieving process and it also lessens the pain the family feels (Partnership for Organ Donation, 1993; Batten & Prottas, 1987). These attitudes are a more complex form of altruism in that the public sees a psychological benefit in kind behavior.

Most of the public also expresses a willingness to donate their own organs. Depending on the survey itself, between two thirds and 80% of the public say they would permit the donation of their own organs (Prottas & Batten, 1991; "Gallup Poll Survey," 1993, p. 14). The most recent national survey was funded by an organization active in promoting organ donation and it reported the lower figure.

This survey and this figure provide an interesting example of the educational as opposed to the marketing orientation of much of the work in this field. In general, public attitude surveys of this sort measure the willingness to donate of the entire population. However, most older people believe they are not suitable organ donors on medical grounds and so, quite reasonably, do not express an intention to donate. When data are disaggregated by age, a 13 to 19 percentage point difference is found between population averages and attitudes of those over 55 years of age (Prottas & Batten, 1991; Partnership for Organ Donation, 1993). The two thirds figure may therefore be a significant underestimation of the willingness to donate among eligible persons.

Preliminary Actions

Moving beyond attitudes, there are two closely related actions that people may take that reflect a willingness to donate. One is simply discussing the matter with their family; the other is signing organ donor cards. As almost all donor cards require a witness and, in most cases, family members are the witnesses, these two actions overlap. Certainly they are meant to. Whereas an organ donor card is a binding legal document, it is never used as a ground for donation. In the first case, standard hospital practices mean that doctor and OPO staff virtually never see the patients' personal property. Moreover, social norms strongly support the right of the family to make a donation decision and so, even in the presence of a signed card, families are asked. Therefore, a signed donor card is relevant only if the family knows about it.

Depending on one's expectations, a surprisingly large or disappointingly smaller percentage of people have discussed their wishes with their families and/or have signed donor cards. Estimates of the number who have signed cards run from about 25% to 30%, and 45% to 50% of the public have discussed their preference with their family ("Gallup Poll Survey," 1993).

Segmentation of the Market

As with virtually everything else in the United States, race matters in organ donation attitudes. On every measure of support for organ donation African Americans are less supportive than White Americans (included are such factors as: general support, willingness to donate one own organs, having discussed donation with one family) (Prottas & Batten, 1991; "Gallup Poll Survey," 1993). To a lesser degree, the same pattern can be seen with regard to Spanish surnamed Americans. Class also matters. When either education or income is used, there is an independent effect of class on donation support. Richer, better educated Americans are more supportive (Prottas & Batten, 1991).

On a practical level, demographic data can be helpful in suggesting what population ought to be targeted, but they are only indicators of differences. They do not explain the nature and source of the differences. Nor should the statistical difference across groups obscure the fact that even among the less supportive support is very high.

A more useful segmentation of the market can be found at the level of willingness to donate a relative's organs and the reasons given for that willingness or unwillingness. It is of more practical importance to understand a person's willingness to donate the organs of their next of kin than to measure their willingness to donate their own organs. Legal formalism notwithstanding, no one ever donates their own organs. (Except, of course, for the living donation of a kidney to a relative.)

In terms of attitudes, the population can be divided into three unequal groups. One group is strongly supportive of donation and has decided to allow it if the issue arises. This group represents 45% to 50% of the population. Another group is extremely uncomfortable with organ donation and would not permit it even if their kin had expressed a willingness. This group represents about 20% of the population. Finally, there is a "swing" group. They are hesitant to donate but, at least on a survey, will change their refusal to donate to an agreement after being provided additional information (Prottas & Batten, 1991).

The reasons each group gives for its decision have implications for the way advertising can be used in support of organ donation. The reasons people give for their willingness to donate have already been alluded to: a desire to help others and a desire to make something positive come out of tragedy (Batten & Prottas, 1987). But, if advertising is to increase permission rates, then it must speak not to those already willing but to those not willing. Reasons for refusal are therefore more immediately important.

These reasons fall into three broad categories. The most common reason given is "I wouldn't want my family member to suffer any more" (63% of respondents). The fourth most common reason is fear that doctors will not try to save a relative if they are an organ donor (46%). Because the dead cannot suffer, these two reasons express the same mistrust of the medical profession and fear for a relative's well-being (Prottas & Batten, 1991).

The second most common reason for an intention to refuse is a sense that the donation process itself is complicated (60%). This reflects both lack of information (the family role in donation is extraordinarily simple) and a degree of alienation and mistrust of medicine-related institutions.

Finally, the third most frequently given reason for refusal is discomfort with the idea of bodily disfigurement of a relative (48%). In addition, substantial portions of those with doubts about donation say that it is against their religion or that other members of their family would object. As no major American religious group objects to organ donation, all these reasons seem to reflect a diffuse distaste for conducting major surgery on a dead body.

IMPLICATIONS FOR ADVERTISING

Taken together, these facts about environment and target populations imply that advertising efforts in favor of organ donation faces three general challenges:

1. It must formulate a message that speaks to the concerns of those now unwilling to give without alienating those already willing to do so.

2. It must overcome the immense psychological distance between the circumstances in which advertising is heard and actual donation decision is made.

3. It must address the cost-effectiveness problem that flows from the very small number of potential donors that become available each year.

Tailoring Messages

If permission rate increases are the test of advertising success, then the proper target of ads are those who do not presently intend to donate. To influence these people, their concerns must be addressed. Nondonors do not reject the moral or social worth of donation, they simply do not find that worth sufficient cause to plan to donate. Their fears for the well-being of the kin and their concern regarding the donation process must be addressed if their willingness is to be increased.

Addressing these concerns is not easy. It is difficult to craft a message to reassure a family that organ donation does not place a patient at risk without acknowledging that this possibility exists, at least theoretically. Moreover, if speaking to the fears of non-donors raises fears among those willing to donate, then this is a bad bargain.

About 60% of families now approached agree to permit a donation. Half of the entire population expresses a willingness to do so on surveys. (Law notwithstanding, not all families are asked for permission. The 60% rate is therefore from a preselected population.) About 20% of those surveyed are strongly opposed and probably cannot—and maybe, ought not—be persuaded. If increasing permission rates among the remaining 30% raises fears among the presently donating population, then the net outcome in terms of donor supply is not likely to be very helpful.

Even more daunting is the possibility that the fears expressed reflect deeply rooted and more broadly applicable mistrust and alienation. A concern that being an organ donor will compromise medical treatment is deeply cynical and shocking. It suggests a perception of the medical system as alien, hostile, and exploitative. It assumes that a hospital and its doctors would sacrifice your relative to help unspecified and unidentified other patients. Yet, more than a quarter of all those surveyed expressed these sorts of fears; more than half of those who said they would not permit a donation gave this concern as a reason.

These reservations are strongly correlated with both race and income. It is more than possible that attitudes toward organ donation are consistent with an entire constellation of attitudes toward American institutions and that lack of support for organ donation merely reflects a more general sense of alienation, exclusion, and discrimination. The social facts underlying these attitudes are not illusionary.

If advertising is to hope to change anyone's willingness to grant permission, it must speak to people's fears. But, if these fears are tied to broader societal divisions and conflicts, then such efforts may have little chance of success. Organ donation occurs in large institutions. It is operated by White, middle-class professionals—the doctors and nurses in addition to the procurement professionals. It may be very hard to separate the mistrust of the context from the narrower concerns about the donation process itself.

Psychological Distance

The psychological distance between the circumstances under which an advertising message is heard and the circumstances under which an organ donation decision is made is unimaginable. Organ donation only occurs as a result of life-shattering tragedy. Donors are generally young and healthy, and their deaths are sudden and unaccepted. Imagine, if you dare, the death of your teenage son.

Although a little is known about who actually makes donation decisions and under what time constraints (Batten & Prottas, 1987), very little (almost nothing) is known about how such decisions are made. How are family dynamics worked out, who acts as opinion leader, what information has the greatest effect, what are the most trusted sources of information, what criteria are used, and so on? More is known about how families decide to buy refrigerators than about how they decide to allow an organ donation.

This ignorance does not mean that a message received from a television while sitting in the livingroom cannot have an effect. But, it does suggest that the relative effect of that message and the message received at the hospital at the time of the donation must be evaluated. Few organ donations are wholly spontaneous. Almost all families are approached by someone associated with the organ procurement system and asked for permission. This permission seeker is often trained to this role and has the assistance of nurses and doctors who may know the family and certainly know the specific circumstance of the tragedy.

It is widely and plausibly assumed that the request process has a more important affect on permission rate than the advertising process. It is also plausibly assumed that prior exposure to advertising facilitates the request process. But how it does so and to what degree is unknown. What part of the living room message carries into the emergency room? Who carries it and how do they share it? Ought the nature of the advertising message change if its goal is to facilitate the "sale" in the hospital after a tragedy rather then motivate action directly?

These are questions more complex than those now addressed in organ donation advertising. The circumstances of organ donation are such that decisions are made under extraordinary stress jointly by a family unit. The process of organ procurement is such that these decisions are made after and during consultations with medical personnel and with organ procurement specialists whose task it is to persuade families to permit donation.[1] Advertising, therefore, must contribute to a positive decision made under unusual and complex conditions. It may be able to do so, but instinct and rule of thumb—the dominate present planning tool—are unlikely to provide much guidance as to how.

Cost-effectiveness

Last year less than 5,000 people became organ donors. Using a 60% permission rate among those asked, this suggests that perhaps 3,500 families were asked and refused. If the role of advertising is to increase permission rates, then its target audience are these families.

The population of the nation is 262 million, representing just under 96 million households (U.S. Bureau of Census, 1995). The percentage of households that had a "opportunity" to donate and refused is therefore .0036%—one in almost 2.8 million. Contrast this to the targets of other public health advertising campaigns: 26% of American adults smoke, 24% have high blood pressure, and 20% have high cholesterol (Public Health Annual, 1994)

Even considered as a percentage of deaths, potential organ donation situations are very rare. Almost 3 million Americans died last year. No estimate of the number of donations suitable deaths places it above 26,000 (Bart et al., 1981) and many place it closer to half that (Nathan et al., 1991). The highest estimate suggests that one death in 11,500 might be medically appropriate to be a donor.

Of course, it's true that the impact of an advertising message does not need to be limited to the year it is heard, and so the number of families refusing in any given year is an understatement of the useful recipients of the pro-donation message. Nevertheless, any consideration of the role of advertising in support of organ donation must take cognizance of the extraordinary rarity of the "opportunity" for organ donation—along with the fact that a large majority already permit donation when asked.

CONCLUSIONS

For amateurs, social marketing and particularly social advertising is easy. One identifies what the public ought to know, tells them, and with this knowledge they act in their own or the public interest. Professionals find the task more difficult. It is hard to get the public's attention, harder to

---

[1] I say "persuade" advisedly—despite the myth that the process only offers a choice. After all, families are approached by employees of the organ *procurement* system.

persuade them of the importance of your message, and harder yet to induce them to change behavior.

Unfortunately, there are no professionals in advertising for organ donation. The core players—organ procurement organizations and their associations and hangers-on—know how to work within hospitals, how to deal one on one with families, and how to move organs from city to city. They lack both formal training and years of experience in social marketing. When they turn to marketing professionals—usually advertising firms—they add an additional kind of ignorance to the mix. When the people they hire are good, they turn to successful models of social advertising for guidance—blood pressure screening, smoking cessation campaigns, and so on. These models provide not an iota of useful information because they lack any overlap in target population, behavioral goals, or knowledge base. There is probably more to be learned in examining why childless couples vote for school bond issues or in discovering why people buy life insurance.

It is impossible to know just why advertising in organ donation is done in such an unsystematic, not to say frivolous, way. But, in fact, one would not undertake to sell soap with so little analysis of the populations targeted, their wants, and how they make decisions. In organ donation, advertising is essentially only a sideline for everyone involved. Perhaps it is partly the result of a suspicion, even among its proponents, that "public education" is of little real use to organ donation programs.

If this is the reason, then they do themselves a disservice. It is quite possible that advertising cannot play a useful role in organ donation programs. It is probable that it cannot play more than a secondary role. But, it is certain that it has never been given a reasonable chance because there has never been a systematic analysis of the problems and a professional approach to their solution. These efforts might lead to the conclusion that little is to be hoped for from advertising, but perhaps well-targeted and skillfully crafted efforts can bring returns.

Ironically, for those convinced that advertising cannot contribute the present system is not so very bad. Present efforts harm no one, and if no real good can come of this advertising, then all that is lost is a relatively small amount of money. However, for those who think there is a contribution to be made, the present system is quite destructive because it preempts better approaches. And without vastly improved, far more sophisticated programs, the intellectual and practical shortcomings of organ donation advertising are probably fatal to this continued funding; indeed, without improvement they certainly should be fatal.

REFERENCES

Bart, K. et al. (1981). Cadaveric kidney for transplantation. *Transplantation, 31*(5), 379–382.
Batten, H., & Prottas, J. (1987). Kind strangers: The families of organ donors. *Health Affairs, 16*(2, Summer).

Centers for Disease Control. (1995). *Monthly Vital Statistics Report, 441*(July 26).

Gallup poll survey on organ donation confirms mistrust among minorities. (1993). *Nephrology News and Issues,* June.

Nathan, H. et al. (1991). Estimation and characteristics of the potential renal organ donor pool in Pennsylvania. *Transplantation, 51,* 148–149.

Partnership for Organ Donation. (1993, February). *The American public's attitudes toward organ donation and transplantation.* Boston: Author.

Prottas, J., & Batten, H. (1986). *Attitudes and incentives in organ procurement.* U.S. Government Report to HCFA. Heller Graduate School working paper, Brandeis University, Waltham, MA.

Prottas, J., & Batten, H. (1991). The willingness to give: The public and the supply of transplantable organs. *Journal of Health Politics, Policy and Law, 16*(1), 121–134.

Public Health Annual. (1994). Washington, DC.

U.S. Bureau of the Census. (1995). *Census and You, 30*(4, April).

Chapter 22

Hippocrates to Hermes:
The Postmodern Turn
in Public Health Advertising

Jerome B. Kernan
Teresa J. Domzal
George Mason University

ABSTRACT

Medicine is becoming a fragmented cultural phenomenon, no longer controlled by sacralized physicians who dictate the meanings of health and sickness. The social sciences have come to influence people's sense of wellness—both the private behaviors sufficient to its achievement and the public conditions necessary for its maintenance. As a result, Hermes (the god of science and commerce) is replacing Hippocrates as the dominant public health metaphor and advertising—the literature of consumption—is beginning to reflect this postmodern transformation in how the human body is construed and its well-being is negotiated. Using public health ads from around the world, this chapter illustrates several markers of postmodernism to highlight how the public discourse over wellness is changing and to demonstrate that contemporary advertising is accommodating this revised health dialogue. Apart from portraying public health campaigns in practice, these examples suggest some strategic guidelines for social marketing programs under the nascent postmodern condition.

Medicine's traditional grand narrative has collapsed. Family doctors, corner drugstores, and community hospitals have given way to exclusive specialists, supermarket pharmacies, and technology-driven medical centers. Third-party payers—both public and private sector—have wrested control of the treatment process from patients while the cost, efficacy, and fairness of the system is debated in a seemingly endless struggle at reform.

Yet, excepting Third World populations, which remain threatened by the natural forces of famine, malnutrition, and disease, contemporary societies' health problems are largely self-imposed. With little material scarcity and a good deal of personal freedom, human beings have developed bad living habits and these have become the principal sources of their morbidity and mortality—as if to reify Eckholm's (1977) claim that each society, in producing its own way of life, produces its own way of death. Our "freedom to be foolish" (Leichter, 1991) also politicizes virtually everything associated with medicine and health care. As regards public health, this has come to implicate advertising, because persuasion is seen as preferable to legislation. Some healthful behaviors are simply too intimate to enforce, so people can only be coaxed to practice them (e.g., safe sex). Other breaches (e.g., environmental pollution) can be punished, but only after the damage has occurred, so it is wiser to induce attitudes that discourage such behaviors.

Advertising has come to be used in the service of both private and public behaviors thought conducive to health. The former is illustrated by encouragements for people to adopt diets low in saturated fats, whereas the latter is exemplified by ads warning of the dangers of secondary cigarette smoke. Although such efforts reflect conscientious attempts to bolster a society's public health quotient, they are not without controversy simply by force of their prescriptive nature. People dislike restrictions to their freedoms and it is easy for them to discount the credibility of such messages, particularly in a pluralistic society. *Hegemony*, controlling the dialogue surrounding an issue, is a prominent idea in postmodernism and there is no reason to suppose that medicine is immune from this condition. Thus, there is debate over advertisements (or any programs) that tell people how to live. (According to whose rules?) Some people hold a conviction that their most intimate possession is their body and they, and no one else (certainly not government bureaucrats), should control it. Doctors are still respected for their technical knowledge, but they have lost much in public esteem and they no longer command the moral high ground. As a consequence, the metaphor for medicine is shifting, from one represented by the benevolent Hippocrates to one characterized by Hermes (the god of science and commerce), all to reflect the fragmented aegis and negotiable condition of what constitutes health and well-being. (The caduceus, with its intertwined snakes, poses an interesting semiotic challenge.) This transformation is a complicated story whose details are beyond the scope of this chapter, but whose occurrence is important to note because contemporary public health advertising cannot be understood apart from the metamorphosis that has affected medicine since World War II.

The primary purpose of this chapter is to illustrate how advertising is used in the service of public health. (By implication, this exposition also reveals lessons for social marketing programs in general.) To accomplish this purpose, however, the phenomena that underscore the contemporary sense of health in general and public health in particular need to be highlighted; the setting in which public health ads operate must be portrayed. This setting is (or is rapidly becoming) one characterized by postmodernism and this backdrop produces some "strange" results—both in the kinds of ads that serve a public health purpose and in their execution styles—so this chapter goes to some length to explain how all this has come about. It begins by reviewing the current conception of health and health care. This is followed by a discussion of the human body and how the social sciences have influenced people to regard it in novel ways. These newer ways of thinking are then related to the phenomenon of postmodernism; in particular, the traditional (modernist) view of life is contrasted with the developing postmodernist conception. It then shows where advertising fits into this newer way of thinking, using contemporary public health ads from around the world. The chapter concludes by suggesting some elements of a "logic" of persuasion to which social marketing programs under conditions of postmodernism might pay heed.

IN SICKNESS AND IN HEALTH

Patrick Henry's disclaimer notwithstanding, most people regard life as absolutely precious. It is just presumed (or hoped) that living implies existence with faculties intact—that people are able to think and do according to genetic requirements, absent threat. This is another way of observing that health is one of life's axial elements. Death is acceptable in the absence of health (e.g., when the terminally ill "have suffered enough"), but otherwise life represents a struggle to maintain health. It goes without saying that this is a consummately important topic.

Generally speaking, humans have overcome the world's other predatory species (wars, ethnic cleansings, and urban violence are another issue) and food/clothing/shelter requirements are not problematic, except in parts of the Third World where the natural forces of disease, malnutrition, and weather still pose real threats. Such health problems are largely expected. Everyone is familiar with the litany—human beings eat poor diets, live sedentary lives, and pollute their bodies with all manner of toxicity. They compete rather than cooperate with their neighbors—sometimes to the point of physical aggression—and most worry too much. In consequence, both private and public health have evolved into expansive concerns; collectively, they have become a significant index of what is regarded as quality of life or well-being.

None of this is a revelation. Policymakers, scientists, caregivers, and ordinary citizens hear about these issues every day; indeed, health has become a major theme in virtually all mass media. What is noteworthy is the massive scope of "the health problem" and how it is coming to implicate so many sectors of society. Health is no longer regarded simply as the absence of sickness; the progressive construal is one of "wellness," which includes physical, mental, emotional, and social facets. People are no longer content with curing sickness; prevention has become the imperative and this dictates both individual and collective responsibilities (to care for oneself and not to prevent others from doing likewise). Finally, concern has evolved into a populist stance arguing that every member of society is entitled to wellness, including those unable to fend for themselves (e.g., fetuses, the halt, the indigent), on the premise that this is both morally proper and otherwise prudent (one person's problem eventually becomes everyone's problem; prevention is less costly than cure, etc.).

The notion of wellness has been portrayed in many models, some descriptive (e.g., Downie, Fyfe, & Tannahill, 1990; Elder, Geller, Hovell, & Mayer, 1994; Evans & Stoddart, 1990; Reinhardt, 1988; Simmons, 1993; Smith & Wesley, 1993; Spector, 1993), others prescriptive (e.g., Baltes, 1976; Bulger, 1988; Freund, 1982; U.S. Public Health Service, 1990; Winett, 1995). Moreover, health conscious segments of consumers have been identified (e.g., Bloch, 1984; Kraft & Goodell, 1993) and there is no dearth of formulae for reaching them as well as their less enthusiastic counterparts (e.g., Block & Keller, 1995; Flora, Maibach, & Maccoby, 1989; Wallack, Dorfman, Jernigan, & Themba, 1993). However, in spite of the social significance of wellness, in spite of the "health industry" being one of the world's largest, well-being is not necessarily enhanced by maximizing prevention and care. There are two reasons why. First, care comes at a cost. This can be regarded as an investment, but even in this sense it must be compared with the worth of alternative investments. (Societal resources devoted to health cannot be devoted to education, for example.) Second, health provision (especially public health provision) can be intrusive and people often prefer individual freedoms to a collective mandate, particularly when the issue is controversial (e.g., flouridated water supplies, passive seat belts). Public health also generates extraordinary passions—and reactance—when it is perceived to be influenced by "marginal lifestyles" (e.g., homosexuality) or to be driven by sanctimony (the rantings of zealots). For these reasons, then, wellness is something to be optimized, in full recognition of its inherent political overtones.

Just as populists argue that education should never be left to educators, many people have come to believe that health is too important to be left to the medical establishment. By and large, doctors no longer hold patients' unequivocal trust; treatment, as well as prevention, is becoming a matter of negotiation and there are many players in the drama. In the United States, this is occurring not only because the traditional population of patients is challenging established rites of medical practice but also as a result of the increase (to some 20%) in the nation's minority populations, whose ethnicities often favor nontraditional prevention and treatment rites (i.e., those not European in origin). As noted earlier, this flux suggests that health should no longer be imagined as a centralized or top-down didactic controlled by a benevolent Hippocrates, but as a multifaceted dialogue, more appropriately portrayed by Hermes (the god of science and commerce). This is where advertising enters the picture. Because persuasion has become part and parcel of the health dialogue, ads are being used to coax consumers to (or not to) do this, that, or the other thing. Advertising is employed by governments, by advocacy/public interest groups, and by corporations— each to promote its particular path to health and well-being. (Some of these efforts are curious from a marketing perspective. For instance, many hospitals and physicians have taken to consumer advertising as a means of promoting their business. Such service-for-fee marketing assumes that target consumers have the latitude to choose their health care providers, however, and that arrangement is likely to dwindle rapidly over the next several years as managed-care programs severely limit such latitude, perhaps usurp it entirely from their subscribing members. As third party payers become more prominent in health care provision, then, the focus of providers' advertising is likely to shift from consumers to those agencies that manage, which is to say control, their care. A diminished consumer market for "superfluous" care—e.g., for cosmetic surgery or deluxe versions of traditional treatment— may remain, but such a remnant is likely to represent only a shard of the current advertising potential.) The totality of such ads produces something less than perfect harmony, of course, because their sponsors tout differing prescriptions for wellness. The fact remains, however, that there is no single source of "health advertising." The consumer might be just as influenced by an ad for an exercise bike (even though the sponsor's motive may be venal) as by one advocating annual physical exams. This is discussed further later, but it is important to establish at this point that the corpus of ads that function in the service of public health cannot be accessed merely by reference to a social marketing or similar index. Health issues cut across many categories of living, often emotionally charged ones (a reason health care reform proposals invariably become controversial), and they can involve life-and-death stakes. Most everyone wants a voice in such matters, so it should not be surprising that advertising is being used to state a variety of positions on and approaches to wellness. "In sickness and in health" may warn of the vagaries of marriage, but it also describes the conditions of daily living. Little wonder, then, that consumers enlist a variety of sources to negotiate their path to a sense of well-being, picking and choosing among them, and according privilege to none, save their own perceptions of what is right.

THE BODY: ALL IN YOUR MIND?

To emphasize the obvious, individuals' bodies are the nexus of all the dialogue concerning health. It is the body that needs nutrition, rest, and protection lest it succumb to disease, fatigue, or accident. It is the body that individuals exercise in the belief that a healthy body is an attractive one. And it is the body that serves as the ultimate artifact (Polhemus, 1988) in social cognition. (Try convincing teenagers that body piercing is something to be eschewed.) All this is a reminder that our corporality remains an obdurate fact—we are formed in the womb, transfigured during life, and then we die. As Frank (1991) noted, bodies can be developed and enhanced. Life can be protected and sustained, but human flesh is not infinitely renewable—everybody must contend with mortality. Thus, the idea of managing the body—of deploying it to impede morbidity and mortality—comes into play. There are many ways to do this (Domzal & Kernan, 1993b), some of them even based on an assumption of class-related bodies. Bourdieu (1984), for example, suggested that bodies are unfinished entities that become imprinted with distinct markings of social class—the result of an interaction among a person's location, habitus, and taste. In consequence, class-related body types and health practices develop. Working-class people regard their bodies as labor instruments, worrying that they will function effectively and accepting illness fatalistically, whereas the upper classes think of their corporality more as a project, actively pursuing its maintenance and trying all sorts of wellness schemes.

The notion of controlling the body is hardly novel; people do this as a matter of routine. In recent years, however, the social sciences have highlighted the extensiveness of body control in contemporary society and the fact that much of it is imposed. (To use the vernacular, individuals may be in touch with their bodies but they are hardly in control of them.) For example, a girl reared in Niagara Falls, NY, in the environs of Love Canal, has little control over her genetic development, given the resident pollution with which her body must contend. Similarly, soft-coal mining areas are not likely to produce adults with healthy lungs. One might enumerate a litany of such controls that technology can visit on people's bodies. Poverty has much the same effect. Poor children commonly experience malnutrition and inadequate health care; yet, this is hardly a condition they chose. Instead, their life chances are controlled by their socioeconomic condition. Even aesthetics are used to control people's bodies. "Overweight" individuals may or may not be somatically sound, but they will be made to feel disruptive, irresponsible, and unnatural for failing to conform to the culture's ideal body proportions. Similarly, the visual history of health and illness reveals a clear, palpable aesthetic divide: Healthy people are depicted as attractive and the ill are portrayed as ugly (Gilman, 1995). It is as though illness is to be avoided because sick people constitute a socio-logical "other." These are just some examples of how people's bodies (thus their health) can be controlled "from the outside." Such forces relegate the body to the status of an object, that is, something to be acted on. Yet, most individuals prefer to regard their bodies as subjects, that is, sentient agents that do the acting. And, the more individuals ponder this distinction, the more they resent being objectified. Insisting on a "negotiated" health dialogue is a way of resisting bodily objectification.

Health consumers' "standing up for their rights" reflects more than political correctness. Historically marginalized people (e.g., women, the disabled) are asserting themselves, but the fragmented nature of the con-temporary dialogue is largely the result of a pandemic recognition that body control has for too long been external and arbitrary. Virtually every-one now finds something about traditional wellness prescriptions with which to disagree; a one-size-fits-all assumption is no longer tenable. And the unrest is not confined to consumers; providers (hospitals, caregivers, drug and equipment suppliers), third party payers, even government agen-cies have expressed misgivings about a system that seems more concerned with order than with efficacy. Health has become a disputatious phenome-non because so many parties are staking proprietary claims on it. No one of these wants to yield to another's control, so evasion, resistance, and subversion have become common; in stark terms, this is a struggle over power. It is easy to recognize in its palpable forms (e.g., the tobacco industry versus the FDA), but a discord no less authentic resides in a variety of subtle forms as well. For example, whenever a talk show sensationalizes a bizarre health regimen, traditional medicine is undermined; people (per-haps only a few initially) are given one more reason to doubt established advice. Every time a poll (or one of those studies in the *New England Journal of Medicine* so dutifully reported by the TV networks) indicates that this, that, or some other behavioral fetish leads to a health advantage, some people are persuaded to try it for themselves. This may seem naive to the cognoscenti, but do not underestimate popular culture's ability to influence people, particularly when these media are perceived as the voice of ordinary folks, the oppressed, or the disadvantaged (Fiske, 1989).

People have an inerrant ability to sense when they are being pushed around, patronized, or otherwise taken for granted and the social sciences have appealed to such frustrations in recent years, particularly in the form of pop psychology and self-help books. Collectively, these epistles (and their accompanying notoriety) stand as a challenge to the medical establishment by suggesting that people not only can, but must, control their own bodies; otherwise, individuals will be precluded from the full measure of physical, mental, emotional, and social health that is their birthright. These popular texts find their grist in the newer (aka postmodern) social theories of health (e.g., Falk, 1994; Featherstone, Hepworth, & Turner, 1991; Foucault, 1975, 1979; Fox, 1994; Lupton, 1995; Shilling, 1993; Turner, 1984, 1987, 1992), which posit that the human body is not only physical but also social. The latter term denotes that the body's natural endowments are shaped by culture and, because that involves human interaction, corporality becomes a political issue—the target of control. Foucault used the analogy of institutionalized bodies (prison inmates, hospital patients) to illustrate that the mere observation of people is sufficient to control them. For example, an 18th-century prison layout advocated by Jeremy Bentham (the panopticon) takes its efficacy from the fact that inmates know only that they might be under watch and they come to discipline themselves out of this fear. Similarly, hospital patients behave in ways they otherwise would not because of the daily rounds made by physicians. In both these cases, an observational "gaze" controls people's behavior, but only because they are co-opted insidiously into their own surveillance. This gaze is effective because of its implied threat and, in this sense, body control is mind control. Foucault argued that such knowledge is power because it allows those so privileged to exert social control (he called it "discipline") over populations, which acquiesce because they have long since internalized the ideal of normalization (i.e., conformity, regulation). The purpose of such discipline is to render people docile, agreeable to the will of those seeking to control them. This is where hegemony arises. The medical establishment is accused of using its superior knowledge of the body to control the health dialogue (what constitutes sickness, treatment, cure, etc.) based on what is best for those who dominate society. Disputing the dialogue is therefore regarded as emancipating by postmodern theorists because it places the individual's rights to wellness over the entrenched comfort of society's power elite. The popular appeal of such ideology is inevitable, because it panders to everyone's sense of freedom and democracy. Indeed, the culture of consumption shifts some of the control of bodies away from traditional health care providers toward the receivers of that care.

So health is about the body, but that prized possession has taken on a multifaceted meaning. The corpus may be flesh, yet the concern is with a biopsychosocial phenomenon, to use Fox's (1994) description. The health dialogue is fragmented because people have come to think about their bodies in novel, nontraditional ways and to realize that well-being is very much a matter of controlling the body. The social sciences have eroded physicians' monopoly on medicine to the point where virtually everyone feels entitled to prescribe and dispute the path to wellness. The credibility of some of the missives (e.g., "brain-surgery-self-taught" manuals, health-related advertisements) may be discounted, but such a concatenation is very consistent with the postmodern condition. Ordinary people are influenced by the cumulative effect.

DIDACTIC AND DISCOURSE:
THE EMERGENCE OF POSTMODERNISM

The health dialogue described here reflects the condition called *postmodernism*, which is a slippery term supported by a vast, complicated literature. This chapter does not presume to explicate even a small portion of that; instead, it focuses on those features of the postmodern condition that underpin contemporary health issues and their apposite advertising.[1]

Postmodernism (postindustrialism, the information age) refers to a *cultural condition* (the setting or environment within which social, economic, and sundry thought and action take place), so it affects many facets of life. For example, there is postmodern art and architecture; postmodern literature, music, and philosophy; postmodern history, economics, and political science; and postmodern anthropology, psychology, and sociology. Each of these is represented by a dense literature, replete with argot couched in arcane writing, so the term is difficult to explicate. (For introductory treatments, see Brown, 1995; Hassan, 1987; Rosenau, 1992; or Van Raaij, 1993). It is helpful, however, to begin with some historical context, which serves as a convenient perspective for understanding postmodernism's many facets.

History (more accurately, Western history) can be regarded as a series of periods, beginning with prehistory and concluding with the present. The first of these periods, the premodern, was characterized by a localized, agrarian economy. Society was hierarchically organized, with a small ruling class of aristocrats and a large class of peasants. Few people were educated and "knowledge" ensued from God or superstition. With the passage of the Middle Ages (circa 1450), however, there was a renewed emphasis on learning and travel and history entered the modern period. The industrial revolution of the 18th century introduced the factory economy (with its need for production workers and far-flung markets) and this saw the rise of a bourgeois class (factory owners and merchants); capitalism arrived as society's organizing basis. Meanwhile, an intellectual ferment—the Age of Reason—was brewing. The likes of Bacon, Descartes, Locke, and Newton argued for man's need to overcome dogma, prejudice, and superstition, and this culminated in the work of Kant and Rousseau (the Enlightenment). The "modern" mentality that grew out of this period—that technology and

---

[1]As the alert reader recognizes, postmodernism is more a collection of ideas than a unified body of knowledge; its advocates often disagree among themselves. Moreover, there are differing approaches to or "takes" on the phenomenon. Firat and Venkatesh (1995), for example, distinguished among celebratory (i.e., affirmative), critical (i.e., skeptical), and liberatory (i.e., emancipatory) postmodernism. Such distinctions are quite beyond the scope of this chapter, however, inasmuch as the objective is merely to introduce the idea of postmodern advertising into the public health domain.

nature exist for man's benefit (and therefore are to be understood and mastered through science), that truth and beauty reveal themselves to rational inquiry, and that man's progress is inevitable because he is perfectible—is sometimes called Cartesian logic (after Descartes) and it survived into the mid-20th century. At that time (roughly, the 1960s), people began to question these tenets and history entered the postmodern period (see Domzal & Kernan, 1993a). Although there is disagreement about whether postmodernism has taken over Western culture or has just begun to exert itself, its presence is unmistakable. (The authors remain detached from this dispute. Moreover, they are not advocates of postmodern philosophy, preferring to regard it merely as a phenomenon to be studied.)

The easiest way to understand postmodernism is to focus on its prefix, to contrast it with modernism. In that context, it is not necessary to be especially sensitive to recognize that contemporary society has drawn sharp limits around technological excess and nature as something to be raped. There is irrefutable evidence that both morbidity and mortality are ill-served by industrial pollution and environmental degradation, hence the postmodern stance that humans must live in harmony with nature, that the second- and nth-order effects of science and technology must be considered before their first-order effects are proclaimed as beneficial. Similarly, truth and beauty are no longer regarded as singular verities whose essence needs merely to be discovered. It is now recognized that what is true, correct, or valid (beautiful, appropriate, or desirable) depends on the context within which inquiry is situated. For example, fetal abortion may or may not be justifiable, depending on which rational criteria are engaged. Curly hair is a problem or a blessing, depending on the cultural standards applied. Postmodernism celebrates pluralism, contending that modernism's singular notion of knowledge (often called "presence" or logocentrism) merely reflects the authority enabled by power. (Medical research has been dominated by masculine concerns because males have held a privileged position historically.) Fragment such power and its authenticity wanes; reality is replaced by multiple realities. Finally, the inevitability of human progress/perfectibility has been challenged on a variety of fronts. For example, is it progress when undeveloped peoples are colonized and thereby exposed to diseases previously unknown to them? Is civilization improved by the technology of nuclear weapons? Is it necessary to threaten every vestige of people's individuality in the name of medical efficiency? Postmodernism disputes the notion of a grand narrative, arguing instead for nonlinear renditions of human history (Lyotard, 1984).

The postmodern world (the ideology has gained a foothold at least throughout the West) is sometimes called the information society, not just to recognize the prominence of knowledge in contemporary life but also to emphasize the agenda-setting role played by the mass media (Vattimo, 1992). Such media consciousness has promoted several characteristic features. For example, advertising, news, and entertainment travel instantaneously, often in the form of snippets (CNN Headline News), and this creates both plurality (anything and everything is topical) and fragmentation (no viewpoint is too bizarre). The incessant symbolism and imagery have transformed reality into hyperreality (Baudrillard, 1983); in semiotic terms, this is a world of signifiers, not signifieds. (Images refer to other images, rather than to something actual.) The consumer world has become a *pastiche* of contradictory juxtapositions (french fries and a diet soda) and this aggravates the fragmentation of logic or rationale.[2] Consumers want self-fulfillment, but this can no longer be anticipated in the traditional way, such as by purchasing a particular product. In the postmodern world, value resides in consumption—one must experience the product before its gratification is apparent—and the result, because it is so contextualized, is difficult to predict. (This phenomenon exemplifies the "decentering" of the subject, to indicate the consumer's diminished control over the process of gratification. But it also emphasizes consumption's domination over production because the former process releases a product's symbolic meanings, which represent its true value.)

All these unlikely features have to do with the meanings people ascribe to their surroundings and to themselves. In postmodernist terms, meaning is always interpreted relative to other meanings and, because these are conventions of language that can be "deconstructed," ultimate meaning must be deferred endlessly (Derrida, 1976). This arguably nihilistic stance leads to communication styles that may seem illogical from the standpoint of conventional rhetoric, but they are effective among consumers who have adopted the postmodern ethos. For instance, postmodern advertising frequently makes use of what Levi-Strauss (1966) called *bricolage* (the commandeering of ideas or materials developed in one context or medium into another, using the resulting intertextuality to convey the desired meaning), as in TV commercials where film stars or sports heroes endorse diet plans. But the biggest effect of postmodernism is ambiguity. People do not have a detached (Cartesian) sense of themselves—they are said to experience "immanence" (a fusing of mind and body with the environment, all symbolically)—and this creates a need for them to consider all sources of self-en-

---

[2]A recent ad for Pepsi features a profile of its can where the sides are in red with stylized logo, and the entire body is black text on white. From top to bottom, the text begins: "I wanna climb Everest. I wanna tie the knot. I wanna sharpen my senses. I wanna be nobody's fool. I wanna hit the snooze button. . . ." Eight of the 154 words of copy appear in red, and these are interspersed over the can—"I wanna" (at the top), "be young" (one third down), "have fun" (two-thirds down), and "drink Pepsi" (at the bottom). Such a do-everything mentality (and never mind that there is no compatability) reflects the youthful, carefree persona of this brand but, just to be certain the message gets across, the red-highlighted copy punctuates it.

hancement, including nontraditional ones. That is why health advertising is not confined to medicine, and why it includes the efforts of brand proprietors in nonmedical categories.

This overview of postmodernism might be summarized with the comment that it has changed (or is changing) the health dialogue, from one characterized by dialectic to one that reflects discourse. The modernist view of medicine (exclusive, rational, and pedantic) is giving way to the postmodernist perspective (inclusive, eclectic, and negotiated), which means that wellness purveyors must persuade consumers about their prescriptions' merits. As "the literature of consumption" (Scott, 1994a), advertising finds a natural place in this discourse, which is illustrated in the next section.

HEALTH ADVERTISING: F/X FOR Rx

The contemporary health discourse still contains marks of its dialectical past, as when official agencies proclaim one or another practice harmful or beneficial to human wellness, based on a body of logical evidence. For example, most people do not dispute the validity of governmental warnings about the dangers of cigarette smoking. Increasingly, however, ordinary people are reserving judgment about what best serves their well-being or quality of life. Such reluctance is prompted not by obstinacy or medical anarchy, but by the creeping effects of postmodernism, where truth is seen as something subjective, reality is regarded as relative, and meaning is characterized by nonfixidness. People are no longer content simply to acquiesce to establishment directives; instead, they are inclined to question them, to compare them with alternatives proffered by less official sources of wellness, and to decide for themselves. Advertising has come to be used as the principal voice of these nonofficial wellness prescribers and for that reason it is very much an element in the health discourse consumers negotiate.

If advertising is considered as social communication, a phenomenon that reflects and affects a society's culture, its place in the health dialogue is easy to appreciate. In a macro sense, advertising tells people what products mean (Domzal & Kernan, 1992). Just as a painting, a play, a musical score, or a movie takes on a public meaning (a consensual understanding), so do commercial products. This is not to say that idiosyncratic interpretations do not exist, but hermeneutics, semiotics, and structuralism all demonstrate that one can approximate (establish an interpretive range for) what various products mean to people. When consumers "read" advertisements, then, advertisers know in general how they interpret them, even though many such meanings represent the idealized versions of products that sponsoring advertisers wish to convey. All this is possible because advertisers understand (and exploit) the visual and textual rhetoric of interpretation (Scott, 1992, 1994a, 1994b). The matrix of rhetoric includes consumer skepticism, as in "this is persuasion, not to be taken at face value"; but, the *generic* argument of most ads is plausible enough to be accepted as reasonable. Thus, when an exercise machine claims cardiovascular benefits, consumers may discount the machine's potential, but they are unlikely to question the efficacy of exercise as a means of achieving a stronger heart. Each time consumers internalize such a generic argument, they add yet another source of wellness information to the set they might consider when making behavioral choices. To be "effective," then, health advertising does not need to convince people; so long as it induces them to consider wellness options, it renders them less compliant as regards establishment prescriptions.

The more consumers are affected by postmodernism, the more advertising influence is likely to occur. The more consumers hold values that are contingent ("it all depends"), ideologically elusive ("don't ask me why; I don't know"), or diverse ("what's good for you may or may not be good for me"), the less they are likely to agree with broad public rationale; and, the less they are likely to accede to universal, societal prescriptions. For such people (the disaffected, the marginalized, or those who for political reasons object to society's incumbent hegemony), the public good is not their good and commonweal appeals go nowhere. Instead, they exhibit a kind of reactance toward most any shard of authority and seem to welcome nontraditional, antiestablishment perspectives (the in-your-face ethos of many teenagers is a good example). Consider Fig. 22.1. This 1995 ad for an "alternative" record shop in Rochester, NY, leaves little doubt that its target audience is young people (Reagonomics as children). Moreover, the ad's message is pretty straightforward: It is structured around food, politics, and

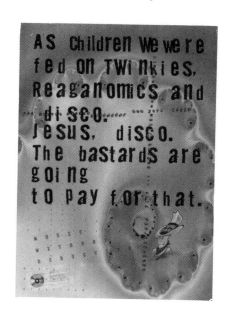

FIG. 22.1. Lakeshore Record Exchange, 1995. Agency: Sda Em Wolb, Rochester. Copyright © ARCHIVE INTERNATIONAL: Used by permission.

music, which together say "we resent our parents' generation." Twinkies being the ultimate junk food, however, that parental indiscretion is forgiveable. And no one (save perhaps liberal Democrats) really gets angry over Reagonomics. Which leaves the music (curiously, the sponsor's product). To young people, disco is so uncool that it needs to be punished. Never again should the earth be contaminated with such cacaphony and stupid looking "dancing." And this will not happen, so long as the Lakeshore Record Exchange has any control over musical matters. (One can only guess at the penalty this ad's readers have in mind for their offending elders.)

Classically postmodern consumers are at once prime targets for advertising (they find "different" messages very accommodating), but they are difficult targets (*which* different messages?). Such people seem to have a sensory inoculation against traditional appeals, which simply do not register with them, yet they are vulnerable to an advertising idiom that is fast, giddy, clever, cynical, and full of irony (Davidson, 1992). It is as though communicating with them requires a particular set of special effects. And that is how, in the extreme, "postmodern" advertising appears to tradition minded people; it looks strange, bizarre, and illogical; it speaks a language unknown to them; it seems to be just style, no substance. To (mostly) older, conservative consumers, such ads often seem vulgar, even reprehensible (as in most anything featuring Madonna). Yet these execution styles are precisely the key needed to reach postmodern segments because of the way they interpret advertising (Goldman, 1992). Figure 22.2 is an apt illustration. This 1995 ad

FIG. 22.2. Minnesota Parent, 1995. Agency: Fallon McElligott, Minneapolis. Copyright © ARCHIVE INTERNATIONAL: Used by permission.

is one in a series for *Minnesota Parent*, a publication that counsels on the "ways of youth," and its execution is classic postmodern: computer-generated iconography, irregular type, a *pastiche* of elements "tossed together," and a vernacular that goes straight to the point. The appeal discourages youngsters through embarassment, by revealing penile insufficiency as one of their unspoken reasons for acquiring an illegal gun. "Get a big gun so you can be a big man," as it were. The man–child *bricolage* is difficult to miss. The character wears the face and clothing of an adolescent city dweller *in situ*, yet he is playing on a skateboard and sucking on a pacifier. ("Grow up!") One can read a good deal of phallic symbolism into the artwork, but suffice it to say that the character's body is obviously distorted for effect (e.g., an outrageously big head). Such postmodern executions take life as it occurs, grab its participants by the throat, and scream at them: "We dare you." However, unless one is streetwise, one is not likely even to comprehend, much less appreciate, an ad such as Fig. 22.2.

Postmodern advertising has its pantheon and David Carson is perhaps its most revered member. (*Graphis* recently described him as a *Wunderkind* and his magazine *Ray Gun* as the home of "fractured layouts and tortured typography—a Rorschach test within the graphic design world.") Such professionals are in very great demand, so their client list is highly skewed toward very commercial products (e.g., Nike, Pepsi), but there is no reason to suppose that such styles will not soon work their way into the heretofore conservative domain of health advertising. It is in this nascent sense that this chapter offers some creeping examples of postmodern-style advertising executions. It should be emphasized at the outset, however, that the principal consequence of postmodernism on advertising—where health does serve as a prominent topic for display—is the diversity of voices on which it confers credibility. It is certainly true that particular execution styles are necessary to attract the dedicated postmodernist segments, but mostly this cultural condition has the effect of legitimizing all health advertising (even that aimed at traditional audiences) by force of its fragmenting of society. More than anything else, postmodernism means cultural diversity—an end to majority privilege—and that opens the health dialogue to competing discourses. It is often said that this is a consumer society, a culture of commerce where plural claims succeed according to the acuity of their enterprise. In health (as in other realms) that implicates advertising, for it is largely through ads that consumers learn of their wellness options.

The following advertisements are taken from an ongoing database of some 4,000, assembled since 1984. They come from Lürzer's International Archive, a retrieval service for multinational ads located in Frankfurt, Germany (see Domzal & Kernan, 1993a, 1994, for details). Although many more (or different) specimens might have been selected, an additional 21 ads were chosen to illustrate how advertising is used in the service of public health. These specimens exemplify five points. First, they indicate that (to labor the obvious) health is everybody's business; the ads are sponsored by private companies, by advocacy groups, and by public agencies. Second, the ads come from around the Western world, which suggests that societies today have a reasonably common sense of their public health problems and how advertising might be used to address them. Third, the ads speak largely to individuals, which implies that "public" health ultimately is a matter of people making private choices. Fourth, some of the ads approach a postmodern-style execution, which illustrates how certain groups must be addressed if they are to be reached. Finally, all the ads reflect a degree of pleading, which implies that public health is something both very important to society yet beyond its ability to influence, save with persuasion. The ads are grouped into three categories, moving from the most person-centered issues (appeals to individual health), through personal/public issues (teenage pregnancy, AIDS issues/safe sex, reckless driving), to public issues (environmental concerns).

Ads addressing personal health (i.e., what *you* can do to prevent illness) range from those implying a relation between diet and wellness to those advocating various medicinal preventatives, explicating the idea that consumers should take control of their own bodies. A 1988 Canadian ad for Campbell's soup (Fig. 22.3), for example, analogizes soup with cold capsules, implying that people (who remain Campbell's kids, according to the tag line) should consume it during the winter months and (to follow the headline's play on words) to ward off the common cold. (Visually portraying the soup cans as capsules is an example of a layout technique called

Take one a day for the cold.

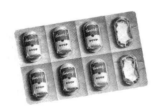

FIG. 22.3. Campbell's Soups, 1988. Agency: Ogilvy & Mather, Toronto. Copyright © ARCHIVE INTERNATIONAL: Used by permission.

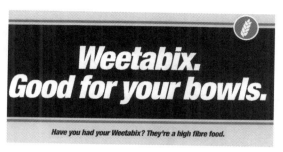

FIG. 22.4. Weetabix Cereal, 1994. Agency: Lowe Howard-Spink, London. Copyright © ARCHIVE INTERNATIONAL: Used by permission.

mortising, thought to guide the ad's interpretation.) Similarly, a 1994 British ad for Weetabix (Fig. 22.4) capitalizes on the textual interplay between the words bowls and bowels to assert this cereal's high fiber content, thus its potency for preventing colonic cancer. Three ads for generic products (i.e., milk, fish, and citrus fruit) get more explicit about the diet/health relation. A 1990 British ad for the National Dairy Council (Fig. 22.5), for example, metamorphizes the contents of a milk bottle to display the food's vitamin and mineral content while the copy reinforces this good-for-the-body claim. A 1992 British ad for Seafish (Fig. 22.6) plays off folklore (thus using *bricolage*) to remind consumers that many kinds of fish (note the tag line which says "There are many more dishes in the sea")

FIG. 22.5. National Dairy Council, 1990. Agency: BMP DDB Needham, London. Copyright © ARCHIVE INTERNATIONAL: Used by permission.

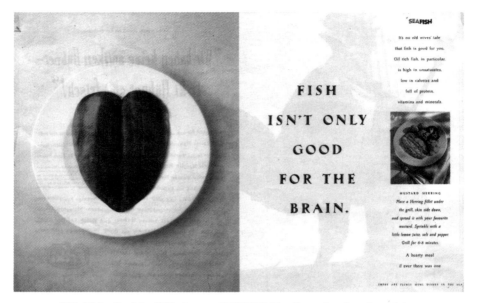

FIG. 22.6. Seafish, 1992. Agency: BMP DDB Needham, London. Copyright
© ARCHIVE INTERNATIONAL: Used by permission.

are good for cardiovascular problems (note the heart-shaped piece of fish
on the plate) and it encourages behavior by including a recipe. And a
1990 ad for the American Cancer Society (Fig. 22.7) portrays an orange
in the form of a stylized bomb (for "navel battle") to be used in the dietary
fight against cancer. (Although the ad focuses on citrus fruit—"Prepare
yourself for Victory at C"—it encourages consumers to eat a variety of
foods thought to be helpful in preventing this disease.) Two other ads
(Figs. 22.8 and 22.9) illustrate how bodily health is addressed blatantly, in
the form of preventive medications. One of these, a 1987 British ad for
Healthcrafts food supplements (Fig. 22.8), speaks to the proclivity of working couples (particularly of men) to eat an excessive amount of junk or
heavily processed food, suggesting that such a diet is nutritionally deficient.
In the best postmodern spirit, however, this practice is not condemned.
Instead, it is accommodated with slight-of-hand: Legitimize your dreadful
diet by consuming these supplements religiously! (Nutrition disappears
into hyperreality.) The other blatant illustration, a 1988 American ad for
Fibre Trim appetite suppressants (Fig. 22.9), appeals to overweight consumers' anxieties about diet pills, specifically the mysterious chemicals that
make these medications work. The play is to people's concern over ingest-
ing "drugs," when with this brand they can suppress their appetite naturally,
using fiber (which incidentally offers additional, colonic benefits). Notably,

THE FIGHT AGAINST CANCER ALSO CALLS FOR A NAVEL BATTLE.

Prepare yourself for Victory at C. Because a diet that includes oranges, peppers and other foods high in Vitamin C may lessen your risk in the battle against cancer. So who else are your allies? Try fiber rich foods, lowfat dairy products, cruciferous vegetables like cauliflower, poultry, fish, and foods high in Vitamin A. They make up the menu in The Great American Food Fight Against Cancer – an American Cancer Society-sponsored program to lessen your cancer risk. You can learn more information by calling 1 800 ACS 2345, or your local American Cancer Society. Before long, you'll C things our way. **THE GREAT AMERICAN FOOD FIGHT AGAINST CANCER BEGINS APRIL 19.**

FIG. 22.7. American Cancer Society, 1990. Agency: DDB Needham, USA. Copyright © ARCHIVE INTERNATIONAL: Used by permission.

FIG. 22.8. Healthcrafts Food Supplements, 1987. Agency: FCO, Ltd., London. Copyright © ARCHIVE INTERNATIONAL: Used by permission.

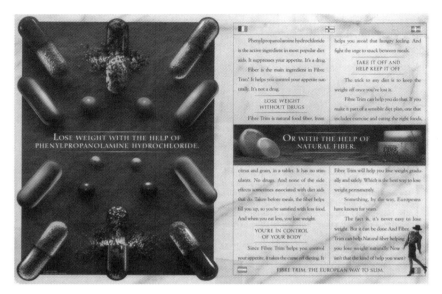

FIG. 22.9.   Fibre Trim, 1988. Agency: Ogilvy & Mather, New York. Copyright
© ARCHIVE INTERNATIONAL: Used by permission.

weight control is taken as a given; indeed, the ad proclaims for the brand's
consumers: "You're in control of your body." Finally, Fig. 22.10 illustrates
a well-crafted warning about the consequences of unhealthy dietary lifestyles. This 1994 execution for the British Heart Foundation uses a variety
of postmodern techniques to convey the ominous nature and alarming
incidence of fatal coronary seizures. The presentation—all in black on

FIG. 22.10.   British Heart Foundation, 1994. Agency: Simons Palmer Denton
Clemmow & Johnson, London. Copyright © ARCHIVE INTERNATIONAL:
Used by permission.

red—is visually arresting (almost hyperreal) as it silhouettes a disassembled (read fragmented), black (read dead) human form on a background of red (read blood). The body outline smacks of a crime scene. But wait; the *bricolage* of intertextualities reveals that the random attack was not perpetrated by a criminal. It was self-imposed by the unsuspecting victim, who ate carelessly and eschewed exercise all his foolhardy life. This random-but-not-really contradiction (explicated by comparing the copy with the tag line) sets up a telling *pastiche.* Moreover, the execution is riddled with resonance (repeated meanings), as the fractured layout and tortured typography reverberate "random."

Ads addressing personal/public issues portray what most people categorize as public health. This section features illustrations, largely admonitions, dealing with teenage pregnancy, AIDS/safe sex issues, the dangers of cigarettes and illicit drugs, and reckless driving. Figure 22.11 (a 1991 effort in behalf of the Children's Defense Fund), for instance, plays on the racial stereotype of African American male athletes to emphasize to girls that they cannot count on the father's help to rear their child. That same don't-be-impetuous admonition is reflected in Figs. 22.12a and 22.12b (1986 ads for The Mayor's Office of Adolescent Pregnancy and Parenting Services of New York City), both of which offer cant-laced counsel to those presumably in need of it. All three ads represent attempts to speak to teenagers who, in postmodern times, have become sexually active to a degree that would have been unimaginable in modern times. AIDS and

FIG. 22.11. Children's Defense Fund, 1991. Agency: Fallon McElligott, Minneapolis. Copyright © ARCHIVE INTERNATIONAL: Used by permission.

A   B

FIG. 22.12. The Mayor's Office of Adolescent Pregnancy and Parenting Services, 1986. Agency: Ketchum Advertising, New York. Copyright © ARCHIVE INTERNATIONAL: Used by permission.

safe sex is a related problem and it is illustrated by Figs. 22.13 to 22.16. Figure 22.13, a 1987 British ad for the Terrence Higgins Trust, uses an epidemiological etiology to emphasize how easily the HIV virus can be transmitted to unsuspecting people, whereas Fig. 22.14 (1991, from the New Zealand AIDS Foundation), Fig. 22.15 (1987, from the British Department of Health and Social Security) and Fig. 22.16 (1994, from the

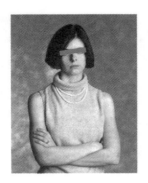

This is the girl,

Who's in love with a man,

Who picked someone up at a party,

Who'd been out with her boss,

Who'd taken a client to Hamburg,

Who'd suggested a tart,

Who'd been with an addict,

Who'd just shared a needle,

With a friend down the road,

Who had AIDS.

SPREAD THE WORD, NOT THE VIRUS.
The Terrence Higgins Trust AIDS Helpline 01-833 2971

FIG. 22.13. Terrence Higgins Trust, 1987. Agency: Mavity Gilmore Jaume, London. Copyright © ARCHIVE INTERNATIONAL: Used by permission.

Life
is cheap.

Every 30 minutes someone somewhere dies of AIDS.
The price you pay for a condom is enough to save your life.

NZ AIDS FOUNDATION

FIG. 22.14. New Zealand AIDS Foundation, 1991. Agency: Ayer New Zealand, Auckland. Copyright © ARCHIVE INTERNATIONAL: Used by permission.

NOW
IT CAN CAUSE
DEATH AS WELL
AS LIFE.

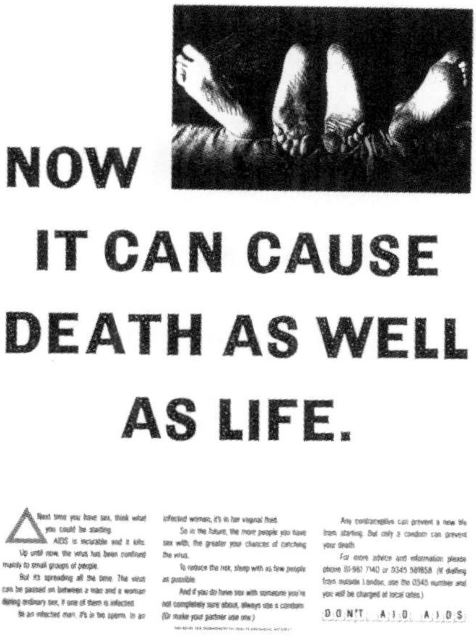

FIG. 22.15. UK Department of Health and Social Security, 1987. Agency: TBWA, London. Copyright © ARCHIVE INTERNATIONAL: Used by permission.

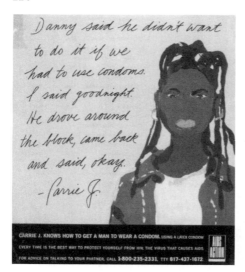

FIG. 22.16. Massachusetts Drug
and Alcohol Hotline, 1994.
Agency: Mullen, Wenham, MA.
Copyright © ARCHIVE INTERNA-
TIONAL: Used by permission.

Massachusetts Drug and Alcohol Hotline) encourage the use of condoms
as a protection against the virus' sexual transmission. Notably, none of the
ads counsels abstinence, presumably because that is regarded as reactionary
in postmodern times. Abstinence is preached with regard to cigarettes and
illicit drugs, however, in Figs. 22.17 and 22.18. Yet, there is no threat in
those antismoking ads (both 1986, for the American Lung Association),

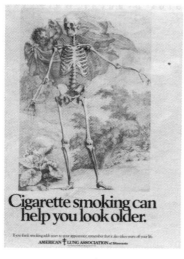

A   B

FIG. 22.17. American Lung Association, 1986. Agency: Fallon McElligott,
Minneapolis. Copyright © ARCHIVE INTERNATIONAL: Used by permission.

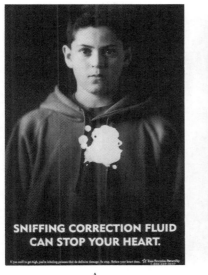

SNIFFING CORRECTION FLUID
CAN STOP YOUR HEART.

SNIFFING SPRAY PAINT
DESTROYS YOUR LUNGS.

A   B

FIG. 22.18.   Texas Prevention Partnership, 1994. Agency: GSD & M, Austin.
Copyright © ARCHIVE INTERNATIONAL: Used by permission.

addressed to teenagers. Instead, they debunk the belief that smoking is an "adult" behavior (Fig. 22.17a) and punctuate the fact that it occasions halitosis (Fig. 22.17b)—both salient issues among such consumers, who imagine death as some far-off, inconsequential phenomenon. Curiously, a virtually opposite tack is evident in the two ads (Figs. 22.18a and 22.18b) done in 1994 for the Texas Prevention Partnership to combat the practice of "sniffing" in the public schools. These ads were directed at children who did not realize the dire consequences of this practice, in the hope that such enlightenment would temper their behavior before it was too late. That forestalling motivation also is evident in this section's final illustration (Fig. 22.19), which is a 1987 Canadian ad about reckless driving. Figure 22.19 is blatantly informative—teenagers' greatest threat to their mortality is traffic accidents. This campaign was deemed necessary because teenagers (especially boys) are not aware of this statistic and generally dispute it (in favor of drugs as a killer). The ad seeks to alert these drivers (and by implication their passengers and parents) to the responsibilities of taking the wheel, to impress on them that a car is not only an expression of freedom but also a means of killing themselves and others and they should think about this as they turn the ignition key.

The final ad presented concerns environmental health. Figure 22.20, part of a 1993 antipollution campaign in New York City, never appeared as a scheduled ad in the media because then-mayor David Dinkins was so alarmed at its potential for shock he took immediate action to correct the

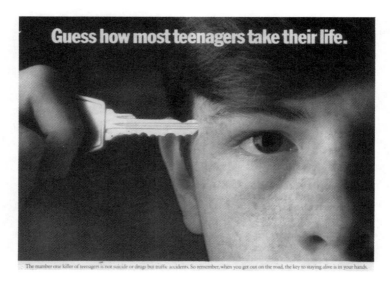

FIG. 22.19. Traffic Inquiry Research Foundation, 1987. Agency: Kuleba Shyllit, Toronto. Copyright © ARCHIVE INTERNATIONAL: Used by permission.

problem highlighted. Figure 22.20 nevertheless remains instructive of advertising's capacity to galvanize environmental health concerns, in this case over the public water supply. Potable water is so intrinsic an element of health it is unimaginable that a civilized society would be without it and to envision a community's drinking water reservoirs polluted with urine is disgusting, if not sickening. The graphic *pastiche* of the ad requires little interpretation, so it is not surprising that this campaign produced such prompt political action.

A POSTMODERN SOCIAL MARKETING?

These illustrative advertisements and the changing health dialogue that underpins them provokes the inevitable question: What does it all mean for public health advocacy in particular and for social marketing in general? It is easy to dismiss the motives of advertisers who urge consumers to buy their branded health products; such efforts are disingenuous because the only interest served is that of stockholders. Similarly, the zeal of advocacy groups can be disputed, discounting their prescriptions as so much fanaticism. But judgments are not the axial criteria; what really matters is how health consumers think about and react to these efforts. If ordinary people achieve a greater measure of wellness as a consequence of heeding these entreaties, then public health has been served; who gets credit for inducing the benefit

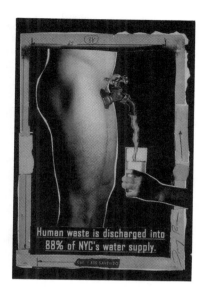

FIG. 22.20. SAVEH20, 1993. Agency: Kirshenbaum & Bond, New York. Copyright © ARCHIVE INTERNATIONAL: Used by permission.

is of secondary concern. This is to say that the result, not the source or motivation of health advertising is what qualifies it, that any ads that function to enhance wellness should be included in the public health set. Wellness is a complicated issue, whose achievement is further tangled by the interactive contingencies of contemporary society; its advocacy should not be expected to be driven by a well-ordered (much less a singular) constituency. It is already clear that the postmodern health care consumer will be (to use Firat & Venkatesh's, 1995, characterization) decentered, communicative, fragmented, liberated, and symbolic—a person who will make sense of the world in terms of symbols, meanings, and experiences. Science will matter, but so will narratives, myths, and symbolic regimes as sources of knowledge and truth about wellness. Thus, there will be fragmenting, if not an actual shift in authority, away from the medical establishment and toward the market as a consequence of postmodernism. None of this will be easy to figure out (and it surely will seem messy), but the consumer will be the beneficiary by the simple expedient of increased choice latitude. People may need to anguish over their decisions in the future, but wellness options such as alternative and holistic medicine, natural healing programs, and a whole range of commercially sponsored self-medications will be accepted as legitimate, which is to say that none of them is likely to produce a privileged symbolism in the consumer culture to come.

On the other hand, the same consumer intractability often encountered in public health advocacy would seem to characterize social marketing endeavors in general. Postmodernism entails societal diversity, fragmentation, and discord and these features aggrevate questions of ontology. Distinctions such as public/private, truth/fantasy, and cost/benefit—all hall-marks of modernism's orderliness—have become blurred with the result that defining commonweal interests is argumentative to say the least. The very idea of social marketing presumes that someone "knows best"; yet that notion is an arrogance (a claim of privilege) in the postmodern perspective. (Family planning is a good example. Who benefits from this practice? What (sub)cultural values does it crush, even ridicule?) As a result, resistance to social change—recalcitrance, in modernist terms—takes the form of evasion or subversion. Resistant groups, moreover, make no apologies for their stance; they see it as an expression of values, a moral response to the oppression of elitists bent on restricting their freedoms, diminishing their identities. Decrees ring hollow with such groups; they are not scandalized by their "aberrant" behavior. Persuasion is the only hope of aligning them with dominant positions, but because their allegiances are so fragmented, the same cacophony of appeals should be expected in the health dialogue to resonate in any movement advocating social change.

The idea of postmodern social marketing may not seem particularly pressing (cf. Kotler & Andreasen, 1987; Kotler & Roberto, 1989; Manoff, 1985) until it is recognized that the groups often targeted for social change campaigns (the poor, the disadvantaged, the marginalized) are those most likely to have embraced the postmodernist ethos. Such people are the most resistant to mainstream ideas, so appealing to them demands a rhetoric different from the customary. These groups are not moved by Cartesian logic and they do not engage traditional schemes of interpretation. If these groups are to be persuaded with advertising, it will be necessary to develop new skills and become comfortable with "weird science."[3] Just as the wellness dialogue gets bogged down by the politics of health care (as though all that mattered was economics), social change can be subverted by a misguided assumption that its targets will respond to syllogisms, so long as they are conspicuous and repeated sufficiently. For good or bad, contemporary society is passing from a top-down hegemony to a commerce of competing wills. The social good has become a matter of opinion and people are more impressed by persistence than by imagination.

REFERENCES

Baltes, M. M. (1976). Health care from a behavioral-ecological viewpoint. In M. Leininger (Ed.), *Transcultural health care issues and conditions* (pp. 149–163). Philadelphia: Davis.
Baudrillard, J. (1983). *Simulations.* New York: Semiotexte.

---

[3]As Petty and Cacioppo (1996) argued, however, this does not mean traditional science should be abandoned in the process.

Bloch, P. H. (1984). The wellness movement: Imperatives for health marketers. *Journal of Health Care Marketing, 4*, 9–16.

Block, L. G., & Keller, P. A. (1995). When to accentuate the negative: The effects of perceived efficacy and message framing on intentions to perform a health-related behavior. *Journal of Marketing Research, 32*, 192–203.

Bourdieu, P. (1984). *Distinction: A social critique of the judgment of taste.* Cambridge, MA: Harvard University Press.

Brown, S. (1995). *Postmodern marketing.* London: Routledge.

Bulger, R .J. (1988). *Technology, bureaucracy, and healing in America: A postmodern paradigm.* Iowa City: University of Iowa Press.

Davidson, M. P. (1992). *The consumerist manifesto: Advertising in postmodern times.* London: Routledge.

Derrida, J. (1976). *Of grammatology.* Baltimore: Johns Hopkins University Press.

Domzal, T. J., & Kernan, J. B. (1992). Reading advertising: The what and how of product meaning. *Journal of Consumer Marketing, 9*, 48–64.

Domzal, T. J., & Kernan, J. B. (1993a). Mirror, mirror: Some postmodern reflections on global advertising. *Journal of Advertising, 22*, 1–20.

Domzal, T. J., & Kernan, J. B. (1993b). Variations on the pursuit of beauty: Toward a corporal theory of the body. *Psychology & Marketing, 10*, 494–511.

Domzal, T. J., & Kernan, J. B. (1994). Creative features of globally-understood advertisements. *Journal of Current Issues and Research in Advertising, 16*, 29–47.

Downie, R. S., Fyfe, C., & Tannahill, A. (1990). *Health promotion: Models and values.* New York: Oxford University Press.

Eckholm, E. P. (1977). *The picture of health: Environmental sources of disease.* New York: Norton.

Elder, J. P., Geller, E. S., Hovell, M. F., & Mayer, J. A. (1994). *Motivating health behavior.* Albany, NY: Delmar.

Evans, R. G., & Stoddart, G. L. (1990). Producing health, consuming health care. *Social Science and Medicine, 31*, 1347–1363.

Falk, P. (1994). *The consuming body.* London: Sage.

Featherstone, M., Hepworth, M., & Turner, B. S. (Eds.). (1991). *The body: Social processes and cultural theory.* London: Sage.

Firat, A. F., & Venkatesh, A. (1995). Liberatory postmodernism and the reenchantment of consumption. *Journal of Consumer Research, 22*, 239–267.

Fiske, J. (1989). *Understanding popular culture.* Boston: Unwin Hyman.

Flora, J. A., Maibach, E. W., & Maccoby, N. (1989). The role of media across four levels of health promotion intervention. *Annual Review of Public Health, 10*, 181–201.

Foucault, M. (1975). *The birth of the clinic.* New York: Vintage.

Foucault, M. (1979). *Discipline and punish: The birth of the prison.* New York: Vintage.

Fox, N. J. (1994). *Postmodernism, sociology and health.* Toronto: University of Toronto Press.

Frank, A. W. (1991). For a sociology of the body: An analytic review. In M. Featherstone, M. Hepworth, & B. S. Turner (Eds.), *The body: Social processes and cultural theory* (pp. 36–102). London: Sage.

Freund, P. E. S. (1982). *The civilized body.* Philadelphia: Temple University Press.

Gilman, S. L. (1995). *Picturing health and illness: Images of identity and difference.* Baltimore: Johns Hopkins University Press.

Goldman, R. (1992). *Reading ads socially.* London: Routledge.

Hassan, I. (1987). *The postmodern turn.* Columbus: Ohio State University Press.

Kotler, P., & Andreasen, A. R. (1987). *Strategic marketing for nonprofit organizations* (3rd ed.). Englewood Cliffs, NJ: Prentice-Hall.

Kotler, P., & Roberto, E. L. (1989). *Social marketing: Strategies for changing public behavior.* New York: The Free Press.

Kraft, F., & Goodell, P. W. (1993). Identifying the health conscious consumer. *Journal of Health Care Marketing, 13,* 18–25.

Leichter, H. M. (1991). *Free to be foolish.* Princeton, NJ: Princeton University Press.

Levi-Strauss, C. (1966). *The savage mind.* Chicago: University of Chicago Press.

Lupton, D. (1995). *The imperative of health: Public health and the regulated body.* London: Sage.

Lyotard, J.-F. (1984). *The postmodern condition.* Minneapolis: University of Minnesota Press.

Manoff, R. K. (1985). *Social marketing: Imperative for public health.* New York: Praeger.

Petty, R. E., & Cacioppo, J. T. (1996). Addressing disturbing and disturbed consumer behavior: Is it necessary to change the way we conduct behavioral science? *Journal of Marketing Research, 33,* 1–18.

Polhemus, T. (1988). *Body styles.* London: Lennard.

Reinhardt, U. E. (1988). Healers and bureaucrats in the all-American health care fray. In R. J. Bulger, *Technology, bureaucracy, and healing in America: A postmodern paradigm* (pp. ix–xxxvii). Iowa City: University of Iowa Press.

Rosenau, P. M. (1992). *Post-modernism and the social sciences.* Princeton, NJ: Princeton University Press.

Scott, L. M. (1992). Playing with pictures: Postmodernism, poststructuralism, and advertising visuals. In J. F. Sherry & B. Sternthal (Eds.), *Advances in consumer research* (Vol. 19, pp. 596–612). Provo, UT: Association for Consumer Research.

Scott, L. M. (1994a). The bridge from text to mind: Adapting reader–response theory to consumer research. *Journal of Consumer Research, 21,* 461–480.

Scott, L. M. (1994b). Images of advertising: The need for a theory of visual rhetoric. *Journal of Consumer Research, 21,* 252–273.

Shilling, C. (1993). *The body and social theory.* London: Sage.

Simmons, S. J. (1993). The economics of prevention. In R. N. Knollmueller (Ed.), *Prevention across the life span: Healthy people for the twenty-first century* (pp. 1–9). Washington, DC: American Nurses Publishing.

Smith, G. R., & Wesley, R. L. (1993). Health promotion: Public policy goal. In R. N. Knollmueller (Ed.), *Prevention across the life span: Healthy people for the twenty-first century* (pp. 97–106). Washington, DC: American Nurses Publishing.

Spector, R. E. (1993). Sociocultural perspective of prevention. In R. N. Knollmueller (Ed.), *Prevention across the life span: Healthy people for the twenty-first century* (pp. 11–19). Washington, DC: American Nurses Publishing.

Turner, B. S. (1984). *The body and society.* Oxford: Blackwell.

Turner, B. S. (1987). *Medical power and social knowledge.* London: Sage.

Turner, B. S. (1992). *Regulating bodies.* London: Routledge.

U.S. Public Health Service (1990). *Healthy people 2000: National health promotion and disease prevention objectives.* Washington, DC: Government Printing Office.

Van Raaij, W. F. (1993). Postmodern consumption: Architecture, art, and consumer behavior. In W. F. Van Raaij & G. J. Bamossy (Eds.), *European advances in consumer research* (Vol. 1, pp. 550–558). Provo, UT: Association for Consumer Research.

Vattimo, G. (1992). *The transparent society* (D. Webb, Trans.). Baltimore: Johns Hopkins University Press.

Wallack, L., Dorfman, L., Jernigan, D., & Themba, M. (1993). *Media advocacy and public health.* Newbury Park, CA: Sage.

Winett, R. A. (1995). A framework for health promotion and disease prevention programs. *American Psychologist, 50,* 341–350.

Author Index

Subject Index

formative research for nutrition and physical activity communications project, 281–284

prevention: framework of integrating marketing and media advocacy, 284–289

using four *ps* in tobacco control programs, 269–272

Challenges

community participation in health programs, 292

future and social marketing to communities of color, 366–368

organ donation, 380–383

Change Your Clock, Change Your Battery campaign, corporate social marketing, 325–326

Character contests, hockey violence, 339

Child Survival Campaign, success of program in Philippines, 53–55

Children

abuse and tolerance of violence in families, 338

health and BASICS program, 300

survival and social marketing programs, 293

Children's Defense Fund, public health advertising, 407

Choice

giving to customers and social marketing, 25–28

latitude and public health advertising, 413

Cholesterol, decline and Stanford Program public health campaign, 48

Churches, mammography compliance in older/poorer populations, 118, *see also* Religion

Cigarettes, *see also* Antismoking campaigns; Behavior, smoking; Cigarettes; Smoking; Tar/nicotine

contraband and antismoking campaigns, 223

low tar, advertising dangers

designing to generate lower machine-estimated yields, 247–249

do smokers equate low tar with safer, 251–253

smokers' understanding and use of advertised tar numbers, 253–260

smokers' understanding of tar numbers, 250–251

value of advertised tar/nicotine levels revisited, 249–250

voluntary disclosure program and smokers' response, 246–247

low yield, lights, ultra lights

filter ventilation effects on standard tar/nicotine yields, 233–234

implications for social marketing, 238–241

significance, 237

ultra light and lights market tar categories, 236–237

understanding before promoting, 231–233

vent blocking, 234–236

pack

size and smoking behavior, 238–239

tar/nicotine yield information, 236–237

youth antismoking campaigns

necessary ratio, 195–198

refusal, 200

sale, 190

Citizen action, *see* Action

Class, advertising role in organ donation, 379, 381

Clinical trials, replication and problems in social marketing, 32

Clinical/pharmacological approaches, tobacco control programs, 272, *see also* Antismoking campaigns

Clinics, mammography compliance in older/poorer populations, 118

Clinton administration, ratio of antismoking to cigarette advertising, 196–198, *see also* Antismoking campaigns

Closed-item evaluation instrument, development for AIDS Community Demonstration Project, 128–129

Coaches, hockey violence, 339, *see also* Hockey violence

Coca Cola, correlation to mammography compliance in older/poorer populations, 116

Coffee Shop Interview (CSI), AIDS Community Demonstration Project, 133, 134–135, *see also* AIDS

Cognitive model, social marketing, 9, 12–14, *see also* Social marketing

Collaboration, successful by social marketers, 70

Color matching technique, social marketing of low yield, ultra lights, light cigarettes, 238–239

DATE DUE

OCT 2 3 1999			
NOV 1 6 2002			
JA 1 3 '04			

Demco, Inc. 38-293